CAREER DEVELOPMENT IN TURBULENT TIMES:
Exploring Work, Learning and Careers

Edited and Contributions by
Rich Feller and Garry R. Walz

With an Introduction by
Dennis W. Engels

ERIC/CASS Publications
School of Education
University of North Carolina at Greensboro
Greensboro, NC 27412
1-800 414-9769

ISBN 1-56109-066-2

This publication was funded by the U.S. Department of
Education, Office of Educational Research and Improvement,
Contract no. RR93002004. Opinions expressed in this
publication do not necessarily reflect the positions of the U.S.
Department of Education, OERI, or ERIC/CASS.

Preface

A decision whether or not to produce a new monograph is a major undertaking at ERIC/CASS. As an organization whose major responsibility is to develop the ERIC database in counseling and student services, e.g., selecting, indexing and abstracting relevant journals and documents, we have an advantage over commercial publishers in that we are committed to producing only a limited number of publications per year. Hence, we can be highly selective and produce only those publications which are ground breaking and unique in their content and perspective. Such recent publications as *Reform in Student Affairs* by Paul Bloland, Louis Stamatakos, and Russell Rogers; *Saving the Native Son:Empowering Young Black Males* by Courtland Lee; *Counseling Employment Bound Youth* by Edwin Herr; and *Family Counseling in the Schools* by Scott Hinkle and Michael Wells are examples we are proud of. They have all plowed new ground and been extremely well received.

Career Transitions in Turbulent Times is the most recent example of an innovative publication. In many ways it is the most ambitious, comprehensive and far ranging publication we have produced to-date. The final product is mind boggling to us: We never intended anything quite so massive. Both its girth and quality pleases us immensely. To paraphrase a well known quote, "never have so many authors responded so well in such a short period of time as they did for this publication." Persons with an interest in career development will surely find this an invaluable resource for many years to come. It has been suggested by a number of NCDA members that this is a replacement for the nineties NCDA decennial volume which never was. However appropriate that is, we have been delighted by NCDA's support and encouragement to produce it.

However rational and systematic one would like to believe their decision making is, I find that in my life it is invariably a significant event, insight or personal contact which catapults me into making a major decision. The inspiration for this monograph came from the publication of a collection of counseling supervision digests edited by Diane Borders. Typically, digests are stand alones with each digest serving to provide a window of R & D information on a single topic. In *Supervision: Exploring the Effective Components*, over twenty separate digests on aspects of supervision were prepared providing a comprehensive and succinct overview of research and practice in the field. The enthusiastic response to *Supervision: Exploring the Effective Components* led me to believe that this format is an excellent way to capture the views of knowledgeable authors in a highly readable fashion. A particularly popular feature of this approach is the brevity and straightforward writing style. Clearly these digests have been read and used, not stored and forgotten.

The second precipitating factor leading to the publication of *Career Transitions in Turbulent Times* was ongoing conversations Rich Feller and I were having about the future. We were concerned about how counseling needs to change if we are to continue being a viable force that shapes career development for the 21st century. During this critical time ERIC/CASS was also engaged with Bryan Heibert and Lynne Bezanson of the Canadian Guidance and Counseling Foundation (CGCF) in producing a monumental collection of digests titled *Exemplary Career Development Programs & Practices: The Best from Canada*. These 48 digests, while covering topics in the broad realm of career development, targeted a particular facet that grew out of a national initiative in Canada.

Both the stimulating nature of Rich and my conversations and the success of the digest collections provided the springboard for *Career Transitions in Turbulent Times*. This publication was particularly exciting due to several innovative features. First, a search of the ERIC database revealed that viewing the emerging future and considering its implications for career development was hardly spoken to in the literature. This surprised us since the many conversations we were privy to on career development inevitably turned to effects of current economic conditions, their effects on career development and what the "turbulent times" meant for career counselor preparation and practice. We believed we were right on target! Secondly, the success of the previously referenced digest collections convinced us that people were highly appreciative of succinct, straightforward written presentations on topics of high priority. We had also learned that readers have special appreciation for pieces in which authors share their reflections, difficulties, and personal beliefs stripped of pedagogics.

Putting the above ideas together led to a strong conviction that what we wanted was a volume of succinct statements on critical needs and promising practices in career development which responded to the turbulent times people everywhere were experiencing. We needed a combination of established leaders in career development who could share the results of their scholarship, and the fresh perspectives of newcomers to the field. Perhaps most of all we wanted authors who spoke with unfettered excitement about their "principle passions," writing papers that were animated discussions on topics they care deeply about.

Indubitably what has made this monograph possible is the contributions of our distinguished group of writers. Persons who have reviewed the manuscript have invariabley commented on how appreciative they were of the high quality articles and the variance in authors' style and approach to writing, which made for interesting reading. It is hard to adequately convey our appreciation, and that of readers to come, of what a useful and vital contribution to the career development field these authors have made.

Readers who are use to highly stylized publications may note that there is more variance in writing style, length and coverage than is usually the case. Many authors have not been the least bashful in expounding on their own products or projects. Welcome to **lite** editing a la ERIC/CASS! I wanted to capture as much of the person behind the writing and ideas as possible, so the editing was done sparingly and with a view to letting the author say it like it is.

One especially pleasing aspect of this volume is that it reached fruition during the celebration of the 30th Anniversary of both the Educational Resources Information Center—ERIC, and the Counseling and Student Services Clearinghouse—ERIC/CASS. Over the decades we have worked with and participated in a large number of projects with NCDA. Appropriately, on this special anniversary we have a most impressive expression of our 30 years of collaboration with NCDA.

I would be remiss if I didn't use this opportunity to share the pleasure I had in working on this project with Rich Feller. We complemented each other extremely well and without his enthusiasm and encyclopedic knowledge of career development it would never have been possible. Thanks Rich, you were great. Let's do another—in a year or two!!

Garry R. Walz
Director & Editor-in-Chief

Celebrating Thirty Years Of Service to Education 1966-1996

ERIC
Educational Resources Information Center
&
CASS
Counseling and Student Services Clearinghouse

In 1966, the Educational Resources Information Center (ERIC) was established by the then U.S. Office of Education. In a national competition, a clearinghouse on Counseling & Personnel Services (CAPS) was established at the University of Michigan under the direction of Dr. Garry R. Walz. Over the past thirty years, ERIC has grown to be the largest educational database in the world with nearly a million entries. It is also the most frequently searched database in college libraries.

ERIC/CAPS, after twenty-seven years at the University of Michigan, moved to the University of North Carolina at Greensboro (UNCG) in 1993 and assumed a new name to reflect its greater attention to college student services, *CASS* (Counseling and Student Services Clearinghouse). Both as CAPS and as CASS, the clearinghouse has won national recognition for its leadership in publications, conferences, innovations in the use of information technologies, and in building a comprehensive database in counseling, guidance and student and adult services at all age levels.

ERIC & CASS are prepared and eager to expand their contributions to the information age and the start of the 21st century, which will bring new challenges to and rewards for the effective utilization of information.

ERIC Clearinghouse on
Counseling & Student Services
Improving Decision Making Through Increased Access to Information

Started here
in 1966

Publications

Website

National Conferences

One of many awards
received by the
Clearinghouse
and staff

...And now in the
School of Education,
University of North
Carolina at Greensboro

ERIC Counseling and Student Services Clearinghouse
School of Education • 101 Park Building • University of North Carolina at Greensboro
Greensboro, NC 27412-5001

Acknowledgements

Producing a monograph of this size and with as many special features is a major task involving the work of many people. Though their names do not appear on the cover, their contributions were essential to its completion. Without their skills, interest, and support, this volume would still be a dream.

First and foremost, I want to express my great appreciation to Kaye Davis for her boundless contributions. She was a desktop publisher, artist, computer specialist, editor and master of all tasks. Her contributions were massive and on-going! If a project of this complexity is to reach fruition, someone must be skilled enough to respond to all the special needs that arise. Sabrina Ross of our staff performed that task with consummate skill. Manuscripts need to be typed and retyped and payments made to keep the office "wheels" moving. Fortunately, in Belinda Madkins, we had a person of great skill to carry out such tasks.

With Rich Feller in Colorado and Garry Walz in North Carolina, a great deal of material had to be sent back and forth. At a time when we seemed overwhelmed with typed pages and discs, Phyllis Beard of Colorado State University, School of Education, stepped in and transferred the editing to a master disc, thereby saving the North Carolina crew countless hours which they really didn't have. Again, thank you Phyllis, for taking on this added task! Jay Malone, an experienced ERIC/CASS editor and history Ph.D. candidate at University of Florida, did yeoman's service in editing the manuscripts. Jillian Joncas, a recent addition to our staff, took on the responsibility of final editing and proofing. So good was her work that we wouldn't let any material go forward until it was "Jillianized." In all matters important, Jeanne Bleuer is there to help where help is needed, and helpful she was at many important times.

As the project moved forward and interest in it grew, it seemed appropriate to see if NCDA was interested in collaborating on the project. They were, and thanks to the continuing support and interest of President, Denny Engels, President-elect, Jo Ann Bowlsbey, and Executive Director, Juliet Miller, the project moved ahead. Without their support and encouragement, we might well have faltered on the way.

Again, it is appropriate to thank our authors for their splendid work. To them for their fine work should go the lion's share of appreciation. Without them there would not be a *Career Transitions in Turbulent Times*.

Garry Walz and Rich Feller

Introduction

On opening this book, the reader may find that one concept lunges out from the table of contents. The rate and magnitude of change today, and many of its side-effects, such as downsizing, outsourcing and incredible growth rates for temporary agencies, might provoke an initial concentration on the turbulence we all hear described in our daily media.

We have all experienced turbulence in weather, perhaps most notably while we have been in boats and airplanes, but recent thrusts into the torrents of the global economy and information society give categorically new meaning to turbulence. As the tidal wave of downsizing continues to overwhelm not only the involuntarily displaced victims but also the working wounded and the working-worried "survivors," we must reassess employer, government, and individual responsibilities and policies and career development practices. Private-sector focus on responsibility to shareholders wrongly suggests that corporations exist in social, cultural, and national vacuums, with no other responsibilities than generating profit. So, too, current and proposed workforce policy, with its simplistic fixation on jobs, tends to ignore the fundamental need for people to have more responsibility for long-term career development.

As job duration shrinks and the safety net of job benefits frays with the "temping" of the workforce, the National Career Development Association's definition of career as our life-long series of experiences, manifest in a variety of activities and settings, has potential value for modifying the turbulence and the turbulence paradigm. If we truly want to promote individual responsibility, virtue, and family values, among other desirous goals, we also need a fuller, life-long and life-roles focus, emphasizing career planning and balancing work roles and responsibilities with other life roles and responsibilities (spouse, parent, sibling, child, citizen, volunteer, citizen soldier, legislator). By looking to our heritage while also looking forward, our authors provide many suggestions for insight, planning, programming, action, and empowerment now and in the future.

As noted or alluded to in various sections, private sector fixations on profit often suggest a false dichotomy. Corporate profit and human resources development need not be mutually exclusive and can be mutually beneficial, as evidenced in many family-friendly, highly successful corporations. So too, a long term focus on employee career development and jobs can be complementary, but only if we disabuse ourselves of the short-term focus so common in business (next quarter) and government (next election) and the longstanding Department of Labor emphasis on macro-economic analysis and employer planning. These common foci encourage little understanding of, or attention to, promoting individual responsibility for personal career planning and decision making.

Thankfully, we need not stay mired in turbulence or remain reactive to economic and other changes in the world of work. As noted in many different ways in this book, our profession has a rich heritage, vision, and strategies for empowerment in and through career development. In some ways, our profession has much in common with the vision shared by the Clinton and Bush administrations in Goals 2000, advocating educational excellence, safe schools, literacy, adult career development, and life-long learning. In the SCANS (Secretary's Commission on Achieving Necessary Skills) competencies endorsed by the Bush and Clinton administrations, major corporate leaders identified real-world individual skills and knowledge needed for U.S. success in the global marketplace. In the National Career Development Guidelines, we have a blueprint for accomplishing these competencies and this vision. Unfortunately, we fall to politicizing and self serving arguments to the distraction of these beacons of our vision, goals, and guidelines for our well being and development. In the U.S., for example, 1996 "Careers/Workforce Development" bills are focused primarily on first-job, next-job placement, rather than on personal responsibility for long and short-term career planning, personal decision making, personal career stewardship, and balancing career and life roles and responsibilities. As noted so frequently and in so many ways in this book, ultimately, the stakes are very high; the issues are simultaneously local, national and international, and we are all shareholders.

In the more than forty essays, we find something for everyone interested in career development. The breadth of coverage is nicely complemented by a brief but intensive, even at times, passionate format of short narratives. It is evident that the editors lived up to their announced goal of having the authors' characteristics, insights, professional intuitions, and values shine through, almost as if the readers were having a conversation with the writers. In combining resources of both the Educational Resources Information Center on Counseling and Student Services (ERIC/CASS) and the National Career Development Association, each with a priority on career planning and decision making, but each with different perspectives, we find a tool well suited for pre-service and inservice education, preparation, and consultation. We are most pleased to be able to join with others around the world to celebrate ERIC's thirtieth anniversary:1966 - 1996. It is especially fitting that this volume, which explores the history and probes the future of career development, should be issued on ERIC/CASS's thirtieth anniversary. It clearly illustrates the high quality of past accomplishments and the potential for future contributions.

Not since the Great Depression have work and jobs mattered so much to so many. But never has career (in the fullest sense of that concept and evolving activity) had the potential to matter so much! This book gives us many suggestions for policies and practices which promote individual career development as a complement to and means of surviving, corporate and governmental policy shifts, by finding balance amidst the turbulence, by finding and maintaining personal empowerment. I salute Garry Walz and Rich Feller for making this book happen. Enjoy!

Dennis Engels, President, National Career Development
Association and Regents Professor, University of North Texas

Table of Contents

*T*urbulence in Career Development: What Changes are Occurring in Career Development & Why?

*I*nnovative Tools and Techniques That Maximize the Effectiveness of Career Development Interventions
....301

A Look to the Future of Career Development Programs and Practices..339

Foundations Revisited

Henry Borow
Norman Gysbers
Sunny Hansen
John Krumboltz
Esther Matthews
Carl McDaniels
John McFadden
Larry Osborne
Sam Osipow
Anna Ranieri
Lee Richmond
Nancy Schlossberg
Anna Miller-Tiedeman
David Tiedeman

1

Vocational Guidance and Social Activism: A Fifty Year Perspective

Henry Borow

This article provides me with a welcome opportunity to reflect on my more than half-century career as a counseling and career development psychologist and to consider how my views of the field may have changed over time. I believe that a fleeting glance at history may help provide some sense of scale concerning how far we have traveled and in what directions.

What were we doing in vocational guidance fifty-some years ago? I was a graduate student/counselor in the Psychoeducational Clinic at Penn State in the early 1940s. Our clients were mostly college students who came to the clinic chiefly for help in choosing academic majors and career fields. We usually scheduled three contacts per client: the initial session an intake interview to hear the presenting problem and to collect some background information, rarely anything in depth; the second session to administer a brief battery of tests, including the original form of the Strong Vocational Interest Blank; and the final session to present and interpret the client's test score profile with recommendations for curriculum and occupational decisions.

> *...it has not been improved technology and intervention strategies so much as the historic emergence of several powerful and liberating ideas...that created the watershed permanently altering the way we view our field and the way we conduct our practice.*

The Strong Blank had to be hand-scored with the aid of two small mechanical counters to tabulate the weighted (plus and minus) item responses. Since hand-scoring required about five minutes per scale, scoring was limited to about a half dozen preselected occupations for each client to conserve time and cost. Group interest scales were at a primitive stage of development, and with the exception of the original 1939 edition of the U.S. Employment Service's *Dictionary of Occupational Titles,* job family schemes allowing counselees to gain a broad overview of the world of work were nonexistent. Interaction in the counseling sessions was generally limited to a few timid client questions and counselor responses. It was tacitly assumed that clients fell into two rather distinct problem categories—those presenting vocational decision-making questions and those with personal adjustment problems—and that dealing with both issues in the same session would ordinarily be inappropriate. There was wide but not universal acceptance of the "test 'em and tell 'em" format of career counseling portrayed here, although we ourselves did not use that unflattering description of it.

The budding field of guidance, lacking a parent discipline of its own, had embraced the psychology of individual differences as its adoptive parent. Guidance professionals championed the truth-disclosing power of objective measurement and flaunted the objective test as their mantra. By measuring the correspondence between personal trait patterns and occupational requirements, vocational psychologists hoped to be able to forecast client probability of success or failure across a wide range of occupations. Choice of occupation was the single-minded goal of vocational guidance, and the calculation of probabilities by objective measurement was the method of choice. Even earlier, intrigued by the prospect of forecasting careers, Hull (1928) had proposed a machine that would furnish differential occupational predictions from aptitude test scores.

I do not consider myself as having made an original contribution to career development theory or knowledge discovery. Rather, I have attempted through my writing to serve as an interpreter, critical examiner, and synthesizer of the contributions of prominent theorists and researchers. I have tried to present ideas and trends in historical perspective, doing so in the belief that, to make sense out of our present and to gauge the future, we must know where we came from and where we have been.

Having held a long-term interest in metatheory—that is, the logic of theory construction— I have looked at extant theories of career development, not so much in terms of how well they mirror reality, but rather to discover how well they conform to the rules of good theory making. I came to the conclusion some years ago that our hypothetical career development models, although helpful, do not represent theories in the formal sense but stand rather as speculative pictures; that is to say, they are "as if" models or accounts of how career-related behavior might unfold. Among their other frailties, our so-called "theories" rely on weak statistical laws (correlational data) rather than on a well-ordered set of cause-and-effect connections induced from replicated baseline data. Failure to concede this limitation exposes practitioners to the error of taking career development theory too literally, as we may have done, for example, in the 1950s with Ginzberg's theory of occupational choice, and again in the 1960s with Roe's theory of child-rearing patterns and personal needs.

On the credit side, the best of our conceptual scenes map out broad schemes for understanding the meaning of human work and career striving. They also provide a rough-hewn frame of reference within which selected research findings and counseling techniques can be provisionally integrated. As in other applied sciences impatient for progress, however, practical gains in career development have often come from exigencies and circumstances devoid of theory. It is not improbable, of course, that the creation of more sophisticated conceptual models can spur significant advances in our career development delivery systems. But I think we have learned not to expect an abundant practical return from theory any time soon.

As I thought about the changes that have taken place during my identification with the career development field, I was initially tempted to identify the new sophisticated information technology, interactive computer-based guidance systems, and an expanding catalog of counseling strategies (examples are career shadowing, guided imagery, paradoxical intervention, skills rehearsal) as the major contributors to progress. But that would miss the mark. In my judgement, it has not been improved technology and intervention strategies so much as the historic emergence of several powerful and liberating ideas, two in particular, that created the watershed permanently altering the way we view our field and the way we conduct our practice.

The first was self-concept theory's bold challenge to the validity of the classical trait-measurement approach to understanding and helping clients. Carl Rogers' (1942) *Counseling and Psychotherapy* sent shock waves through the counseling community and generated intense and prolonged controversy. Rogers, who preferred to think of his person-oriented posture as a point of view rather than a theory or technique, placed client feelings and thoughts at the core of the counseling encounter, and he pointedly questioned the effectiveness of testing and diagnosis in the helping relationship. Although he was speaking out of his experience as a psychotherapist, it was clear that Rogers believed his argument to be valid for all forms of counseling. Among the resultant changes in manner of operation that we conventional practitioners learned to make, and not without some resistance and discomfort, was closer attention in the counseling interview to the dynamics of affective behavior and to verbalized feelings as a critically relevant source of information about the client.

The notion of developmental stages was a second seminal concept that significantly modified our picture of the occupational exploration and choice process. The idea of studying behavior by means of a life-stages paradigm had been advanced by Charlotte Buehler in Europe, and by Erik Erikson and Robert Havighurst, but it was expressly set in a career framework by Donald Super. His astounding productivity on this fruitful theme over the last forty years of Super's life dramatically redefined and durably altered the course of career development research and practice. I was fortunate to spend a year as research associate during the early phase of Super's longitudinal Career Pattern Study, and I became a confirmed advocate of the developmental focus upon career exploration research.

I drew on the child development literature for indications that career-relevant behavior characteristics might have roots in childhood socialization. This was an investigative theme that had received scant attention from vocational psychologists, probably because vocational guidance had been traditionally fixed on the act of choice which typically occurred at school-leaving in middle or late adolescence. What I discovered in the journal literature of early childhood was a rich vocabulary of connected constructs that looked very much like the connotative markers of adolescent and young adult career maturity: ability to delay gratification, internal controls, self-management, readiness to explore the environment, coping behavior, Laura Murphy's progressive mastery, Robert White's effectance motivation, personal autonomy (sense of personal agency), achievement motivation, and the like. At the invitation of the Society for Research in Child Development, I published "Development of Occupational Motives and Roles" as a chapter in the society's 1966 handbook, *Review of Child Development Research* (Borow, 1966). I resynthesized my interpretation under the title "Occupational Socialization: Acquiring a Sense of Work" in the National Career Development Association's third decennial volume (Borow, 1984).

New empirical support for the claim that childhood variables are strong predictors of later career-related behavior has come from a recent longitudinal study by Clausen (1991), an occupational sociologist. Clausen, who employs the construct "competence" as a near synonym for Bandura's "self-efficacy," concludes that adolescent competence is powerfully influenced by family (parental) socialization and related childhood conditions and that, in turn, competence level at high school age has consequences for later educational and career attainment. I believe that claims of this kind make a strong case for revitalizing the school-based elementary grades curriculum in career education that seemed so promising in the 1970s.

The boundaries of the knowledge terrain that career development investigators cultivate are too constrained. Several social science fields, among them occupational and industrial sociology and labor economics, offer clarifying descriptions and insights on the structure of work and the operation of the labor market, but regrettably, we in career development have established little intellectual engagement with these disciplines. In particular, occupational sociology contributes images of work life, work style, and career histories that pose a challenge to some of the commonly held assumptions and priorities of career development counselors and researchers (Hotchkiss & Borow, in press). Sociologists are far less optimistic than career development theorists about the degree of control available to individuals for implementing career plans and aspirations. They assert that labor market forces and conditions related to socioeconomic status are major determinants of career outcomes and, as such, seriously constrict the decision-making process. Further, whereas psychologists and career counselors are interested in how the individual's overall makeup, including cognitive and personality traits, will influence job performance, sociologists reverse the two sides of the equation and emphasize the effects that workplace rules and conditions and market circumstances exert on worker satisfaction and performance.

Career counselors may infer from the sociological perspective on work that the conventional objective of helping clients find a harmonious match with occupational choice should be brought into more realistic balance with the teaching of client coping strategies that are needed to surmount the formidable barriers clients are likely to encounter. The current widespread trends toward corporate downsizing, wholesale layoffs, and drastic reductions in long-term, career-ladder positions, and toward part-time jobs carrying no benefits and no future . . . these grim developments call into question the idealized picture of the career counseling and planning process that our textbooks and journals often present. Twenty years ago, Charles Warnath (1975) published a controversial paper entitled "Vocational Theories: Directions to Nowhere" in which he charged that career development theories and career counseling ignore the reality that "jobs . . . are designed to meet the needs of production and profit . . . not to meet the personal needs of the people who fill those jobs." We can dismiss Warnath's polemic if we choose, but we do so at our own peril.

As for the future of career development, I have a brief but urgent wish list. These hopes center on the need for renewed social action and advocacy and heightened attention to our accountability. If impediments to hygienic work socialization and to entrance into and advancement in a career are as disquieting as my statement has suggested, counselors will need to take on a more forthright and assertive demeanor. They can learn to be more frank about representing work for what it is . . . sometimes growth producing and self-fulfilling but often not. School counselors do not always speak candidly to students about the depersonalizing character of many types of work. I would welcome a resurgence of the spirit of social activism that caught the attention of many counselors in the tumultuous 1960s. In my scenario, a new breed of counselors, through direct intervention, mentoring, and cooperative efforts with community service centers, will provide career survival skills and damage control to our most vulnerable clients: school leavers caught in the void between school and work, part-time employees in dead-end jobs, and discouraged, unemployed job-seekers.

Secondly, our work is under scrutiny. Given the mounting competition for shrinking budgetary resources, we can no longer expect society to support our counseling enterprise on the strength of our verbal assurance that what we do is worthwhile. Legislative bodies, school boards, and funding agencies are asking insistent questions about the returns on their monetary investment in human services, including career counseling. It is probably safe to say that public policy makers are not greatly impressed by paper-and-pencil improvements in self-insight and self-esteem ratings; they want more pragmatic results. For those students exposed to career education programs, is the school dropout rate lower? Do more of them complete diploma requirements? Do more of them find gainful employment after school completion? Oliver in 1969 and Hotchkiss and Vetter in 1987 have made clear how difficult are the problems of research on outcomes of career counseling. Nonetheless, we must find ways to produce more convincing evidence of the worth of our endeavor.

References

Borow, H. (1966). The development of occupational motives and roles. In L. Hoffman & M. L. Hoffman (Eds.), *Review of child development research,* Vol. 2, pp. 373-422. New York: Russell Sage Foundation.

Borow, H. (1984). Occupational socialization: Acquiring a sense of work. In N. C. Gysbers (Ed.), *Designing careers (*pp. 160-189). San Francisco: Jossey-Bass.

Clausen, J. S. (1991). Adolescent competence and the shaping of the life course. *American Journal of Sociology, 96,* 805-842.

Hotchkiss, L., & Borow, H. (in press). Sociological perspectives on work and career development. In D. Brown, L. Brooks, & Associates (Eds.), *Career choice and development* (3rd ed.). San Francisco: Jossey-Bass.

Hull, C. L. (1928). *Aptitude testing.* New York: World Book Co.

Rogers, C. R. (1942). *Counseling and psychotherapy.* Boston: Houghton Mifflin.

Warnath, C. F. (1975). Vocational Theories: Directions to Nowhere. *Personnel and guidance journal, 53,* 422-428.

2

Beyond Career Development—
Life Career Development Revisited

Norman C. Gysbers

Twenty years ago an article titled "Beyond Career Development—Life Career Development" written by myself and Earl J. Moore (Gysbers & Moore, 1975) appeared in the *Personnel and Guidance Journal.* In it we proposed the concept of life career development in an effort to expand and extend career development from the historical occupational perspective to a life perspective in which occupation (and work) had connection, meaning, and place. We defined life career development as self-development over the life span through the interaction and integration of the roles, settings, and events of a person's life. The word "life" in life career development was used to focus on the total person—the human career. The word "career" identified and related the roles in which individuals are involved (e.g., worker, learner, family member, parent, and citizen), and the settings where individuals find themselves (e.g., home, school, community, and the workplace), and the

> *By adding the four factors of gender, ethnic origin, religion, and race and their potential influences on the original life career development perspective, a broadened real-life structure is available on which clients can better understand their life career development.*

events, planned and unplanned, that occur over their lifetimes (e.g., job entry, marriage, divorce, and retirement). Finally, the words "life career development" brought these separate meanings together, but at the same time a greater meaning emerged. Life career development as a concept was created to describe people and their development, unique people with their own lifestyles.

The need for extending and expanding the conception of career development from a work-and-occupation-only perspective to a life perspective, at that time, was based on the many substantial changes that were occurring in society during the 1970s. Vast and far-reaching changes were taking place in the nature and structure of the social systems in which people lived and the economic systems in which they worked. Also, the values and beliefs individuals held about themselves, about others, and about the world were changing. And, finally, more and more people were searching for meaning and coherence in their personal and work lives.

Because the 1990s is witnessing similar changes but at an even more accelerated pace, it is appropriate to revisit the original conceptualization of life career development. Is the concept still relevant? Are modifications needed? This essay responds to these questions by first briefly showing how the broadened view of career evolved over the past ninety years to establish the background and context for the revisit. Then attention is turned to describing a major modification in the original 1975 conception of life career development. Next, the essay focuses on how the now even broader conception of life career development provides individuals with greater explanatory power to understand their past and present life career development and to visualize and plan for their life careers. Finally, emphasis is given to the utility of the now even broader view of life career development as a perspective on human development and behavior from which to develop and manage comprehensive school guidance programs for children and adolescents.

Changing Views of Career Development: Then and Now

In his book *Choosing a Career,* Parsons (1909) used the terms vocation, career, and occupation. For example, on page four of his book he used the term vocation as in "the choice of a vocation" and then in the same paragraph he used the phrase "working career." Later, Parsons used the phrase "scientific choice of occupation" (p. 99), "building up a successful career" (p. 100), and "building a career" (p. 101). While it is unclear as to the meanings Parsons attached to the words vocation, career, and occupation in these contexts, it is interesting to note the use of the word career.

Following the work of Parsons, the terms used by others to describe this phenomenon over the next few decades seemed to settle on the words vocation, occupation, and vocational. Occasional use of the term "career" occurred as in "the life-career motive" and as in "life career classes" in schools that focused on the study of occupational opportunities and problems. Even then however, the term seemed to have mostly an occupational connotation.

Vocational guidance during the 1920s, 30s, and 40s, following Parsons' lead, became the means or the process to assist individuals to choose an occupation, prepare for it, enter it and make progress in it. This was the mainline definition of vocational guidance that persisted during the 1920s, 30s, and 40s (with minor revisions during this time span). Occasionally, the term career was used but when it was, it continued to have an occupational emphasis.

The beginnings of current conceptions of career development began appearing in the literature during the early 1950s although, as we have seen, the precursors of these conceptions seemed to have been present in the work of Parsons and other professionals who followed him. During the 1950s however, theorists began to emphasize a broader and more developmental view of occupation (vocation) and occupational (vocational) choice. It was during this period of time that the term "vocational development" became popular as a way of describing the broadened view of occupational (vocational) choice and the many factors that influenced it. At the same time, the word career was being used with increasing frequency.

During the 1960s and 1970s the word career began to displace the word vocations in definition and use. For example, in 1973, the National Vocational Guidance Association (NVGA) published a paper (done jointly with the American Vocational Association) that defined career and career development. In essence, it defined career as "a time-extended working out of a purposeful life pattern through work undertaken by the individual" (1973, p. 7). Career development was defined as "the total constellation of psychological, sociological, educational, physical, economic, and chance factors that combine to shape the career of any given individual" (p. 7). In 1976, Super defined career as:

The sequence of major positions occupied by a person throughout his preoccupational, occupational and post-occupational life; includes work-related roles such as those of student, employee, and pensioner, together with complementary vocational, familial, and civic roles. Careers exist only as people pursue them; they are person-centered. (p. 20)

By the 1980s, the broader, more encompassing definitions of career and career development were in place including the definition that I, along with my colleague Earl Moore, proposed. Correspondingly, the words "career," "career development," and "career guidance and counseling" had almost completely replaced the words "vocation," "vocational development," and "vocational guidance and counseling" in the literature and in use. One important piece of evidence of this occurred on July 1, 1985 when the National Vocational Guidance Association (NVGA) changed its name and became the National Career Development Association (NCDA). Another important piece of evidence occurred in September of 1986 when the *Vocational Guidance Quarterly* became the *Career Development Quarterly*.

Life Career Development Today and Tomorrow

Is the 1975 conception of life career development still useful? Does it provide sufficient explanatory power to facilitate our understanding of human development and behavior in career terms in the worlds of today and tomorrow? I believe that the basic configuration of life roles, life settings, and life events unfolding over a lifetime is still valid. However, it is clear that there are important factors at work that influence the life career development of individuals that were missing from the 1975 conception. What are these factors? What influence do they exert on the lives of individuals?

McDaniels and Gysbers (1992) answered these questions by adding the factors of gender, ethnic origin, religion, and race to the 1975 conception of life career development. The addition of these factors underscored their importance in shaping the life career development of individuals of all ages and circumstances. These factors provided greater explanatory power to the life career development conception to increase individual understanding and program relevancy.

Before I focus on how the explanatory power of life career development can be increased by adding the factors of gender, ethnic origin (ethnicity), religion, and race to the original conception, it is first necessary to define two of these terms: ethnic origin and race. Ethnic origin or ethnicity refers to a group of people who share a unique social and cultural heritage. The sociocultural customs (e.g., language, religion, food, dance, values, etc.) of ethnic groups are passed down from one generation to the next. Examples of ethnic groups include Italians, Ethiopians, Sioux, and Koreans. The term African American (Black) can be used as a racial or ethnic classification. Race on the other hand, refers to a group of people who share various physical characteristics such as hair texture, body types, facial features and skin pigmentation (e.g., Negroid, Caucasoid, Mongoloid). Race also refers to the shared socio-historical experiences of a group of people based on their physical appearance (e.g., the enslavement of Blacks). Although race as a biological construct has no implication for human behavior, race as a social construct significantly affects one's experiences, beliefs, behavior, and social interactions.

Individual Understanding

Providing individuals with the ability to more fully explain and understand the what, why, and how of their overall life career development, the career goals they may have, or the career concerns they may face, is important, particularly in today's complex society. We live in a nation that is a part of a world economy. We live in a nation that is increasingly diverse racially, religiously, and ethnically, and yet has common themes that connect us all. We live in a nation that is continuing to change its views on what it means to be female or male educationally and occupationally. Religion continues to be an important part of many individuals' lives. Thus, the influences of all of these factors on the life career development of individuals must be understood more completely and reckoned with more directly if individuals in our society are to achieve their career goals or respond effectively to the career challenges they face.

Since one of the purposes of a theoretical concept such as life career development is to help explain human development and behavior, the more effectively it does so for individuals, the better. The life career development view of human development and behavior was created to provide clients and counselors with a way to analyze and understand clients' development and behavior in career terms; to expand their vision of career, from a work only focus, to a broader view involving life roles, life settings, and life events, all interacting over the life span. This allows them to focus on a specific role but, at the same time, connect that role to other roles, to appreciate the influence various life settings may have on life roles, and anticipate the possible impact that planned and unplanned events may have on career planning and decision-making. By adding the four factors of gender, ethnic origin, religion, and race and their potential influences on the original life career development perspective, a broadened real-life structure is available on which clients can display, organize, and understand the impact these factors have on their socialization—their life career development.

To illustrate the potential of this conceptualization consider clients who are struggling with work and family issues and concerns. It is sometimes difficult for them to identify, sort out, and understand the dynamics involved. What is required is a way to conceptualize these dynamics and to have a structure on which to display them. Often the issues and concerns involved pertain to more than work and family. They also may involve other life roles, settings, and events. Hence, the conceptualization used needs to be broad enough and sensitive enough to identify and respond to these related problems. Life career development is such a conceptualization, and as such, is a lens through which clients can view and understand work and family concerns. Add the factors of gender, ethnic origin, race, and religion and the lens becomes even more powerful. Now clients have a way of bringing their personal histories and the histories of their reference groups into focus. Now they can see how these factors have directly or indirectly influenced them, their views of themselves, others, and the world in which they live. Now they have four additional factors to use to understand and respond to their struggles with work and family issues and concerns.

Program Relevancy

By adding the four factors of gender, ethnic origin, religion, and race to the life career development conception, we have seen that its explanatory power can be greatly increased. It becomes more personally relevant because it provides individuals with ways to make direct and meaningful connections among their past and present life experiences, using the real-life, real-world factors of gender, ethnic origin, religion, and race as lenses to understand and appreciate their personal histories (their socialization) and how these histories have impacted their views of themselves, others, and the works in which they live. Now the question is, can this expanded view of life career development provide school counselors with new insights concerning the needed nature, structure, and content for school guidance programs? The answer is yes.

If the expanded view of life career development is a way of describing, understanding, and guiding human development, then it has particular relevance to school guidance program development and management (Gysbers & Henderson, 1994). It has particular relevance because the expanded view of life career development provides a perspective, a point of view, about human development and behavior that can guide school counselors as to the needed nature, structure, and content of the school guidance programs. It provides a perspective from which to identify the knowledge, skills, and attitudes (competencies) that students need to facilitate their personal, educational, and occupational development, their life career development. By adding the factors of gender, ethnic origin, religion, and race to the roles, settings, and events configuration of life career development,the effects of one's socialization, one's reference groups, and one's history can be identified and can be taken into account when designing and putting into operation the activities of the program. Thus, the expanded view of life career development that can provide personal relevance and empowerment to individuals can also be incorporated directly into the design and operation of a school guidance program.

How can the expanded view of life career development be incorporated into the design and operation of a comprehensive school guidance program? It begins with the insights generated by school counselors concerning the needs of students as these are revealed by the lenses of the four factors of gender, ethnic origin, religion, and race, overlaid on life roles, settings, and events. Because of the possible effects of these factors on the lives of students, students may lack knowledge about personal, educational, and occupational options. Or, what knowledge they may have may be stereotypical. Both conditions may lead students to believe that because of the socialization they have experienced some roles are closed to them or at least entry into them is severely restricted. Other students may not be aware of what is possible at all so that the adage "an opportunity unknown is not an opportunity at all" becomes an unfortunate reality.

Based on the insights of school counselors concerning the needs of students, based on school counselors' knowledge of the impact that the four factors have on students' socialization, and based on school counselors' full understanding of how these factors have created intentional and unintentional personal, educational, and occupational biases and barriers for some individuals, the next step is to select and put in operation the content and activities of the guidance program. While the content and activities of the program will vary by building location, level, and population, there are common guiding principles that are important for school counselors to keep in mind. These guiding principles that follow were adapted from the work of McDaniels and Gysbers (1992, pp. 295-296).

1. *School counselors should consider their own values and prejudices.* This may mean doing some real soul searching, carrying out some assessment of personal positions, getting involved with encounter groups, or maybe doing some serious reading and talking. Another way to approach this could be through professional conferences, workshops, and the like. Taking stock of personal attitudes and prejudices and finding out what to do about them if some changes are in order will allow school counselors to function more effectively with *all* types of clients.

2. *School counselors should strive to seek a deeper level of understanding of various population groups with special needs.* Counselors should make this a comprehensive, ongoing effort at building a knowledge base about gender, racial/ethnic groups, and disabling conditions—that is, about the people involved and their cultural, sociological, psychological, and economic background.

3. *It is important for school counselors to be in a constant state of growth.* The completion of a class, degree, certificate, workshop, or whatever does not mean that a counselor has arrived! Instead this should set the stage for the next level of professional and personal advancement and should provide a basis for better service to others.

4. *School counselors must work aggressively with family members in promoting better career development for all populations.* It is increasingly evident that school counselors cannot relate solely to a student/client in isolation. The family system must be considered as fully as possible in the total picture. This is a *must* consideration.

5. *School counselors should promote the visibility of career models wherever and whenever possible.* This is very important for young people. They are in need of strong career (and personal) role models close to their own situations that they can believe in and relate to.

6. *It is important to find career mentors for students.* Career Models can bepeople who are far away, but they must be available as a source of encouragement, support, and nurturance to the extent possible. Finding and promoting career models and mentors represent highly desirable interventions.

7. *School counselors should stand out and stand up as advocates for everyone in special population groups.* Action-oriented school counselors—the ones who constantly go to bat for students—are likely to produce the best results.

A Concluding Thought

I have labeled the phenomenon of life career development unfolding over the life span as the drama of the ordinary because it happens each and every day, often unnoticed by the individuals it is effecting directly. And because it does, it appears to be mundane, not often appreciated by individuals. It is often veiled by ordinariness. As a result, individuals may fail to understand its dynamic nature and the substantial impact it has throughout their lives. By using the broader concept of life career development (the four factors of gender, ethnicity, religion, and race added to life roles, settings, and events) as a way to understand human development and behavior—the human career—life career development becomes the drama of the extraordinary.

References

Gysbers, N. C., & Henderson, P. (1994). *Developing and managing your school guidance program* (2nd ed.). Alexandria: American Counseling Association.

Gysbers, N. C., & Moore, E.J. (1975). Beyond career development-
-life career development. *Personnel and Guidance Journal, 53*(9), 647-652.

McDaniels, C., & Gysbers, N. C. (1992). *Counseling for career development.* San Francisco: Jossey Bass.

National Vocational Guidance Association (1973). *Position paper on career development.* Washington DC: Author.

Parsons, F. (1909). *Choosing a vocation.* Boston: Houghton Mifflin.

Super, D. E. (1976). *Career education and the meaning of work.* Washington, DC: U.S. Government Printing Office.

3

ILP: Integrating Our Lives, Shaping Our Society

L. Sunny Hansen

How do we as professional helpers assist people in making life choices and decisions in these changing times? Aren't our models of fitting people into jobs still the best way to provide career counseling, especially with so many workers losing jobs and needing help finding new ones? With greater numbers of ethnic minorities and women seeking an equal place in the opportunity structure, more women and men wanting to work but also wanting more time for family, and many citizens feeling cynical about the political climate and discouraged by violence in local and global communities, the need for individual and community development is critical.

What do we need to know and do to add to our theories, strategies, and interventions to help individuals and families make more effective life planning decisions? How can this be done for their own self interest and with consideration for community needs?

The essence of my response to these questions is that, while we will always need and use the matching or trait-and-factor approach to vocational guidance and career counseling, it is not sufficient. With the enormous changes occurring in society, in individuals, families, and work, my thesis is that we need to help students, clients, and employees more fully understand those changing contexts and that we must consider a more holistic and integrative approach to human development.

> *Integrative Life Planning is a complex, comprehensive process of examining critical themes influencing our lives and identifying patterns and strategies which can help us to understand, manage and perhaps even shape those influences.*

Besides the changing life patterns in the Information Society, there are also changes in knowledge systems—in what we know and how we know it—with a growing body of literature in contemporary psychology on "ways of knowing." In the field of counseling (including career counseling), for example, new theories of multiculturalism, feminism, contextualism, and wholism have been created which suggest alternatives for practices with increasingly diverse populations. It is my belief that these new ways of knowing are essential, not to replace but to complement traditional empirical approaches.

What I see as needed in the new millennium is an alternative frame of reference for career development. Dramatic changes in this global village require new ways of solving problems or what some call paradigms and paradigm shifts. In this article I propose one such framework called Integrative Life Planning (ILP).

Discussion

The work of the late Donald E. Super (1990) has had the most influence on my thinking about career development. In graduate school, when I was making major decisions, including that I did not want to choose between career and family but wanted both, I was introduced to his concepts of career as more than occupation. His notions that roles and theaters of a person's life (the Life-Career Rainbow) are important as developmental tasks to be mastered over the lifespan made sense to me then as they do today. His expanded concept of career undergirds the "Career Development Curriculum" my colleagues and I developed at the University of Minnesota in the 70s, as well as the *BORN FREE* program, and his life-roles framework has influenced those who have begun to approach career development from a broader life-roles and work-family linkage context.

While there is much in the work of Super and associates that is still valid today, our ways of looking at people's lives and at society in the next century may be very different from the way they were at the turn of the last century or in the 1950s. Increasingly, surveys of people's needs indicate a desire among people of all backgrounds and life circumstances for development in several aspects of life—

what some call the mind-body-spirit connection—not just focused on career or work, but also across cultures. New theories such as holistic, feminist, and multicultural counseling, and concepts such as positive uncertainty, spirituality and work, male-gender-role strain, the construction and deconstruction of gender, and racial, gender, and cultural identity development need to be added to a new framework for career development in the 21st century.

Counseling and career development theory and research are changing (albeit slowly) and beginning to recognize the need for alternative frameworks for practice. Psychologists and counselors have begun to question the fragmentation which has occurred in the past and to examine different kinds of integration, congruence, and convergence of career theory and practice. Many female and multicultural theorists are moving from the separation, autonomy paradigm to one which is relational and connected. Some suggest that American society needs to discard the old self-focused, egotistical approaches to life and life planning to other-focused choices and decisions based on societal needs—choices which could make a positive difference in families and communities. To some, this may seem to be just a variation of Super's well-known definition of career development as the implementation of a self-concept "with satisfaction to self and benefit to society." Amitai Etzioni calls it "communitarianism," a concern for not only individual rights but also community responsibilities. Integrative Life Planning (ILP) is the framework I am proposing to make our career development practice more congruent with future changes in society and in human development. The remainder of this article will briefly explain that concept.

Integrative Life Planning (ILP)

Integrative Life Planning is a complex, comprehensive process of examining critical themes influencing our lives and identifying patterns and strategies which can help us to understand, manage, and perhaps even shape those influences. It is a concept which views career professionals as change agents, helping students, clients, and employees to see themselves as change agents shaping life for themselves and others.

Traditional approaches to career planning rely heavily on tests to predict which occupation is best for a person, it assumes there is one perfect job to be selected from a shrinking occupational pie. They ignore the multipotentialities and transitions of people's lives and the work-family-leisure-learning changes expected to make life more difficult in the Digital Age. They also seem to assume that career decisions are solely individual decisions without recognizing that such decisions are made in context, influenced by race, gender, class, beliefs, and culture, and affect other parts of our lives, especially our families and the communities in which we live.

ILP is intended to complement more traditional approaches by providing a "Big Picture" framework for career counselors and other helping professionals to assist their clients to see the larger picture within which they work, love, learn, and play. It provides a comprehensive conceptual model along with qualitative tools to stimulate thought and action on topics important in people's lives today, topics not always addressed in the career literature, such as spirituality, inclusivity, pluralism, and community—all being extremely relevant to life planning.

It is important to understand that Integrative Life Planning is still a concept in **process**. While it draws from related theories and practice and is based on a considerable body of research on the various topics included in it, it does not offer definitive answers or "findings." It is still a conceptual framework, but one with a number of new ideas which professionals can take and develop into their own action plans. It represents the progression of my thinking over the past 30 years, from my own career decisions, to the Minnesota Career Development Curriculum, to the BORN FREE program which promoted expanded options for women and men, to the current integrative and comprehensive focus on life planning. It represents my interpretation of the expanded concept of career, drawn from my own life and family context as well as from the literature.

ILP is a concept which fits well with the new paradigms in the behavioral and social sciences and will appeal to those who believe that new paradigms are also needed in career and life planning. It recognizes the shift from segmented, objective, fragmented thinking to more integrated, subjective, and holistic world views. Although most approaches to career planning have focused primarily on the work role, ILP specifically addresses the connections between work and family, women's and men's development, personal and career counseling, spirituality and community, inclusivity and multiculturalism, and the intersections of these. While it presents a contemporary philosophical framework, it also offers a solid knowledge base, as well as both original and adapted tools for professionals to use in an integrative approach to career counseling and career workshops. Let us look then at the six life themes which comprise the framework for ILP.

Changing Global and National Contexts

An overwhelming number of issues are affecting us as we become more of a global village. My hope is that career counselors and others will identify those most relevant to their clients to determine how such issues and trends may affect their lives. In writing about global challenges that confront humanity, Johnson and Cooperrider (1991) list 10,233 global issues; in a more modest vein I have selected ten which seem most important to me: Technological Change, Environmental Degradation, Human Rights, Multiculturalism, Migration, Changing Gender Roles, Violence, World Population Issues, Spirit and Meaning, and New Ways of Knowing. Similarly, on the national scene, I believe that changes in the demographics of the population, the movement toward adult development and lifespan learning, the existence of multiple family types, and, perhaps most important, the changes in workers, the workplace, and work patterns, present contextual challenges which will require additional life-planning knowledge and skills on the part of both clients themselves and their professional helpers.

Holistic Development

In a society which has focused so strongly on work, it may appear naive to suggest that holistic life planning—which includes mind, body, and spirit, and social,intellectual, physical, emotional, and career development— is possible. But there is growing recognition that our lives do not fall conveniently into little boxes and that what happens in one part of our lives affects other parts. The best example of this is in the counseling field where leaders increasingly are writing about the connection between career and personal counseling and challenging the distinction between the two. Counselors have known for a long time that good career counseling is very personal.

Other signs of integrative thinking include the increase in articles linking at least the work and family parts of life (we have long linked work and education and work and leisure). When we think about the major life roles, what I call the 4L's of love, labor, learning, and leisure, it is usually the labor (work) and learning (education) roles which get the most emphasis. Many feel that work cannot meet all needs and express a desire to balance work and other life roles, to see "work within a life" and to become more integrated persons. Since it is difficult for individuals to develop in all of these areas at once, they need help in priority setting according to the individual, family, and community needs and values. Integrative Life Planning is one approach to help people move toward more holistic lives.

Work-Family Roles and Relationships

As part of the movement toward wholeness, much more attention needs to be given to reforming gender roles, male-female relationships, and the connection between family and work. The BORN FREE program promoted equal partnerships and expanded options for both women and men. It is now being "re-visioned" to include culture, gender, and career. Although interest in this area was heightened in the 70s and early 80s, and many work-family task forces were formed in business and industry, that interest seems to have diminished in the 90s as people face job loss, reduced incomes, and job uncertainty. While excellent studies and conceptual literature have been produced, misplaced anger toward women and minorities has slowed progress in helping women and men of all backgrounds to work out new patterns, roles, and relationships in the multiple family structures of our society.

Issues in dual-earner and dual-career families comprise much of the literature, and many gender role dilemmas, both in families and in the workplace, cause considerable stress. Some of these relate to work-family balance, which is hard to achieve, especially when organizations usually expect workers to put work before family (Hall, 1989). Others have been exacerbated by recent changes in work and the new psychological and economic contract between employers and workers.

Gender roles are changing across cultures, and career counselors need greater understanding of the power of gender, race, and class in careers as well as of men's and women's differential socialization and life planning, and of ways to facilitate mutual planning and partnerships. I define partnerships as those relationships in which each partner: 1) treats the other with dignity and respect, 2) demonstrates flexibility in negotiating roles, and 3) enables the other to choose and enact roles and fulfill responsibilities congruent with his or her talents and potentials and the two partners' mutual goals for the relationship, the family, and society.

Inclusivity and Pluralism

The need for human beings to incorporate into consciousness the critical issues of demographics, dignity, difference, and diversity can best be described with the term "pluralism" and "pluralistic development." This requires an acute awareness of all kinds of difference— racial, ethnic, class, religious, gender, age, disability, and sexual orientation. Such awareness is essential to our interpersonal interactions and inclusive attitudes and environments of the future. Business organizations have recognized this need through extensive attention to diversity training, helping workers and managers to learn to value differences and to develop effective, diverse work teams. New multicultural counseling courses, political action for change, and other initiatives in our field also represent a constructive response to these critical issues. While developing positive interpersonal relationships on and off the job always has been an important component of the broad concept of life planning, with the social, economic, and political issues facing our society, it is imperative that we help people learn not only to understand but to accept, value, and celebrate diversity.

Spirituality and Community

Spirituality is a theme central to the lives of many but often missing in the career development literature. I link spirituality with meaning and purpose, the core of one's self that gives meaning to one's life. It relates to the search for self-actualization, personal values, and wholeness. I use the term as a yearning for something larger than oneself, the need to give back to society, to contribute one's talents to the improvement of community, and achieving a sense of connectedness with others. Our logical approaches to career development in the past have allowed for little attention to the place of the spiritual in life. Counselors and career development specialists can play an important role in helping clients explore the larger meaning and purpose in their lives, including the meaning of money and materialism in relation to life purpose and community.

Transitions and Personal and Social Change

The theme of transitions and personal and social change is one of the most important in ILP. Several models exist which career specialists can use to help clients or workers both think about and successfully negotiate the transition process. Schlossberg's (1981) detailed model of "human adaptation to transition," with its focus on not only triggering events but "non-events," is especially useful, particularly in today's climate of involuntary job transitions, the de-jobbing of America (Bridges, 1994), new psychological and economic contracts between employers and workers, and large numbers of contingency or temporary workers.

Transition counseling will be an important field in the future, not only "outplacement counseling" but counseling which helps students, clients, and workers make transitions at all stages of life. It will be a challenge to career professionals to help people in transition integrate those most important parts of their development in their own contexts at different life stages. Clients will also need to be taught the relationship of decision-making to transition-making, utilizing new decision models such as Gelatt's (1989) "positive uncertainty," which combines both reason and intuition and can help prepare people for the change and instability which they may face in the new millennium.

An equally important aspect of transitions is helping people to become change agents in their personal lives and in their organizations. A rich body of literature on organizational development and systems change can be helpful in this process. Moving from where we are in our lives and organizations to where we would like to be can be facilitated by any of several models of change process. I believe we can be change agents in our own lives, in our interpersonal relationships, and in our institutions. Identifying both the "inhibitors" and "facilitators" of change can be helpful in implementing the change process.

Recommended Course of Action

It is difficult to recommend a single course of action for Integrative Life Planning. Within the concept, to be described fully in a forthcoming book (Hansen, in press), is an extensive delineation of the themes along with strategies for translating them into action in career counseling and in career development and human resource development workshops. Obviously, it will be important for both counseling practitioners and counselors-in-training to be exposed to this "contextual-developmental" approach to career planning and for counselor education institutions to incorporate this integrative philosophy and concept into their graduate preparation programs. Career planning increasingly will need to be viewed as life planning with new tools developed to assist in the process.

Conclusion

By its nature, an Integrative Life Planning approach to career development is comprehensive, interdisciplinary, and inclusive. It is a systems approach, connecting many parts of our lives and society. No counselor, career development professional, or career planner could be expected to absorb the whole concept at once. Each counselor will have to select those themes which are most important or meaningful at a given time and work with them. In the concept, I try to connect the life roles (the 4L's), development domains (social, intellectual, physical, spiritual, emotional, and career), and identity dimensions (ethnic, racial, gender, class, abilities, beliefs, and sexual orientation) of people's lives.

Six life themes form the framework for ILP, and, because they have been so neglected in career counseling, I put a great deal of emphasis on spiritual and pluralistic development. My hope is that this inclusive concept will provide a "value added" dimension to those theories and practices which have been demonstrated to be effective and, when implemented, help people move toward more holistic lives as well as toward unity within diversity and more caring communities in this changing global community.

References

Bridges, W. (1994). *Job shift: How to prosper in a workplace without jobs.* Reading, MA: Addison-Wesley.

Etzioni, A. (1993). *The spirit of community: Rights, responsibilities, and the communitarian agenda.* New York: Crown.

Gelatt, H. B. (1989). Positive uncertainty: A new decision-making framework for counseling. *Journal of Counseling Psychology, 36*(2), 252-256.

Hansen, L. S. (in press). *Integrative Life Planning (ILP): Work, family, and community.* San Francisco: Jossey Bass.

Johnson, P. C., & Cooperrider, D. L. (1991). Finding a path with heart: Global social change organizations and their challenge for the field of organizational development. *Research in Organizational Change and Development, 5,* 223-284.

Schlossberg, N. (1981). A model for analyzing human adaptation to transition. *The Counseling Psychologist, 9*(2), 2-18.

Super, D. E. (1990). A life-span, life-space approach to career development. In D. Brown and L. Brooks, *Career Choice and Development* (2nd ed.). San Francisco, CA: Jossey Bass.

4

Learn, Yearn and Earn

John D. Krumboltz and Anna M. Ranieri

As Pat Powar approached the counselor's door, he felt anxious. So much was at stake. He opened the door to Maria Perez's office. Maria greeted Pat warmly. "You look troubled, Pat. Tell me what's on your mind."

Pat swallowed, then blurted out, "I want you to give me a test that will tell me the right occupation for my life's work."

How should Maria respond to Pat's request? Like many others before him, Pat has asked for something that career counselors can never provide. Should she tell him that no such tests exist, never have and never will? Should she tell him that an occupation that seems right to him now may be completely wrong for him in a few years because his interests and skills will

> *The Learning Theory of Career Counseling affirms counseling practices that recognize the world of work as a changing environment in which workers continue to learn and develop personally and professionally over the course of their careers.*

almost certainly change? Should she tell him that occupations are undergoing such rapid change that a good choice now may soon be obsolete?

Maria sighs, thinking to herself, "Pat is another victim of a theory."

Overview

Pat has adopted the theory that there is one right job for him which he will find by matching his own characteristics with the characteristics of that job. It's a theory that's been around for a long time. Trait and factor theory was the foundation for career counseling, and still serves as the basis for the thoughts and actions of counselors and clients today.

When Frank Parsons (1909) developed the theory, the industrial revolution had created workplaces that required standardized kinds of people in rigidly defined positions. If people could be matched to jobs efficiently and effectively, it was thought that both employees and employers would be satisfied with the results for years to come.

Today's workplace, however, is vastly different. In post-industrial times, occupations and the settings in which they're performed change rapidly. The needs of employers and the roles of employees are not static. The very concept of a job may become obsolete (Bridges, 1994) as employees move beyond job descriptions to a more fluid process of doing whatever needs to be done. People are adapting to changing technologies by retraining. Lifelong learning is a necessity. But people may also change careers because their own professional interests and personal desires change.

No wonder Pat is apprehensive! He still believes he has to find today the answer that will serve him for the next forty or fifty years. If his counselor could give him that answer today, it would be out of date tomorrow, when Pat, his environment, or both, have changed.

We advocate that counselors use a Learning Theory of Career Counseling (Krumboltz, 1996) to respond to the needs of Pat and others like him. It's a theory that says "Learn, Yearn, and Earn." By learning we can formulate new aspirations and fulfill them through a variety of work experiences. We can continue to learn and grow both professionally and personally as we continually interact with our environment.

Discussion

If Pat had lived at an earlier time, Maria might have used some assessment instruments to determine which of Pat's traits would be relevant to him in his career. She would have evaluated his current interests and aptitudes. Then she and Pat would have searched for the name of an occupation that would have provided the best fit for Pat's current characteristics. Having discovered the best match, Maria's work with Pat would have ended. Instead...

"I have some good news and some bad news for you, Pat," said Maria. "The bad news is that there is no test that can tell you what your life's work should be. The good news is that we can find out more about who you are now and identify some areas in which you want to learn new skills and interests. Then, we will explore some possible learning experiences that will help you grow in the directions you want. You will be trying out possible career-related opportunities so you can evaluate their value for you. I am willing to stick with you as you go through this entire process and monitor your progress as long as you like."

Using trait and factor theory, the desired outcome was a decision. Indecision was a sign of failure. Learning theory, on the other hand, acknowledges the role of creative indecision in helping to pave the way for learning and growth. The Social Learning Theory of Career Decision Making (Krumboltz, 1979) showed how an infinite number of accumulated learning experiences resulted in one's current occupational placement. The Learning Theory of Career Counseling (Krumboltz, 1996) builds on that view by specifying what counselors can do now to promote further learning.

Are there career counselors who already use learning methods for helping their clients? Yes. Whether or not they've heard of the theory, these counselors' actions demonstrate that they acknowledge the importance of helping clients plan for change. Maria is such a counselor, as she made clear during Pat's first visit.

"Pat, I'd like to find out more about your current interests, skills, values, and beliefs about work, and about your life outside of work. I have some assessment tools that will help us discover more about what you have learned so far and what you might want to learn next."

Assessment instruments can be used to help people experiment with new learning opportunities, rather than merely diagnose their current state. Vocational assessment instruments summarize some part of what clients have already learned. They can then be used as a jumping off place for continued learning.

The instruments themselves do not provide the needed learning experiences. They can serve as tools, however, for the counselor and the client to use together to identify the preferences, skills, and beliefs that the client has learned so far and to suggest additional interests, skills, beliefs and values that the client might want to acquire in the future.

This idea that interests, beliefs, and values can be changed may sound surprising to some. After all, skills can be learned, but interests, beliefs and values? Many feel that these are static predispositions that people carry with them as they move through life. But interests are acquired, social learning theory tells us, as individuals have experiences that are personally enjoyable to them. New beliefs are acquired as people encounter information that causes them to reassess old beliefs. Values change with life experiences and personal contemplation.

The career counselor's use of assessment instruments can help to frame a discussion of "where to go from here." They serve as a basis for appropriate interventions that foster learning. That's how Maria used them in counseling Pat.

"Pat, one of your scores on the *Career Beliefs Inventory* indicated that it's important for you to have the approval of others as you consider career opportunities. Why don't we spend some time exploring that belief and discussing whose approval you're seeking? Then we can find out about the learning experiences you would like to have and how they fit in with your relationships with others."

A host of interventions can facilitate the learning process. The methods appropriate for most clients can include career education, study materials, and computer-based occupational simulations. Interventions tailored to the characteristics of the individual client may include goal clarification, cognitive restructuring, countering troublesome beliefs, narrative analysis, bibliotherapy, role-playing, paradoxical interventions, and the use of humor. All these interventions are linked by their capacity to promote learning and change.

But is the counseling process working? The evaluation of career counseling outcomes should be appropriate to a learning model. Success for the client is much more than making a decision about a desired occupation; it's the acquisition of new learning that is personally and professionally relevant. Maria evaluates her work with clients by observing how much effort they devote to exploring alternatives and how pleased they are with their own growth and accomplishments.

"I will be working with you, Pat, over an extended period of time as you try out some new ideas and get additional information about yourself and about the world of work. I'll be there to encourage you, and to learn with you. I'll consider our work together successful if you are launched on a continuing learning process."

Recommended Course of Action

The Learning Theory of Career Counseling affirms counseling practices that recognize the world of work as a changing environment in which workers continue to learn and develop personally and professionally over the course of their careers. Maria Perez recognizes that the processes of career counseling can be expanded and redefined in serving her clients as they embark on, or redirect, their lifelong journeys of learning. What actions do we recommend?

Assessment

Use assessment instruments to identify new areas for learning. These areas may center around preferences, skills, interests, beliefs, values, work habits, and/or personality characteristics. Today's clients are seeking to build lives in which their work goals are in accord with their other aspirations and needs. Assessment will take into account clients' experiences both inside and outside the workplace, in relationships, and avocations. Counselors can use assessment instruments as a springboard to suggest additional experiences that will help clients formulate possible future identities. Assessment also will be sensitive to the social and cultural experiences of clients from diverse backgrounds, taking into account their group memberships and their individual identities. The counselor will seek to learn with the client, without using preconceived notions about the client's experiences or desires.

Interventions

Use a variety of educational interventions to foster clients' learning and growth. Consider interventions that will help the client clarify personal and professional aspirations and begin taking action to achieve them. For example, counselors can use techniques to help clients overcome phobias related to interviewing or contacting potential employers. Counselors can design role playing experiences to help clients learn how to ask the boss for a raise. Counselors can help clients dispute irrational beliefs about taking risks in the face of possible failure.

Using learning theory, career counseling becomes far more comprehensive. The counselor can take into account personality and adjustment on the one hand and global labor trends on the other. Maria says, "This complexity is what makes my job so fascinating. I am learning along with Pat as he identifies new areas to explore."

Evaluation

Judge success by measuring the outcomes of learning and the effort devoted to it. The learning process is a highly individual one, but the counselor can measure the amount of effort expended in exploration as one determinant of a successful outcome in counseling. This requires that the counselor trust in the process more than was required in the days when the success of counseling was determined by client decisions. Pat says, "I'm still not sure where I'll end up, but I know what I'm going to try next. Maria has really helped me to open up my thinking, about myself, about work, and about my life as a whole. I've changed a lot since the day when I was hoping she'd match me up with my whole life's work."

Summary

The Learning Theory of Career Counseling takes into account the realities of the workplace and the workers of today. It postulates that learning is the process that has enabled workers to get where they are now. It advocates that counselors can continue to use the learning process to help their clients create satisfying lives for themselves.

Counselors, in applying this theory, use assessment instruments not merely as tools for diagnosis and prediction, but as stimuli for new learning. They can devise a variety of educational methods to help clients master new skills, develop new interests, challenge old beliefs and values, and strengthen effective work habits and personality patterns. Counselors can then evaluate their clients' progress by assessing the degree to which their clients have exerted effort and actually achieved these outcomes.

Lifelong learning is needed in the present age for workers to develop their capabilities and to adapt to a changing workplace. This learning theory confirms and celebrates what some career counselors already do—facilitate clients' new learning—while putting forward a more encompassing view of career counseling as integrating personal and career concerns. Clients thus will be better able to participate effectively in a changing workplace as well as to create more satisfying lives for themselves.

References

Bridges, W. (1994). *Jobshift.* Reading, MA: Addison-Wesley.

Krumboltz, J. D. (1979). A social learning theory of career decision making. In A. M. Mitchell, G. B. Jones, & J. D. Krumboltz (Eds.), *Social learning and career decision making* (pp. 19–49). Cranston, RI: Carroll Press.

Krumboltz, J. D. (1996). A learning theory of career counseling. In M. Savickas & B. Walsh (Eds.), *Integrating career theory and practice.* Palo Alto, CA: Davies-Black Press.

Parsons, F. (1909). *Choosing a vocation.* Boston: Houghton Mifflin.

5

Change and Continuity: Themes of a Lifetime Career

Esther E. Matthews

In 1941 I began my professional education in a master's degree program in counseling and career development. My mentors and role models were exclusively men, who supported my career development at every turn. Women role models in this field were virtually nonexistent. One exception was Anne Roe, who served on my doctoral committee in 1960. From 1959 to 1963 she was Lecturer on Education at Harvard and in 1963 she became the first woman professor in the Graduate School of Education.

Each stage of my career testified to the enormous support of men of vision, perception, and intelligence, who recognized competence without regard to gender. One of the great dangers of some phases of the Women's Movement (1963-on) has been the tendency to minimize or reject the absolute necessity for the understanding, cooperation, and support of both men and women. An exclusive,

> *My professional life themes can be summarized as: 1. career development of girls and women, 2. an individualized philosophy of learning, 3. attention to all facets of understanding human possibilities and, 4. understanding world futurism.*

defensive, parochial attitude paradoxically creates reverse discrimination and delays necessary change and progress. The serious problems that women face are real, but the solutions demand the attention and intelligence of both women and men.

Role models and mentors are fundamentally connected to the professional preparation phases of a career. Later on, the work of innumerable colleagues becomes influential. For example, the many authors represented within the NVGA/NCDA Decennial Volumes, edited by Henry Borow, 1964; Edwin L. Herr, 1974; and Norman C. Gysbers and Associates, 1984, illustrate such influence.

My views on career development have evolved over many decades. Those beliefs have enriched my life and mind, and, I hope, have enhanced the lives of those I have tried to serve. Beliefs grow from interests that are ignited by respected role models and mentors. Eventually these tenets translate into enduring life themes that deepen, expand, and illuminate all aspects of life in unpredictable ways.

My fundamental beliefs are clearly mirrored in professional service through teaching, counseling, supervising, consulting, and writing. In each of these areas of concentration an integrated and definitive philosophy of life has gradually emerged. That philosophy has found expression in four major emphases that were continually shaped by the forces of historical change and continuity. Although I have listed these concentrations separately, they need to be viewed as an interdependent and interrelated matrix.

Professional Life Themes

Theme One: An Enduring Commitment to the Career Development of Girls and Women

I was fortunate to have a doctoral advisor, Dr. David V. Tiedeman, who encouraged my dawning attention in the career development of girls and women. His support was most unusual since interest in the career development of girls and women, in the late 1950s, was virtually nonexistent. It is of interest that the dissertation theme that he supported focused on marriage-career conflict in girls and women (Matthews, 1960). Although through succeeding decades that theme has been affected by great changes in society, it has far from vanished.

Theme One was powerfully supported by my long-term affiliation with the National Career Development Association (formerly The National Vocational Guidance Association). In 1968 NVGA President Norman Feingold asked me to chair the newly-founded Commission on the Occupational Status of Women. The history of that Commission is of considerable historical importance because it reflected the changing attention to, and growing importance of, women's career development. The activities of the Commission involved every part of America and utilized the energy and talents of many people. A comprehensive report on the first twenty years of the Commission covered the period from 1968 to 1988 (Matthews, 1989).

NVGA also helped to sponsor four national conferences on many aspects of the career development of girls and women (Eugene, Oregon, 1970; Boone, North Carolina, 1973; Rutgers University, N.J., 1975; and Hartland, Michigan, 1977). The conferences eventually produced three useful monographs containing a number of articles by a variety of authors. From 1960 to 1995 I have contributed over 30 papers and articles on many aspects of this fascinating topic.

Theme Two: An Individualized Philosophy of Learning, Teaching, and Counseling

Over the years I have thought more and more about the commonalties, as well as the differences, between learning, teaching, and counseling. I have had the opportunity to work with people of various ages, in many settings, and in different cultural and geographical areas.

For me, the key to understanding resided in how to *individualize* learning, teaching, and counseling. I decided to try first to understand how I learned, from childhood onward. Then, perhaps, I would have a deeper understanding about the learning *process* in each individual with whom I worked. This kind of knowledge, of course, drew together many insights from my long experience in education and counseling.

The result of my introspection translated into a book (Matthews, 1988). The book contained an extensive chronology of life experiences and a detailed analysis of how one person came to individualize learning for many people.

Theme Three: A Powerful Concern and Attention to Understanding Human Possibilities Over the Life Span

It is nearly impossible to summarize the depth and extent of my focus on human possibilities. It seems to have been, in part, a reaction to the heavy emphasis on pathology in psychology and in society.

The long-ago roots of my attention to this theme were planted by the gentle, scholarly genius of Robert W. White. Succeeding editions of his classic, *Lives in Progress* (1952, 1966, 1975) made an indelible impression on my mind, because White clearly illustrated the possibility of hope and change as lives unfolded. You can well imagine his dynamic effect on my teaching and counseling.

White's contribution greatly enhanced my understanding of the monumental contributions of Erik H. Erikson. Erikson's knowledge, experience, and insight would deeply affect my writing, teaching, and advising. It is unfortunate that, as with all great theorists, his contributions were not always adequately understood by some people. Several of his classic contributions have, and will, stand the test of time and the verdict of history—for example: *Childhood and Society* (1950) and *Identity and the Life Cycle* (1959). Readers will be appreciative of the book edited by Stephen Schlein (1987) that contains selected papers of Erikson drawn from 1930 to 1980.

As the years raced on, I translated my learning about human possibilities into seminars and papers. I also became committed to autobiographies and biographies as a means of making an unmistakable translation of my own theory and philosophy of human possibilities.

Theme Four: A Sustained Commitment to Understanding all Facets of World Futurism

I found that world conferences on futurism were extraordinarily energizing and inspirational. These meetings directly supported my interests in work, career, and human possibilities. Everyone should have the opportunity to meet with like-minded people from around the globe, who are working to improve the lives of humans and to protect the earth for future generations (Matthews, 1984).

Many of my students became fascinated with the astounding scope of R. Buckminster Fuller's creative vision, by first reading his *Operating Manual for Spaceship Earth* (1968) and then studying his lesser-known, but equally important, *Ideas and Integrities* (1963). Fuller was truly the greatest futurist of this century. The vast productivity of his mind became central to my vision of the future.

Present Thoughts

It is hard to condense one's life into a few thousand words. Yet, I have lived long enough to see, and to be amazed, at the confluence of my life energies and interests. I still maintain a strong commitment to each of the four themes. However, reading, thinking, and writing, at this stage, seem to focus on two factors: the critical impact of the earliest stages of life, and the evolution of the intellect (mind) in girls and women. The latter topic seems to be a neglected area of study due to the massive research devoted to the innumerable unresolved issues in women's lives.

In conclusion, I share the mystery that surrounds the creation of a lifetime career. How does a person intuitively recognize the important thoughts, ideas, and directions offered by learning and experience? Why do particular books, of the hundreds read, stand out in memory decades after they have been absorbed into the mind? What explains one's readiness to be influenced, in a powerful way, by a writer, a student, a colleague, a friend? How are these influences permanently etched upon the fabric of a life? Readers are encouraged to study their *own* career development and to recognize the themes that have characterized their life stages and professional contributions. Young researchers may become involved in carrying on the never-finished work represented by the themes that have formed the base of my work:

- concern for the career development of girls and women,
- respect for learning as a highly individualized process,
- recognition of the evolution of human possibilities over the life span ,
- commitment to understanding world futurism.

References

Borow, H. (Ed.). (1964). *Man in a world at work.* Boston: Houghton Mifflin Co.

Erikson, E. H. (1950). *Childhood and society.* New York: W. W. Norton.

Erikson, E. H. (1959). *Identity and the life cycle.* New York: International Universities Press.

Fuller, R. B. (1968). *Operating manual for spaceship earth.* Carbondale, IL: University of Illinois Press.

Fuller, R. B. (1969). *Ideas and integrities.* New York: Macmillan.

Gysbers, N. C. (Ed.). (1974). *Designing careers.* San Francisco: Jossey-Bass Publishers.

Herr, E. L. (Ed.). (1984). *Vocational guidance and human development.* Boston: Houghton Mifflin Co.

Matthews, E. (1960). *The marriage-career conflict in the career development of girls and young women.* Unpublished doctoral dissertation, Harvard University.

Matthews, E. (1984). The creative utilization of mature intelligence and experience. In H. F. Didsbury (ed.), *Creating a global agenda: assessments, solutions, and action plans* (222-233). Bethesda, Md: World Future Society.

Matthews, E. (1988). *Learning, teaching, and counseling: An individual perspective.* Unpublished manuscript.

Matthews, E. (1989). *Perspectives: Occupational status of women, 1968-1988.* Paper presented at a meeting of the American Association of Counseling and Development, Boston, Mass.

Schlein, S. (Ed.). (1987). *A way of looking at things: Selected papers from 1930 to 1980 of Erik H. Erikson.* New York: W. W. Norton.

White, R. W. (1952). *Lives in progress: A study of the natural growth of personality.* New York: Dryden Press [2nd ed., 1966; 3rd ed., 1975). Holt, Rinehart and Winston.

White, R. W. (1972). *The enterprise of living: Growth and organization in personality.* New York: Holt, Rinehart and Winston.

6

Career = Work + Leisure (C=W+L):
A Developmental/Trait
Factor Approach to Career Development

Carl McDaniels

Introduction

The model approach advanced in this paper is that there can be convergences of trait factor and developmental theories into an amalgamation called a Developmental Trait Factor or C=W+L approach to career development. This position rests directly on Frank Parsons' turn-of-the- century work, *Choosing a Vocation* (1909), and on the seven-decade contributions of Donald Super, perhaps best summarized in his chapter "A Life-Span, Life-Space Approach to Career Development" in Brown and Brooks (1990). Interestingly, a thematic issue on the "Life and Work of Frank Parsons" came out in the Summer 1994 *Journal of Career Development* when a similar retrospective of Donald Super's work was published

> *...each person's career involves the continuous interaction of work and leisure across the life span in a series of transitional situations.*

in the September 1994 *Career Development Quarterly*. The point is, there is ample current material on which to base a comparison and possible merger of their work. The convergence of these two approaches seems to offer a more holistic approach and better explain what actually occurs in people's lives.

My own journey toward the Career = Work + Leisure (C=W+L) over the Life Span Model started with a deep appreciation of the work of both Parsons and Super. It always seemed to me that they came together in my own counseling. I first illustrated this in a presentation at the APGA (now ACA) Annual Convention in Minneapolis in 1965 which resulted in a paper entitled "Vocation: A Religious Search for Meaning" (McDaniels, 1965). Since then I have been investigating the work/leisure connection and interaction and brought those ideas up to date in the 1984 NCDA decennial volume *Designing Careers* in a chapter called "Work and Leisure in the Career Span" (1984). More recently the entire matter is integrated and illustrated in much greater detail in the book *Counseling for Career Development* by McDaniels and Gysbers (1992). Essential to all of this discussion is a core set of definitions which have emerged over the years.

Some Essential Definitions

For purposes of this model, definitions of *work, leisure, career,* and *career development* are essentially taken from a report by Sears (1982, p. 139), which was reviewed by a panel of career guidance experts, the NVGA (now NCDA) board of directors, and *Vocational Guidance Quarterly* editorial reviewers. The definitions are

> WORK—a conscious effort, other than having as its primary purposes either coping or relaxation, aimed at producing benefits for oneself and/or for oneself and others.
>
> LEISURE—relatively self-determined activities and experiences that are available due to having discretionary income, time, and social behavior; the activity may be physical, social, intellectual, volunteer, creative, or some combination of all five.
>
> CAREER—the totality of work (*and leisure*) one does in a lifetime.
>
> CAREER DEVELOPMENT—the total constellation of psychological, sociological, educational, physical, economic, and chance factors that combine to shape the career of any given individual over the life span.

For adequate attention to be given to the concept of leisure, it is essential to add the words *and leisure* to Sear's definition of *career*. Over the years a number of articles, special journal issues, chapters, dissertations, and books have examined leisure. The coupling of work and leisure as the basis for a career over the life span brings all three elements together in a holistic framework. Obviously, other roles can also be incorporated into the career concept. Super included nine roles in his life-career rainbow: those of child, student, worker, leisurite, citizen, spouse, parent, homemaker, or pensioner. Super made a strong case for his broader concept, but in this model the focus is on C=W+L. Through this linkage, leisure can be placed in the proper perspective as an important component of career development over the life span. Counselors and teachers can recognize the importance of leisure in elementary school, middle/junior high school, senior high school, post-secondary education, and beyond. Counselors and other service providers can assist all adults in dealing with the interaction of both work and leisure in one relationship—a career.

The Essential Trait Factor Approach

Parsons (1909) provided a clear and succinct three-part suggestion for career development:

In the wise choice of a vocation there are three broad factors: (1) a clear understanding of yourself, your aptitudes, abilities, interests, ambitions, resources, limitations, and their causes; (2) a knowledge of the requirements and conditions of success, advantages and disadvantages, compensation, opportunities, and prospects in different lines of work; (3) true reasoning on the relations of these two groups of factors. (p. 5) A developmental component can be integrated into Parson's ideas by adding time, process, and change to the tenets above.

First, Self Understanding

1. Self understanding should be a PROCESS occurring over the life span—not the momentary outcome of a PRODUCT (one or more standardized assessment tests).
2. Self understanding can best be developed with the individual as an active participant in multi-faceted investigations and inquiries which are continuously updated and revised.

3. Self understanding goes beyond the single one-time choice of an occupation or a leisure activity to having the ability to self assess one's dynamic relationship to both work and leisure over one's life span.
4. Self understanding looks carefully at the various roles played in life and especially gives consideration to the interaction of work and leisure throughout one's career.

Second, Knowledge of Career Opportunities

1. Learning continuously about educational, occupational, and leisure opportunities.
2. Using a WIDE variety of cognitive, affective, and behavioral sources.
3. Seeking as much personal first-hand experience as possible in learning about opportunities in a wide variety of career exploratory activities.
4. Updating continuously one's knowledge of career opportunities over the life span.

Third, True Reasoning Through Counseling

The counselor is a primary facilitator in both of the processes above and he or she is key in the effort to help individuals establish a career which unfolds in a broad, holistic fashion throughout their entire life. For, in my judgment, each person's career involves the continuous interaction of work and leisure across the life span in a series of transitional situations.

As counselors we should strive to help others seek *satisfaction from both work and leisure in their careers.* We should seek ways to empower our students and clients by helping them use "true reasoning," both cognitively and affectively, to understand their emerging sense of self in the context of a changing and interacting world of work and leisure. All of this should occur in conjunction with the special client considerations we have grown to respect, such as gender, race, religion, national origin, and persons with disabilities. More recently we also have been challenged to consider generation differences by Strauss and Howe in their 1991 book, *Generations—*

The History of America's Future, 1584-2069. So, true reasoning/ counseling for the future must help people weigh considerations ranging from generational concerns to fitting their individual characteristics, as they understand them, into the mosaic blend of work and leisure.

The Essential Developmental Approach

The work of Donald Super, dating from 1939 to 1995, is both extensive and expansive. The notion of a Life Span - Life Space is central along with the multiple roles he stressed in his famous life career rainbow. The Career = Work + Leisure Through the Life Span Model approach acknowledges the many life roles we all play to some degree, but it emphasizes the interacting and principle influence of work and leisure that form the main components of one's career. Indeed, Super's first book in 1940 dealt with leisure interests and he wrote frequently on the relationship of work and leisure in the career span. His equal consideration of work and leisure in one's career was all too often over-looked.

The Importance of Work and Leisure

No one argues, at least not much, about the importance of work in one's career. Some tend to merge work-occupation-job-career into one synonymous glob of terms although it appears the terms are clearly different or should be. As we reach the close of the 20th century there is a growing debate about work: its current status, its fairness, its pay, and its future. There is a spate of new books out on the topic, such as Bridges' *Job Shift,* Glassner's *Career Crash,* Fox's *The Reinvention of Work,* plus the usual forecasts by the World Future Society in *The Futurist* and the Department of Labor's biannual *Occupational Outlook Handbook* and other reports. In spite of dire predictions, like Rifkin's *The End of Work,* it still appears work will be a part of nearly every adult's future well into the 21st Century. In short, there is plenty of what appears to be factual information and forecasting by a wide variety of sources about work now and in the future.

Leisure, on the other hand, does not come in for nearly as much reporting of factual information or speculation as to its future role in the USA or in individual lives. A consideration of the key aspects of leisure indicated above (physical, intellectual, volunteer, creative, social, or some combination of all five) clearly reflects an increased level of activity and interest by nearly everyone. A sense of the importance of leisure in people's lives was reflected in several recent labor disputes—even strikes over forced overtime and seven day-a-week work schedules. Union members were saying loud and clear that extra hours and pay are important only up to a certain point, then one wants a certain amount of leisure and they are willing to strike to get it.

One aspect of leisure which is growing in terms of national importance is *volunteering*. This clearly should be viewed by counselors and other helping professionals as a significant part of career development. Instead, counselors are seldom involved in one of the major career development opportunities of the past half century--volunteering for community service through the Peace Corps, or thousands of local, state, national, and international opportunities as well as the new Americorp which is part of the larger Corporation for National Service. In its first year, 1994-95, Americorp enrolled about 20,000 volunteers. Volunteering is also increasing in grades K-12 as well as in higher education (where it is called "service learning"), business, industry, and government. Several recent Gallup polls indicate well over 50% of all adults are volunteering at least four-hours-per-week in regular on-going leisure activities.

Work-Leisure Dichotomy

The juxtaposition of work and leisure in one's career development may be a struggle for some counselors. There are those who would hold out for a "purist" position that leisure is for its own sake—pleasant to anticipate, take part in, and recall—a separate entity in life, unrelated to other activities, including work. For example, you learn weaving for the joy of it, and should not think of it as a possible source of income, either full- or part-time.

Along this same line of thought is the work only—marketable skills—position. This is most visible in secondary school vocational education programs where many courses are promoted primarily as preparation for direct employment, *not* for leisure. People who hold this position argue that persons should not take home economics, auto mechanics, or agriculture simply because they want to learn to cook, fix their friend's car, or grow a small garden. It is contended in this article that maybe after some years and appropriate skill maturation, students may want to put these leisure activities to work--or maybe not. Possibly, they will just enjoy being the best weekend cook on the block or relish tinkering with the family car, or having a landscaping scheme that is the envy of the neighborhood.

The people with whom counselors and teachers work do not seem to want artificial separations between work and leisure. Why should positions be forced on individuals by organizations and associations? Instead, many counselees and students with whom we work see the natural relationship between work and leisure better than the professionals who are sometimes blinded by tradition, legislation, territorial boundaries, or, worse yet, simple protection of the status quo. It is advocated here that the work/leisure dichotomy simply be eliminated.

The Work/Leisure Connection Through One's Career

After 30+ years of studying the work/leisure relationship, I have become increasingly convinced of the closeness of the connection. I spent a sabbatical leave some years ago driving 20,000 miles across the U.S.A. to observe the work/leisure connection in people's lives. I saw countless people who were working at part-time jobs which had grown out of leisure interests. I saw many others who moved from casual interest, to beginning skill, to mature skill, to part-time, then to full-time employment in a leisure-related area. There was ample evidence of former volunteers who had made a smooth transition to full-time employment at the same location, doing essentially the same tasks for pay (work) that they had done for free (leisure). There were also plenty of people who lived for their leisure, who might not have liked their work at all, but were satisfied with leisure activities. For a detailed description of the interaction across the life span and illustrations of dozens of successful employment transitions, see

McDaniels' *The changing workplace: Career counseling strategies for the 1990s and beyond* (1989).

Perhaps a few illustrations can serve as the best argument for a case of Career = Work + Leisure. What follows are several actual situations which show the work/leisure connection in people's lives.

• *Busy in the Southwest* —A couple in the their 70s, both are retired as park naturalists. They are busy with interests developed through earlier work and leisure. They commented that they had *no leisure* in their busy lives. They are active with a local group of bird watchers. They tour the national parks frequently and recently returned from a two-week trip to Mexico. The husband plays the piano and they both play bridge once or twice a week (when at home). They walk 2-3 miles daily no matter where they are. Oh yes, they are in a cooking club that exchanges dinners twice a month.

• *Volunteer in Vermont*— A 55-year-old woman volunteered with a local fire and rescue squad she helped organize. For several years she enjoyed the challenge of emergency health care. After her husband died suddenly, she was contacted by a physician nearby who asked her to come to work in his office for 25 hours a week. He told her that the experience and training she gained on the rescue squad made her an ideal candidate. She was then able to put her leisure to work in his office. She had been a pre-med major in college and, after dreaming of a health related occupation for more than 30 years, finally found herself working exactly where she wanted.

• *Transition in Tennessee*—A 45-year-old, laid-off factory worker named Bill learned about upholstery through a recreation department class. He discovered that he was good at upholstery and actually enjoyed restoring old furniture. Suddenly, he found himself busy while "officially unemployed" with upholstery work in his basement, fixing up a half dozen pieces a week for family and friends. Now, he has his eye on a small storefront nearby where he plans to establish his growing work-at-home small business.

• *Art in Arkansas*—A 30-year-old housewife and mother of three children is on the verge of a new direction for her career. After spending several years at home with young children, she took a calligraphy course (the art of beautiful handwriting) just to explore an interest in improving her penmanship. She did well, took several more courses from a local community college, gained confidence and skill. First, she did printing on cards and announcements for friends, then she started selling some of her work at local craft fairs. Now she does certificates for a nearby university and bids on contract work and finds herself busy working at home about 30 hours a week.

• *A Runner in the Mid-West*—A teenager has been a runner for 5 years. He also has been working in a sporting goods store as part of his high school marketing education program. The student mainly sells shoes and advises customers on running apparel. He has even tried his hand at designing some running outfits. Now he is trying to decide what to do after high school graduation. He knows that he wants to do something which keeps him close to running activity. He seems to understand clearly how his part-time employment in a leisure-related area is helping to establish better-defined career options and goals.

Career = Work + Leisure

In closing, four reasons will be advanced as to why the work/leisure relationship should be blended into the career formulation.

1. *Combining Work and Leisure is More Holistic.* Currently, professionals are making genuine efforts to deal with people on the broadest possible scale. It is a time to incorporate as many factors into counseling as possible: the physical, the social, the spiritual, the cultural. It seems only professionals tend to "carve" people up and see them through separate pairs of glasses—instead of one pair—a holistic approach pair.

2. *Combining Work and Leisure is Life Span Oriented.* At last, there is recognition of continuing career development after high school or college. There is a strong life span, life role influence on teaching and counseling, advanced mainly by Donald Super (1990). This is all to the good and allows one to see the ebb and flow of leisure and work in life. In the early and late stages of a 70- to 80-year life expectancy, leisure activity tend to dominate. In between, there is a long period of work and leisure interaction.

3. *Combining Work and Leisure is Future Oriented.* The rapid pace

of change in the second half of the 20th century has shaken many of our American traditions and values. Currently, roles for families, education, work, and leisure are changing. The future is likely to hold more leisure for people of all ages—and from all indications, much more! The need to integrate leisure together with work into one's career development seems all the more important in order to face the challenges of life in the 21st century.

4. *Combining Work and Leisure is Ever Present.* Of all the changes which have come about in the past 100 years, few have been as swift and steady as the increased acceptance of leisure as a way of life. Clearly, leisure has been legislated in large amounts by moving around holidays and creating longer and more favorable vacation periods. Daylight savings time is routine six months of the year in most parts of the USA which provides more opportunities for leisure, including on-the-job wellness programs. Many people of all ages have more money for leisure. Also, there are increasing facilities for leisure, ranging from Walt Disney World in Florida to small wilderness areas in Appalachia. At the same time, there is an ever-growing social acceptance of a variety of leisure roles from a former professional football player doing macrame to women running in the Olympic marathon.

Summary

Individuals play many roles in their lives. Two of these roles—worker and leisurite—have been viewed as having a significant part in career development. It was pointed out that professional counselors and educators often view work and leisure as a dichotomy. Some examples of how people satisfactorily live out the work/leisure connection in their life span were provided. Finally, four reasons for the Career = Work + Leisure were offered.

References

McDaniels, C. (1965). Vocation: A religious search for meaning. *The Vocational Guidance Quarterly, 14,* 31-35.

McDaniels, C. (1984). Work and leisure in the career span. In N. Gysbers, & Associates (Eds.), *Designing careers.* San Francisco: Jossey-Bass.

McDaniels, C. (1989). *The changing workplace: Career counseling Sstrategies for the 1990s and beyond.* San Francisco: Jossey-Bass.

McDaniels, C., & Gysbers, N. (1992). *Counseling for career development.* San Francisco: Jossey-Bass.

Parsons, F. (1909). *Choosing a vocation.* Boston: Houghton Mifflin. (A 1989 reprint is available from Garrett Park Press, Garrett Park, Maryland.)

Sears, S. (1982). A definition of career guidance terms: A National Vocational Guidance Association Perspective. *The Vocational Guidance Quarterly, 31,* 137-143.

Super, D. (1990). A life span, life space approach to career development. In D. Brown, L. Brooks, & Associates (Eds.), *Career choice and development,* (2nd ed.), San Francisco: Jossey-Bass.

7

Values and Career Development through Transcultural Counseling

John McFadden

Overview

Contemporary counselors consider the formulation of a worldview in counseling as a prerequisite for effectiveness. This worldview should incorporate how individuals perceive themselves in relationship with the surrounding world — physical, social, political, aesthetic, intellectual, psychological. To counsel clients efficiently in a multicultural and multiethnic environment is to demonstrate a commitment to helping counselees regardless of race, gender, religion, nationality, sexual orientation, or disability. Career development represents a primary focus of the mission of many counselors. In order to provide optimal services for a diverse population through transcultural counseling, counselors must develop awareness, knowledge, and an action-oriented base of cultural diversity.

In order to provide optimal services for a diverse population through transcultural counseling, counselors must develop awareness, knowledge, and an action-oriented base of cultural diversity.

This essay generates ideas and activities which may be useful as counselors and counselor educators facilitate career development for their clients and students in a rapidly changing environment. Transcultural awareness is an ongoing process and transcends differences among individuals and groups. It acknowledges, appreciates, and advocates cultural and unique identities. Transcultural counseling epitomizes a level of cultural transcendency in the midst of transnational perspectives. Thus, transcultural counselors understand and elevate themselves beyond debasing idiosyncrasies of a particular cultural group.

Challenge and complexity characterize career development of today's youth. Traditional theories of career counseling might not be relevant for practice across cultures as we advance toward the twenty-first century. Strategic analysis and skillful application of more appropriate theories may be adapted for use in a variety of cultural settings. Therefore, it becomes important in transcultural counseling for helping professionals to have knowledge of some non-traditionaltheories and models of cross-cultural counseling, i.e., transcendent (Harper & Stone, 1986), systemic (Gunnings and Simpkins ,1972), stylistic (McFadden, 1993).

Counselor/Client Values

Values play a significant role in establishing helping relationships for transcultural counseling. Both clients and counselors maintain values that evolved from their life experiences, and these core values support the formation of behavior toward select perceptions and attitudes about careers. Although clients are generally grounded in their own set of values, counselor values also have a major impact as the counseling relationship is formulated. Moreover, in relationships where counselors and clients represent different cultural values, it is vital for counselors to remain cognizant of their own values and those of their clients.

Sue (1978) identifies characteristics of culturally effective counselors in developing a worldview for career development:

1. recognizing their own values and assumptions about human behavior and acknowledging those that are different as legitimate;
2. being aware that no theory of counseling is politically or morally neutral;
3. understanding that sociopolitical forces have influenced minority groups;
4. having the ability to share and respect their client's worldview;
5. having practices and mastered a variety of counseling skills

regardless of theoretical orientation and having the ability to choose the most appropriate for each individual client with respect to cultural background.

Counselor Cultural Awareness

The span of counselor cultural awareness is quite varied, from extremely positive to extremely negative. At one extreme end, exist those counselors who could be described as being culturally encapsulated, believing in universal truths that justify and perpetuate ethnocentric worldviews. These culture-bound practitioners may have an implicit disregard for cultural diversity and, thus, may approach counseling from a stymied technique orientation rather than a culturally aware perspective (Carter, 1991). Such cultural bias is extremely difficult to overcome since it frequently is not that counselors are operating from a lack of awareness but rather from the extent to which cultural assumptions and values are held outside conscious awareness. This is primarily due to the fact that it is not readily apparent to most people how cultural values or worldviews are related to human interactions or how they influence behavior, thoughts, perceptions, and assumptions regarding career development.

Cultural awareness by counselors allows them to discover their roots. Among the assumptions of cultural bias made frequently in counseling, according to Pedersen (1978), are that all people share a common measure of what constitutes "normal" behavior; there is a dependence on linear "cause and effect" thinking; people of all cultures understand the intended meanings of abstract words frequently used in Western culture; counselors are already aware of their assumptions. It seems clear that the expectations with which individuals perceive and organize their world are learned and are directly related to their personal and cultural background. Assumptions by human beings and their thinking patterns are acquired through a socialization process which represents culture. Fundamental cultural assumptions depict the perspective or the filter used to perceive the world, the self, and others. Individuals are typically not conscious of the systematic, organized, and abstract cultural values and assumptions which guide their perceptions and thinking (Stewart,

1972, cited in Carter, 1991).

Client Cultural Values

Counselors and clients may come from different cultures. Misunderstanding, rejection, distrust, and negative transference are likely to occur as a result of perceived cultural differences (Todisco & Salomone, 1991), undermining the most basic tenets in the development of therapeutic relationships. Effective transcultural counselors, therefore, should be familiar with the cultural background and value system of their clients in order to diminish misunderstanding and to nurture effective client-counselor relationships.

For example, when dealing with Maori clients, there could be a considerable discrepancy between two counseling outcomes where counselors incorporate knowledge of the Maori culture as a people reluctant to express feelings in exchange for politeness and agreeableness. They should not overlook such relevant information in working with Maori clients and counselors should not function under the assumption that this cultural group operates from frames of reference similar to those of the counselor. What are the ethical considerations when counselors decide to help African American clients work toward independence and away from feelings of being externally controlled when, inherent to the cultural environment of the clients, there is a high regard for group interdependence? Parallel to the noble intentions of counselors is the implied statement that it is better to function independently of others and with an internal locus of control. This is a clear illustration of how client values are considered secondary to those values which dominate the worldview of helping professionals.

Counselors should also attempt to recognize how dominant cultural values, imbedded in the institutions of society, clash with values by minority groups. Schools have been and are now fertile ground for indoctrinating culturally enriched persons with platitudes that perpetuate a monocultural worldview even in career planning. Native American students who belong to a culture that possesses deeply ingrained beliefs in the concept of sharing are "righted" by reprimands when they are tardy to school because they were asked to share in morning household responsibilities (Griggs & Dunn, 1990). Such actions could deny the sources of strength in humanity and divert potential for successful career development and enhancement.

Implications

Being aware of and understanding one's values and how they relate to one's physical environment, social environment, and personal environment, counselors can commence tounderstand the values of others and strive to bridge differences between themselves and others.

Through awareness, transcultural counselors can help create unity through diversity and be more effective in selecting appropriate goals and processes with clients for career development. Sue and Sue, (1990) include the following partial list of competencies applicable to transcultural counseling:

1. Culturally skilled counselors have moved from being culturally aware to being aware and sensitive to their own cultural heritage and to valuing and respecting differences.
2. Culturally skilled counselors are aware of how their own cultural background and experiences, attitudes and values and biases influence psychological processes.
3. Culturally skilled counselors are able to recognize the limits of their competencies and expertise.
4. Culturally skilled counselors are comfortable with differences that exist between themselves and clients in terms of race, ethnicity, culture and beliefs (pp. 167-168).

Understanding the worldview of culturally different clients includes being aware of negative emotional reactions toward other racial and ethnic groups. Being competent as transcultural counselors will demand the willingness and commitment to confront such reactions when they obstruct the counseling process.

Counselor-Client Relationship

The complexity of the counselor-client relationship in transcultural counseling features different factors, such as the barriers which affect career decision making. Generally, most theories of career development are psychologically oriented, emphasizing personality.

In addition, each individual is influenced by biological factors, and human functioning is backdropped by inherited physical, emotional, and mental characteristics which are acted upon by the environment. Career development is also influenced by social, political, geographical, economic, and intellectual issues. These factors mingle with values which historically shape the lives of individuals and are guided by political and economic variables.

Removing Barriers to Career Development

In order to eradicate some of the barriers across cultures, including racism, sexism, and economics, to career development, counselors should function as advocates for students. Counselors may also find themselves in situations requiring that they assist clients so as to enhance client identity and self-esteem and to work concurrently toward a success-oriented model. The concept of extended family, therefore, becomes an enlivened reality, for the whole "village" — parents, siblings, and community— becomes involved.

Williams (1979) suggests that a graded career education program is necessary and should include the following parameters in minimizing barriers to career development:

1. concepts of career development;
2. requirements for entering an occupation;
3. characteristics and life patterns of adults who are involved in particular occupations;
4. activities that require students to imagine their role according to certain occupations;
5. an imaginary society to project, explore, and speculate about the kinds of skills and occupations that will be needed in the 21st century;
6. actualization of experience between classroom information and the world of existing occupations. (p. 180).

Course of Action

An important aspect of aiding our youth with career insights is to expose them to successful role models from their own ethnic or cultural group. This happens to be one of the most effective means of directly and indirectly influencing young people in careers. For example, The Benjamin E. Mays Academy for Leadership Development at the University of South Carolina is a concept in transcultural career mentoring for middle and high school students. It is designed to help outstanding youth develop leadership skills and achieve career excellence in a number of scientific, literary, technological, mathematical, social, and cultural areas.

Axelson (1985, p. 210) has suggested some activities and techniques for career development designed specifically to help clients "define personal expectations and goals in relation to who and what they are, in harmony with their own background of cultural experiences." These include the following:

1. Identifying and reinforcing self-perceived qualities and self-movement;
2. Blocking negative thoughts;
3. Practicing positive visual imagery;
4. Validating self through identification with others;
5. Learning self-assertion skills;
6. Understanding and using the system;
7. Acquiring knowledge and information through career guidance and education.

"CD's in Transcultural Counseling—A Career Development Quadrant" represents a model for transcultural "career developments" (CD's) to which counselors may refer in forming constructs and arriving at implications for counseling. Through devising this model, the author recognizes that one's values lie at the core of career development in a transcultural society.

The model reflects an indication that values which individuals hold are primarily influenced by family, school, peers, and members of a community. For purposes of this concept, these four quadrants are identified as: (I) Family, (II) Peers, (III) School, and (IV) Community. Each quadrant is vital in deciding values. For example, faculty and staff in a school represent a great influence when individuals are exploring values of self-worth and respect for others. However, depending on the culture of a person, one or more of these quadrants

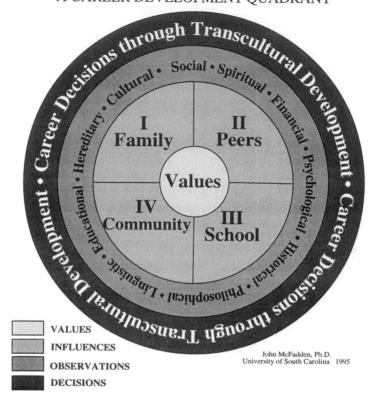

John McFadden, Ph.D.
University of South Carolina 1995

VALUES
INFLUENCES
OBSERVATIONS
DECISIONS

may be more influential than others in the determination of values.

Among other conditions, societal observations impacting on decisions in career development by clients include dimensions such as the spiritual, financial, historical, social, educational, psychological, etc. When interfacing with these variables, reassessment may occur. Depending on the decisions in related experiences, one's present value system may change. However, the values, influences, and observations undergird career decisions through transcultural development.

The "Transcultural Counseling Model of Career Development" is based upon each individual's value system. Experiences are united with choices made through encountering life situations and interfaced with the influence of family, peers, school, and community to decide the value system. The combination of "significant" people and experiences together contribute to the formation of one's value system.

Summary

Career development in the context of values and transcultural counseling can be a rather complex process. Inherent in unraveling this complexity is an immediate awareness and clear understanding of cultural values, which is the fundamental being of individuals. To know your clients is to master insights into their cultural background and values associated thereto. It is generally an accepted fact that, if counselors do not have some understanding of the values, beliefs, frame of reference, and cultural mores, of their clients, a major gap between the counselor and client could evolve. Career development through transcultural counseling encompasses broad aspects of cultural diversity to the extent that values drive perceptions and behavior which ultimately influence career choice.

References

Axelson, J. A. (1985). *Counseling and development in a multicultural society.* Monterey, CA: Brooks/Cole.

Carter, R. T. (1991). Cultural values: A review of empirical research and implications for counseling. *Journal of Counseling and Development, 70*(1), 164-173.

Griggs, S. A., & Dunn, R. (1990). Is this the counselor's responsibility? A step by step guide to dealing with shifting cultural and family values. *School Counselor, 38*(1), 24-33.

Gunnings, T. S., & Simpkins, G. (1972). A systemic approach to counseling disadvantaged youth. *Journal of Non-White Concerns in Guidance, 1*(1), 4-8.

Harper, F. D., & Stone, W.O. (1986). Transcendent counseling: A multimodal model for multicultural counseling. *International Journal for the Advancement of Counselling, 9*(3), 251-263.

McFadden, J. (1993). *Transcultural counseling: Bilateral and international perspectives.* Alexandria, VA: American Counseling Association.

Pedersen, P. B. (1978). Four dimensions of cross-cultural skills in Ccounselor training. *The Personnel and Guidance Journal, 56,* 480-484.

Sue, D. W. & Sue, D. (1981). *Counseling the culturally different: Theory and practice.* New York: John Wiley & Sons.

Sue, D. W. (1978). Word views and counseling. *The Personnel and Guidance Journal, 56,* 458-462.

Sue, D. W., Arrendondo, P., & McDavis, R. J. (1992). Multicultural counseling competencies and standards: A call to the profession. *Journal of Multicultural Counseling and Development, 20(2),* 64-88.

Todisco, M., & Salomone, P. R. (1991). Facilitating effective cross-cultural relationships: The white counselor and the black client. *Journal of Multicultural Counseling and Development, 19 (4),* 146-157.

Williams, J. H. (1979). Career counseling for the minority student: Should it be different? *Journal of Non-White Concerns, 7,* 176-182.

8

Donald E. Super:
Yesterday and Tomorrow

W. Larry Osborne

Donald E. Super, who died on June 21, 1994 at age 83, was a giant in the career development field for half a century. He served as a Visiting Distinguished Professor at my university. I had the pleasure of working with him and, during the last several years of his life, the enjoyable opportunity both to relive the history of the career development field, and to hear his hopes for the future. This article will review some of Donald E. Super's work, and attempt to speculate about its future directions.

Yesterday

Beginning in 1940, Super tried to understand the various determinants of career development; his findings eventually resulted in a "segmental theory" to explain career development. Many of his insights came from the Career Pattern Study, a quarter-of-a-century longitudinal study of more than 100 men from the ninth grade through 35 years of age and beyond, as they went about occupational choice, preparation, and participation in work (Herr & Cramer, 1992).

> *There may be no greater legacy of Donald Super than the commitment by those who knew him to continue and extend the work which occupied most of his life, and produce the career development researchers, theorists, teachers and counselors of the future*

Super was quite proud of the holistic, integrative nature of his theorizing about career development which came from this research. One representation of this is the Life Stages and Substages model (Super, 1990; see Figure 1), which suggests that people move

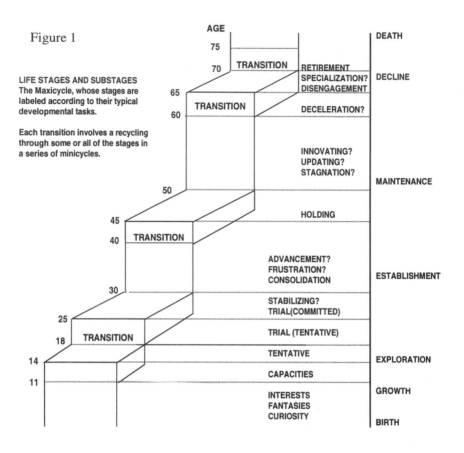

Figure 1

LIFE STAGES AND SUBSTAGES
The Maxicycle, whose stages are
labeled according to their typical
developmental tasks.

Each transition involves a recycling
through some or all of the stages in
a series of minicycles.

through the stages of Birth, Growth, Exploration, Establishment, Maintenance, Decline, and Death, and encounter various developmental tasks along the way. The extent to which one is ready to cope with these tasks is an indication of the individual's career maturity.

As one moves through these stages, various factors influence his or her ability to cope with developmental tasks. These are represented by A Segmental Model of Career Development (Super, 1990; see Figure 2) and portrayed on a Norman arch, which was inspired by a church door in Cambridgeshire, England during Super's appointment as Visiting Fellow at Wolfson College from 1976-1979— this following his "first retirement," from Columbia University at the mandatory age of 65.

Figure 2

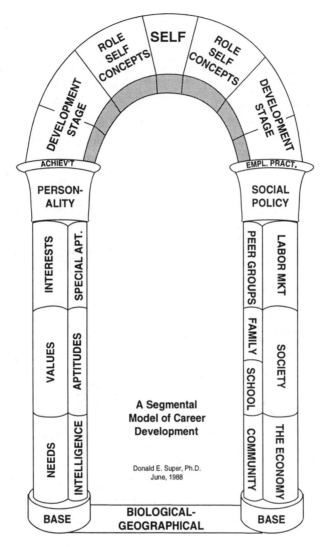

The right side of this arch consists of geographical factors that influence career development, including the community one comes from and lives in, schools attended, the family, peer groups, the economy, society, the labor market, social policy, and how all this interacts to affect employment practices.

The left side of the arch portrays biological matters that influence development, these consist of one's needs, intelligence, values, attitudes, interests, and special aptitudes, all of which come together to represent personality and the resulting achievements of the individual.

The factors represented on both sides of the arch influence how one copes with developmental tasks at each stage of his or her development, and they affect role self-concepts. All of this is brought together through decision making by the self, which is the keystone of the arch.

Another example of Super's attempts to integrate what is known about career development into a holistic perspective of the process is The Life-Career Rainbow (Super, 1990), a model which portrays the dimensions of one's life career from birth until death.

The Rainbow suggests that, as one moves through various stages of career development, copes with developmental tasks, and makes decisions influenced by geographical and biological factors, he or she engages in six life roles. These include child, student, leisurite, citizen, worker, and homemaker. How much one participates in these roles, is committed to them, and expects to be involved with each in the future, affects the individual's career development.

The Rainbow model clearly was one of Super's favorites. He often remarked about the "poetry" of it, particularly when referring to the colorized version of the Rainbow. In this version, the arc for spouse, for example, was colored purple—a deep purple during the couple's courtship and early marriage, a paler purple while they experienced marriage difficulties, and a deeper purple again after they had undergone a genuine reconciliation. The other arcs had similar color configurations to portray particular roles and the intensity of involvement with these roles during various stages of one's life. Super wanted to extend this model through a computer program he called "Paint your own rainbow." The program would enable a user to color both an actual and ideal Rainbow which could then be used to make decisions about how the individual wanted to live her or his life.

Super's integrative nature was evidenced in other ways, too. He wrote an article in the fifties (Super, 1955) about a vocational counseling case ("John Stasko") that demonstrated how vocational and personality development are interrelated. Actually, according to

Super, this was a reiteration of writing he had done a decade earlier. One of his last articles, "The two faces of counseling: Or is it three?" (Super, 1993), which was included in a special issue of *The Career Development Quarterly* and entitled "How personal is career counseling?", made the point that there are two kinds of counseling—situational and personal—and that these are on a continuum, rather than being dichotomous. Clearly, Super thought more about the similarities between things and how they fit together, than about the differences that exist and the uniqueness of matters.

Most of Super's work, then, can be summarized in a three-fold progression: 1) trying to understand the many determinants of career development, 2) tying all these together into a "segmental theory," and 3) devising a career counseling approach that addresses these determinants, while recognizing the interrelationship of personal and vocational development.

Tomorrow

Let me now try to take the risky position of speculating on what Donald E. Super would want for the future of the career development field. Those of you who knew Donald Super know that few spoke for him; I hope he would have considered my views to be at least somewhat representative of his.

Toward the end of his life, Super expressed one of his wishes in a 1991 videotape which was introduced by Tom Sweeney, moderated by Nicholas Vacc, and distributed by the American Counseling Association as part of Chi Sigma Iota's Distinguished Scholars Interview Series. Super wanted to convene all major career development theorists and arrive at an integrated view of the process. He thought enough research and speculating about career development theory had been done to provide a more holistic picture of the process so that no view stood alone, and all views stood in relation to others. However, I think he also believed, since his approach is developmental and integrative in nature, that most other theories of career development could be nicely fitted within his own understanding of the process (Super, 1994).

Other directions for Super's work reflect his self-concept, which demonstrated that one's age is not necessarily related to the career development stage he or she may be living. Super did not think of himself, until the last year of his life, as being in the Decline stage of his model, generally characteristic of people from ages 60 to 70. He described himself, rather, as always "innovating" and as one who wanted to be on "the cutting edge" of his specialty, a developmental task of people typically aged 40 to 60 found in the Maintenance life stage.

Part of the way he accomplished this was through advancement of the Career Development, Assessment and Counseling (C-DAC) model (Super, Osborne, Walsh, Brown, & Niles, 1992), a practical approach to career counseling based upon his research and theory.

The C-DAC approach is built on the recognition that no simple process of matching people and jobs can adequately meet the needs of individuals and society, while taking into account the possibility and the likelihood of changes in individual needs, values, interests, and circumstances, and the changing nature of work, as people go through life.

The approach makes use of five assessment tools, including the *Adult Career Concerns Inventory, the Career Development Inventory,* the *Strong Interest Inventory, The Values Scale,* and *The Salience Inventory.* These instruments help clients focus on their career stages and each stage's corresponding developmental tasks. The tools also help clarify clients' attitudes and knowledge; their vocational interests which arise from their attitudes and knowledge; the values they may express in their interests; and the extent they might participate in five life roles, be committed to them, and expect to be involved with them in the future. These instruments may be used in different sequences for particular clients—they are supplemented by the *Myers-Briggs Type Indicator* at The University of North Carolina at Greensboro when working with college students. The *Occupational Stress Indicator* is substituted for the *Career Development Inventory* at The University of Virginia when the C-DAC model is used with adults reentering the workplace. (For more detail about these instruments and how they are used, see Super, et al., 1992).

Super was interested in further studying this approach to understand how it could be more effectively used in career counseling. To that end, a research team consisting of Steve Brown (The University of Georgia), Spencer Niles (The University of Virginia), Claire Usher-Miner in Austin, Texas, and Larry Osborne was formed to conduct various studies. Research has been done on the relationship of *Strong Interest Inventory* "flat" profiles to career maturity, adults returning to the workplace have been profiled on the *Adult Career Concerns Inventory,* two studies on how personality preferences relate to career maturity have been conducted, and a book manuscript about the C-DAC model and how it can be used with college students, adults, and high school students is near completion. This team will continue to pursue Super's interest in understanding the applicability of the C-DAC approach, and intends to extend research focused on applications of the C-DAC model with undergraduate students, adults, and high school students.

Beyond this, however, Super was curious about how the C-DAC approach could be used with various groups, including Mexican-Americans, African-Americans, clients in other countries, and women. His earlier research, as part of the Career Pattern Study, was with a group of young men, and Super continued to be interested in how his model of career counseling could be extended to a wider variety of people.

The effort to achieve this has resulted in a number of convention and conference presentations at the state, regional, and national levels. These conferences focused on the theoretical basis of the C-DAC approach and on how to use it in case studies involving clients of differing gender and culture. Research describing the career development characteristics of Mexican-Americans has recently been done—a doctoral student has completed a dissertation on the relationship of personality preferences to the career maturity of Mexican-Americans and Anglo-Americans—and other research on the career development of women and African-Americans is under way and will continue.

These are notable attempts at extending Super's ideas to a broader range of people. It is also important, however, to pursue this interest of his to understand the usefulness of career development theory and traditional career counseling procedures for other countries.

At the time of Super's death, an international consortium of 14 nations called the Work Importance Study was exploring applications of the C-DAC model to other cultures. The initial work of this consortium resulted in *The Values Scale* and *The Salience Inventory.* This effort should proceed to explore the appropriateness of career development theory for other populations, devise ways to provide effective career counseling for persons of varied backgrounds, and modify the C-DAC instruments for the widest possible use. To date, no one has assumed leadership for this important venture. Colleagues in other countries, including England and Spain, who have shown great interest in Super's work, may do so, and it is hoped that they will; there definitely is a need for someone to carry forward this part of his vision.

There is at least one more wish that I believe Donald Super would have had for the future of the career development field. This involves the further popularization of study and professional practice in this aspect of our profession, and the nurturing of young professionals to carry on this endeavor. He was fond of saying that he had more colleagues collaborating with him during the last fifteen years of his life than he ever had before. His interest during this period was in identifying beginning, and sometimes plateaued, professionals who could benefit from being involved in his work and, perhaps, in helping them to find a mission of their own.

That focus needs to continue. There may be no greater legacy of Donald Super than the commitment by those who knew him to continue and extend the work which occupied most of his life, and produce the career development researchers, theorists, teachers and counselors of the future. He would have wanted no less.

I hope the views described here have fairly represented those that Donald Super would have expressed. If they do not, I'm sure that, just as was true when we worked together, I will somehow hear about it.

And nothing would please me more.

References

Herr, E. L., & Cramer, S. H. (1992). *Career guidance and counseling through the life span: Systematic approaches* (4th ed.). New York: Harper Collins Publishers.

Super, D. E. (1955). Personality integration through vocational counseling. *Journal of Counseling Psychology, 2,* 217-226.

Super, D. E. (1990). A life-span, life-space approach to career development. In D. Brown & L. Brooks (eds.), *Career choice and development* (2nd ed., pp. 197-261). San Francisco: Jossey-Bass.

Super, D. E. (1993). The two faces of counseling: Or is it three? *The Career Development Quarterly, 42,* 132-136.

Super, D. E. (1994). A life span, life space perspective on convergence. In M. L. Savickas & R.W. Lent, (eds.), *Convergence in Career Development Theories* (pp. 63-74). Palo Alto, CA: Consulting Psychology Press.

Super, D. E., Osborne, W. L., Walsh, D. J., Brown, S. D., & Niles, S. G. (1992). Developmental career assessment and counseling: The C-DAC model. *Journal of Counseling & Development, 71,* 74-83.

9

The Importance of Focusing on the Macro and Micro Aspects of Career Psychology

Samuel H. Osipow

Overview

When I started my career in vocational psychology in the late 1950s and early 1960s, I thought that the major problem in career psychology was devising improved ways to measure interests and as a result aid people, especially young people, to find satisfying careers. In holding that belief, I failed to realize the importance of the social context of

> *Attempts must be made to develop and extend theory that successfully takes into account life's uncontrollable events as well as those that are based on individual differences.*

work that has since influenced my thinking. At that time, the United States economy was about to begin a long period of growth. Although that growth was not without occasional decline, over the long perspective the economy grew significantly. This economic expansion created conditions that reinforced my original belief. Expansion created career opportunities, especially for talented individuals, creating the need to have a method that these individuals could use to screen their options . From my perspective as a youthful professional, the way I perceived the world seemed to be the way it always was and would be forever.

Among the important vocationally related factors I failed to consider as I developed my initial understandings and approach to vocational development was the impact of the low birthrate of the 1930s on my generation. Between an expanding economy and a dip in the labor pool of those in their twenties, opportunities seemed unending. The economy was expanding, opportunity was everywhere, and the major problem I thought people needed to face was selecting from among the many choices they had in connection with their entry into the labor force.

Because of this, my early work focused on career indecision . With so many options available (I thought) to young people, many had trouble sorting out the best direction in which to head. In addition, I was entering the field just at the time there was a shift from a "hands on," practical, empirical approach to understanding vocational choice, development, and counseling, to one that would emphasize the creation of concepts to account for the diversity that clearly existed in the process of career development.

Discussion

When young adults had what seemed to be limitless career opportunities, a major problem was identifying where to enter the labor force and what sort of education/training to obtain. Thus, a review of the literature of the 1960s and 1970s reveals considerable interest in helping adolescents understand and deal with career indecision. One important endeavor was a continuing effort to improve the reliability and validity of interest measures. A second needed aspect was a sensible and reliable way to measure career indecision. As a result of the second need, the efforts of many investigators, my own work included, were expended on the development of career indecision measures. Two early measures of the 1970s were Holland, Daiger, & Power's (1980) "My Vocational Situation" and Osipow, Carney, Winer, Yanico, and Koschier's (1976) "Career Decision Scale." For many years these two measures were the primary ones used to study career indecision . Recently, several second generation measures of career indecision have been devised (for example, Chartrand, Robbins, Morrill, and Boggs', 1990, "Career Factors Inventory"). These instruments have been, and continue to be, useful in helping us to understand the basis of career indecision and to identify issues in career counseling.

However, one assumption underlying the statement of the problem, that is, that the major problem of career entry for many is deciding what career to follow, fails to acknowledge the lack of viable and attractive career options for many adolescents of the present time as well as of the earlier era. As a result, too great an emphasis on career indecision may result in a failure to serve populations with more fundamental career needs: that is, good basic education, career options available in the labor force, and access to a wide range of careers. Access to, and options to consider, a wide variety of occupations are often severely reduced as a result of gender, racial, and ethnic bias. As a consequence of these limitations, even though career indecision remains a significant problem for many young people, it has become apparent that adolescents have many problems that must be addressed related to their career entry.

Career Options and the Economy

How is the nature of the economy and the resulting labor market likely to affect career decision making? One major aspect influencing the answer to this question is how the nature of work evolves. It appears that in many developed countries, a bi-model work force is emerging where one segment of the population is highly educated and has access to a wide range of technical and professional careers which require long periods of training and commitment but lead to psychologically and economically satisfying careers. For these people, career decision and indecision is and will remain a significant problem. They need the means to help them choose from among a bewildering array of attractive career choices . However, for another large portion of the emerging labor force, the issue is and will be how to find meaningful and economically viable work. Good jobs will be harder to find for individuals with limited education and few work skills, and the career patterns that will result for these people will resemble the most undesirable of those described by Super (1957). It might even be appropriate to say that because of this bi-model distribution of career opportunities, careers in twenty-first century America will have a "split personality."

It should be remembered that Super was one of the first to bring our attention to the notion of the career life span, a concept which can be useful in many ways. Super's theoretical writings focus on career developmental tasks (1963) and his later works place those clearly in a life-span context (Super, 1980). For example, a life-span approach helps us to understand the developmental tasks associated with vocations and careers at different life stages. Children's and early adolescents' tasks are to observe, learn, accumulate knowledge, develop constructive attitudes toward work, and simulate experiences that may be useful when they later choose and implement careers. At a slightly older age, preliminary decisions must be made about work entry, ideally based on information and attitudes learned earlier . Such decisions should rely on emerging self knowledge about skills, aptitudes, interests and opportunities. Later, career advancement and establishment is important. This phase requires the individual to understand the workplace mores, and to develop skills to implement those understandings. The establishment period is followed by a period of "stability," during which the worker extends and refines career skills and progress. Finally, comes the disengagement and retirement phase. This phase requires former workers to adjust to diminished influence, income, health, energy and many other factors. However, life does not proceed linearly from stage to stage as that sequence implies. People enter and leave and re-enter the labor force many times throughout their work lives. Sometimes the departures are voluntary, sometimes involuntary. Some of the people who depart do so to get trained for a new vocation and must start their career at the entry level of the new field. Some of the people who depart involuntarily seek additional training as a necessity. Many people retire and later return to work either to provide some stimulation in their lives or to add to retirement incomes that are not sufficient to support them. We know that people leave their jobs for a host of reasons, only a few of which are indicated above. In order to help someone make sound career decisions it is important to take into consideration their personal reason for leaving the work force.

It should be obvious that the way individuals progress through the career life stages is a jumble of mixed events that, sometimes, involve career decisions (and indecision) at mid-life as well as during adolescence. Retirement, for example, is an event that means many different things. Some people retire from their career early to pursue other careers (e.g., military personnel), some people are forced to "retire" either by accepting incentives or reacting to threats. Others retire by choice and later decide retirement was premature and re-enter the work force. The retirement of a 52-year-old is likely to reflect very different circumstances than the retirement of a 68-year-old; premature retirement because of illness or disability is not the same as retirement at the end of a long, productive career, and men and women are likely to experience retirement very differently.

Furthermore, industry and government seem ambivalent about the most appropriate retirement age. The motives of these organizations are often internally inconsistent. On the one hand, organizations may provide incentives to encourage older workers to leave their job early, thus, cutting costs and perhaps providing opportunities for younger individuals. At the same time, problems retirees may face in maintaining health insurance provide an incentive to remain at work. Also exerting a pull toward delaying retirement is the potential government decision to delay the onset of full social security benefits in order to encourage people to work longer and save that system from financial ruin.

Another important factor warranting the attention of career psychologists results from the expansion and extension of technology in the work place. It is becoming increasingly clear that jobs are shaped by technical advances. These advances require workers to update their skills frequently, and even prepare for totally new occupations. The pattern of job recycling and retraining is accelerating. One result of this pattern is that many individuals face not only one period of career decision making, in adolescence, but face the need to make significant career decisions during several periods, occurring at various points in adult life. This suggests that new measures and procedures should be developed to be used in helping adults deal with career indecision.

Our theories have assumed that career options exist and that work is an attractive option for all people. However, the social factors of unemployment and underemployment have major consequences for our conceptions of career development. These factors are producing a vocational underclass which has increasing difficulty in finding economically viable work. Ways must be found to deal with the frustration and loss of hope that this underclass experiences. What are the tasks the career psychologist can take on to help society deal with this problem?

Summary and Recommended Courses of Action

There is no doubt that career psychologists cannot solve all the problems faced by individuals in their careers. These difficulties stem from a multiplicity of forces, ranging from individual problems to social and economic barriers far beyond the individual's power to control. Attempts must be made to develop and extend theory that successfully takes into account life's uncontrollable events as well as those that are based on individual differences.

At present, Social Learning Theory (Krumboltz, 1994) represents the best approach that integrates individual and societal factors (e.g., labor market and economics). The application of Social Learning Theory in its new, cognitive mode (Lent, Brown, & Hackett, 1994) may provide a workable framework to be used in extending the reach of career psychologists' influence on the career lives of individual workers.

References

Chartrand, J. M., Robbins, S. B., Morrill, W. H., & Boggs, K . (1990). Development and validation of the Career Factors Inventory. *Journal Of Counseling Psychology, 37,* 490-501.

Holland, J. L., Daiger, D. & Power, P. G. (1980). *My vocational situation.* Odessa, FL: Psychological Assessment Resources.

Krumboltz, J . (1994). Improving career development theory from a social learning theory perspective . In M. Savickas & R. Lent, (Eds.), *Convergence In career development theories.* Palo Alto, CA: Consulting Psychologists Press.

Lent, R. W., Brown, S. D., & Hackett, G. (1994). Toward a unifying social cognitive theory of career and academic interest, choice, and performance. *Journal of Vocational Behavior, 45,* 79-122.

Osipow, S. H., Carney, C. G., Winer, J., Yanico, B., & Koschier, M . (1976) . *The career decision scale .* Odessa, FL: Psychological Assessment Resources.

Super, D. E. (1957) . *The psychology Of careers* . New York: Harper & Row.

Super, D. E. (1963) . Vocational development in adolescence and early adulthood: Tasks and Behaviors. In D.E. Super, R. Starishevsky, M. Matlin, & J.P. Jordaan,(Eds.), *Career development: Self-concept theory* . New York: College Entrance Examination Board Research, Monograph No. 4.

Super, D. E. (1980). A life-span, life-space approach to career development. *Journal Of Vocational Behavior, 16,* 282-298.

10

On The Way to Somewhere Else: Beliefs About Career Development that Have Shaped My Contribution

Lee J. Richmond

I entered the field of career development by accident, not design. Therefore, my earliest thinking about occupational choice is one of serendipity. Ironically, my major contribution to the field of career development is designing, developing, piloting, and eventually teaching theory- based career programs for various adult populations.

Early on, I dreamed of being a medievalist and a poet. In my retirement years, I may fulfill that dream. However, as a young woman with four young children, I augmented my sporadic income as a freelance writer with a part-time English and world history teaching position at a Catholic girls' high school.

> *...the answer to impermanency in the marketplace is not only personal flexibility, but also trust in one's own being. Emphasis needs to be placed on self-conceiving rather than the self-concept, and new technology and virtual reality simulations can aid us.*

Through a series of events, more circumstantial than planned, I took a Master's Degree in Counseling, took a counseling job in an urban public school, trained at the specialist level in psychology, and eventually took a job teaching psychology in a community college in order to obtain a flexible schedule while earning a Ph.D. in Counseling. In my heart, I still wanted to be a poet and medievalist, but recognized that I had little talent for the former, and that the latter offered little remuneration.

My community college was one of the first to receive a federal grant to train women in their middle years for the work force, and I was chosen to develop and manage the program. I knew nothing about continuing education programs for women, so I studied the existing few programs at the elite, select four-year colleges that received the first federal dollars, and learned that the most successful programs combined course work with guidance and counseling. I adapted that model, and developed a program for women returning to community college.

That program enjoyed success, and many schools copied it. The program contained regular academic coursework, but the guidance and counseling component involving assessment of interests, aptitudes and skills, individual and group counseling, and optional personal career development workshops accounted for its favor.

The women taught me that a little confusion is a wonderful thing. I saw multi-potentiated, high-need, achieving women coming to the program looking for the one thing they could do outside of the home. After seven or eight weeks, they were confused by a multitude of choices. From counseling sessions with the women, I learned that society, sometimes family, and, in a few cases, even their psychiatrists, had "done a mean number" on these, supposedly, "unfulfilled women" who, with a little encouragement, could accomplish almost anything. My experience as program director, counselor, and teacher of these women taught me that I could, too. Through a set of what seemed like circumstantial events I became, not a poet or medievalist, but a very good teacher, program developer, and counselor of women. Without dream or design, I decided that I adored my work.

By studying a large number of workers, I learned that women frequently think that the occupational roles that they assume are insufficient for their talents. Also, many women experience greater personal strain than men because of their dual roles as homemaker and worker. Nevertheless, they handle stress better than male counterparts because they exceed them as rational, cognitive copers. Without an "old girl network" or much time for social activities or recreation, women are, nevertheless, good copers because of the way that they are able to frame and reframe ideas about self and world.

Two examples follow. A fifty-two-year-old worker, housewife, and mother of an eighteen-year-old mentally retarded son had enrolled in a social work program. At a time when others retire, she would be starting a new career. Her point was that, with a little luck, she would be fifty-five years old anyhow. Why not be fifty-five with a professional degree?

A female minister, told me that her husband went through a period of sexual impotency after she was ordained because he could not behave in a sexual manner with "a woman of God." After going through therapy with him, she said that he was doing better, but she added that the world would be in a sorry place if women filled their heads with some of the silly mythologies that men hold.

Despite the fact that women are good, cognitive copers, many sadly call themselves "justas"—justa housewife, justa mail handler, even justa counselor. I also know that the notion of being a "justa" needs to be dispelled, and will only be erased when people are valued more for what they are than what they do, and when all work is respected.

Subsequently, I received a series of grants to develop community counseling programs for people with special needs. At the same time, The School of Continuing Studies at The Johns Hopkins University embarked on a major organization and development project that involved training people to design such programs. I was asked to come to Hopkins for a year. I stayed for eleven years, and my scope of work broadened to include developing and coordinating their graduate programs in counseling.

While at Hopkins, I received a research grant to ascertain the counseling needs of students in vocational education. I had a captive sample of more than 2,000 students. John Holland also used my sample because I agreed to couple my questionnaire with "My Vocational Situation," a test he was then norming (1980). Dr. Holland told me that most people thought his work related to occupational interest, but he saw himself as a personality theorist: his hexagon organized information about interests so people could learn about themselves. Dr. Holland taught me that career development and personality development inextricably relate to a person's mental health.

From my own research, I learned that the personal and career-counseling needs of students in vocational education looked similar to those of their college-bound counterparts. Over 90% of the voc-ed students intended to continue their education, and even a greater percentage of academic students had immediate concerns about the world of work. So much for stereotypes!

By 1980, I knew the following to be true: It isn't smart to hold to stereotypic beliefs about what people will or won't choose, do or don't need; work satisfaction and general well-being are closely related; occupational involvement may be due to factors that seem accidental, but personality factors determine how fulfilled one will be; all people are multi-potentiated and are capable of self-organization, leading to personal satisfaction; and counseling can be helpful to many people.

Some Changes Over Time

During the next ten years, I learned that things which appear accidental are really not. The universe is synergetic, and its physical laws of dissipative structures, uncertainty, and complimentarity apply to all humans. Based on both research data and deep personal experience, I also learned that, in stressful situations, women exceed men as rational cognitive copers — a fact that runs contrary to popular opinion.

In the 1980s, I grasped the importance of having a mentor. Dr. Kitty Cole was such a mentor, and my work with professional associations, is largely due to her. Dr. Cole realized that, as a profession, career counseling needed standards, programs needed accreditation, and professionals needed credentialing. The year that she served as NCDA President, she appointed me Chair of the Standards, Accreditation and Credentialing Committee. That provided the push behind both the NCDA Standards (1981) and the NCCC credential. From this, I learned that professional associations sometimes do important things.

The 1983 ACA Convention theme was, *Counselors Help America Work,* and I was program chair. As a result of the convention, I met two other important mentors, Richard Bolles and David Tiedeman. I called Dick Bolles and asked him to keynote, and he told me straight-out that he was against the credentialing effort. He asked if he could speak against it. I said that if he would agree to keynote, he could say whatever he wished. In an auditorium full beyond the doors with people crowding the aisles, Dr. Bolles mesmerized the mob, and never did he say a word about credentialing. To this day, I think his question was some kind of test.

David Tiedeman, a major presenter for NCDA, talked about process —being in the act of becoming—and about valuing persons, not because of what we do, but because of what we are. He spoke of connectedness and consciousness. Not a traditional career theorist, David was on to something different, and he spoke daringly of it before his colleagues. Both Dick and David lent a spiritual element to my vision of career.

In May 1983, I attended the Assembly to Advance Career sponsored by the National Institute for the Advancement of Career Education, of which David Tiedeman was the President. At this Assembly, I learned that much that David was talking about related to Lifecareer®, a theory and philosophy of his wife, Anna Miller-Tiedeman, who presented her life as process ideas at the Assembly. Impressed, I invited both Miller-Tiedeman and Tiedeman to teach a special course at Hopkins. One of their students, Linda Kemp, career development specialist for the U.S. Postal Service, had the task of developing a program that would change the career philosophy of the postal service and eventually affect the corporation's 800,000 workers.

Another student in the same class was the Reverend Dr. Harvey Huntley, whose job was to design a career program to ease the pain of workers during a merger of the Evangelical Lutheran Church and the Lutheran Church of America. This program also adopted the Miller-Tiedeman model. Was it purely an accident or marvelous synchronicity that the ideas of the Tiedemans provided structure for the paradigm shift that these programs introduced to corporate America?

Along with Dr. Carole Rayburn, I have been engaged for the past twelve years in research involving differential stresses on males and females in religious occupations. From our studies, we learned that women in clergy positions suffer overt and covert discrimination from both the institutional church and from parishioners. Female clergy frequently work as assistant pastors rather than pastors, often doing the scut work of the church. However, they, and other women in religious vocations, such as nuns, cope far better than male clergy.

They excel in rational-cognitive coping, a fact that breaks the stereotypic notion that women rely on feeling more than rational thought. This research, coupled with my earlier experience with women's programs, taught me to respect women immensely, that their stories, often filled with spoken injustice and non-spoken courage, are infinitely worth hearing.

Current Thinking

For the past 10 years, as president of NCDA and of ACA, I have traveled extensively. Some of the travel has been to third-world countries. These travels profoundly influenced the development of my current thinking about career development and career counseling. Thinking globally has made me aware of the limitations of much of current theory, and the non-applicability to third-world people of some good career instruments and tools. As modernization comes, educated people from third-world nations turn to the United States for career expertise, and I wonder whether we are wise enough to know what we do not know.

My work with the postal service has taught me that no work today is totally secure, and that sometimes people need to change their paradigms. Old patterns of loyalty do not suffice when large companies restructure. Conversely, I learned the danger of "golden handcuffs" that cause people to stay in places, unfulfilled.

With the rapidity of change that marks the information era, the answer to impermanency in the marketplace is not only personal flexibility, but also trust in one's own being. Emphasis needs to be placed on self-conceiving rather than the self-concept, and new technology and virtual reality simulations can aid us.

People can recognize a remarkable synergy in their lives when counselors help them tune in to their own processes. Occupation, education, leisure activity, and family experience are not roles that people play, but rather the very essence of the grand career that we call life. One may change occupations or be out of work, but one is never out of career so long as one lives.

Decisions can no longer be for all time. People cannot remain vital and change less rapidly than does the world around them. Because the role of women world over is changing, our cultural optic must also change. The economy is such that women's work is permanent; therefore, it cannot be secondary.

Furthermore, it is important to understand that the powerless are powerful. A global community cannot safely exist when there are "haves" and "have nots." Nations cannot survive at the expense of other nations. It serves individuals and nations well to help others. My current interest is with those who are developing collaborative and cooperative models, rather than competitive ones. In my opinion, human survival depends on this.

Twenty-first Century career development theory will, I feel certain, be the kind of process theory that turns people, corporations, and nations to collaborative models dedicated not only to production, but to the well being of workers. Such theory will challenge old models

References

Holland, J. L., Daiger, D. C., & Power, P. G. (1980). *My vocational situation*. Palo Alto, CA: Consulting Psychologists Press.

Rayburn, C. A., Richmond, L. J., & Rogers, L. (1986). Men, women and religion: Stress within leadership roles. *Journal of Clinical Psychology, 42*(3), 540-545.

Richmond, L. J., Johnson, J., Downs, M., & Ellinghaus, A. (1983). Needs of non-caucasian students in vocational education: A special minority group. *Journal of Non-White Concerns, 12*(1), 13-18.

Tiedeman, A. M. (1992). *Lifecareer®: The quantum leap into a process theory of career*. Vista, CA: Lifecareer Foundation, 1-800-366-8612.

Vacation/career counseling competencies (1981). Alexandria, VA: National CAreer Development Association.

11

A Model of Worklife Transitions

Nancy K. Schlossberg

The world of work is a world of starts and stops, of accelerations and waiting periods. Careers have never followed blueprints; unfortunately, the ranks of the jobless and underemployed are still swelling. Most of us know somebody who's out looking for work—or praying that a job already in hand won't disappear. And the ongoing layoffs are affecting everyone; whether you're a top or middle manager, a front-line supervisor, or a blue collar worker, job security is likely to be on your mind.

> *...almost everyone in our society is in transition—moving in, moving through, moving out, or trying to move back into the workforce. Since individual needs differ depending where someone is in the transition process, interventions must also differ.*

Despite the gloomy economic picture, many people are still getting, losing, and changing jobs—that is, building careers. How do careers develop, especially in times of considerable economic uncertainty?

Transitions: The Common Thread

Thinking about adult career development as a *transition process* of moving in, through, and out of the workforce helps explain what is, in essence, a highly fluid process. The length of time someone stays in each phase depends on the person, and his or her subgroup, career plan, and available and perceived options. Each individual's needs, along with appropriate interventions, will differ depending on where the person is in the system (See Figure 1).

Moving In

People who move into a new situation, be it marriage, the Peace Corps, a first job, or new job in mid-life, have certain common agendas and needs. They need to "learn the ropes"—to become familiar with the rules, regulations, norms, and expectations of a new system.

Meryl Louis (1980) refers to this as a process of acculturation—a period in which newcomers, like ethnographers, are attempting to understand and see the organization as an insider does.

Take Mary, whose first job was that of a camp counselor. After college, she worked as a sales clerk in a bookstore; then came her first "real" job as a secretary, then as director of admissions of a trade school, then as a professor, then as the first woman executive of a major educational association, then as a professor again. All these experiences involved moving into new roles and Mary needed help orienting herself to each new job and new setting.

WORK TRANSITIONS	ISSUES FOR INDIVIDUAL	INTERVENTION	OUTCOME
Moving In • Newly employed	*"Learn the Ropes"* • Expectations re: job, culture • Explicit and implicit norms • Marginality, at the edge	• Expectation exchange • Formal socializing agent	The
Moving Through • Fast-tracked • Plateaued • Caught in between	*"Hang in There, Baby"* • Loneliness and competence • Bored, stuck • Competing demands	• Networking • Job enrichment • Policies like family and Medical Leave Act • Redefining /Restructuring work	feeling you
Moving Out • Laid off • Retired • Making a career change	*"Leaving, Grieving, Striving"* • Loss and reformation of goals • Articulation of ambivalence	• Teaching about transitions • Rituals • Life Planning	matter to
Trying to Move In Again • Unemployed	*"Falling Through the Cracks"* • Frustration • Despair	• Support • New Options • Retraining • Financial assistance	others

Figure 1. A Model of Worklife Transitions

As Mary looks back on two of the jobs that didn't work, the reasons she gives are simple: unrealistic and unmet expectations, and lack of adequate socialization. She was fired from the first job she took after college graduation, because her expectations were out of line with the realities of her new workplace. Mary forgot that while she'd left college as a leader with access to power on campus, she began work as a salesperson at the bottom of the ladder. So when she complained about the lack of a storm door and the cold store, she misunderstood her manager's sarcasm when he told her to take her complaints to the company's president. Mary went immediately to the president, who told her to dress more warmly—and when she wore a ski cap, long socks, and boots, Mary was fired.

Years later, she became the first woman to serve as a senior executive at a major educational association. She left after less than a year. First, she had no idea that she would have to raise money for her office. The organization expected that its staff would know this; however, this had never occurred to Mary, who was startled when after several months she was questioned about her fundraising efforts. What's more, she had no idea what the organizational norms were. For example, in Mary's case, no one served in the socializing role; thus, she did not realize that all the executives went to the men's room 10 minutes before noon, met in front of the elevator at 5 minutes to noon, and went to a local cafeteria at noon. She later found out that the other executives thought she was standoffish. Mary, however, felt rejected and marginal.

Mary's experience confirms a well-known phenomenon. As many as 50% to 60 % of all new hires leave their jobs within the first seven months. Because the revolving door is spinning so fast, the issue of managing the "joining-up process" has risen high on the agenda of many corporate HR departments (Liebowitz, Schlossberg, and Shore, 1991).

Most new employees talk about marginality—the feeling that they're at the edge, on the fringe. For many bi-cultural individuals, marginality is a way of life. But all of us, whether poor or rich, "minority" or "majority," feel marginal when we move into new roles. We aren't who we were, nor are we clear about who we should be and what's expected of us. And this feeling of marginality recurs at different points throughout our working lives.

Moving Though

If the motto for those moving in is "learn the ropes," the motto for those moving through might be "hang in there." Of course, some people are on the fast track, moving up and right along. Others are caught between work and family demands, pulled in many directions, while still others are bored, burned out, and plateaued. Each of these groups has different needs.

Fast-track fallout. Excitement and pleasure invariably accompany a big promotion. But these feelings are often followed by complaints of loneliness and the fear of being "found out," of a lack of competency.

Caught in-between. Many people aren't on the fast track; rather, they're caught between numerous competing demands. Susan, a graduate student in her fifties, explained why she dropped out of graduate school. In the past five years, the following family events occurred: her parents died; her daughter, unable to find employment, moved back home after receiving a M.A.; and her married son lost his job. As if that weren't enough, her husband's parents, in their nineties and living in another city, could no longer manage on their own. Should Susan move them in with her? Should the elderly couple try to manage in a structured living environment in their own city or move to Susan's family's city? Susan's husband was really the sole support of this increasingly needy and stressed family. So Susan changed her schedule as a part-time church counselor and orchestrated her in-laws' move into her home.

Susan is fairly typical of the "middle" generation, often stuck between the needs of parents, children, spouses, and bosses—and too busy to attend to their own needs. Sociologist Gunhild Hagestad has labeled these people "kinkeepers": they will experience the burdens and joys of living in three-, four-, and even five-generation families (1986).

Other caretakers include sons and husbands who account for close to 30% of all caretakers, and a growing corps of grandparent caretakers who are raising grandchildren. These caretakers range in age from 40 to 80, many of whom need to work for financial reasons but who have great difficulty "hanging in" the workplace (Pinson-Millburn, Fabian, Schlossberg, & Pyle, in press).

Plateauing. Almost the opposite of the "sandwich" group are individuals who are bored, plateaued, discouraged. Judith Bardwick (1986) differentiates among three types of plateauing: structural, content, and life. According to Bardwick, "of 100 people who are hired because they have all the right qualities and look outstanding, only one will reach any level of middle management, and only one will reach the executive level." Such people are plateaued for structural reasons.

In contrast, many workers are bored because of job content. They've been doing the same job for a number of years; they know what to expect every day. There is nothing new to learn.

A mid-life man working as an engineer fits into what Bardwick labels a life plateau. Such a person might summarize his frustrating situation in this way: "I have a house, a mortgage. I don't have the freedom to move as [others] do, yet I get passed over for promotions. I come to work, I do my job, I go home—there's no challenge, no excitement at home or work."

This man is bored with his life; he's experiencing a non-event. His daily routines aren't changing, but something more basic is changing--the way he sees himself. He is beginning to view himself as a loser, a person with no future. Many plateaued employees are experiencing their careers and lives as non-events. Unfortunately, they often lack the support that comes with more observable career transitions. (Schlossberg and Robinson, 1996).

Moving Out

Changing jobs or leaving the world of work are transitions that often result in a perceived or actual loss of goals, friends, and structure. The feelings of grief that go along with this often surprise people, especially if the transition has been initiated by the individual. The process of leaving a job differs, of course, depending on what the person's work role is, why he or she is leaving, and where the person is going. Is it for retirement, because of being fired, or being promoted?

Organizations do not pay the same attention to helping employees move out as they have to helping them move in. Often, leave-taking is symbolized by a single ritual, the retirement dinner. Yet, we know that leave-taking is a process occurring over time. Sociologist, Rose Fuchs Ebaugh (1988), interviewed ex-nuns, ex-CEOs, ex-transvestites, and many other ex-groups as a way of identifying the process which starts with the first thoughts of leave-taking—up through its occurrence. She also found that after one leaves the role, one holds onto a "hang-over identity." For example, the college president who was once a nun has a different identity from the college president who was formerly a CEO of a major company.

One study of men, whose jobs were eliminated, highlights some issues in the moving out process. The study's subjects reported feeling as if they had been "slapped in the face" or "kicked in the back," and they feared that their age would make it tough to get another job. These men were angry at not having control of their transitions and felt shamed that they were creating hardships for their spouses (Schlossberg & Leibowitz, 1980).

Jeffrey Sonnenfeld (1988) describes the reluctant farewell of 50 prominent former CEOs. The shift from "who's who" to "who's that" was nearly unbearable for many of these individuals. They found it especially difficult to exchange the CEO's lofty status for the image of a passive retiree dealing with non-negotiable limits for the first time. But the issue of leaving isn't restricted to executives; it's difficult even when voluntary. Workers aged 55 and older constitute only about 13% of the labor force; by the year 2000 they'll make up only 11%. Often older employees' attachment to work is weakened by the encouragement of early retirement as a cost-saving device, by downsizing, and by stereotypes about work and aging as well as choices in leisure activities.

One engineer who left by choice for a better job reported that her biggest surprise was depression. "What I didn't expect," she said, "was that the pain would continue." And a Peace Corps retiree reported that she felt purposeless and depressed. These are typical responses to the complex process of taking one's leave.

Change of any kind can create anxieties, forcing a person to establish new roles, relationships, routines, and assumption. Graduation from college forces a reformulation of goals. As one set of goals is reached—finishing a degree—there is an inevitable let-down, for once again a sense of purpose must be reconstructed. The learners moving on are giving up classes, advisors, and the goal of becoming but have not yet moved to a new set of activities and self-definition. Grief is the inevitable response to loss—even when the loss is chosen.

"Falling Through the Cracks"

What about the millions of unemployed people who are searching for jobs—some of whom become depressed, some homeless, some forced to take jobs at much lower levels? We're facing the fact that people from all walks of life can be in the position of trying to move in again. Simply stated, an enormous group is falling through the cracks.

Tying Interventions to the Transition Process

As we've seen, almost everyone in our society is in transition—moving in, moving through, moving out, or trying to move back into the workforce. Since individual needs differ depending where someone is in the transition process, interventions must also differ. Tying interventions' flexibility to differing needs allows for more systematic evaluation and program development. What follows are general descriptions of interventions appropriate for different points in the transition process.

Interventions for Moving In

For most people moving in, the overall issue is the need to learn the ropes. Orientation programs for new faculty, for new students, and for parents of new students exist in almost every college. A growing number of businesses are confronting the issue of how best to socialize new recruits. To help with this process, Conceptual Systems designed a self-guided learning tool, *The Joining-Up Process* (Leibowitz, Schlossberg, and Shore, 1992). This tool addresses practical ways to help organizations and newcomers understand and navigate the joining-up process. Through an expectation exchange process, managers and newcomers periodically and systematically exchange expectations and discuss how they are and are not being met—a crucial element of acculturation.

Corning Glass is an example of a company that makes a concerted effort to assist new employees. Before a new employee's arrival, managers are given guidelines and checklists which are used for the first 12 to 15 months. Everyone, starting with Corning's CEO, is committed to this process. With this kind of buy-in, Corning has already seen positive results.

Interventions for Moving Through

There are many scenarios for those moving through and each scenario needs a different intervention. Let's start with the loneliness that can accompany the big promotion. The American Council on Education, through its Office of Women, initiated a 20-year project to move women into presidencies of colleges and universities. These new presidents needed help in dealing with the major responsibilities and often the isolation of being in a visible place. The office organized a summit meeting of women college presidents. At that meeting, a major point of discussion related to their feelings of isolation. The opportunity to talk with other women in the same boat was reassuring.

Another group, those described as caught-in-between, can be helped to "hang in there" through workplace reform. To date, only three percent of U.S. companies have designed programs and policies to help the balancing act performed by caregivers. These programs range from brown-bag lunches, hot lines, flexible work schedules, cafeteria benefit packages, unpaid leave, and family care days, to Stride Rite Corporation's inter-generational daycare center—a real first. The benefits of workplace reform can be immediately seen. In fact, when Aetna Life and Casualty extended its family leave from several weeks to a year, turnover of caregivers dropped from 22% to 13%.

The Family and Medical Leave Act (H.R. 770/S. 345) requires companies of over 50 employees to grant unpaid leave to care for ill relatives, including parents, siblings, aunts, and uncles. The act provides a period of up to 12 weeks of unpaid leave without job loss or loss of health benefits for employees who participate in the care of newborn or newly adopted children—or children of any age—or who look after parents when there is a serious health problem. The connection between family and work productivity is underscored when data is examined documenting the high cost to employers of not having parental leave.

For plateaued employees, intervention strategies can include refocusing the individual's notions of success so that they include "slower-track" paths and careers, "growing in place"—enrichment of the current job—and so on. We know up is not the only way to grow. Especially in today's economy, "downshifting" is becoming more common. Helping employees deal with lost dreams is a must.

Intervention for Moving Out

Whenever possible, interventions need to be designed to take into account the fact that leave-taking is a *process*. A one-time ritual doesn't address the importance of grieving and of reformulating next steps. One organization established a process (lasting two months in each instance) of helping "riffed" employees find new situations. The results were heartening; with this intervention (limited but intensive), many former employees were able to find new opportunities. One man reported in the six-month follow-up that learning to handle his leave-taking had prepared him to handle anything (Schlossberg & Liebowitz, 1980).

Organizations typically devote far more energy to recruiting and retraining than to leaving. To counteract this complaint, the Peace Corps has initiated a program designed to help volunteers better understand the transition process; face up to the losses they will feel; and begin to reinvest in new activities.

Interventions for Moving Back in Again

In recent years, mechanisms for helping people move back into the workforce have undergone tremendous growth. Job clubs, employment services, newspaper ads, word of mouth, support groups, churches and synagogues, bookstores and libraries—all are trying to help people move back in.

One interesting experiment in Palm Beach, Florida, is "Adopt a Family." A professional staff of three reaches out to community and church groups that then recruit and select families willing and able to "adopt" another family. The adopted families are given money, but more importantly, their sponsors help them work on a plan to get back on their feet.

One single mother (whose husband had deserted his family) was helped with baby-sitting while she attended school to become a bookkeeper. A laid-off father of five was helped (by a former CEO) to get a job and a new home—and was planning to open his own small business in the future.

The Bottom Line: Mattering and Hope

It's axiomatic: when the needs of individuals are addressed, they feel appreciated, noticed, and respected. This is what the late sociologist Morris Rosenberg (1981) called "mattering"—a construct designed to document that adolescents who feel they matter are less likely to commit delinquent acts. This suggests an interesting question for further study: do adult employees who feel they matter to others produce more effectively, show more commitment to the organization, and feel better about themselves?

Today, an increasingly large number of employees feel betrayed by their organizations. They sense that they don't matter, that they're insignificant. We can't solve the underlying economic and political problems that have created both underemployment and unemployment, but we *can* work to help people "hang in there" and stay hopeful.

Specifically, we can do the following:
- Show the difference between a long-term dream (employment in a career I want) and short-term realism (sweeping floors while waiting for the job market to change, or sweeping floors and studying for a more marketable career.)
- Reframe the issues so an individual sees that "it's not just me" but also the system that needs to change.
- Provide emotional and informational support.
- Encourage libraries, community centers, churches, and

synagogues, and community colleges to establish job-networking groups.

- Assess individuals' commitment to their goals and ability to attain them. Snyder designed a scale to reflect an individual's ability to focus on goals and his or her capacity to find means of solving problems. Targeting the individual's particular difficulties in losing sight of his or her aims, or not having viable strategies to reach them, helps counselors, HR personnel, supervisors, and others intervene to turn helplessness into hopefulness and optimism.

Practitioners face a large and exciting challenge as they attempt to empower employees and managers alike for the long haul. For most of us, the track is likely to be neither fast not slow, but full of unexpected obstacles, a windfall or two (if we're lucky!), and hard-earned rewards.

References

Bardwick, J. M. (1986). *The plateauing trap.* New York: American Management Association.

Ebaugh, H. R. F. (1988). *Becoming an ex: The process of role exit.* Chicago: University of Chicago Press.

Hagestad, G. O. (1986). Dimensions of time and the family. *American Behavioral Scientist, 29* (6), 679-694.

Leibowitz, Z., Schlossberg, N. K., & Shore, J. E. (1991,February). Stopping the revolving door. *Training and Development Journal,* 43-49.

Leibowitz, Z., Schlossberg, N. K., & Shore J. (1992). *The joining up process: A guide for new employers.* Silver Spring, MD: Conceptual Systems.

Louis, M. R. "(1980, June). Surprise and sense making: What newcomers experience in entering unfamiliar organization settings. *Administrative Science Quarterly, 25,* 226-251.

Pinson-Millburn, N. M., Fabian, E. S., Schlossberg, N. K. and Pyle, M. (in press). Grandparents raising grandchildren. *Journal of Counseling and Development.*

Rosenberg, M., & McCullough, B. C. (1981). Mattering: Inferred significance to parents and mental health among adolescents. *Research in community and mental health* (Vol. 2). Greenwich, CT: JAI Press.

Schlossberg, N. K., & Leibowitz, Z. B. (1980). Organizational support systems as buffers to job loss. *Journal of Vocational Behavior, 18,* 204-217.

Schlossberg, N. K., & Robinson, S. P. (1996). *Going to plan b: How you can cope, regroup, and start your life on a new path.* New York: Simon & Schuster.

Snyder, R. (1989). Reality negotiation: From excuses to hope and beyond. *Journal of Social and Clinical Psychology, 2,* 130-57.

Sonnenfeld, J. (1988). *The hero's farewell.* New York: Oxford University Press.

12

Surfing The Quantum: Notes of Lifecareer® Developing

Anna Miller-Tiedeman

Moving on from Traditional Career

Many people believe, if you don't know where you're going, you'll probably end up somewhere else. My experience suggests that even if you do know where you're going, you'll still probably end up somewhere else. Wherever you end up, if you work with the life force, you'll enjoy the journey. That's more likely to happen when you follow your own inclinations and live your life as career.. I believed that before I ever knew a field of career development existed. I still believe it, perhaps even more. I believe that life is much more creative than any of us humans, fortunately. I also believe that life is in charge, not us.

In graduate school, no one hinted that life might qualify as the Big Career. That omission opened up my life work, although I didn't know it then. The following story recounts my deliberate living of life as process, what I ran up against and what I learned.

> *...life-as-process, like the bread crumbs dropped by Hansel and Gretel, leads those ready for the personal journey back to their own knowing.*

After graduate school, I worked in the Appalachia Educational Laboratory in Charleston, West Virginia. My first year I researched the decision-making literature. This raised more questions than answers for me. While there, I met David V. Tiedeman, the career theorist whose writing I found most fascinating in graduate school. I discussed with him my concern that teaching about good and best decision making lacked something. David listened, I talked, but no answers formed. (In a magical turn of life, David and I later married.

But that's another story.)

Next, I worked in a middle school observing decisions about individual differences and tolerance. Then I moved to high school, my interest in decision making still strong, I developed the *Pyramidal Model of Decision Making* (1977). I took the styles of Lillian Dinklage (1968), the stages of David Tiedeman (1961), and the levels created by Eugene Wilson (1971), and merged them into a working whole which I used to teach students decision making. When students didn't enjoy learning about decision making, I realized something wasn't right.

Most of my learning and formation of beliefs concerning career development came from listening to students and clients, asking questions, opening my awareness, working to break out of the limited focus of the traditional career paradigm, and letting time pass. Not exactly a walk in the park, but a good way to let life teach you experientially.

In my reading, I discovered a strong link existed between time urgency and increase in blood pressure, blood cholesterol, heart and respiratory rate, the blood levels of insulin, and other physical factors. So, I stopped formal career development activity, which I thought increased students' stress, and started to review their four-year plans with them. Voila, a sparkle appeared in their eyes.

In the meetings that followed with each of my 300 students during each of their four years of high school, many exciting things happened. I watched as they followed their own experience, intelligence, and intuition. (I didn't know it at the time, but this started my work on a process theory/philosophy.) While observing the decision process in action, I encouraged and facilitated self-chosen next steps, whether an A student wanted to avoid college or a D+ student vowed to go. I cared more about students learning from their own experience than from authoritative pronouncements. I only wanted to encourage the next step and drop concern about long-term goals, thereby enhancing health.

Working that way, I discovered I valued intentions more than goals. I watched students set goals, and, partially as a result of unmet goals, saw them worry, stress, and experience physical problems, not to mention depression and lowered self esteem. Goals tend to run in very narrow channels as Deepak Chopra, MD and author of *Creating Health: How to Wake Up the Body's Intelligence* (1991) suggests, but the river of life doesn't work that narrowly. He further notes that the highest state of attention goes beyond goals and anchors internally with a balance between rest and activity. Both goal setting and traditional career attitudes encourage activity, with little focus on rest. Without the rests in music, little melody would emerge. The same holds true for a career developing.

In my work with students' four-year plans, I found they liked their decisions as much as any of us. One of them said, "If it doesn't go right, then I'll make another choice. And I do that as well as anyone." Student comments gave me courage to return to my own personal theory of career as did the comments of many counselors who told me that they never took a decision-making class nor did they ever want to.

That raised more questions concerning why career professionals placed a standard on students that they didn't follow themselves. It seems students received the same admonition Buckminster Fuller did as a youth, "Darling, never mind what you think. We are here to teach you" (1981, p. 56). Of course, about decision making.

Clearly, all the traditional career thought converged into the belief that if you plan well, all will work out. No fuzzy logic here. Business followed with, "if you fail to plan, you plan to fail" which currently falls on hard times as noted by a recent CEO of Hewlett Packard. Furthermore, the information used to make plans came in Department of Labor and related kinds of publications and computer programs. Internal information, particularly that going counter to common wisdom, didn't usually enter into the equation of life direction, not to mention the information in the collective intelligence—probably the two best sources of life-direction information available to each person. But here you run into belief systems once again. If you don't believe in invisible information, you don't see it.

Considerable time passed, and I didn't know what to do next. I couldn't relate to the traditional and nothing else existed. I almost decided to switch into another discipline. Then Dr. Tom Kubistant sent me Zukav's, *The Dancing Wu Li Masters* (1979). That started me on a reading odyssey into the new science, a trip that continues to this day. One of Zukav's most important ideas is that it's not possible to observe reality without changing it. "According to quantum mechanics there is no such thing as objectivity" (p. 56). That idea liberated me from all those individuals in the past who had admonished me to be objective. Knowing that can never happen freed me even more to my own thought.

Then I read Joseph Campbell's *The Power of Myth* (1988). He reminded me that none of us can know reality directly. We only construct ideas about it which represent our individual myths. Another paradigm (belief) breaks up when you realize all we hear from anyone about anything represents their beliefs and myths which often have little basis in our individual realities.

I continued to read in the new science. I discussed the ideas with my students. I attended workshops offered by physicists, several of them Nobel Prize winners. I tried my idea out on just about anyone who would stand still for discussion. All my reading in the new physics validated my experience of life—life patterns and works, not always the way we want it to, but it works.

The Life-As-Process Surfboard

In 1981, I moved with David (V. Tiedeman) to Los Angeles, and worked with him in the National Institute for the Advancement of Career Education. With time to think over my questions about traditional career, the idea of living life as process started to take shape in my mind, but not all at once. I'd like to think I started out with this great idea, but it only came in bits and pieces. I would write down each idea and place it in a folder, not knowing it would ever be worth anything later. Fortunately, an organization later appeared. I didn't know it then, but those bits and pieces contained my life mission. Granted, it took a long time to find it and an even longer time to develop it, but like it or not (and sometimes I didn't), I stopped off in the career development field to initiate thinking about life as process. I then knew that life-as-process, like the bread crumbs dropped by Hansel and Gretel, leads those ready for the personal journey back to their own knowing.

In constructing a process theory, I wanted it to:

1) empower the career theory of each individual;
2) be open, varied, and free, rather than limited by parts, levels and stages;
3) encourage flexibility rather than depend on pattern and prediction; and,
4) work well for all people in any situation.

And it does!

Reason and Rowan in their book, *Human Inquiry: A Sourcebook of New Paradigm Research* (1981) said, we need "to put people in positions where they may learn truth about themselves." Process theory does just that.

With no idea of the fear-raising impact of this idea on many counseling professionals, I jumped in, optimist that I am, and put my money on my belief in writing and publishing. In retrospect, I resembled the daring young professional on the Quantum trapeze. But I put *How NOT to Make It...And Succeed: Life on Your Own Terms* (1989) into the popular market. Then I wrote *Lifecareer®: The Quantum Leap Into a Process Theory of Career* (1988) for the academic community. Finally, I wrote *LIFECAREER®: How It Can Benefit You* (1989, 1992), an application book.

At the beginning of each of the fourteen chapters in *How NOT To Make It...And Succeed...* I specify a difference between Traditional career and Lifecareer. Several such key differences in belief are

Belief Differences

Traditional Career	Lifecareer®
Career as job	Career as life
Supports career theorists	Believes that each person is his or her own best theorist
Emphasis on self-concept theory	Emphasis on self conceiving
Control of life—make it happen	Cooperation with life
Suggests parts equal the whole	The whole organizes the parts

Control of life using goal setting and planning	Cooperation with life using the Career Compass® for setting intentions and organizing
Knowing where you're going is a first condition in getting there	Learn as you go
Getting a job	Making a life versus making a living
Focus on right and wise decisions	Honors decisions that go right as well as those that don't work out
Trends and former patterns guide	The understood life from personal experience
Career is made	Career is lived in the moment and becomes the path you leave behind

When you live life as process, you free up considerable energy. You gain a sense of balance and harmony. You don't rehearse what didn't work. You take the learning and move on. You don't sweat about finding a career or worry about a second or third career. All that becomes irrelevant when you live life as the Big Career. You learn that life works, not always the way you want it to, but it works. You know that cooperating with the approaching forces, while thinking, makes for less stress which enhances the immune system.

Surfing Life

As you can see in my tale, I first anchored the career development process in life making it primary and job secondary. What do you gain when life takes primary position? First, less stress that translates into a stronger immune system; second, a sense of satisfaction whether or not you experience a positive outcome in what you do; and third, an endorphin high when both health and satisfaction emerge.

Many dictionaries list as their first definition of career—a course or path through life. That responds to my passion for helping each individual live his or her own note while watching for life's signals that point to activities that fulfill the life mission. In this way, the individual adapts his or her choices to life, not the reverse. This offers good potential for better lab reports on blood pressure, cholesterol, and other biomarkers of wellness.

Second, I value individuals learning from experience of making decisions, from which they can then use to learn. I'm told that research indicates that we remember 20 percent of what we hear, 40 percent of what we hear and see, and 85 percent of what we hear see and do. That's why I want individuals to experience their decisions and speak from that experience. Further, I believe it important to embrace all of life, loving both the right and left decisions. Those left decisions teach us. They also add spice and challenge to life, when not denied. Besides, they provide employment for all of us.

Third, I now focus on the health benefits of living life in accordance with its own adaptive responses. This approach lowers stress and impacts the immune system in a positive direction. This frees up creativity and supports job-related activities whether a job search or on-the-job work.

Questions My Work Now Addresses

I now want to accommodate Quantum processes where the whole organizes the parts, not the reverse as in traditional career. For instance, I now wait for the questions to arise rather than ask block-busting questions in the beginning. Further, I only pay attention to the questions that keep returning. One such question: What format will offer an *a ha* experience about beliefs that limit our life direction? That led to a paradigm shift in my consulting and speaking. I now do interactive presentations that offer the audience an experience (and I did this with an audience of 300 on one occasion) not a telling of how their life-direction beliefs impede rather than advance their progress.

A second major question also kept visiting me: How can I offer counselor educators a user friendly text around the idea of life as process? With my partners from the beginning of this odyssey— David V. Tiedeman and Lee Joyce Richmond—I now lead the construction of such a manuscript on process living.

A third major question keeps my attention as well: Since I value each individual living his or her own career theory, how can I encourage each individual to ask his or her own questions and derive personally acceptable answers, and not depend on answers from those perceived as authority. It's all too easy to get caught in our own paradigms about authority, what it can or can't do for us. For instance, had I listened to David's doctor in 1990, David would not be here today.

Finally, the fourth major question persists: How can we raise question forming to equal status with question answering? In a world where answers can manifest in nanoseconds, question forming far outruns the time of getting answers. But here's where development comes in and that's a tomorrow's discussion.

So What?

The last fourteen years represent a dedication to quantum surfing the life process. An important rule in surfing is never surf alone. As you can tell from this story, I quantum surfed with all kinds of knowledgeable people. Each of them added to my understanding.

Real winners understand the importance of help. This suggests that, contrary to rugged individualism, none of us has all it takes to realize our dreams—another paradigm in need of shifting. For anyone who makes it, you can list from ten to twenty plus people who supported that journey. It's as natural as the late Lewis Thomas claims:

> The urge to form partnerships to link up in collaborative arrangements is perhaps the oldest, strongest, and most fundamental force in nature. There are no solitary, free-living creatures; every form of life depends on every other form.

> We should go warily into the future, looking for ways to be useful, listening more carefully for the signals, watching our step, and having an eye out for partners.

References

Campbell, J. (1988). *The power of myth.* New York: Doubleday & Co.

Chopra, D. (1991). *Creating health: How to wake up the body's intelligence.* Boston: Houghton Mifflin.

Dinklage, L. (1968). *Student decision-making.* Photocopy.

Miller-Tiedeman, A. (1989). *How NOT to make it...and succeed: Life on your own terms.* Vista, CA: Lifecareer® Center.

Miller-Tiedeman, A. (1988) *LIFECAREER®: The quantum leap into a process theory of career.* Vista, CA: Lifecareer® Center.

Miller-Tiedeman, A. (1989). *LIFECAREER®: How It Can Benefit You.* Vista, CA: Lifecareer® Center.

Reason, P., & Rowan, J. (1981). *Human inquiry: A sourcebook of new paradigm research,* New York: John Wiley & Sons.

Tiedeman, D. V. (1961). Decision and vocational development: A paradigm and its implications. *Personnel and Guidance Journal, 40,* 15-20.

Wilson, E. H. (1971). *The development and pilot testing of a system for the teaching of decision making.* Cambridge, MA: Harvard University (Unpub. doc. dissert. Harvard University, Cambridge, MA)

Zukav, G. (1979). *The dancing wu li masters.* New York: William Morrow and Company.

13

The Quantum Career Floats Through the Air ...?

David V. Tiedeman

Foundations

My Professional Credo

I am passionate about three professional matters based upon half a century's service in guidance. First, guidance is the potential catalyst for personal, social, and universal growth and development. Second, present guidance theory (with the exception of Miller-Tiedeman's process theory, 1988) is too narrow, too shallow, and too thoroughly ignored to meet the world's momentary crises. It takes a world unafraid of universe-responsible creativity. Third, work on a general theory of career development, already started by Miller-Tiedeman (1988, 1989), should be given first priority on a universe agenda. Miller-Tiedeman chose a scientific world view for her process theory. She learned from several physicists including Capra (1975, 1982), Prigogine (1980), and Bohm (1980). Since that time other physicists joined into study of the evolving Quantum paradigm and its parallelism with life and consciousness paradigms— read across disciplines to locate these sources. Zohar (1990) and Zohar and Marshall (1994) offer particularly broad, deep and practical accounts of the parallels between concepts of Quantum Mechanics and of self and society. A forthcoming Zohar book on *The Quantum Spirit* is to complete this trio on Quantum's new and dazzling social

> *...a general theory of career grounds in two faiths: i.e. (1) faith that each individual has a personally learned and empowered career, willy nilly: and (2) faith in the "comprehensive, intellectual integrity manifest by the universe."*

vision.

Some Principles of Faith

In 1981, Miller-Tiedeman and I interviewed the late Buckminster Fuller. I asked him if he believed that universe would support work of integrity. He replied that a difference existed between belief and faith. He went on to say that he had faith based in his experience. Fuller continued instructing me on faith while writing this inscription on the flyleaf in his *Critical Path* we had come to discuss: "With faith in the comprehensive, incisive, intellectual integrity manifest by the universe."

Presuming Fuller's "faith" to have its first meaning in my *Random House Webster's College Dictionary* (1992, p. 479)—namely, "confidence or trust in a person or thing" (including oneself)—a general theory of career grounds in two faiths: i.e. (1) faith that each *individual* has a personally learned and empowered career, willy nilly; and (2) faith in the "comprehensive, intellectual integrity manifest by the *universe*."

Since you can't fool Mother Nature, don't trouble to lie to her. Particularly don't lie about your personal career. In the universe, what goes around comes around. A lie to yourself about your personal career gets doctored by your own body. As Miller-Tiedeman contends, our hospitals are our best career re-direction centers.

Career involves action, particularly the action of making a living while making a life (Miller-Tiedeman, 1989). This principle makes inheritance, investment (learning and monetary kinds, for instance), labor, work, job, occupation, position, vocation, career and the like fair game for the lexicon of a general theory of career. It pays to know which one is addressed in a "career" conversation.

Career evolves both in humans' lifetimes and in cosmological time. Furthermore, at the level of personal consciousness, understandings can and do change instantaneously. It all depends on the situation. Nevertheless, career understandings tend toward complexity with a surprising coherence and clarity emerging as complexity gets closer and closer to the individual's nature and emerging life direction.

Career understandings emerge as a succession of changes in intellectual process(es). Each understanding, in potential, (1) integrates to a new unity, (2) differentiates from the rest of the system, and (3) re-integrates into the larger system. These re-organizational steps in an open, self-organizing system appear evident in a first cut at a general theory of career (Miller-Tiedeman, 1988). Personal understanding marches towards more and more coherence of the individual's system with that of the rest of universe. That's why it can't be determined by pronouncements. It comes from the person.

The self is a process, a figment of intellect. To Quantum Selves (Zohar, 1990) the self is potentially everywhere, not just in the "brain." Consciousness probably functions Quantum-like itself (Zohar & Marshall, 1994).

Self, consciousness, career, and society become separate concepts when discussed but they function holistically in a career developing. For your own career and in empowering the careers of others, pay careful attention to the functioning of this principle. An individual's perception of it makes considerable difference in the ease with which that person's cosmological paradigm will change.

The universe is unity. We form part of that unity. Quantum Mechanics offers today's best lexicon for universe functioning a la process lexicon. de Saint Exupery's (1971) little fox offers his Little Prince friend this telling explanation of that imparted lexicon principle. "It is only with the heart that one can see rightly; what is essential is invisible to the eye" (p. 87). There's Quantum functioning in a nutshell.

The Arrow of Time in My Career Development Faith
Model Builder Me

Joseph Campbell, author of *The Power of Myth* (1988), said, "People say that what we're all seeking is a meaning for life. I don't think that's true. What we're seeking is an experience of being alive so that our life experiences on the purely physical plane will have resonances with our innermost being."

My professional life work of a Campbell nature started in constructing models that resonate coherently with *both* people's external worlds *and* their internal functioning which illustrates a good Quantum principle. With several colleagues from Harvard, the Newton (Mass.) School Department, and the New England Education Data

System, I undertook construction of a model interactive, decision-guiding computer—the *Information System for Vocational Decisions*(ISVD)—to assist individuals in turning facts/data into personal information while instructing them in the principles of personal decision making.

ISVD modeled how a person can relate to an informing process in order to inform the individual about a decision under consideration, as well as facilitate moving the person forward in understanding the process of deciding all at the same time. That process of deciding leads to the development of purpose and a sense of agency, both of which manifest Quantum properties.

Transformation in My Career

Miller-Tiedeman and I joined forces in career development research in 1971. We both initially worked with career decisions in the commonly held paradigm—as if such decisions penetrated the individual from just the society, neither from the reverse nor from both. As such, we inadvertently favored a period of conformity which in the United States starts in family and is reinforced in schools. Remember that schools first came on the scene to train people to conform so they would make better industrial workers. Education was a by-product. So, in our beginning we cooperated with the conforming mindset.

Within a few years, Miller-Tiedeman began giving the two of us the added advantage of her knowledge and exemplification of intuition and its power in defining a life and/or career decision. I gradually found myself more and more guided by her knowledge and creativity. As I considered her thought carefully, I increasingly grasped the needed implication of the individual in comprehension of career: (1) as a continuous life process; (2) integrating in coherence with an emerging life direction while; (3) simultaneously differentiating from circumstances debilitating to its realization, and; (4) re-integrating into the individual's personal re-organization of the self at a higher level of consciousness.

Miller-Tiedeman's (1988, 1989) demonstrations that life and career function as a seamless, continuous process, not as isolated conditions, constitute a change in career development theory analogous in power and value to Einstein's uncovering of a special theory of relativity. Like the relativity work of Einstein and other scientists, her life-process work presently enables further development of a general theory in career.

I have wholeheartedly joined her purpose.

Present Impressions and Queries

How should training in career research allow for an individual's participative presence, along with measuring devices, when the researcher wants to transition to a Quantum environment from today's Newtonian one? A necessary condition of Quantum thinking is that the individual wholeheartedly implicate him or herself in the process of understanding. This will cause Quantum-committed researchers to rethink quantitative and qualitative research as a set, not as discrete categories. Researchers and citizens will then have to move up in awareness during psychological research and daily living and take responsibility for relevant perceptions as a common practice. This means coming to terms with the illusion of objectivity in a subjective human cosmology. For instance, Brian Swimme, a physicist, once remarked that the definition of objective is subjective. That's the magnificent jump in cognitive development I seek in facilitating the development of a life direction grounded in Quantum principles.

Given the fact that an interested person's presence is necessary to infer a Quantum situation, what facilitates the move up from conformity to self awareness? It seems you only need examine your cosmological paradigm ever more carefully and ask yourself, what and how much of what you then do patterns another's or society's belief system? When you can adequately distance yourself from your conformity upbringing and schooling, you can be "choiceful" and take full responsibility for your projections and perceptions.

In reading yourself into your career as a unity of Quantum phenomena, you will also move toward a Quantum Society. In doing so, you have to accept movement and its new, sometimes momentary, generalities, letting intuition unabashedly enter your processes of decision making and appreciation of universe as "all." This happens most easily in the Exploration stage of my seven stages in decision making (Miller-Tiedeman & Tiedeman, 1990) because that is the only one of the seven stages of decision making free from pre-set conditions as intuition requires.

As you bless universe by returning your experience, intelligence, and intuition in service to all universe, avoid an earlier mistake of mine. While marshaling determination and courage to explore in the process of deciding, stand up diplomatically to the pains of committing to a potential ideal; don't expect just joy as the emotion of exploration. Joy resides in exploration, but not all the time.

From Trapeze to Trapeze in Personal Quantum Leaping

He floats through the air with the greatest of ease, that daring young man on the flying trapeze (of Quantum, that is).

Quanta continually leap about universe with ease—naturally. In the above excerpt from the Trapeze song, a young man "... floats through the air ... with the greatest of ease," as well—if he has perfected "floating" through the air, that is. If so, Quanta and skilled high-wire aerialists both have easy floating knocked. The young man's high-wire mastery test comes as he seemingly "floats" from trapeze to trapeze in imitation of Quantum leaping. Master aerialists do this "...with the greatest of ease."

As Quantum aerialists release existing support and hurtle through space to some landing arrangement, trust, courage, confidence and skill are surely called into play, whether consciously or not. When these qualities come into doubt, living the Quantum Career becomes more stressful. That is the risk ending to my song, the ending I'd prefer we avoid. But on the other hand, that's the part we learn from.

Some After-Words

At this juncture in my own Quantum Career, I join my faith with Miller-Tiedeman and Dr. Lee Richmond, who has worked with us for a decade, to leave posterity what we three believe will have endless life for those daring young professionals on the Quantum trapeze— an appreciation of the 99% invisible in universe. As you walk courageously into the new:

May the road rise up to meet you as you entertain Quantum.
May the wind be always at your back as you reach for higher
ground.
May the sun shine warm upon your face when you need
support.
The rains fall soft upon your fields when you need
nourishment.
And until we meet again, may God hold you in Quantum
consciousness —
today's ultimate state of oneness.　　(Adapted from an old
Irish poem)

References

Bohm, D. (1980). *Wholeness and the implicate order.* London:
Routledge & Kegan Paul.

Brown, D., L. Brooks & Associates. (1990). *Career choice and
development: Applying contemporary theories to practice.* San
Francisco: Jossey-Bass.

Campbell, J. (1988). *The power of myth.* New York: Doubleday.

Capra, F. (1975). *The tao of physics: An exploration of the parallels
between modern physics and eastern mysticism.* Boulder:
Shambhala.

Capra, F. (1982). *The turning point: Science, society, and the rising
culture.* New York: Simon and Schuster.

de Saint Exupery, A. (1971). *The little prince. New* York: Harvest/
HBJ Books.

Fuller, R. B. (1981). *Critical path.* New York: St. Martin's Press.

Miller-Tiedeman, A. (1988). *LIFECAREER®: The quantum leap into
a process theory of career.* Vista, CA

Miller-Tiedeman, A. (1989). *How NOT to make it ... and succeed:
Life on your own terms.* Vista, CA: LIFECAREER® Center.

Miller-Tiedeman, A., & Tiedeman, D. (1990). Career decision making: An individualistic perspective. In D. Brown, L Brooks, & Associates. *Career choice and development.* (pp. 308-337). San Francisco: Jossey-Bass.

Prigogine, I. (1980). *From being to becoming: Time and complexity in the physical sciences.* San Francisco: W. H. Freeman.

Random House and Webster's college dictionary(1992). New York: Random House.

Tiedeman, D., & Miller-Tiedeman, A. (1994). *Consciousness and the human career: An evolutionary journey.* Vista, CA : LIFECAREER® Center.

Zohar, D. (1990). *The quantum self: Human nature and consciousness defined by the new physics.* New York: Quill/William Morrow.

Zohar, D., & Marshall, I. (1994). *The quantum society: Mind, physics, and a new social order.* New York: William Morrow.

Turbulence in Career Development: What Changes are Occuring in Career Development & Why?

William Charland
Cal Crow
Rich Feller
Tom Harrington
Kenneth Hoyt
Frank Jarlett
Richard Knowdell
Juliette Lester
Rodney Lowman
George Ritzer
Jane Walter
A.G. Watts

14

Careers in Changing Times: Learning What Comes Next

William A. Charland, Jr.

Labor market analysts estimate that each year in America one-third of our job roles are in transition, one-third of our technical skills turn obsolescent, and one-third of our workers leave their jobs. For the rest of our careers, you and I will be working in the midst of an economic revolution. We can't control the pace of a changing economy. But we can try to grasp the shape and direction of change: the shift, for example, from pyramid to diamond-like organizations. Moreover, we can learn to grow with the times.

Skills are the bridge to learning what comes next in an economy where we must reconsider many traditional assumptions. Today, jobs are joint ventures and employers are partners in the problem-solving process. Much as we're accustomed to thinking of

> *We're living in a time when jobs are joint ventures, employers are partners, and careers are continuing education. It's a day of transition and a time for new learning.*

a prospective employer as a fatherly fellow who's prone to hire the candidate with the best-shined shoes, nowadays that's mostly not the case. Employers are more like partners in a joint venture.

Careers are different, too. Nowadays, a career is basically a continuing education. The bottom-line benefit in most jobs is what we learn, not what we earn. As an instructor in aviation mechanics told me the other day, "Our field is changing so fast that a diploma is nothing but a license to keep learning."

That's why a good short term strategy in seeking employment is to look for a good learning environment in an industry where one wants to be— even if the first available job isn't one where one wants to stay. The point is to hire on and learn the ropes in a good learning community.

Learning is closely related to networking in new fields. Schools, professional associations, and other learning organizations are wonderful places to network—especially if we're unemployed. That's a time when most of us need all the support we can get when it comes to making connection.

Sometimes I think of that problem as the Senior Prom Syndrome. Remember how it felt when you had to get a date to a big dance? Looking back on that teenage trauma, it's a wonder we all weren't undone by it.

The reason we survived was that dating had a context. Getting dates was only one strand in the larger fabric of high school life. We made contact with the opposite sex and got clues as to who might be available as we mingled in the halls each day at school. High school provided a support system for traumatic events such as finding a date to the prom.

As adults, our needs are not so different. We all still need some systems of support and points of connection with others. The difference is that, as we grow up, those contacts are harder to come by. In adulthood we're much more isolated than we were in our teens.

That's one of the strongest arguments I know for pursuing some course of study when we're unemployed: not just to learn new skills, but to make contact with others whose interests are leading them in a similar direction. Learning is the leading edge of our experience, and education is a great source of community.

Pyramids to Diamonds: How the Workplace Is Changing

It's hard to make career decisions in changing times—not that it's ever been easy. Even in periods of economic stability, careers aren't static. People can outgrow their work. Elementary school teachers and pediatricians may find they're less motivated to work with small children once their own kids are grown and gone. Dancers need new careers when their legs go.

Not only do the needs we bring to work change, but the workplace shifts as well.

Set your sights on a job as a sushi chef, and suddenly the American taste for Japanese food sours. Learn to program in ADA and the computer industry turns to C++.

That's what it's like to make plans in the midst of an economic revolution.

For that's what we're living through today. Whatever people say about an economic recession, what we really have in this country is a radical revision of the way we're doing business. It's a change in the rules of the game.

For some time now, I've been aware of three pronounced trends that seem to be affecting most people's working lives:

- the shift from pyramid to diamond-like organizations
- from specialized careers to new jobs for generalists
- with new support systems in reorganized labor.

I first recognized the diamond-shaped organization when I was conducting a study of employment trends in Colorado a few years ago. I'd developed a questionnaire to find out the principal kinds of jobs found in key industries within our state.

As I interviewed employers in these fields—everyone from hospital directors to hotel managers—I asked about the levels of workers they employed. 1) How many were full-time executives and managers? 2) How many were directly involved in producing goods or delivering a service? 3) How many were in clerical or custodial jobs?

The pattern emerged slowly, but it was clear. In most organizations, the great majority of jobs were in the second category; most employees were producers of goods or services. They were customer service representatives, for example, or consulting engineers.

They were not full-time managers: vice presidents of this or that. Most of the organizations I surveyed had cut management staff to the core and not many people were paid just to supervise the work of someone else.Nor were there many support staff jobs at the low end of the scale. Some companies employed no clerical support staff at all.

These new organizations were shaped like diamonds. They were thick in the middle with service providers and other workers who produced revenue while supervising themselves. They were thin at the bottom and the top.

Compare that pattern with the economy we grew up in. Twenty or thirty years ago, most major companies were shaped like pyramids. They were thick at the bottom and narrow at the top. Those were organizations that people could enter through low level jobs with minimal skills, and work their way up. Careers were based on the familiar blue-collar to white-collar ladder.

Corporate pyramids were tiered. The lowest jobs were for blue collar workers who were directly involved in production. They made things with their hands. To progress in a pyramid, one worked up into the ranks of white collar positions. Those were the jobs for supervisors and managers who no longer had to work with their hands but supervised others who did. In a typical corporation there were about half as many white collar as blue collar jobs. Life in a pyramid organization was a lot like the military. You entered as a private, then made corporal, and rose up through the rungs.

Like any powerful institution, the corporate pyramid made a deep impression on the values of our entire society. That's why most people who grew up in the corporate era still value upward mobility at a gut level and secretly hope to find themselves climbing up some sort of ladder in their careers.

That view can be disorienting today, for despite the scarcity of corporate jobs, we continue to spawn white collar specialists. Law school enrollment is at an all-time high (129,580 at last count), and MBAs are multiplying like rabbits. That's not to say that the education these people have received is without value. Most specialized academic fields are personally enriching: it's stimulating to be able to think like a lawyer, conceive designs as an architect, or plan a media campaign as a public relations specialist might do.

The problem is finding work in white collar professions. Traditionally, highly-trained professionals have relied upon large corporate employers to employ them in specialized niches such as managerial development or strategic planning. But today the corporate economy is fading. Analysts estimate that America lost one million corporate white collar jobs a year in recent times, and that one-third of all middle management jobs are history.

The bottom line is that the day of the protective corporate employer is past. We're living in a time when jobs are joint ventures, employers are partners, and careers are continuing education. It's a day of transition and a time for new learning.

Lifelong Learning

Learning is as natural as breathing. Watch an infant develop or consider the incredible range of competencies of a two-year-old, and it's impossible to doubt that human beings have a strong interest in acquiring new skills. It's a need that doesn't diminish with age.

But adult learning is complicated; as grown-ups we have other roles and responsibilities in our lives. Beyond that, there are tough choices involved in continuing one's education. What if the skills we learn should land us in a dead-end job? Or in no job at all?

David Kolb, a social psychologist, became interested in learning styles when he served as an academic advisory at the Massachusetts Institute of Technology. Kolb noticed that many bright students dropped out of MIT not because they couldn't do the work required but because they learned in a different manner from the engineers who ran the school. He went on to study various ways in which specialists in different fields pursue learning. Some interesting differences turned up.

He found that engineers tend to follow a very concrete learning style; they like questions that can be answered right-or-wrong. Social workers, on the other hand, do better with creative material such as case studies, rather than black-or-white, true-or-false exams.

Kolb's research suggests that all of us should pay attention to our comfort zones in learning. Be it small seminars or large lecture classes, independent study or on-the-job training, we each ought to find the mode that fits us best.

Some of us will do better in active styles, while others need time for quiet reflection. Wherever possible, we ought to negotiate for a style of learning that matches our strengths.

Kolb seems to view learning as a form of problem-solving. We learn in order to get past some impediment in our lives—whether it's setting up a computer or just crawling across the living room to pull down a lamp. He believes there are four phases in a typical problem-solving/learning cycle.

First, we perceive the problem to be solved, then we process what we've seen and heard to form a concept or theory of it. After that, we produce some sort of solution to the problem; and, finally, we promote our solution to the problem to others.

Just as we each have preferences in the four phases of the problem-solving cycle, so our skills follow different patterns. We each tend to develop skills that follow our most comfortable style of learning. As a result, we develop distinctive weaknesses and strengths. That's why we need to recognize our strengths and get help in the areas where we're less comfortable: both in our work and in our learning.

Just as individuals differ in learning styles, so do professional groups. Professions tend to cultivate the same core competencies, so when a profession changes, co-workers often have common learning needs. That's why some of the most dynamic learning today is occurring in professional associations.

All of which raises the question of academic credentials. In a society where there's so much informal learning in professional associations, as well as other groups such as franchising organizations, small business organizations, and even temporary employment services, do college and graduate degrees matter anymore? It's a question worth considering.

On the one hand, it's important to note that more and more Americans have college degrees. In 1970, there were 11.8 million college graduates in the United States. By 1990, that number had increased almost three-fold, to 32.5 million. The fastest-growing group of students was women aged 35 and older.

Another related argument is that college graduates seem to be doing much better than non-grads. According to figures compiled by the Center for Labor Market Studies at Northeastern University in Boston, the income gap between male college graduates and high school graduates more than doubled between 1973 and 1986. Paul Harrington, a labor economist at Northeastern, is quick to point out that colleges may not be entirely responsible for the relative success of their graduates. "The main reason the rate of return is so good for college grads," he observes, "is that the labor market treats everyone else so bad."

Harrington believes that non-college graduates have suffered from the loss of "bridge jobs" in manufacturing—the kinds of jobs where people could learn basic skills and work their way up the ladder of pyramid organizations.

Look at the jobs in diamond organizations, and it's easy to see why more people are returning to college. For the points of entry in those firms are not at the bottom of some work-your-way-up ladder, but in the middle of the organizations—where new workers must be able to hit the deck running, with marketable skills in place.

But can adults balance college with the rest of their life? In recent years, many colleges and universities have taken steps to recognize the skills that mature students bring to the classroom. Mid-career adults now find they can receive academic credit for non-classroom learning through procedures known as "prior learning assessment." They can cut the time required to earn a degree and avoid sitting through classes they actually might be qualified to teach.

According to the National University Continuing Education Association, 97% of America's higher education institutions now grant credit for prior learning. The methods they use differ, as do the amounts of credit they assign.

Those are two arguments for completing a college degree: more of our competitors in the workplace have one, and through prior learning assessment it's possible to earn credit for what one has learned in the school of hard knocks. So it's possible to argue that anyone who can possibly earn a college sheepskin ought to.

Other questions surface when one considers the relationship between the places where today's college graduates are employed on the one hand and their major fields of study on theother. With the exception of a few occupations in the health sciences, it seems that college graduates with the same degrees are scattered all over the map.

According to the economists at Northeastern, only one journalism graduate in four is employed in publishing five years after graduation, and only 17% of banking and finance graduates are working in commercial banks.

I'd say that today the basic purpose of a college education is to generate long-term generalists. That is, if one can leave college with enough skills to gain a foothold in some occupation learning to do research as a journalist, for example—then it may be possible to expand upon those skills as one shifts to other fields. A good education is one that enables a person to recycle skills repeatedly.

And I do mean "repeatedly". For, in more fields, higher education has become a life-long process—whether or not one has a degree. A college education is not so much a possession as a process.

That's especially evident in community colleges. Today there are some 1200 community colleges across the country. Their enrollment has been growing twice as fast as in four-year colleges, and their mission is much more diverse. The typical community college student today is 30 years of age and 20% of entering students already have undergraduate degrees. The main emphasis at most of these schools is providing technical training for occupations that require not four years but two years worth of skills. That includes many of today's most promising jobs.

Don Goodwin calls the workers in these new two-year-training jobs "technoprofessionals." He believes they're vitally important to America's new economy. Goodwin serves as director of a new community college program at an abandoned air force base in Denver. The mission of this new school (The Higher Education Advanced Technology Center at Lowry) is to produce graduates for new jobs as technoprofessionals.

Today, in one field after another, some of the best-paying and most satisfying jobs involve skills drawn from the traditionally separate realms of manual and intellectual occupations. Neither blue collar nor white collar, they're jobs for new generalists.

Compare the earning potential and job security of these skilled technicians to traditional white collar professionals such as lawyers and architects, and it's evident there's no comparison. The outlook for technoprofessionals is much more favorable.

One reason for the shift to technical generalist jobs is the influence of advanced technology in all sorts of industries. Automotive technicians are paid to service on-board computers that have doubled the gas mileage cars got 20 years ago while drastically reducing pollution. There are more of these computers in many cars than on the earliest flights into space, which is why automotive maintenance has become such a high-tech occupation.

That's one reason we're seeing more generalists in the American workplace: because technology is changing. Another reason is the change I've noted in organizations, from corporate pyramids to diamond-shaped organizations. In today's flatter, more flexible firms, workers must perform a wide range of functions that are constantly changing.

Above all, whether or not one is pursuing a degree, it's vitally important to find a learning place one enjoys. Education is not a one-size-fits-all exercise, as it may have been back in school. It's a basic human function that combines the "holy curiosity of inquiry" with the benefits of staying current. Lifelong learning is a way of living fully in our time, and that is the gift of a changing economy.

15

Transitions in Turbulent Times: A Case for Education Reform

Cal Crow

He was an unhappy young man. Holding a low-wage and—in his mind—dead-end job, he saw little hope for the future. It had not always been this way. After completing a good training program and landing the job he wanted, he assumed that he had "arrived." Soon, however, came mergers, takeovers, buyouts, bankruptcies, and massive layoffs. He joined the growing ranks of the unemployed and had no idea what to do. At age 28, during a chance encounter with his high school counselor, he wanted to talk seriously about his experiences. He had few nice things to say about the education his high school had provided him.

> *...as we move into a post-industrial, global economy, much of what America's young people learn and experience as students is almost totally disconnected from what they will be expected to know and do as adults.*

More than a decade later, another discouraged young man sat before the same counselor, this time at an adult career/life planning center. More than a year after earning his bachelor's degree, he had not been able to find a job that could support him. Choking back the tears, he described the disappointment, humiliation, anger, and, more recently, the depression that overtook him when he thought about "wasting" $40,000 on a college degree. He felt cheated, and wondered if things would ever work out for him.

The messages from these two twenty-somethings were almost identical: *Their educational experiences had done little to prepare them for the world they were encountering.* They had done all of the right things in school, only to discover that courses, credits, grade points, test scores and diplomas didn't seem to matter once they left the classroom. This disparity between what occurs in school and the repertoire of skills people need outside of school is growing at an alarming rate. In fact, as we move into a post-industrial, global economy, much of what America's young people learn and experience as students is almost totally disconnected from what they will be expected to know and do as adults.

The problem is serious. It is not new and it is not going away. Since at least the early1980s, we have known that America's economy was changing. Structural unemployment, corporate downsizing, technological advances, and a growing reliance on a contingent workforce have made it clear that traditional models of education and training are no longer adequate, and, in many cases, are preparing people for a world that has ceased to exist.

From *America's Choice: High Skills or Low Wages* (1990), we learned that the United States has one of the worst school-to-work transition programs and the most unequal distribution of wealth among the world's industrialized nations; that a high school diploma has little or no meaning for the majority of the nation's employers; and that up to 70% of our citizens may be in serious economic difficulty by the end of the decade. From the SCANS Report (1991) we learned that the majority of our young people leave school without the skills and know-how to support themselves.

Research in the cognitive sciences tells us that people do not predictably transfer school knowledge to everyday practice, do not predictably transfer sound everyday practice to school, and do not predictably transfer their learning across school subjects. These findings suggest the need for more applied, experiential learning, i.e., cognitive apprenticeships, to help students see the connections and develop the skills necessary to make the transition from school to work (Berryman & Bailey, 1992).

School-to-work legislation and other education reform efforts are attempts to address these issues, and to help shrink the widening gap between school and the rest of the world. The operant word here is *reform,* because nothing short of a major overhaul will work. Tinkering with the existing system (e.g., increasing the number of graduation requirements) certainly won't do it (especially when we know that school knowledge does not predictably transfer anyway). Neither will adding a few new courses or providing a career unit in one or two classes.

If we are serious about helping people survive in turbulent times, we must be equally serious about ensuring that their educational experiences reflect the world they will be entering. This will require a willingness to question everything we do in the name of education, and what we ask of students. What does a credit mean? What are students *learning*? Why is it important that they know this? How do we expect them to use it when they leave school? Why do we have departments in our high schools? Why do we have six fifty-minute periods in a typical high school day? What does it mean to be a fifth grader, other than being ten or eleven years old and a former fourth grader? Do students really know why they are in school? Does anybody?

To get an idea of the type of restructuring that is necessary—and possible—imagine two different school systems. The first system is driven by a mass-produced, textbook-driven curriculum, which all students are expected to learn within a given time frame. Those who don't are described as "not capable," "unmotivated," or "not really trying." Standardized tests are used to rank, sort, label and place students, and to compare schools. Instructors hired to teach specific grades or subjects work with many of the same students, but rarely with each other. Neither students nor teachers are expected to show how levels or courses are connected. Because this system is organized around content and time, "extraneous" activities such as career development are viewed as an encroachment, taking time away from the real curriculum.

The second system utilizes a customized curriculum, reflecting what is known about learning and learning styles, motivation, multiple intelligences, and cultural differences. Textbooks are viewed as just one resource among many, and the purpose of testing is to improve instruction and increase learning. In this system it is assumed that all students can learn and perform, and want to be successful. Schools are organized into multilevel, interdisciplinary learning communities where the operant word is learning and everyone learns from everyone else. Students frequently work in teams on projects designed to show how things are connected in school, and how school is related to the world at large. Learning occurs both in the classroom and in the workplace, and career development is viewed as an integral part of the curriculum.

High schools in the first system have tracks for different students, e.g., college bound or non-college bound, academic or vocational, regular or special. The tracks are vertical, with one always "above" the other. The education system itself is also organized vertically. Major decision makers are at "the top," while instructional staff and students—who are at "the bottom"—are rarely asked to suggest strategies for systemic change. As a result, most do what is expected of them, but rarely do they think creatively about improving the status quo.

In the second system, all high school students select and enter broad horizontal career pathways which reflect their interests and enable them to develop a wide array of applied skills, regardless of future educational or career plans. Because this system embraces a philosophy of continuous improvement, students and staff regularly initiate discussions about how to improve learning for everyone.

In the first system, students are viewed as *products* who enter at age five or earlier, then "move through the line," occupying a new position each September. The purpose of school is to help them negotiate the line successfully. "Passing" or "failing" depends on the judgments of individual teachers. Because it is assumed that large numbers of students can't perform at high levels, a passing grade is set at 65% or 70%, or lower. In this system, the purpose is to "get through." Success is determined by the number or percentage of students who graduate "on time."

In the second system, students are *customers*, and the educational program is the product. This results in educators continually asking whether their product is meeting customer needs. Students are expected to perform at high levels so they will have the knowledge and skills necessary to succeed in an increasingly competitive global economy. Because the focus is on achievement rather than time, success is determined by the number or percentage of students who have demonstrated mastery of essential learnings.

In the first system, students "take courses" which may or may not be related to post high school career plans. Their bottom line is graduation, or perhaps college entrance. They are puzzled if someone asks them to describe their "program." When asked why they are doing an assignment, they will reply, "Because the teacher told me to," or "Because it is required," or "Because I need the credit." Rarely will they describe what they are learning, or why, or how they can use it once they leave an educational setting. Students who complete the requirements for this system receive a diploma, based on time in class and credits earned. However, no one is quite sure what these young people know and can do as a result of receiving this document. Even many diploma recipients ask, "Now what do I do?" "What does this mean?" Both of the young men mentioned earlier are good examples of this.

In the second system, students begin a career portfolio no later than sixth grade, and career development—including mastery of the SCANS skills and the National Career Development Guidelines competencies—is an integral part of the instructional program. When asked to describe their "program," they respond by explaining their current career pathway, and the decision making that led to their selecting it. When asked why they are doing an assignment, these students reply that they are developing knowledge and skills consistent with their career plans, and they are able to support this with concrete examples. Students in this system always know what they are learning, why they are learning it, and how they can use it, because their teachers regularly discuss this with them. Students graduating from this system receive a certificate of mastery indicating what they know and can do, and they leave with a clearly delineated career plan that includes at least one year beyond high school.

Most Americans will recognize the first system, designed decades ago to mirror the prevailing industrial view of the world. Reich (1991) described it as providing " . . .a standard assembly-line curriculum divided neatly into subjects, taught in predictable units of time, arranged sequentially by grade, and controlled by standardized tests intended to weed out defective units and return them for reworking" (p. 226). Many successful completers of this system—including large numbers of educators—see little or no need to fix it. In their minds, "It ain't broke. It worked just fine for us."

In actuality, the traditional American education system has never worked well for large numbers of students, especially the "defective units" who exited early (during mid-century this was about half of them) or those who went through the motions without ever becoming actively engaged in learning. In fact, many young people left school questioning their ability to learn. (Why do so many dislocated workers become agitated at the thought of returning to school for retraining? Why do so few adults take advantage of company-sponsored tuition reimbursement education programs?)

For decades the weaknesses in our education system were not a serious issue. Even those who were "not good students" could leave school and find family-wage jobs in factories, mills, forests, stores, warehouses and other workplaces reflecting the industrial way of doing things. Teenage dropouts could earn more than their teachers. Many of those who couldn't find jobs were welcomed into the Armed Forces.

Educators were seldom required to show a direct link between their programs and the knowledge and skill base required of students when the latter left school. Although there were many excellent vocational programs, they were seldom considered part of the fiber or mission of the school. They were offered for students who "weren't going on." The real purpose of education was to teach basic skills and to prepare students for more education. Third-grade teachers prepared students for fourth grade. Fifth-grade teachers prepared them for middle school, which prepared them for high school. Many of the nation's high schools adopted the demeanor of prep academies, devoted to preparing most of their students for college. Readying them for work or for a life of learning outside of school was not a high priority. It was assumed almost without question, that this was a good system which would lead to successful adulthood, if students would only do what was expected of them.

That has changed. Being well-schooled, like the two struggling young men mentioned earlier, is not enough. People must also be well-educated, which means developing the knowledge, skills, and world view required to function in a post-industrial economy. For this to occur, we must move from the first education system described above into something that looks more like the second. This, at least in part, is what education reform is all about.

The issue is not whether education needs restructuring—not to change is not a viable option—but rather the direction it will take. This will depend on who assumes leadership and who controls the agenda. True education reform will be a tough sell. Many oppose it because they have a vested interest in the existing system. Some are simply afraid of change. Others are hesitant to support it because they do not fully understand its connection to our nation's economic survival, or to individual student success. Advocates for change will need to recruit others who sense the urgency of the situation, and who can explain it in terms that others will understand and support. A good starting point might be to pick up on the "double helix" image selected by Berryman and Bailey (1992). It leaves no doubt that education and the workplace are intertwined, and makes it clear that attempts to effect education reform must emanate from a context of economic change in order to be successful.

The turbulent times are already here. America's schools must gear up to meet them. To do otherwise would leave thousands of young people trying unsuccessfully to apply an industrial model of education to a post-industrial world. And that would be unconscionable.

References

Berryman, S., & Bailey, T. (1992). *The double helix Of education and the economy*. New York: The Institute on Education and the Economy, Columbia University.

Commission on the skills of the american workforce. (1990). *America's choice: High skills or low wages*. Rochester, NY: National Center on Education and the Economy.

Reich, R. B. (1991) *The Work Of Nations.* New York: Vintage Books.

U.S. Department Of Labor. (1991). *What work requires of schools: A SCANS report for america 2000.* Washington, DC: U.S. Government Printing Office.

16

Redefining "Career" During the Work Revolution

Rich Feller

In large measure vocational identity shapes how we define ourselves. "What do you do?" follows most social greetings. The route to identity was enhanced by a stable work place which rewarded endurance, loyalty and rank. For many "the job I do, is who I am."

> *Since information drives the new work place, the timeliness of a worker's information impacts their ability to add value. Accessing information via technology and learning on demand creates unlimited growth oppotunities*

"Jobs" traditionally defined careers. A strong work ethic meant working harder rather than smarter. The American Dream encouraged acquiring and consuming more than one's neighbor. Material comfort and financial security were deeply held aspirations, yet saving was rewarded little. The U.S. dominated the world economy and large corporations provided jobs matching ages to wages. Local communities believed that "what was good for G. E. must be good for us." College degrees equated with professional job titles and tickets to social mobility. All of this is changing and so will career development as it helps develop human resources, foster a higher quality of life, and promote a more humane society.

While there is plenty of work to be done, there are not enough good jobs to provide the fulfillment of those seeking them. This realization creates a sense of questioning, a search for alternatives, and personal responsibility for choices shaping careers.

Because of a revolution in the present work place fewer workers are defining themselves through their jobs and many are seeking a better quality of life by redefining their "career." David Tiedeman taught me early on that careers were the sum of one's journey as we are much more than our job titles. His words are even more telling today.

History Reworks Itself

Present dislocation, downsizing, and job elimination is causing many to question assumptions about their future, community and lifestyle. Just as the agriculture-to-industrial transition brought technological change, economic growth and downward mobility, the present global-technological revolution brings pain to many and opportunities for others. Debates about the changing nature of jobs range from the impending end of a civilization to the beginning of a marvelous social renaissance. As in any time of great change, new structures, insights and options will replace the old, and career development will never be the same.

In the 1880's the Luddites protested industrial capitalism and technology and their ability to turn self-sufficient, self-directed citizens into dependent laborers. Others anticipated consumer goods, expanded markets, high-value jobs and an increased standard of living.

Today authors like Rifkin (*The End of Work: The Decline of the Global Labor Force and the Dawn of the Post-Market Era,* 1995) and Aronowitz and DiFazio (*The Jobless Future*, 1994) and a growing labor voice call for more equitable distribution of gains from technology enhanced productivity. David Korten in *When Corporations Rule the World* (1995) suggests that we face problems that can only be resolved by changing the structures and rules of the larger economic and political system within which business operates. He argues that within the present business system, it is impossible for even the most ethical and socially minded managers to lead firms with a community interest, and still survive. Lester Thurow in *The Future of Capitalism: How Today's Economic Forces Shape Tomorrow's World* (1996) concedes that while no system provides the efficiency and technology of capitalism, it is driven by avarice.

He sees a world of growing economic imbalances which may lead to a dark ages.

Economic war has replaced the Cold War and global corporations see less interest in national or community development. Multiple mailboxes throughout the world and electronic mail make it easy for transnational companies to overlook human problems left by downsizing, restructuring and acquisitions. Communities often reduce quality of living and environment standards in a race to restore jobs. Often those same jobs return to the global turnstyle. As a result, conservative and liberal philosophies begin to question the tradeoffs of the "survival of the fittest market system."

Politicians slowly respond to real wages, family income, and poverty rates which have flattened or declined since the 1970s. Social activists direct attention to the consequence of wage disparity from international trade, erosion of the minimum wage and declining union membership. Educators create new models to empower the underclass as much of the income inequality comes from technological changes that benefit the better educated. Consumers start to note that the pay ratio of chief executives to average workers in big corporations has gone from 41:1 in the mid 1970s to 187:1 in 1995.

Futurists bring ideas like workplace communities (Nirenberg, 1993) and wholelife economics (Brandt, 1995) to the popular press which can move us from disempowering jobs to empowering work so that more can find opportunities and personal fulfillment. Citizens speak out about the concentrated economic and political power of organizations as it reduces government's ability to provide a check and balance. As history demonstrates, adjustments to keep influence-rich corporations from threatening human interests can work.

Without a civil society committed to supporting workers in transition through voluntary associations, churches, and public education, class tension will rise. Without family income rising or parents free to raise children, class divisions expand. Commitment to the displaced or attention to the social fallout from technology's replacement of labor seems limited. Yet the *New York Times'* seven day front page feature ("The Downsizing of America," 1996), and full page ads on behalf of ATT's laid-off workers are encouraging.

It is no secret that the rules of the global marketplace are transforming work, learning, and careers. As the Luddites learned, while many were left behind, others reinvented themselves. As a result, the true meaning of a fulfilling career can unfold for those who are disciplined, agile, and resilient about learning and work in the new work place.

Transforming the New Work Place

Technology which raised the standard of living for so many makes it possible to produce things anywhere, using resources from anywhere, to be marketed anywhere. Cheaper labor accessible worldwide invites corporate and investment mobility overnight. Manufacturing workers and relatively low skilled, middle wage jobs increasingly disappear. Those lacking basic skills or disenfranchised from learning find the new work place offers little patience. Becoming agile regarding change, decision making processes and technology's potential are a prerequisite for finding good opportunities.

The work place structurally changed while creating new jobs, holding unemployment to half of that in Europe, and creating wage stagnation for those least educated. It transformed from a traditional, industrial, low performance work place to one that "reprofessionalizes" workers by expecting behaviors from all workers formerly expected of professionals.

In *Career Shifting: Starting Over in a Changing Economy,* Bill Charland, one of my best teachers, helped me understand most of my insights about the turbulent work place. Within it he ably illustrates the shift from the pyramid to diamond-like organizations. From his work I have tried to integrate new notions. The traditional triangle-shaped work place honored the top 15% of workers as the professional-managerial class (see Figure 1): those who made the decisions and exerted control. Work design was driven by engineers who removed responsibility and judgment from craft workers. Success was driven by efficiencies of higher volume at lower cost. Intelligence and talent were assumed to reside only at the top. Testing and sorting strategies served as gatekeepers to social mobility. At the other end of the triangle, the 85 percent of "blue collar" workers took direction, followed orders, and were reinforced for "leaving their brains at the door."

By meeting highly specialized job distinctions and stable skill requirements, and following clear lines of authority, there were ample entry-points. Beginning and low skilled workers entered manufacturing and public utilities in great numbers with no distinction between youth and adult labor markets.

North America's domination of the world economy and its competitive advantages led to significant job creation. Through seniority, collective bargaining, and continuous economic growth, workers obtained more than average world wages. In the 1990's the prohibitive cost of management's many layers and the computer's ability to disseminate information in "real time" shattered assumptions about job security, the structure of work, and company loyalty.

In the emerging diamond shape configuration, the new work place rewards different skills and broader responsibilities from more flexible workers but fewer supervisors. Supervisors "coach" a greater number of more broadly skilled workers while farmers carry computers to the fields and direct satellites to pinpoint which acres need attention.

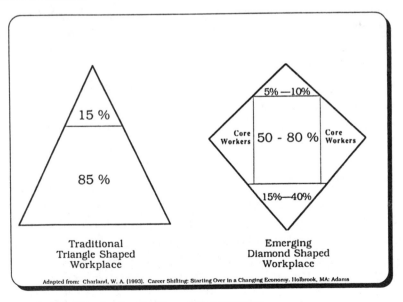

Figure 1. Traditional Triangle to Emerging Diamond Shaped Work Place

The emerging diamond shaped workplace as illustrated in Figure 1 mandates lifelong learning as workers adopt principles of global competition. Continuous improvement, international quality standards, self-management, teamwork, and high skill-high performance expectations are the norm. Time-compressed distribution, product development, and process innovation have literally created a work place revolution and transformed the worker's relationship with the company.

In terms of job options, the new work place requires moving supervisory and quality control tasks to all workers. Fewer primary, family wage, entry level jobs are available for students or low skilled adults. The fastest growing and economically most promising positions are technical jobs requiring training beyond high school but less than a four year degree. Increasing numbers of college graduates end up without the credentials to get professional level or "core competency" jobs. Many have found it impossible to predict the earning power of a particular degree.

The unemployed and those with "limited resources" face fewer opportunities at the base of the diamond. Those expecting job security or job entitlement face frustration, alienation and discouragement. However, within the diamond shaped configuration many become empowered through freedom, independence and flexibility. Risk and entrepreneurship are welcomed, personal investment and self-direction become a priority, and variable compensation rewards high performers. At the far right and left points of the broad portion of the diamond, a number of "core employees" find greater attention from employers. They possess skills central to the companies' achievement and mission. Their work is not threatened by out-sourcing or temporary contract labor. Figure 2 lists a review of work place shifts anticipated as one moves from the old to the new work place.

In my own consulting I find numerous examples of formerly displaced employees of bureaucratic risk-adverse companies, invigorated within small start-ups that maximize individual creativity. However, not everyone can easily adapt. Those who can recognize that learning is a job requirement. While business commits added resources to training, traditional public education works to preserve democracy by preparing students to be lifelong learners, economically

Characteristics of the Shift from the Old to New Work Place

Traditional Triangle-Shaped Work Place	Diamond-Shaped Emerging Work Place
command control supervision	supervision as "coaching"
authority invested in supervisor	authority delegated to workers
centralized control	decentralized control
fragmentation/individual worker tasks	work teams, multiskilled workers
"that's not my job" view	increased "dejobbing" view
mass production	flexible production
long production runs	customized production
fixed automation	flexible automation
end of line/process quality control	on line/within process quality control
"entitlement ethic"	"psychology of earning ethic"
company dependent career	"own your own job, skills, and career
labor management as enemies	view"
minimal qualifications accepted	labor management as allies
workers as a cost	screening for basic skills
internal labor market	work force as an investment
advancement by seniority	limited internal labor market
information to decision makers	advancement by skill documentation
minimal training for selected workers	information to all
narrow skills for some	training essential for all workers
broad base of primary entry-level jobs	broader skills for all
little concern for foreign markets or labor	fewer primary entry-level jobs
easy access to primary labor market jobs	great attention to foreign markets and alliances
	previous experience, temporary employment,employment, or occupational proficiencies before access to primary labor market job
Worker "classes" by title and degree	workers appreciated by degree of core skills

Figure 2. Characteristics of the Shift from the Old to New Work Place

self-sufficient and responsible citizens. However, schooling and learning face a transformation as well.

Transformation: School is No Longer a Place

As U.S. Education Secretary Richard Riley says, "The era of semi-skilled factory worker making good pay is simply gone forever." Good paying jobs require those who know math, can read and write, are part engineer, part salesperson, understand software or robotics, can solve problems and get along with others.

So where do students learn these skills? While Berliner and Biddle (*The Manufactured Crisis: Myths, Fraud, and the Attack on American Schools* , 1995) take education critics to task and celebrate public education's success, *Breaking Ranks: Changing an American Institution* (NASSP, 1996) calls for making way for electronic learning. At the same time, the Western Governor's Association has initiated a Virtual University (1996) affirming that the barriers to time and place are eroding. Opportunities to learn are everywhere. Regardless of the learner's age or need, technology can enhance learning anywhere. Software has replaced schools as the key factor shaping when and where learning occurs. Teachers can no longer own the content or compete with technology's ability to present information. It makes instruction more student-centered, encourages cooperative learning, stimulates increased teacher/student interaction, and helps students take more responsibility for their own learning.

Since information drives the new work place, the timeliness of a worker's information impacts their ability to add value. Accessing information via technology and learning on demand creates unlimited growth opportunities. More flexible, efficient, and customer friendly learning systems are becoming accessible and competency based. Figure 3 illustrates factors impacting how learning and work is changing.

Understanding relationships among the factors shaping learning and work can empower clients and students as they seek jobs and plan for career fulfillment.

151

Learning and Work in the New Work Place

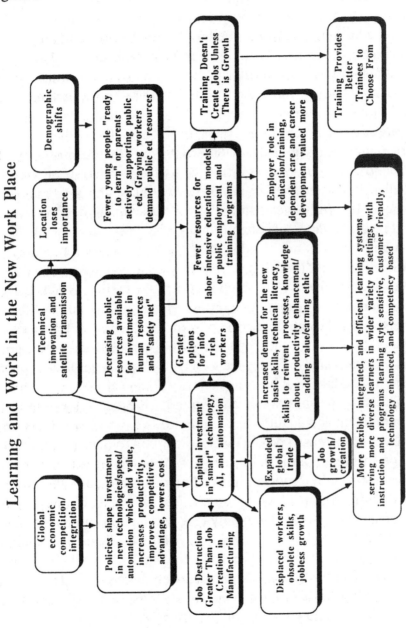

Figure 3. Learning and Work in the New Work Place

Transforming Careers: Defining Success On Schedule

Providing good career development requires recognizing that success and fulfillment is individually defined. The dominant culture and media suggest "more is better," "up is the only way to go," and "surpassing the Jones" is Americans' favorite pastime. However, the assumption that everyone wants to get ahead, climb the corporate ladder, or live to work, is not always true as careers are redefined and career values transformed.

Brooklyn Derr's (1986) identification of five distinct career orientations among today's workers suggests there are benefits and tradeoffs of each success strategy. As the psychological contract (Feller, 1995) between employers and workers is broken, some find, or seek, less fulfillment within jobs. Reassessment of career values and time commitments often follows.

Many workers are at odds with society's values. *Yearning for Balance* (Merck, 1995) suggests they want to achieve more balanced lives and provide a cleaner environment for their children. Eighty-five percent of respondents cite responsibility, family life and friendship as key guiding principles for themselves. Yet they believe others do not share their priorities. This gap between what people say they value and how they see society's values suggests many clients are off schedule with how the majority define success.

The way people work and spend time shapes community commitment and quality of life. Previous workers gained leisure as a result of increased productivity. According to Shor (1991), recent wage increases almost exclusively fueled increased per capita consumption. She suggests many Americans are both working and consuming themselves to death. Yet upwards of half of her respondents say they'd willingly take less pay for more free time.

Redefining careers in search of fulfillment demands evaluating one's relationship to money and materialism. The growing popularity of *Your Money or Your Life* (Dominguez & Robin, 1992) suggests that striving for a simpler, more frugal lifestyle is an increasingly valued career strategy. They report an average of 20-25% decrease in expenses as a result of following a nine-step plan. Such a plan promotes conscious responsibility in choice making. Reassessing one's addiction to money, material things, and job identity at the expense of finding balance, community and fulfillment can lead to personal freedom and a redefinition of "career." I suggest even a more humane society!

Conclusion

The global and technological revolution is making fewer good jobs available. Yet there is plenty of work to be done. Fortunately changes in organizational efforts and structures, and personal insights on the part of individuals can empower workers and expand opportunities. These can lead to redefining identity, values, and time commitments as one confronts the present "survival of the fittest market system."

As the traditional triangle work place transforms into a diamond shaped configuration, many will prosper. Others will take the opportunity to reassess personal choices. This will enhance career development specialists as they help clients explore unlimited and on-demand learning options, personal freedom, and new forms of fulfillment. With this a new definition of "career" can evolve—careers that can include more learning power, responsibility for conscious choice making about community, and hopefully a better quality of life.

References

Aronowitz, S. & DiFazio,W. (1994). *The jobless future*. Minneapolis, MN: Regents of the University of Minnesota.

Berliner, D. & Biddle, B. (1995). *The manufactured crisis: Myths, fraud, and the attack on american schools*. Reading , MA: Addison-Wesley.

Brandt, B. (1995). *Wholelife economics: Revaluing daily life*. Philadelphia, PA: New Society Publishers.

Charland, W. (1993). *Career shifting: Starting over in a changing economy*. Holbrook, MA:Adams.

Derr, B. *Managing the new careerists* (1986). San Francisco, CA: Jossey-Bass.

Dominguez, J. & Robin, V. (1992) *Your Money or your life.* New York, NY: Penquin.

Feller, R. (1995). Action planning for personal competitiveness in the "Broken workplace." *Journal of Employment Counseling, 32,* 154-163.

Korten, D. (1995). *When corporations rule the world.* San Francisco, CA: Berrett-Koehler.

Merck Family Fund. (1995). *Yearning for balance.* Takoma Park, MD: Author.

National Association of Secondary School Principals. (1996). *Breaking ranks: Changing an american institution.* Reston, VA: Author.

Nirenberg, J. (1993). *The living organization: Transforming teams into workplace communities.* New York, NY: Irwin.

Rifkin, J. (1995). *The end of work: The decline of the global labor force and the dawn of the post-market era.* New York, NY: Putnam.

Schor, J. (1991). *The overworked american: The unexpected decline in leisure.* New York, NY: Basic Books.

The downsizing of america. (1996, March 3-9). *New York Times.*

Thurow, L. (1996). *The future of capitalism: How today's economic forces shape tomorrow's world.* New York, NY: Morrow.

Western Governor's Association. (1996). *From vision to reality.* Denver, CO: Author.

17

Is Job Dissatisfaction Related to Changing Values?

Tom Harrington

Have you considered that the reason work is no longer satisfying may rest more with the person than the job? As people age and change, they often fail to realize that their values also change. People are aware that organizations have downsized, merged, committed to affirmative action, and increased the amount of work workers are expected to do. People are working harder and with more diverse people, but is the work itself really different or demanding different skills?

People do not socialize at the workplace as they previously did. Children have to be picked up at day care and endless commuting is less appealing after a few drinks. With job loss, sometimes internalized as "something is wrong with me," people become depressed and financial and marital problems soon follow. While media has focused on jobs and how they have changed., another perspective is whether people have examined what is important to them, whether what they value has changed. We know work practices have changed, but have personal values changed to adapt to the economy?

Recently after an interview, a journalist reduced years of work with the bold caption, "People Value Money More", aggravating the

> *A surprising and most troubling finding was that working with one's mind and leadership were not highly valued by adolescents or even college students. These two values are frequently mentioned in connection with the jobs of the future and are associated with attributes of extensive effort, delayed gratification and persistence.*

researcher. Isn't that statement common sense and true? Yes, it is true for adolescents, but not for adults, according to some research. The headline then sent an incorrect message. So, why does a researcher travel to South Africa and survey over 23,000 people from the United States, Australia, Japan, Israel, Norway, and Great Britain to learn that, among adolescents, money is the foremost job value across the globe, spanning professions from lawyers to travel agents and, to a lesser extent, bricklayers? The answer is based upon examining the belief that cultures and people differ in what they value. But how much diversity of values exists among people of different traditions, ethnicities, and cultures?

Diversity is an increasing reality. The media markets uniqueness and differences. Psychologists focused on individual differences fcor years. Finding ideas and things that people in general agree upon is a challenge. A critical review of observations and assumptions that different values are held by various groups is warranted and by implication favors change if these observations and assumptions prove to be wrong.

The Importance of Examining Values

A major assumption in career counseling is that examination of one's values is an important goal. How many work-related values are there? Twenty-eight values were identified in a U.S. Department of Labor-based publication, the *Guide for Occupational Exploration* (Harrington & O'Shea, 1984). Such a listing, however, raises a question about the theoretical definition of a value and its differentiation from an interest. Values were defined as objectives that one seeks to attain to satisfy a need (and that) interests are the specific activities and objects through which values can be attained and needs met.

The significance of examining values is the belief that satisfaction with one's career, including retirement, is related in part to the degree to which values are recognized and satisfied. The writer's experience is that, while most people agree that values are important to know, few people have examined theirs extensively and find it enlightening to do so. They often highlight reasons for their stress. Life transitions are those points when people become involved in others' value clarification. Transitions are opportunistic periods for reflection, reviewing, discovery, rediscovery, and prioritizing what people believe is most important. All approaches to decision making consider assessing one's values as a critical step.

Some Research

Students from seven nations showed remarkable uniformity in prioritizing their job values in data collected over ten years. Some specific findings revealed U.S. English- compared with U.S. Spanish-speaking rank ordered value correlations were .82; U.SEnglish-speaking compared with Canadians were .87; and U.S. with Japanese adolescents were .81 (Lebo, Harrington, & Tillman, 1995). Females showed a greater homogeneity than males in value rankings across cultures. A median rank-ordered correlation of .83 between females and males reveals a high degree of commonality among adolescent value rankings.

Top values for students transnationally were: good salary, job security, variety-diversion, working with people, and high achievement. Money dropped as the number one value for U.S. adults and was surpassed by the need to achieve. If adults have abilities and skills that are not utilized, their focus shifts more to achievement and ability utilization. The workers surveyed were employed in 53 occupations, many in national companies (Harrington & O'Shea, 1993). Among adolescent values, albeit a commonality exists, differences were found between countries. For example, in Finland and Japan, variety was the top value. While Japanese respondents ranked creativity in 3rd place (a surprise contradicting a common stereotype), creativity ranked 6th in Australia and Finland, 7th in Canada, and 9th in a listing of 14 values in the United States. Independence, working with hands, prestige, and working with one's mind were in the mid-range of popularity. The values least important to youth, consistently across cultures, were physical activity, leadership, physical risk, working outdoors, doing repetitive work, and being supervised.

A surprising and most troubling finding was that working with one's mind and leadership were not highly valued by adolescents or even college students. These two values are frequently mentioned in connection with the jobs of the future and are associated with attributes of extensive effort, delayed gratification, and persistence. They also have relevance to national goals and competing within a global society. Could the new jobs of the future, which emphasize mental involvement and the challenge to assume leadership roles within organizations, be at odds with individual personal values? The data point to a major discrepancy between individual and organizational expectations. Adolescent's high values of people involvement and job security are not being met in many organizations.

Elizur, Borg, Hunt, and Beck (1991) also studied work values across eight cultures: Germany, Holland, United States, Israel, Korea, Taiwan, China, and Hungary. The samples were mostly male, the modal age group was 21-29, about a third were supervisors and managers, and a half were college graduates. They found that the highest ranked of 24 values were: achievement, interesting work, advancement, personal growth, and esteem. Salary was ranked in the middle with the lowest ranked values being job status, contribution to society, work conditions, opportunity for people interaction, and influence in the organization. The above top selections characterize the intrinsic and the bottom rankings the extrinsic dichotomy of the conceptual structure of work values. It is noted that the researchers had expected similarity between the West European and North American samples and anticipated a contrast between Western and Eastern culture. Elizur et al. expressed surprise when they found that the intercultural differences were "far and away only minor variations within a much broader pattern of structural similarity."

These three studies fit Super's (1989) summary of cross-culture value studies. "Values are essentially the same structurally and in content in all major countries, although they differ in their relative importance with the traditions and economies of the country." Super's conclusion, however, does not mean that everyone has the same values profile.

Various job clusters were found to differentially satisfy different values, according to a study by Harrington and O'Shea (1993) of the values profiles of trainees and workers in 106 occupations. However, some jobs were noted to only satisfy one or two of a person's values.

Theory and Practical Implications

Values, needs, skills, and abilities are key aspects of one of the four major career development theories—the theory of work adjustment (Osipow, 1994). This theory allows careers to be examined by focusing on what happens to adults under various workplace conditions. According to Dawis (1994), "Abilities and values are seen as providing the structure of personality. Thus the operative set of skills and needs may change with time or with a given situation, but the source—personality structure—remains essentially the same" (p. 35). Thus values inform needs and needs reflect values. Reinforcer preferences for a person's psychological needs represent a basic concept of the theory. Values relate to assessing the importance and the strength of a reinforcer to reinforce specific behaviors.

Values clarification then plays a significant role in career planning through recognizing what the major values are, the relative importance attached to them, and how they are reflected in what we do. For example, all of us fill many roles in life, some roles can conflict and many individuals are constantly striving to achieve a balance in relationships, work, and our sense of self identity. Caring for an aging parent, children, or a mate; maintaining a desired lifestyle; desiring to do a good job at work; having private time; and keeping physically attractive all reflect values, potential conflicts in time demands, and are sources of personal satisfaction and dissatisfaction. Since values are so highly personal, different people will satisfy different needs performing the same activity. The articulation of people's motivation is good for consciousness raising and fostering communication skills when values are shared. An end goal in values clarification is to help people establish a hierarchy that reflects a personal reality, is comfortable, and identifies potential conflicts and stress.

In summary, when one considers the relationship between values and job satisfaction, it is helpful to recognize that (1) prioritization of values shifts with age; (2) values are essentially the same structurally across cultures; (3) different values are satisfied in various job clusters; (4) values are a recognized part of enhancing career development; and (5) clarification of values plays an important role in self awareness and self direction.

Conclusion

While values have been studied, their interaction effects still are unclear in three areas: the environment, personal meaning, and decision making. First, context or environment may be a reinforcer of values. In the 1950s education was rewarded financially but people were not punished if they did not get an education. Currently, education may be rewarded but people can be severely punished for not pursuing schooling throughout life. Jobs of the future, as well as present job shifts, directly challenge and, I suspect, will change adolescents' present low value for working with the mind. Do societal values follow personal values or vice versa? For example, Gail Sheehy, in her new book *New Passages: Mapping Your Life Across Time* (1995), issued a wake-up call for a personal choice—to reject the reproductive revolution that might make females mothers anytime, regardless of their biological clock. Second, while a similarity of values may exist among adolescents and cultures, that does not mean people attach the same meaning to the same value. Individuals must be encouraged to tell their own stories to learn their personal meaning. Third, decisions need to be conceived within a cycle, not a single event as some have incorrectly learned. Initially, it is valuable to explore and weigh options and then to make a commitment. But most people learn that the environment also makes or deals out decisions that impact individuals more than personal choices. The key point is to realize individuals need to reexamine the initial decision, along with the response from the environment, and again proceed through the decision-making steps with this new information. As decisions can be reevaluated, the search for the meaning of values in relation to the environment will continue.

References

Dawis, R. V. (1994). The theory of work adjustment as convergent theory. In M. L. Savickas & R. W. Lent (Eds.), *Convergence in career development theories.,* Palo Alto, CA: Consulting Psychologists Press.

Elizur, D., Borg, II, Hunt, R., & Beck, I. M. (1991). The structure of work values: A cross cultural comparison. *Journal of Organizational Behavior, 12,* 21-38.

Harrington, T. F., & O'Shea, A. J. (Eds.). (1984). *Guide for occupational exploration* (2nd ed.). Circle Pines, MN: National Forum Foundation.

Harrington, T. F., & O'Shea, A. J. (1993). *The Harrington-O'Shea career decision-making system revised manual.* Circle Pines, MN: American Guidance Service.

Lebo, R. B., Harrington, T. F., & Tillman, R. (1995). Similarities in selected work values of high school students from seven cultures. *The Career Development Quarterly.*

Nevill, D. D., & Super, D. E. (1989). *The values scale: Theory, application and research.* Palo Alto, CA: Consulting Psychologists Press.

Osipow, S. H. (1994). Moving career theory into the twenty-first century. In M. L. Savickas & R. W. Lent (Eds.) *Convergence in career development theories.* Palo Alto, CA: Consulting Psychologists Press.

Sheehy, G. (1995). *New passages: mapping your life across time.* New York: Random House.

Super, D. E. (1989). *Values: What they are, how we judge them, and some things we know about them.* Paper presented at the annual American Association of Counseling and Development convention, Boston, MA.

18

Preparing the "High Skills" Workforce

Kenneth B. Hoyt

Introduction

It is widely believed that America's occupational structure is rapidly moving from being industrial based to being a post-industrial, information-oriented, knowledge-based society. It is further widely believed that the rate at which these changes are taking place is much swifter than occurred when America moved from being primarily an agricultural to an industrial-based society. Finally, many believe that if America is to compete successfully in the emerging international marketplace, there will be a great need to produce a "high skills"

> *...the declining middle, the secondary labor market, and the power of education—all hold serious implications for changing the role and function of career counselors in general and secondary school counselors in particular.*

work force that will allow us to produce both goods and services that are *better, cheaper,* and delivered more *quickly* than those of other nations (Marshall & Tucker, 1992; National Center on Education and the Economy 1990).

To the extent these beliefs are true, major changes in the knowledge, skills, and activities of career development specialists are needed. These changes can be understood in part in terms of basic concepts regarding (1) the "declining middle" controversy, (2) the "secondary labor market" phenomenon, and (3) the importance of education in the emerging society. Each of these three concepts will be briefly discussed. Following this, some implications for how career counselors can best help their clients will be presented. Finally, one possible solution will be provided.

The "Declining Middle" Controversy

The July 1983 issue of *The Atlantic Monthly* contained a prophetic article by Bob Kuttner entitled "The Declining Middle" . In this article, Kuttner predicted and illustrated with a series of then current examples that America's occupational society, in an economic sense, will rapidly lose its "middle class" occupations. He further predicted that, as a result, both "high skills-high paid" and "low skills-low paid" occupations would increase at a rapid rate with the gap between the "high paid" and "low paid" workers average income becoming increasingly wide. More recently, the dangers of becoming a two-tiered society with a few winners, lots of losers, and an eroding middle class have been emphasized by Secretary of Labor Robert Reich (1994).

The accuracy of these contentions has been seriously questioned by Mishel and Teixeira (1991). They provide DOL data demonstrating that the predicted change in percentage of jobs requiring a "high" (+2.2%), "middle"(-0.8%), or "low"(-1.3%) level of education will be minimal between 1986 and 2000. Further, their data demonstrate that the widening gap in wages between those with a "high" amount of education as opposed to a "low" amount is due primarily to decreasing wages for the less educated, not because of increased wages for the more educated.

The existence of a *trend* toward creating conditions leading to a "declining middle" has been recognized in a very thoughtful article by Drucker (1994). However, Drucker does not see this as something that is occurring rapidly on a wide scale. My reading of the literature forces me to agree with Drucker on this point. Career counselors must keep clearly in mind the concept of the "declining middle" and the broad trends leading toward this situation. It is far from being a sure thing but it is an important topic to be discussed with clients in many counseling conversations.

The Concept of the Secondary Labor Market

The concept of the "secondary labor market" was apparently first developed by Piore (1970). According to this concept, "secondary labor market" jobs are identified primarily as ones that are dead-end, low pay, short tenure jobs in organizations not supplying entry-level workers with such things as sick leave, annual leave, hospitalization plans, or retirement plans. "Primary labor market" jobs, on the other hand, are either union-organized or professional with relatively good wages and benefits, fairly predictable ways of moving up in the organizational structure with recognized *career* development, and good job security. The emerging information-oriented, knowledge-based occupational society is obviously one holding little promise of good jobs for those in the secondary labor market. Not many persons can be expected to *choose* a career in the secondary labor market.

Still, for those youth seeking to enter the labor market with no more than a high school education, it seems probable these are the typical kinds of jobs they are most likely to find. It appears that, of the 26.3 million new jobs projected to be created between 1992 and 2005, 10 million will require only a high school diploma or less (*Occupational Outlook Quarterly,* 1994). Large numbers of these are almost sure to be secondary labor market jobs. The other 16.3 million new jobs will all require some form of postsecondary education or training and so are unlikely to be available to youth with only a high school diploma.

Career development assistance to *all* high school leavers should include a strong emphasis, beginning in the elementary schools, on such things as equipping pupils with (a) the basic academic skills; (b) a set of productive work habits; (c) a strong and personally meaningful system of work values; (d) a set of job seeking/finding/getting/holding skills; and (e) basic career decision making skills. It appears likely that youth equipped with such skills will have little difficulty finding jobs in the *secondary* labor market. It seems safe to say that, while not all persons with a high school education or less can be expected to find themselves in the secondary labor market, most persons in the secondary labor market have a high school education or less.

For those seeking to enter the *primary* labor market, these basic skills are best thought of as being *necessary* but not *sufficient*. Most such persons will find it essential to *add* to these skills a set of specific occupational skills to be acquired in some kind of postsecondary education institution.

The Importance of Education in the Emerging Society

Both the Kuttner (1983) and the Mishel and Teixeira (1991) publications contend that a strategy of investing large amounts of money into providing prospective workers with the occupational skills needed for economic success in the emerging "high skills" society is unwise. Their point is that, if very large numbers of persons sought "high skills" training, it is unlikely they could all find job vacancies simply because of the relatively small numbers of "high skill" jobs predicted to be available.

Recently published data can be used to illustrate this point. The Spring, 1994 issue of the *Occupational Outlook Quarterly*, on page 52, contains two charts. One of these provides data showing the projected *numerical* change in employment during the 1992 - 2005 period for persons with varying amounts of education. An increase of 26.3 million persons is expected during this period, 3.0 million of whom are projected to have received some kind of postsecondary training at less than the bachelor's degree level and 8.0 million at the bachelor's degree level or higher. This leaves 15.3 million persons projected to enter new jobs that require no formal postsecondary education. Under these circumstances, many will question the wisdom of urging almost all high school leavers to secure *some* kind of postsecondary education prior to entering the work force.

On the other side of the coin, the currently popular publications by Marshall and Tucker (1992), the National Center on Education and the Economy (1990), and Drucker (1994) all strongly emphasize the need for greatly increased numbers of high school leavers not headed for four year college/university settings to secure some set of high-level, specific occupational skills at the postsecondary sub-baccalaureate level. All three of these major publications point to the need for this to happen if the United States is to compete successfully in the international marketplace. They also point to the great need for persons to acquire such skills if they are to function effectively in the emerging information-oriented, knowledge-based occupational society. All three of these publications deserve careful study by career counselors.

One source supporting their claims with reference to the growing importance of some form of postsecondary education can be seen in the Spring, 1994 issue of the *Occupational Outlook Quarterly*. This document provided data showing that, between 1992 and 2005, the number of jobs requiring specific occupational skill training at the sub-baccalaureate level will increase by 34%—more than for any other level of education reported.

To whatever extent the United States occupational society is currently experiencing a "declining middle," those favoring great increases in the percent of both youth and adults who acquire some specific set of occupational skills at the postsecondary sub-baccalaureate level look to such increases to result in the reemergence of an economic "middle class" for the U.S. occupational society.

A recent national survey of employers with 20 or more employees indicated that 33% of these employers reported using "technical and vocational institutions" and 30% reported using "community and junior colleges" as training sources (National Center on the Educational Quality of the Workforce, 1995). If recent high school leavers secure specific occupational skills in these kinds of institutions, it appears their chances of finding employment in the primary, rather the secondary, labor market are likely to increase. Of course this expectation ignores whatever biases employers may have with respect to employing youth. The National Career Development Association publication reporting results from the 1993 Gallup Poll (Hoyt & Lester, 1995) contains impressive data illustrating the problems experienced by persons in the 18-25 age range with respect to meeting their career development needs. This is a serious matter.

Challenges to School Counselors

A variety of evidence is available indicating that America's occupational structure is changing toward becoming what Drucker (1994) has called a "knowledge society." Increasingly, the education system is being expected to help persons solve problems related to both the "declining middle" and the "secondary labor market" concepts. Education will, increasingly, be counted on to help create a "high skills" occupational society that can compete effectively in the international marketplace. A variety of challenges now face school counselors as they seek to help youth cope with these changing conditions.

First, with respect to the "declining middle" concept. This concept appears to be legitimately considered as only a faint trend unlikely to have serious consequences for a number of years. In spite of this, the tendency for more and more jobs to be at the top *and* at the bottom end of the wage scale distribution is clear. This is emphasized several times in the Reich (1994) paper in which he cites such figures as: (1) the top 5% widened their lead last year by taking home 48% of the nation's total income; (2) men who lack college degrees have suffered a 12% decline in average real incomes since 1979; and (3) 47% of those displaced workers who found new jobs are now earning less than they did before.

Problems associated with the growing numbers of workers at the bottom end of the wage scale are especially serious challenges for career counselors to consider. It is clear that, in order to survive at anything close to a comfortable standard of living, more and more dual career couples must be created. Neither partner will be able, on his/her own, to earn enough money to support both of them. The range of jobs available to one partner will increasingly be limited by factors associated with the job held by the other partner. Full freedom of career choice for such persons is almost sure to be more limited than we would like it to be.

Second, challenges associated with the "secondary labor market" concept. Data found in the Fall 1989 issue of the *Occupational Outlook Quarterly* show the numbers of workers in occupations typically considered to be in the "secondary labor market" are increasing at a relatively rapid rate. This can be seen by noting that projected increases in only three occupations likely to have large numbers of persons in the "secondary labor market" - retail salespersons (730,000), janitors and cleaners (556,000), and waiters and waitresses (551,000). These three occupations are expected to total more of the new jobs projected during the 1986-2000 period than the 20 fastest growing occupations (1,580,000 new jobs) put together. Several other occupations in the list of the 20 occupations predicted to provide the largest numerical increases in employment during this period also appear to include many workers in the secondary labor market such as (1) general office clerks, (2) nursing aides and orderlies, (3) receptionists and information clerks, (4) cashiers, (5) food counter, fountain and related workers, and (6) food preparation workers.

Most youth are unlikely to fully understand the implications of choosing an occupation predicted to have many workers in the "secondary labor market" as opposed to the "primary labor market." Further, it is primarily jobs in the secondary labor market that are readily available to today's high school leavers who seek immediate employment. The frequency with which persons change jobs in the secondary labor market make it difficult to conceptualize what is happening as a form of true career *choice*. Instead, secondary labor market jobs appear to be ones persons *settle* for when they cannot find a job in the primary labor market. Many persons with jobs in the secondary labor market appear highly likely to find "drudgery," as opposed to true "work," in their job duties (Hoyt, 1991). They may have to meet the human need to work in other parts of their lives. Counselors must do all they can do to help their clients avoid entering the secondary labor market under circumstances that make it appear this to be their prime career choice.

Third, with respect to level of education. Reich (1994) cites statistics showing that every year of education or job training *beyond high school* increases average future earnings by 6 to 12%. If America is to move toward becoming a "high skills" nation able to compete effectively in the world marketplace, it is essential that almost all high school youth (except those headed only toward the secondary labor market) consider enrolling in some kind of postsecondary educational institution prior to entering the work force. As Drucker (1994) contends, education will be the "coin of the realm" in the knowledge society. The days when a high school leaver could appropriately ask the question "should I go to a four year college or should I go to work?" are past. The question today's youth must ask —and answer—is "should I go to a four-year college or to some other form of postsecondary education prior to seeking entry into the work force?"

Helping today's youth answer this question poses a variety of serious challenges for school counselors. Among these are the challenges to (1) increase both counselor and student knowledge regarding the variety of kinds of postsecondary educational opportunities, (2) helping high school pupils seriously consider *choosing* some form of postsecondary sub-baccalaureate education rather than *settling* for it when they either can't get in or can't remain in a four-year college or university, (3) helping parents realistically accept and help their children consider a variety of postsecondary educational options—*not just* those associated with four-year colleges; and (4) helping youth, parents, and the general public understand that the question "Which is the best occupational choice?" is very limited in meaning. The proper question to ask is "Which is the best occupational choice *for Person #N*?

The Counseling for High Skills Project:
One Approach to Meeting These Challenges

A beginning attempt to contribute toward meeting these challenges can be seen in the operation of the Counseling for High Skills (CHS) project at Kansas State University. This project has been funded as a $3.3 million demonstration grant by the DeWitt Wallace-Reader's Digest Fund. Its goals are the production and use of information aimed at helping the 70% of high school leavers not bound for four-year college/university settings to consider, choose, and enroll in some other form of postsecondary education prior to seeking entry into the labor market.

The prime kind of information being accumulated is, in effect, a "customer satisfaction" approach to describing specific programs in specific postsecondary institutions. This approach involves asking present and former students in these programs to supply answers to questions high school youth, considering enrollment in such institutions, most often ask. It is assumed high school students will value answers to these questions given by persons like themselves who are now experiencing what the high school student is considering.

As high school students consider enrolling in a specific program in a specific institution, here are some examples of major questions we have discovered they often ask:

1. What kinds of persons will I find as classmates?
2. How do current students rate this program at this institution?
3. What do current students feel will be the *total* (not just tuition) cost to take this program?
4. How do current students pay the costs of taking this program?
5. What kinds of housing problems, if any, are current students experiencing?
6. What are chances of getting a full-time job for students completing this program?
7. Does the institution help former students find jobs?
8. Are the jobs former students find directly related to the education they received?
9. Is this program equally available to men and to women? To minority and non-minority?
10. How do former students rate this program at this institution?

A crucial component of the CHS project is its procedure calling for a "partnership" arrangement between the Project and the State Division of the American School Counselor Association (ASCA) in each participating state. Teams of ASCA members serve as official data collectors in each participating postsecondary institution. To do so, these counselors must actually visit each participating institution, interact with both staff members and students there, and observe the institution's facilities. This is aimed at helping them become better informed and less biased regarding these institutions and programs. It is also aimed at helping counselors judge for themselves the validity of the information they collect.

Once collected, the data received from present and former students in each participating program at each institution are processed at the American College Testing Program (ACT) and placed on computer disks along with data collected from other students in other programs and institutions in the state. A separate computer disk is prepared for each participating State. These computer disks are distributed free of charge to all ASCA State Division members in the State who attend a short professional development session aimed at helping counselors learn how to best use the data. Counselors who have these disks can share data with both students and their parents. By doing so, it is hoped that both student and parental biases against the generic notion of postsecondary sub-baccalaureate education can be reduced and eventually overcome.

To date, data have been collected from approximately 18,000 students enrolled in about 800 programs in about 230 institutions in 13 states with about 750 school counselors involved as actual data collectors. It seems safe to say a *beginning* has been made.

Concluding Remarks

The three basic concepts discussed here —the declining middle, the secondary labor market, and the power of education—all hold serious implications for changing the role and function of career counselors in general and secondary school counselors in particular. A partial set of answers to these challenges can be found in the Counseling for High Skills project at Kansas State University. I hope that consideration of these concepts will motivate many counselors to study more carefully and consider participating in this program. The challenges are real. The time to move toward making the kinds of counselor changes that will enable us to meet these challenges is now.

References

Drucker, P. E. (1994, November). The age of social transformation. *The Atlantic Monthly,* pp. 53 - 80.

Hoyt, K. (1991). The concept of work: Bedrock forcareer Development. *Future Choices, 2(3),* 23 - 30.

Hoyt, K., & Lester, J. (1995). *Learning to work: The NCDA Gallup Survey.* Alexandria, VA: National Career Development Association.

Kuttner, B. (1983, July). The declining middle. *The Atlantic Monthly,* pp. 60 - 72.

Marshall, R., & Tucker, M. (1992). *Thinking for a living.* New York: Basic Books.

Mishell, L., & Teixeira, R. A. (1991). *The myth of the coming labor market shortage: Jobs, skills, and incomes of america's work force 2000.* Washington, DC: Economic Policy Institute.

National Center on Education and the Economy. (1990). *America's choice: high skills or low wages.* Rochester, NY: Author.

National Center on the Educational Quality of the Workforce. (1995). *EQW Databook.* Philadelphia, PA: The Center.

Occupational Outlook Quarterly, (Spring, 1994). Occhart. <u>38</u>(1), 53.

Occupational Outlook Quarterly, (Fall, 1989). Occupational Employment. <u>33</u>(3), 30-31.

Piore, M. (1970). Manpower policy. In S. Beer et al. *The State and the Poor* (pp. 50-83). Boston: Winthrop Publishing Company.

Reich, R. (1994, November 22). *The revolt of the anxious class.* Remarks presented to the Democratic Leadership Council. Washington, DC.

19

Jobs, Small Businesses and the New Workplace

Frank E. Jarlett

Overview

Global competitors with lower wages and high-quality products are pushing the United States towards a new workplace dominated by small businesses and sophisticated products/services. The key to success is an organization's attitude towards its future: if it is proactive and creates its own future, then it will likely succeed. The career counseling profession has unique skills to help businesses upsize not downsize; the profitability of these upsizing employers creates employment, provides tax dollars, and is the source of *your* income. The future of the career counseling profession is *in* the workplace helping employees upgrade their skills.

> *The best practitioners of the career counseling profession are supporting employers that upsize and not supporting employer strategies of downsizing and outplacement*

Many traditional career counseling functions havebeen automated—these functions are both opportunities and threats to the profession. Career counseling activities should be reapportioned to the employment/unemployment ratio: 93% on the workplace to help employers/employees improve their workplace by not downsizing, and 7% on issues that help the unemployed/underemployed understand workplace issues. The information in this paper is part of a program at the University of California San Diego (UCSD) for a certificate in career counseling.

The Changing U.S. Workplace

We read the headlines about the big layoffs by prestigious employers such as IBM, General Motors, Sears, and the federal/state/local government. However, they often bungled their downsizing and many of those laid-off did better than the survivors. One-third of management jobs have been eliminated and the 30-year-job-to - retirement has gone. In reality, the U.S. workplace grew by 24 million jobs in the 1970s, grew by 18 million jobs in the 1980s, and is still growing at the 18 million rate in the mid-1990s and is projected to continue at the same rate for the next 15 years. Why? Because the downsizings of large employers was totally overwhelmed by the upsizings of small businesses. The best practitioners of the career counseling profession are supporting employers that upsize and not supporting employer strategies of downsizing and outplacement (U.S. Department of Commerce, 1993; Maddux, 1992; Stevens, 1994).

The New Workplace
Most employers, large and small, navigated successfully through these recent turbulent times and their techniques constitute a "new workplace." Their keys to success include:
- Innovation of high value-added products and services for niche markets;
- Use of the best technology from anywhere in the world;
- knowing that the only way to compete and pay high wages is to use high-productivity tools such as robots;
- First-time quality;
- Care of customers;
- Timeliness of deliveries (first to market);
- Project organization with autonomous teams having interpersonal skills, adaptability, creativity, initiative, goal-setting, leadership, cooperation, and continually added skills;
- Organizational changes such as virtual corporations, core + outsourcing, reengineering, autonomous business units, empowered employees, self-managed teams, TQM, managing change, learning organizations, cross-training, adaptable employees, career resilience, and family-friendly policies;
- A typical work life is now 15-20 increasingly sophisticated

projects each lasting about two years. Additional skills must be gained in those two years so that each employee is ready for the next significantly different project.

How an organization responds to these issues is key to its survival. In Denmark, Oticon's motto is "think the unthinkable"—informal groups initiate projects and do them, keeping costs down and sales up: profits increased 25% in two years. In Brazil, Semco's "natural business" is self-governing and features an increasing competence, a 7-fold increase in revenues, high profits, and assist with self employment. In the U.S., 3M has 90,000 employees, sells 60,000 products around the world, and 30% of its sales come from products introduced in the past four years. Intel's highest achievement is to unseat a currently successful product. These are examples of the crazy new management of "flatten, burn and rebuild." Career counseling professionals must help their clients understand and respond positively to these workplace issues (Peters, 1994).

Managing Change

Career counseling professionals need to know how employers manage change because it is the foundation of employment. The successful completion of large, sophisticated, international projects occurs every day in the United States' workplace. System engineering techniques conduct tradeoffs of customers' conflicting technical and operational needs and optimize the total system; then project management techniques keep the program within budget and on schedule until final delivery. Of course, each project is different, but their common thread is the six-step process described below (don't ask for source documents because they are proprietary to private businesses and are buried in the voluminous procurement regulations of government agencies). The six steps include lessons learned from the past, uses the present to analyze future options, and plans/manages to achieve the best possible future:

1. Trends: Changes occurring outside of the organization such as technology, economic, social, political, and environmental trends;
2. Status:Core capabilities, patents, copyrights, employee skills,

equipment, facilities, management, uniqueness, strength/ weakness of competitors;

3. Goals:Values, mission, vision, short/long term, current/new customers;

4. Options: This step is the key to good decision-making. An organization creates a range of future options (from "do nothing" to "what is the best possible outcome") and then evaluates them versus all the multi-disciplines that are impacted. The best future is selected—often an intermediate option;

5. Plan:The resulting plan includes engineering, procurement, manufacture, sales, and customer support. It must be updated periodically to reflect changes taking place both outside and inside of the organization;

6. Manage: Human resource policies, training and skills upgrade to match new business opportunities, leadership, future tasks, schedules, work-arounds, cost controls, management information, and managing backwards.

Career counselors should help their clients understand these ideas because workplaces that use these six-steps upsize—workplaces that don't, downsize. The six steps combine left-brain and right-brain activities and creative thinking, but have little to do with "long range strategic planning," five year plans, and other inflexible approaches.

Small Businesses

Counselors and their clients need to know that small businesses are the only group reporting a net gain in job creation. Currently, 75% (and increasing) of all jobs are in businesses with less than 500 employees whereas 25% (and decreasing) of the jobs are in larger private business, federal/state/local government and public education. Forecasts call for 18 million additional jobs during the next 10 years, same as in the past 20-30 years—all in small businesses. The primary beneficiaries of this sustained job creation are women, minorities, and the foreign-born. For example, in 1960, less than 20% of married women with children under 6 years old worked, today it is over 60% and rising. The best workplaces are becoming family-friendly (U.S. Department of Commerce, 1993).

In some regions of the U.S., 12% of the workforce are self-employed and another 12% are in 2-5 person businesses. Of course, there is volatility in these small enterprises: some go from 2 employees to 100 in 5 years, others grow slower, others grow to their comfort zone and level off, others grow and retrench, some die. Their focus is to survive and expand; they hire people who have multiple skills, who can function in a wide variety of workplace environments, and who respond positively to recurring crises.

Why this trend towards small employers? Because "new workplace" qualities are instinctive to small businesses—to compete against low-cost global competitors. Large organizations are often too slow. As an example, virtually all of the new successful biotechnology companies are small start-ups, the large organizations are left behind. Counselors need to understand the modus operandi of these small businesses.

Future Work

As part of their strategic focus, employers know what workers they need in the next few years, the skills they want, and the wages they expect to pay. ERISS (Employment Research and Information Supply System) is a new, powerful, user-friendly, computer program that contains the most advanced occupational information available today; it meets the Clinton Administration's call for a one-stop-access to re-employment. ERISS contains:

- Over 120,000 pages of information, all linked and cross-indexed for instant retrieval. It contains more than 37,000 occupations and cross references;
- Complete and detailed job descriptions, requirements, projections, and characteristics for about 13,000 jobs;
- National, state, and local labor market information, projections and wage data;
- Typical career ladders, working conditions, benefits, and skills employers are looking for and where to find the jobs;
- Listings of local training providers, and programs matched to the skills needed for each job;
- Graphical displays showing highest wage jobs, fastest growth,

most openings, best self-employment, and cross-county comparisons;
- Transferable Skills Analysis module, correlation between data/ people/things and listing of all compatible employment, recommendations based on work history, autopilot that guides anovice user, and pre/post injury calculations;
- Actual employers (name, address, phone, principals, industry, DOTs);
- Community-based service providers;
- Coming soon: "the explorer"—a Windows-based product designed for the job seeker (ERISS).

Counselors: many traditional career counseling functions have been automated. You could be in the workplace using ERISS to help employers do skills upgrade planning for each employee, then target the appropriate training so that future workplace skills will be there when needed. ERISS could result in unemployment for counselors who stay with the old tools.

Getting Work

The unemployed and underemployed must understand that the only openings are in small businesses or in big ones trying to look small. They need to stop focusing on themselves and their mindset of "getting a job, tweaking resumes, getting interviews, etc."; instead, they need to focus on the needs of the workplace by doing three things:
1. Identify a few specific local employers and find out about their products, markets, competition, organization, culture, key persons, revenues, profitability, and what they need to accomplish their goals;
2. Use career counselors to identify their own transferable skills and see if their skills are compatible with the future needs of the organization. Then decide what they as an individual will do to help the organization survive near-term and thrive long-term;
3. Mesh these issues together and build a "forward-looking capabilities brief" rather than a "backwards-looking resume." Get business cards and a brochure and see themselves as self

employed, ready to help solve an employer's problems.

Suggested Priorities for the Career
Counseling Profession

The above changes in the workplace are opportunities for counselors who are aware of them, but they are threats/uncertainty for counselors who cling to the old tools. Specific recommendations include the following:

1. Help employers accept the realities of the "new workplace." The global workplace is performing low and moderate skill jobs for less than 1/10th of our minimum wage. The U.S. workplace is moving inexorably towards higher levels of sophistication in technology, management, and team skills. Help employers and employees move gracefully into their new workplace. They are desperate for your expertise.

2. Build your own data base of workplace information and help employers survive near-term and thrive long-term (Jarlett can get you started).

3. Help the 93% of the workforce who are employed become creative, productive individuals by continuous skills upgrading —their only employment security.

4. Some traditional career counseling techniques have been automated and are being used in the workplace; acquire these techniques.

5. Help the 7% who are unemployed (and others who are underemployed) acquire the skills that employers say they want. Steer them towards small businesses and away from middle management. Career ladders and training programs are an integral part of your local data base of future employment.

6. With the above strategies, it is easy to get zero unemployment. One unemployed person is assigned to each 15-person team for on-the-job training. Each workplace inherently knows the skills that are needed. Appropriate incentives would be given to the employer and to the unemployed person. If this happens, are you ready?

References

ERISS Corporation. *Employment Research and Information Supply System* (ERISS). 9968 Hibert Street, Suite 103, San Diego, CA 92131-1035. Phone (800) 491-ERIS, Fax (619) 566-1707.

Maddux, R. (1992, November). *Lessons learned: Dispelling the myths of downsizing.* Presentation at the 1992 California Career Conference, Sacramento, CA.

Peters, T. (1994). *The tom peters seminar - Crazy times call for crazy organizations.* Vintage Books.

Stevens, P. (1994, November). *Differing motives for career development systems within organizations.* Presentation at the 1994 California Career Conference, San Francisco, CA.

U.S. Dept of Commerce (1993). *Statistical abstract of the United States, Annual Updates.*

20

Perspectives Shaping Career Planning in The Future

Richard L. Knowdell

Career decision-making has evolved from an event to a process; it is no longer a once-in-a-lifetime event. In 1950, at the midpoint of the twentieth century, planning, acquiring, and maintaining a career was very much like boarding and riding on a train.

When you wanted to use a train to go somewhere you purchased a ticket for your destination and boarded the train at the gate with your destination printed on a sign. The train moved steadily along the fixed and stable tracks until it reached your destination. No detours. No changes in the route. Just sit back and relax. The engineer, conductor and crew would take you to your destination. In 1950 I was a plumber's helper. I boarded the "plumbing train" and expected to move from plumbers helper, to apprentice plumber, journeyman plumber, foreman plumber, master plumber, and maybe even plumbing contractor. I was sure that the nature of the job wouldn't change. The career path wouldn't change. My career route was as predictable as the train route. And that was the way everyone in 1950 viewed careers and jobs. But the train view or metaphor had become obsolete by the 1960s and 1970s.

In 1970 we needed a new metaphor to describe the dynamics of career and job decision-making. Career decision-making was now like riding a bus.

When you boarded your bus for work each day, you didn't get on a

> *I believe that career development is in the eye of the beholder. The way that we view career development depends on our position in the organization and our experience in the world of work.*

vehicle that operated on fixed and stable tracks. With the bus, you were on a vehicle that could change its route when the road conditions and traffic patterns changed. You were now on a vehicle that could change its ultimate destination. You could even transfer or change buses in mid-route if you desired. Career decision-making in the 1970s became much more flexible, allowing the occupation to change with the technology and economy and permitting the individual to make mid-career changes or transfers. But, like the train, we still relied on the bus company to set the schedule and route as they could be heard to say "leave the driving to us." As we approach the year 2000, we need a new and different metaphor that will describe career planning and decision-making for adults in the workplace during the next century.

To successfully navigate the career and job world of the 21st century we need to move to the "all terrain vehicle" or "ATV" as our metaphor for career planning.

The ATV is flexible and fast. It doesn't require fixed tracks. It doesn't require fixed transit schedules or even paved roads. Routes can be changed or modified every year, month, week, day, hour or even minute. And the ATV has one other distinguishing difference from the train and bus. When you ride the train or the bus, someone else is in the "driver's seat."   But, in the all terrain vehicle (ATV), the individual needs to take charge of the situation and control his/her own course. In career planning, the individual needs to take the controls and "drive" toward his/her own unique career toward success.

The careers in the 21st century will not be steady and fixed The computer technology of the 1950s and 1960s brought us thousands of key punch operator jobs. That same technology has now eliminated all of those jobs. A combination of an emerging technology and changing social habits may replace bank teller positions with automatic teller machines. We can't predict the specific jobs that will emerge in the 21st century, but what we do know with a high degree of certainty is that those employees who have learned to "drive their own careers" will be able to prepare for, acquire and master the careers and jobs that emerge. A major challenge for today's career counselor is to inspire employees to take control of their careers and to steer and drive those careers toward attaining their own personal satisfaction. The possibility exists to the degree the following seven trends can be personally accommodated.

Rolling Recessions and Up and
Down Labor Market Demand

At a StanfordUniversity conference several years ago, economist and futurist, Richard Carlson predicted that the recessions and downsizings of the late 1980s were not a temporary economic anomaly, but represented a pattern of regular fluctuations that will be with us for the predictable future. Management training programs are now including how to deal with layoffs and downsizings as part of their curriculum. Even the most healthy of companies are learning to plan to contract as well as expand.

The Two-Tiered Work Force

Not many years ago companies advertised Temporary and Permanent positions. No more! Corporate counsels are careful to advise their corporate clients that if they refer to a job as permanent they will be facing law suits if they try to terminate employees from these "permanent" jobs. So now we have two distinct types of workers: the "regular" employees who will hold the jobs as long as they perform satisfactorily *and* as long as the company needs them; and the temporary or "contingent" employees who are hired for a specific project or assignment and who can expect to be terminated or reassigned at the conclusion of the project. The general expectation of most corporations is that the "regular" or core workforce will be retained during recessions and downsizings while the contingency employees will be laid off. There are pluses and minuses to this two-tiered workforce. On the positive side, there will be many temporary and part-time jobs available for those workers who choose not to commit themselves to a long term relationship with an organization and value the freedom and independence of being able to move on to new challenges and environments. On the negative side, many of these jobs do not contain benefits as those in the "regular" workforce do. More importantly, we are facing the dilemma of creating a category of second class workers, an under-class who will be paid less, have less benefits, and perform the less desirable tasks on the job. The two-tiered workforce is here now. The question is Where are we going with this new phenomena?

The Changing Technology

Whenever I attempt to predict the future, I remember reading about the prediction of the head of the U.S. Patent Office during the last two decades of the 19th century. That department head, whose name has long since been forgotten, sent a letter to the President of the United States recommending that the Patent Office be abolished because "obviously, everything that can be invented has already been invented." I do not purport to know what will be invented during the next two decades, but, if we just look at what has changed in our lifetimes: from wristwatches with hands to tell the time to digital readouts and calculators; from carbon paper to copy machines; from telegraph lines to mobile telephones; from paying extra for air mail to instant fax machines.

The De-Layering of Middle Management

As the twentieth century comes to a close, most successful companies (and some government agencies) are eliminating several layers of redundant middle management. Peter Drucker has predicted that the organization of the future will look much less like the hierarchical military chain-of-command and more like the symphony orchestra. Decision-making authority will be moved down in the organization and the span of control and authority of any manager will be greatly expanded. The new manager will not be expected to be a technical expert who will teach and monitor the workers very closely, but rather like the symphony conductor who facilitates the actions of dozens of musicians, each of whom knows his or her instrument better that the conductor, in order to create a product that no single individual could have created on their own.

New Work Options

For several years western society has had the means to restructure where and how we do our work. Job sharing has been instituted where two part-time workers share a single position or assignment. Flex-time, where the start or finishing time is modified from the traditional nine to five pattern, has been successful in numerous organizations. Telecommuting is slowly gaining in popularity. Organizations have been slow to respond to any of these new work options when they have been considered at the request of employees, i.e., when the working single mother asks to schedule her work time around her children's school schedule. On the other hand, many organizations have changed starting time to non-peak hours when they found that reduced bumper to bumper commute times for employees increased productivity. With the availability of the new wireless technology and mobile fax machines, we should see a marked increase in telecommuting during the next few years.

Low Skill Jobs With Low Pay

The willingness to "just work hard" used to be the ticket to success in the Western world. Now, every job in the 21st century will require computer skills. It was not long ago when the only people who were expected to understand and use computers were computer programmers. Today, ride in any big city taxi and you can observe the driver entering data about the number of passengers and their destination in a dashboard computer. Check your baggage at the airport curb and the skycap enters your name into the computer and your personalized baggage tags with the correct destination are instantly produced. You will even find a computer in the cab of a tractor cultivating a wheat field in Kansas. We are moving swiftly toward a society of high skilled "haves" and low skilled "have nots." And I believe we have a choice of which group we want to belong to.

The Knowledge Worker

Gone are the days when the young entry level worker, with little education, went to work for a company, learned and mastered their product, and lived "happily ever after." Overspecialization without a broad foundation of knowledge can lead to obsolescence. Security for the knowledge worker (if there is such a thing anymore as security) rests not in the mastery of a specific job at a specific organization, but in personally developing a body of knowledge and skill that is transportable across organizations and occupations. A case in point would be the "Lockheed" engineers who flourished before the aerospace downsizings of the late 1960s and early 1970s. The Lockheed engineer (which is a generic term for overspecialized engineers at any number of aerospace companies) joined the organization in boom times with little education and no experience. But they were quick learners and hard workers and quickly became narrow experts. They knew virtually everything about the base of the rear antenna on the L-2 rocket powered satellite, but very little else about engineering. They were very valuable employees while that particular product was being built but very expendable when the company moved on to a new product line.

The First Line Supervisor's Increasing
Span of Responsibility

The traditional span of responsibility and control of the first line supervisor has been to select, hire, train and monitor five to seven workers—workers who couldn't do the job as well as the supervisor, who needed to be watched and showed how to do the job. Recently, Peter Drucker has painted a different picture of the successful manager of the 21st century. In this new model, each of the workers, like musicians in an orchestra, will know their specific jobs better than the manager or orchestra conductor would know them. And the orchestra leader's span of control is much too broad to spend time looking over the shoulders of individual musicians (or workers).

How is Career Development Viewed by the
People in the Workplace?

I believe that career development is in the eye of the beholder. The way that we view career development depends on our position in the organization and our experience in the world of work. I have frequently been disappointed when I've looked at books that were advertised as being about career development and found them to be about job change, job search, job rotation, job enrichment or career paths—all of which can be aspects of career development—but none of which is career development by itself. Here are three views of career development.

The Worker's View of Career Development

This was the first view I was exposed to twenty years ago, when I started delivering career development programs in organizations. I came in as a consultant from an educational setting—the way many consultants get involved in career development. The first people I was exposed to, who had a view of career development, were the workers and employees at the bottom of the organizational pyramid. Being at the bottom of the pyramid, the only direction the employee can look is up. When we talked about career development, they were hearing "these are the career paths; this is how you move up; these are the skills you will need to move up in these paths; this is where you can get training and how you can move up; this is how long it will take you to move up?" And the employee hopes it won't take longer than a year to move up.

When I go into any organization and talk to the rank-and-file employees about career development, the employees don't hear career development, they hear *"upward mobility."* In their minds eye, career development equals upward mobility. In most of today's organizations, we don't have the traditional pyramid structure anymore. Organizations are flattening out. The time is long past when a large segment of the employee population just waits for a higher level job to open. Even if organizations still looked like pyramids, we would still have a lot of impaction, plateauing, stagnation, or attrition because there is clearly not enough room at the top for everybody.

As career counselors or human resource professionals, when we talk with employees, or when we hang out our shingles that say "career development provided here," the employees will view that shingle differently than we do. To the employee, the shingle will say "Promotions and Upward Mobility Offered Here." Unfortunately, that is the only thing many employees are willing to see. As a professional career counselor, I tend to think of career development in terms of a process that requires hard work and discipline and involves assessment techniques, exploratory research, goal setting, planning activities and continuing education. But, that's just our view. The reality that career development professionals must deal with in the workplace is the employee's view of career development.

The Supervisor or First Level Manager's View of Career Development

A second view of career development is the supervisors' view. They are closer to the center of the organization pyramid, and the supervisor views career development differently than the employee does. When supervisors hear "career development," they visualize "motivation." "How can I motivate my employees? How can I work to coach my employees? What can I do to keep good workers? How can I get rid of the poor performers?" Supervisors are very interested in retraining good workers and ask, "Is there some class that I can take to learn how to motivate my employees?" When career development professionals start working with supervisors and first line managers in organizations, the supervisors really aren't thinking about upward mobility. They're thinking, "I've got these very real problems right now. I've got these employees I'm trying to motivate. I've got some good employees that I certainly don't want to lose. This career development stuff might mean that the Human Resource office is trying to move good people out of my department. I don't want that to occur. What do you mean, you people from HR want to do career development? I'm the one that's responsible for career development in my troops, because I work with them every day. So you give me some tools I can use."

Top Management's View of Career Development

Let me move to the next level of the organization, and examine their view of career development. This is the top management of the organization. Top management thinks of career development in terms of identifying potential managers. Their focus is on identifying which employees have the right skills to meet the challenges that the organization will face in coming years. Top management is worrying about how to get employees trained to move into new positions, and to determine when those employees will be ready to move. So what happens when I talk with top managers about career development? When I say "career development," they hear "succession planning." Unlike the first line supervisor who asks "What do I need immediately?" the top manager asks "What do we need to do in the next three to five years in order to have the right people with the right skill mix in the right place?"

The above are sketches are of three different groups of people in organizations. Each group, depending on their level in the organization, views career development differently. The employee who is looking at upward mobility wants to move within the next year; the first level manager or the supervisor, feels an immediate need for assistance and worries about motivation, productivity and performance. Top management takes a long range view of three to five years in the future, is focused on the big picture and is concerned with the selection and identification of people to move up in the organization. Ironically, the top management is not really concerned about people moving out as much as lower management is. First-line supervisors are concerned about letting a person leave this week because they have to get production out this week. Top management understands that, in order to get the right people in the organization, some people have to move on. Top management is much more receptive than the other sectors to what I call "open" career planning and career development.

The ride into the 21st century is an uncertain and turbulent one. Those who learn to "drive" their own careers will get there. Those who don't may crash in flames. The role of the career development professional is clear: to teach and empower employees to take control and responsibility for their own careers. Understanding trends that shape the workplace allows career development specialists to confront clients with reality. Regarding the varied ways career development is viewed increases their potential to reach workers at different levels. As both occur, career planning will lead to greater success for the counselors and clients.

21

Turbulence at the (Gallup) Polls

Juliette N. Lester

"Education is affected by larger trends—forces beyond the classroom and the campus that determine, inevitably, the destiny of our schools. No debate about the nation's schools can be conducted without reference to the larger context within which each school carries on its work."

> Ernest L. Boyer, President
> Carnegie Foundation for the Advancement of
> Teaching

Flugzeug im Bauch

Turbulence in career development: an image flashes to mind of the proverbial sweaty palms and butterflies produced by a job interview... the headaches of facing a deadline and the computer locks up... the worry over rumors of staff cuts, reorganizations, lay-offs... the stress of being stuck in the wrong job... the strain of looking for a new one. Anyone who works with first-time job seekers, displaced workers, or career changers knows the personal turmoil a career transition can produce. For

At least half of all adults surveyed in the latest NCDA Gallup Survey said high schools were not doing enough to help students choose careers, develop job skills, and find jobs after they leave school. Carpe diem.

many Americans in today's workforce, the German metaphor may be more fitting: *Flugzeug im Bauc—*airplanes in the stomach.

The word "turbulent" is cropping up more and more to describe contemporary America (Carnevale, 1994; Doeringer, 1991). Is our rhetoric running amok, or are the times we live in more turbulent, in terms of work, learning, and careers, than for earlier generations? What can our public agencies and schools do to prepare a workforce reeling through cyberspace for the turbulence ahead?

Surfing History

One might contend, in thinking back over the growth of the American economy, that some turbulence in the workplace is good. Job and career changes have been essential to economic progress and income growth in the U.S. To a large extent, the flexibility and adaptability of American workers contributed greatly to higher living standards for larger and larger segments of the population.

How many of us would trade an RV for a covered wagon? Yet how many blacksmiths had to learn new skills or switch careers when the automobile replaced the horse and buggy? True enough, many individuals and their families suffered from shifts in the economy and the labor market. To survive, they had to learn new skills, take other jobs, or find new markets for their wares and services. Mobility was often westward, not necessarily upward.

Let me scroll quickly through history and click briefly on the turbulence that accompanied the rise of industry at the turn of this century. Problems in other countries and promises of opportunity in America increased the flow of immigrants. Many job seekers from rural areas and from abroad were attracted to cities, where the growth of large scale manufacturing and construction offered employment opportunities to unskilled and semi-skilled workers. During this period, the early foundations of career development were established by pioneers like Frank Parsons in Boston and Jesse B. Davis in Detroit. In 1913, the forerunner of the National Career Development Association (NCDA) was formed.

Throughout this century, Americans have experienced periods of social and economic turbulence that affected their education and their careers. Public policies and programs responding to their needs have had an impact on the field of career development, directly or indirectly, as well. Among remedies to address the turmoil of the Great Depression, for example, the Wagner-Peyser Act established a nationwide employment service system, with agencies in every state to help the unemployed find jobs.

Fifty Years, Lester's Tablets

Plato once envisioned memory as wax tablets in the human mind. On these tablets are imprinted the images and perceptions of significant events that have marked our lives. Culled from memories of major national events in my lifetime, I offer Lester's tablets on turbulence in careerdevelopment. Other people might choose different tablets, but these will illustrate how major forces or trends can affect public policy and private lives. They also can have far-reaching implications for educational institutions, social service agencies, and the career development profession.

World War II and the GI Bill

My first example is the GI Bill. It expanded dramatically the career opportunities for veterans returning from the battlefields of World War II. After the war, the Veterans Administration also set up centers for career counseling nationwide. As Halberstam (1991, p. 61) notes, ". . . the GI Bill democratized the educational process as the New Deal had democratized the workplace." It enabled a generation of young Americans to go to college. Many of them were the first in their families to do so.

Remember Sputnik?

When the Soviet Union (USSR) launched the first Sputnik in 1957, the satellite's impact reverberated in the schools and research laboratories of the United States. In response, the *National Defense Education Act,* passed in 1958, established scholarships to encourage talented young Americans to study mathematics, science, and foreign languages. This opened doors for many students who otherwise might have lacked the interest or the resources to pursue careers in science, technology, or international relations. By 1969, Americans were walking on the moon and working in space.

Civil Rights and Educational Opportunities

The migration of African Americans from rural south to urban north and rising expectations for fair treatment and a better life lent momentum to the movement for civil rights in the late 1950s. It became a powerful force for changes in employment and education. The *Civil Rights Act of 1964* helped expand opportunities for African Americans, other racial and ethnic minorities, women, older Americans, persons with disabilities, and other special populations who had suffered from discrimination.

Also in the early 1960s, the *War on Poverty* produced programs like Head Start, Upward Bound, and the Job Corps to give economically deprived children and youth a better chance in life. The *Higher Education Act of 1965* created educational opportunity grants (the forerunner of today's Pell grants) and established programs like Talent Search. This encouraged a broader segment of the population to pursue postsecondary education and provided financial aid to those who did. Counseling, support services, and educational materials were designed to help people take advantage of these opportunities.

Click on the 1970s

Consider the turbulence of the early 1970s. Americans felt the pain of war in Vietnam, the Watergate hearings, the first OPEC oil shocks, and the ensuing energy crisis. Double-digit inflation and high unemployment had far-reaching consequences in education, employment, and career development. In the midst of this turbulence, the *career education movement* was born (Hoyt, 1994). For the first time, Congress authorized the use of federal funds to demonstrate the effectiveness of career education. The emphasis was on incentives, not mandates, for state and local demonstration projects.

Other education and labor legislation called for efforts to prepare Americans, especially young ones, for better job and career opportunities. Among these laws were the *Education Amendments of 1976* and the *Comprehensive Employment and Training Act Amendments of 1978.* These two laws also established the National and State Occupational Information Coordinating Committees, known today as the NOICC/SOICC Network.

Recession in the 1980s

By 1976, the "misery index" (inflation plus joblessness) had jumped to new highs and grew even worse in the early 1980s. Overvaluation of the dollar led to factory shutdowns and increasing competition from foreign markets. The U.S. deficit zoomed upward. Recession had a chilling effect on employment. The Trade Adjustment Assistance program, originally designed in the 1960s to help workers displaced by foreign competition, was expanded in 1974 and cut back in 1985. It was modified in 1986 to provide more retraining for dislocated workers and to require those receiving assistance to participate in job search programs (Reynolds, Masters, & Moser, 1991).

1990s: Good News—and Bad

The turbulence of the 1980s has continued into the 1990s. Germany was reunified, the Soviet Union collapsed, and the Cold War ended. We are witnessing the downsizing of the defense establishment and sharply rising import levels, particularly from Asia. It is becoming increasingly difficult for U.S. industries needing less skilled workers to meet foreign competition.

On the whole, however, the economic picture has improved. Many U.S. manufacturers have increased their productivity and competitiveness. Inflation and unemployment are running at much lower rates than in the 1980s. In March 1995, the unemployment rate dropped to 5.4 percent, down from a high in 1983 of 10.3.

Nevertheless, more than 7 million people were looking for work and unable to find it. Others were working reduced hours or in part-time or temporary jobs. Many Americans feel they are working harder and longer, but falling further and further behind. Real wages have not risen since 1973 (Reynolds, Masters, and Moser, 1991). Job insecurity has.

Yes, We Do "Windows"

The pace of technological change has accelerated. So have massive restructuring and downsizing of major U.S. corporations. Americans are being urged to prepare for a different kind of work life and for lifelong learning. That is easier to say than to do, especially for those who are already working full time to support a family.

Workers are told that they must be flexible, continually learn new skills, and work in teams. They must expect to change from one task to another, from one software system toanother, from one company to another. "Cross-training" isn't just for athletes. "Multi-tasking" is not merely computer jargon. With cellular telephones, notebook computers, and modems, white collar workers have more flexibility— and less free time, as workdays stretch into nights. *Flugzeug im bauch.*

Tool Kits for Current and Future Workers

Carnevale (1994) warns of the dilemma of maintaining "the strengths inherent in our flexible labor markets without creating an economy that fails to provide job security. . . . If we truly want American workers to be flexible, we must provide them with a tool kit that increases opportunity rather than economic failure in a turbulent labor market." Among the contents of the "tool kit," he lists portable health care and pensions, education and training, counseling and job search assistance, and accurate labor market information.

Recognizing the importance of a highly skilled workforce, federal initiatives launched in the early 1990s made workforce development and education a priority. Career development is an essential component of state and local programs authorized by the *School-to-Work Opportunities Act of 1994*. The Labor Department's *one-stop career centers* would provide an array of employment-related services, including occupational and career information.

The NOICC/SOICC Network has resources to support these and other efforts to provide tool kits for workers. State computerized career information delivery systems (CIDS), for example, are ideally suited to meet needs in one-stop career centers. The National Career Development Guidelines provide a framework and related materials for building career development into School-to-Work systems. These resources are described briefly in Figure 1.

Figure 1: Sampler of Career Development Resources

The NOICC/SOICC Network has worked with private developers and leaders in career guidance and counselor education to produce resources and training programs to meet career information and development needs. The resources listed in this sampler are keyed to the National Career Development Guidelines and can be used to form a complete career development package. Specific information about these and other occupational and career information resources in your state is available from your State Occupational Information Coordinating Committee.

> • **National Career Development Guidelines** provide a framework for planning, developing, and implementing comprehensive, competency-based career guidance programs at many levels and in a wide range of settings. The Guidelines identify competencies that participants should gain in the areas of self-knowledge, educational and occupational exploration, and career planning. Local handbooks contain competencies for six levels: elementary schools, middle/junior high schools, high schools, postsecondary institutions, and business or community organizations. A state resource handbook, trainer's manual, and videotape also are available.

> • **Planning to Meet Career Development Needs: School-To-Work Transition Programs** can help school districts and schools build career development into plans for school-to-work transition programs. This program guide identifies strategies and existing resources that can be used in implementing grants awarded under the School-to-Work Opportunities Act.

> • **Get a Life: Your Personal Planning Portfolio** is a career planning journal to guide students through the career development process. It helps them relate their education to career interests and aptitudes as they progress through school and beyond. The Portfolio can be used in classroom activities or individual and group counseling sessions. Individual Portfolios are available in file-folder format or as a computer software program. A facilitator's manual for counselors and teachers and an introductory videotape are available. The *School-to-Work Transition Planner,* a supplement to the

Portfolio, is designed for students in grades 11 and up who are enrolled in tech prep and other school-to-work programs. A portfolio for adults will be available in the fall of 1995.

• *Workforce in Transition* is a training program and curriculum package for career and employment counselors, job-search trainers, placement specialists, and others who work with adults in career transition. Developed by NOICC's Career Development Training Institute, it can help practitioners help adults learn how to find and keep jobs.

• *Improved Career Decision Making in a Changing World* (**ICDM**) is an inservice training program for counselors and other career development facilitators. It helps them become more skilled in using occupational and labor market information to help students with the career decision making process. ICDM training is available through SOICCs.

Computer-Based Information Systems

Since the late 1970s, NOICC and the SOICCs have worked with public and private developers on implementing and enhancing state-based, computerized information delivery systems. These systems supply information tailored for specific purposes and customers, for example:
• **State occupational information systems (OIS)** are used in planning programs in vocational-technical schools, postsecondary institutions, and employment and training agencies. Other delivery systems provide data needed by employers and economic development agencies. Most of these systems provide computer software and user guides; in some states, data also are available on electronic bulletin boards.
• **Career information delivery systems (CIDS)** serve

individuals making personal education or career decisions. These systems are a resource for counselors and teachers. Using computers and other media, CIDS supply schools and community agencies with information on occupations, educational programs, and labor market opportunities and requirements. They are user-friendly systems that allow individuals to relate personal characteristics, such as interests, aptitudes and educational goals, to compatible job, career, and training opportunities.

A Public Stake in Information

In a turbulent workplace, public needs for information about opportunities in employment and education are broad based and persistent. One federal response to the demand for such information was the creation of the National and State Occupational Information Coordinating Committees. Our mission is spelled out in our name. Briefly, it is to see that useful information about education, occupations, careers, and training reaches individuals who need it, either in their work or for their own personal career decisions.

NOICC is a small but unique link in a complex multi-agency data chain. What has set it apart for me is the involvement with our partners—in federal and state agencies, professional associations, universities, and the private sector. By working with all the stakeholders, NOICC and the SOICCs have helped their member agencies and others respond to their customers' needs. As a result, the public has access in most states to

- computerized career information systems, newspapers, and handbooks for career exploration and counseling;
- curriculum, instructional materials, and training programs to strengthen career development programs;
- conferences, training workshops, videos and teleconferences for professional development and networking;
- occupational and labor market information for business and education planning.

Some of the major resources developed with leaders in education and counseling and related to career development are described in Figure 1. In more than 40 states, the National Career Development Guidelines have been used to formulate state guidelines for career guidance or to establish local career development programs in schools, community colleges, and adult education centers.

CD=*Carpe Diem*

Washington, DC, is the capital of "capitals." In different circles, the same acronyms have different meanings. CD can stand for certificates of deposit, civil defense, compact disks, CD-ROM, or even career development (as in NCDA). Within career development circles, CD should be shorthand for *carpe diem*—seize the day.

I believe the career development process is vital for today's workers, especially young ones, to navigate successfully in the job market and even more so in the uncharted territory of the future workplace. In this turbulent moment of history, millions of Americans need career development assistance. They might not recognize it by that term, but they are concerned about changes in the workplace and in their own careers. The need is especially widespread among young adults between the ages of 18 and 25.

Helping youth move from school to stable and satisfying employment is high on the public agenda. At least half of all adults surveyed in the latest NCDA Gallup Survey said high schools were not doing enough to help students choose careers, develop job skills, and find jobs after they leave school. *Carpe diem.*

Necessary Connections

Parnell (1994) argues that the greatest sin committed in today's schools is their failure to help students make *connections* between information and experience, between school and the world, between their past knowledge and present challenges—and between those challenges and their future responsibilities. I believe the career development process is one way to help students make these necessary connections.

Career development is a skill-building process. It should begin early in the school years rather than occur as a crash course for seniors. By then, students will already have made many important decisions that affect their future. The process is concerned with expanding opportunities and aspirations. It should open doors for all young Americans and keep them open for as long as possible.

Personal Coda

In 1995, as we note the 50th anniversary of the end of World War II, memories abound of horrors and victories, of Glenn Miller's Army Air Force Band, and—for me—the role of music and nursing. I was 8 years old when the war began, and my career goal was instant: a nurse in uniform. While I played military songs on the piano, my passion was to be a nurse. (Little did I know that nursing was one of the top five "traditionally female" occupations.)

At 17, I turned down a music scholarship, enrolled in a women's liberal arts college, and worked summers in a doctor's office and a hospital. At 19, I transferred to a large university, turned away from an opportunity to pursue law school, and decided to become a teacher of my favorite subjects, history and government. By 1960, I had been a high school teacher for five years and became the director of student activities at the very hospital in which I had tried out my abandoned nursing career.

Fifty years later, the nurse, the musician, and even the lawyer are distant memories. My career aspirations were set in the larger picture of the nation, along with the expectations and possibilities for women of the 1950s. For me, the scale to climb began in teaching. By the 1960s, women had more educational opportunities, including financial aid, and by the 1970s, jobs to match these opportunities. My career was affected by larger trends and events.

Life works in wondrous ways. For the past nine years, I have led an agency with the unique mission of delivering occupational and career information to students and adults in our nation. That seems a very appropriate ending for my chapter in the history of career development. My tablets of national events may not be yours, nor are they all of mine. I chose them, for brevity's sake, to illustrate the impact public policy can have on education and careers. For myself, I would like to be remembered for climbing the NOICC scale with the passion of a musician and the foresight of a lawyer. The rest is history.

References

Carnevale, A. (1994, November 27). Trickle down and out. *The Washington Post*, p. C1.

Doeringer, P. et al. (1991). *Turbulence in the american workplace*. New York: Oxford University Press.

Halberstam, D. (1991). *The next century*. New York: William Morrow and Co., Inc.

Hoyt, K. (1994). Career education and transition from schooling-to-employment. In *Youth Policy*, vol. 15-16, no. 12 & 1. Washington, DC: Youth Policy Institute.

Parnell, D. (1994). *LogoLearning: Searching for meaning in education*. Waco, Texas: Center for Occupational Research and Development.

Reynolds, L.G., Masters, S. H., & Moser, C. H. (1991) *Labor economics and labor relations* (10th ed.). Englewood Cliffs, New Jersey: Prentice Hall.

22

Who Will Help Us Work More Functionally?

Rodney L. Lowman

Overview

The times *are* turbulent—traditional definitions of work are unreliable and the implicit assumptions about the nature and of design work, which have been made for decades are now under constant challenge and revision. The more advanced societies have increasingly moved into dichotomous cultures: the career "haves," who have been able to meet the demands of an increasingly intellectually demanding and automated society, and the career "have nots" whose skills,

> *The working role, and what can go wrong with it, should...be a standard part of any mental health professional's training, in the same way and manner that being able to address the sex role is integrated into professional training...*

abilities, and interests increasingly relegate them into low-paying jobs, such as those in the service industry or those involving physical labor. The presumption is that workers can simply retrain to meet changed characteristics of work challenges the accumulating evidence of a strong genetic component (Bouchard, Lykken, McGue, Segal, & Tellegen, 1990) in all three major domains affecting career choice: interests, abilities, and personality (Lowman, 1991).

Transitions to this new world of work will be strained, awkward, and there will likely be increasing disparity among the developed and developing nations, accompanied by greater polarization within the "developed" nations. Societal benefit from this new order will include more fantastic possibilities than perhaps ever before imagined, occurring at an almost super-human pace. The costs, among others, will be considerable social strain.

If, as I contend, humankind is neither infinitely nor readily malleable, especially in adult years, and if society's work roles are changing rapidly, beyond the individual's capacity to adapt, it follows that individuals will suffer transitional casualties: persons will be unable to work at levels compatible with their economic wants and demands. Depression, anxiety, and other mental disorders related to work will accelerate under such circumstances, and mental health professionals will be increasingly called upon to address career and work-related issues. These professionals, already the perceived victims of a revolution not of their own making (managed care), are, by and large, ill prepared to address such concerns among their clients.

This article, therefore, makes three major assertions: a) most mental health professionals are poorly trained in career and work issues; b) specialists in career and work issues are often unschooled in individual psychological dynamics and, too often, are unfit to address the affective aspects of work issues; and c) both groups need quickly to become more competent in their areas of missing expertise if they are to be able to address the needs of an increasingly work-displaced, potentially alienated society.

Discussion

Consider this not a typical case. A badgering, seemingly never happy, boss continually pressured an employee (we'll call him Hal) to improve his sales productivity. The ever-escalating quotas, rising to twice what they had been just a year ago, when the now-berated employee had been rated "outstanding" by his supervisor, seemed impossible to meet.

Anxious, tense, unhappy, and angry, Hal quit after yet another confrontation with his boss over Hal's reportedly poor sales productivity. The employee announced his resignation politely and without apparent malice, but internally he was filled with rage and secretly hoped that his resignation would not be accepted, that his boss's supervisor or that other higher ups would come to his rescue. Had he not given what he regarded as the best years of his life to this company? Under the company's new administration, however, the resignation was accepted, and Hal left, without even being the beneficiary of a farewell party.

The employee had been well regarded in his chosen field of industrial sales, but, in a tight job market, he could not find new employment as fast as he had imagined. In time, he filed for unemployment benefits. His former company refused to pay the claim without a substantial waiting period since the termination had been voluntary. Increasingly anxious, depressed, and angry, he found it harder and harder to initiate job search activities. As his limited savings dwindled, he finally sued his former employer for harassment and also filed a claim against the company for having created a hostile work environment.

In its defense, the company stated that not only had the former employee resigned voluntarily, but also that he was someone with an ongoing history of psychological problems. He had been anxious in many meetings, had at best an erratic sales performance (admitted highs followed by non-productive slumps). While he had indeed been an excellent employee a year before the termination, his performance at the time of the departure was far from outstanding and, since his last job performance rating, sales expectations had risen. Hal had become a disgruntled employee, unable to keep up with the company's rising expectations and standards.

Did the behavior of Hal's supervisor *cause* him to experience psychological difficulties? Or, was Hal someone with a chronic mental disorder whose serious psychological problems caused him to become a liability to his company? Or was some complex interaction at work? Given such an individual as a client, how should a mental health professional proceed?

The relationship of traditional diagnostic categories of psychopathology and work is surprisingly uncharted. In the case example, it might be argued that a hitherto apparently well-adjusted individual was made depressed and anxious by the external characteristics of the workplace. However, we do not know the individual's prior psychological history and there is evidence that persons with histories of mental disorders, even in youth, are at higher risk of experiencing later problems on the job. Needed research will expand our understanding of the relationship between work demands and psychopathology, but it seems unlikely, as I have argued at length (Lowman, 1993), that existing taxonomies of mental dysfunctions will adequately address work issues. The capacity to work may be high despite psychopathology; conversely, work dysfunctions may occur without any evidence of traditional mental dysfunctions.

The need for mental health professionals to become competent in treating work issues is further fueled in the United States by the inauguration of the Americans with Disabilities Act (Jones, 1990), and its extension to mental disorders (Fiedler, 1994). This Act specifies that employers may not rule out potential employees with certain mental disorders (depression and the like). With some exceptions, employers can only consider such conditions at the post-conditional offer stage and must then be able to prove that there is a connection between the condition and the capacity to work at the specific position under consideration. If researchers will not determine the relationship between work and psychopathology, lawyers will.

Recommended Course of Action

Understanding work and career issues should not be an optional course of specialization for persons in a few mental health training programs, such as social work or counseling psychology. Each mental health professional should be competently trained to assess and to understand work issues and, if not themselves competent to assess or treat such conditions, to know where to send clients who need specialized services.

However, it is not enough simply to adopt existing diagnostic taxonomies to the issues of work. The fit is too often Procrustean, and the research linking psychopathology and work is notoriously limited (Lowman, 1989). Mental health professionals need to push forward the frontiers of the psychopathology of work and of work dysfunctions. This should start with taxonomies of work dysfunctions developed for purposes of classifying what can go wrong in the work role (Lowman, 1993), not simply applying existing taxonomies to new purposes.

Summary

Working functionally will be an increasing casualty of societies such as ours that are rapidly redefining what constitutes work and what constitutes work organizations. Increasingly the mental health consequences of work upheaval will become apparent, but at the moment we have few mental health professionals competently trained to diagnose and ameliorate such issues.

The working role, and what can go wrong with it, should therefore be a standard part of any mental health professional's training, in the same way and manner that being able to address the sex role is integrated into professional training and is a routine part of standard training programs. We also need more career specialists who are trained to handle the important emotional aspects of career and work.

Bibliography

Bouchard, T. J., Lykken, D. T., McGue, M., Segal, N. L., & Tellegen, A. (1990). Sources of human psychological differences: *The Minnesota study of twins reared apart. Science, 250,* 223-228.

Fielder, J. F. (1994). *Mental disabilities and the americans with disabilities Act: A concise compliance manual for executives.* Westport, CT: Quorum.

Jones, N. L. (1990). *The Americans with Disabilities Act. An overview of major provisions.* Washington, DC: Congressional Research Service, Library of Congress.

Lowman, R. L. (1989). *Pre-employment screening for psychopathology: A guide to professional practice.* Sarasota, FL: Professional Resource Press.

Lowman, R. L. (1993). *Counseling and psychotherapy of work dysfunctions.* Washington, DC: American Psychological Association.

23

McJobs

George Ritzer

Overview

McDonaldization is the process where principles of the fast-food restaurant come to dominate more and more sectors of society and the world. The concept is derived from the work of the German sociologist, Max Weber, on the rationalization of the West. To Weber, the paradigm case of rationalization was the bureaucracy. While the bureaucracy remains an important site of rationalization, almost a century later, the fast-food restaurant has emerged as an even better model of that process. To Weber, the distinctive development in the West was a type of rationality (formal rationality) in which individual choices of means to ends are guided by social structures, rules, and regulations. It is this type of rationality that lies at the base of the process of McDonaldization.

> *It is important that we see McJobs for what they are...low-status, poorly paid and dehumanized jobs...that tend to offer dead-end careers that serve to a large degree as impediments to one's ability to acquire the higher-status, higher-paying, more complex and more human post-industrial jobs.*

McDonaldization involves five basic dimensions. First, there is an emphasis on *efficiency,* on finding the best means to whatever end we may choose or have selected for us. Second, *calculability* involves an emphasis on things that can be quantified, often to the detriment of the quality of production and product. Third, a McDonaldized world is one which is *predictable,* in which things like products and services are the same from one time or place to another. Fourth is *control,* especially over people (workers *and* customers), through the substitution of non-human for human technology. The immediate objective is to use technology to regulate what workers do. The longer term goal is to reduce workers to human robots and once that is accomplished, to replace the human robots with mechanical robots. The fifth and paradoxical dimension of McDonaldization—the *irrationality of rationality*—is in many ways the most interesting and important. In spite of their goals, rational systems seem inevitably to spawn a series of irrational consequences. The most important of those negative effects is the dehumanization of both the people who work in McDonaldized systems and those who are served by them.

In recent years the spread of McDonaldization has led to the creation of an enormous number of jobs. Unfortunately, the majority of them can be thought of as McDonaldized jobs, or "McJobs" (one of every eight Americans has worked at McDonald's at some time in their lives). While we usually associate these types of positions with fast-food restaurants, and in fact there are many such jobs in that setting (over 2.5 million people worked in that industry in 1992), McJobs have spread throughout much of the economy with the growing impact of McDonaldization on settings which had previously experienced relatively little rationalization. Good examples of the latter are the McDonaldization of banking (and credit, more generally) and the rise of what has been labelled "McUniversity."

Discussion

McDonaldization is manifest at all levels and in all realms of society. However, the work world has played a particularly pivotal role in this process. On the one hand, it is the main source of many of the precursors of McDonaldization, including bureaucracies, scientific management, assembly lines, and so on. More recently, the kinds of jobs, work procedures, and organizing principles that have made McDonald's so successful have not only affected the larger society, they have also influenced the way in which many businesses now organize much of their work. In fact, it could well be argued that the primary root of the McDonaldization of the larger society *is* the work world. On the other hand, the McDonaldization of the larger society has, in turn, served to further rationalize the work world. That is, we have come to value McDonaldization in general, as well as its specific components, and these values have manifested themselves, among other places, in the work world. We thus have a self-reinforcing and enriching process that is serving to speed the growth and spread of McDonaldization throughout the social world in general and the work world in particular.

Among many other things, the process of McDonaldization is leading to the creation of more and more McJobs. For one thing, many of the new jobs that are being created can be thought of in this way. The service sector, especially at its lower end, is producing an enormous number of jobs, most of them requiring little or no skill. There is no better example of this, of course, than the mountain of jobs being produced by the fast-food industry. However, new occupational creation is not the only source of McJobs. In fact, many extant low-level jobs are being McDonaldized. More strikingly, large numbers of middle-level jobs are also being deskilled and transformed into McJobs.

McJobs are characterized by the five dimensions of McDonaldization outlined above. First, the jobs tend to involve a series of simple tasks in which the emphasis is on performing each as efficiently as possible. Second, the time associated with many of the tasks is carefully calculated and the emphasis on the quantity of time a task should take tends to diminish the quality of the work from the point of view of the worker. That is, tasks are so simplified and streamlined that they provide little or no meaning to the worker. Third, the work is predictable; employees do and say essentially the same things hour after hour, day after day. Fourth, many non-human technologies are employed to control workers and reduce them to robot-like actions. Some technologies are in place, and others are in development, that will lead to the eventual replacement of many of these human robots with mechanical, computerized robots. Finally, the rationalized McJobs tend to lead to a variety of irrationalities, especially the dehumanization of work. The result is an extraordinarily high turnover rate and difficulty in maintaining an adequate supply of replacements.

While the growth of McJobs characterizes a significant portion of the work world, it certainly does not describe all of it. Clearly, alongside the spread of McDonaldization is the growth of the post-industrial society with its highly skilled tasks requiring high levels of education and training. In the main, these are far from McJobs and lack most, or all, of the dimensions discussed above. In spite of appearances, there is no contradiction here; McDonaldization and post-industrialization tend to occur in different sectors of the labor market. However, the spread of McJobs leads us to question the idea that we have moved into a new post-industrial era and in the process have left behind the kind of deskilled jobs we associate with industrial society.

While they have much in common with them, McJobs are not simply the deskilled jobs of our industrial past in new settings; they are jobs that have a variety of new and distinctive characteristics. Industrial and McDonaldized jobs both tend to be highly routinized in terms of what people *do* on the job. However, one of the things that is distinctive about McDonaldized jobs, especially since so many of them involve work that requires interaction and communication, especially with consumers, is that what people *say* on the job is also highly routinized. To put this another way, McDonaldized jobs tend to be tightly scripted. In fact, McDonaldized jobs tend to be characterized by *both* routinized actions (for example, McDonald's hamburgers are to be put down on the grill moving from left to right, six rows of six patties, and the burgers are to be flipped beginning with the third row, with the first two rows to be flipped last) and scripted interactions (examples include, "May I help you?"; "Would you like a dessert to go with your meal?"; "Have a Nice Day!").

The claim usually made by spokespeople for McDonaldized systems is that they are offering a large number of entry-level positions that help give employees the basic skills they will need in order to move up the occupational ladder (and many of them do). This is likely to be true in the instances in which the middle-level jobs to which they move, for example, assistant manager or manager of a fast-food restaurant, are also routinized and scripted. In fact, it turns out that this even holds for the positions held by the routinized and scripted instructors at Hamburger University who teach the managers, who teach the employees, and so on. However, the skills acquired in McJobs are *not* likely to prepare one for, help one to acquire, or help one to function well in, the far more desirable post-industrial occupations. Experience in routinized actions and scripted interactions do not help much when one finds oneself in post-industrial occupations that require thought and creativity.

Recommended Course of Action

As a general rule, high school and college students who can afford it should be counseled that it would be best to avoid McJobs during the school year. Not only are many of the skills acquired not very useful for post-industrial jobs, McJobs take time and attention away from the educational process that could help young people to acquire creative occupations. Research has generally shown that McJobs, especially those involving 15 or more hours per week, have an adverse effect on grades, academic performance, and the dropout rate. While many teenagers need McJobs in order to survive, for others, such jobs represent a triumph of short-term rationality that may adversely affect their occupational prospects in the long term.

If there are skills to be acquired on such jobs, they tend to be of the interpersonal type. Young people should be counseled to avoid tightly scripted jobs and to use their work to hone their interpersonal skills.

Clearly, McDonaldized systems and the McJobs they produce are going to continue to expand and there are people who are going to fill them, at least for a short period of time (the figure one usually hears is that the turnover rate for the industry is 300%-400%). For those with little education, and few occupational prospects, a McJob may prove useful in helping them to acquire such fundamental skills as learning to arrive at work on time, to look presentable, to learn to deal with superiors and peers, and so on.

It is getting increasingly difficult for adults to find jobs that have not been McDonaldized, at least to some degree. To avoid disillusionment employees should be better prepared to face the McDonaldized aspects of their jobs. Those who cannot face a work life dominated by McDonaldization would be well-advised to search out organizations that provide non-rationalized niches or to create a non-McDonaldized business of their own. The great success of Ben & Jerry's should stand as a model for those who want to create a successful, non-McDonaldized business (although even Ben & Jerry's is, of late, showing signs of becoming McDonaldized).

Although they are poorly paid, McJobs might be more advisable for senior citizens interested in filling some of their idle hours with work.

Given the projected increase in McJobs, at least until advanced technologies designed to supplant them are created and prove viable economically, it might be advisable to counsel people to find non-McDonaldized leisure time activities in which they can express their more creative capacities. The problem here is that the world of leisure (Disney World is a wonderful example) is being McDonaldized at least as rapidly as the work world.

Summary

The McDonaldization of society and the McJobs it tends to produce are going to be with us, probably in expanded form, for the foreseeable future. It is important that we see McJobs for what they are and not accept the romanticized image of them presented by the fast-food industry and other McDonaldized systems. These are low status, poorly paid, and dehumanized jobs that stand far below the similarly burgeoning post-industrial occupations. There is a wide chasm between these two types of occupations and, as a rule, McJobs do not represent a stepping stone to post-industrial work. Rather, they tend to offer dead-end careers that serve to a large degree as impediments to one's ability to acquire the higher-status, higher-paying, more complex and more human post-industrial jobs.

McJobs seem alluring to young people since they are an integral part of, and fit nicely into, their McDonaldized lives. Furthermore, there are many such jobs and they are readily available and easy to acquire. The jobs are also attractive because they provide pocket money to spend on a range of McDonaldized activities. McDonaldized systems tend to romanticize their jobs and they even create programs that seem to help young employees combine work and school and achieve ultimate success in the work world. In the face of all of this, young people need to be counseled about the liabilities of McJobs and the fact that experience in them is unlikely to be helpful in acquiring more satisfying, meaningful, and lucrative occupations in later life.

Bibliography

Fjellman, S. M. (1992). *Vinyl leaves: Walt Disney World and America.* Boulder, CO: Westview Press.

Hage, J., & Powers, C. (1992). *Post-Industrial lives: Roles and Relationships in the 21st century.* Newbury Park, CA: Sage.

Kablaoui, B. N., & Pautler, A. J., Jr. (1991). The effects of Part-Time work experience on high school students. *Journal of Career Development, 17.*

Lager, F. (1994). *Ben & Jerry's: The inside scoop.* New York: Crown.

Leidner, R. (1993). *Fast food, fast talk: Service work and the routinization of everyday life.* Berkeley: University of California Press.

Luxenberg, S. (1985). *Roadside empires: How the chains franchised america.* New York: Viking.

Parker, M., & Jary, D. (1995). The McUniversity: Organization, management and academic objectivity. *Organization 2,* 319-337.

Ritzer, G. (1993). *The McDonaldization of society.* Thousand Oaks, CA: Pine Forge Press (revised edition forthcoming, 1996).

Ritzer, G. (1995). *Expressing America: A critique of the global credit card industry.* Thousand Oaks, CA: Pine Forge Press.

Reiter, E. (1991). *Making fast food.* Montreal and Kingston: McGill-Queen's University Press.

Shlaes, A. (1995, August 15). About those McDonald's jobs..., *Wall Street Journal,* A17.

Weber, M. (1968). *Economy and society* (3 Vols.). Totowa, NJ: Bedminster Press.

24

Shifting the Paradigm: a Managerial Plan for Effective Downsizing

Jane H. Walter

Tyler Maxium, manager of a production department in a high-tech manufacturing organization, has just been informed that his department will be cut 20% in one month. Maxium is charged with developing a plan for continuing productivity and efficiency while maintaining high morale. The scenario is familiar, but the difference is that this manager has been given detailed guidelines to achieve these results.

Organizational assistance to managers in such crisis situations has traditionally been lacking. These lessons of silence have created a gap of often four to five years before the goals of increased profits are realized. The myth of becoming more competitive has been exploded as two-thirds of the downsized organizations experience no increase in productivity and 50 % see no improvement in profits.

> Dependent employees will resist being in charge of their careers...a strong proactive message [determining their own career needs] ...with a strong sense of what is needed in a competitive organization

But the human shrinkage factor will continue as reduced profits are attributed to overstaffing instead of to the real issue--not responding earlier to changing markets. Reducing staff has led to increased stress, role confusion, overload, reduced risk taking, ambiguity, and insecurity. Managerial leadership has lagged because managers experience the same symptoms as co-workers, as well as the burden of providing undefined leadership, during the transition period. The failure of most organizations to confront these outcomes directly by establishing a positive plan for action is legendary. Cutting staff without stabilizing those who remain is like changing a chemical formula and expecting the old results. Guidelines expected from upper management are missing because of the failure of upper management to grasp the significance of the transition impact on all employees. "They're lucky to still have a job" mentality prevails. The most prevalent problems are lack of planning for the transition and lack of open communication during this period. To complicate matters further, interdepartmental turf wars often erupt as insecurity permeates the organization.

How can managers and employees collaboratively develop and implement a successful strategic plan for organizational restructuring? At first glance, the expectations of managers and employees are diametrically opposed. Managers need flexibility and dependability; employees need fulfilling work and security. Despite this apparent dichotomy, collaborative planning for and during the transition is essential and possible.

The following six components represent a paradigm shift which supports managers and employees in times of organizational transition.

I. Open Communication Channels
II. Internal and External Options
III. Individual Employability
IV. Morale, Motivation, and Recognition
V. Work Redesign
VI. Employee Development Programs

This paradigm denotes organizational commitment to provide direction, support, and strong, open communication. As a result the organization will emerge stable, productive, and profitable from severe cutbacks.

I. Open Communication Channels

It has often been stated that when communication is most needed, it is most lacking. During periods of transition, it is especially important that management be visible and sensitive to responding to the impact of the change. This responsiveness means being honest and direct about what is known and unknown. Assuring everyone that those affected by cuts are receiving outplacement services should be documented by explaining both the extent of the services and ways that remaining employees can assist departing employees. Conveying that outgoing employees would be welcomed back if conditions warrant is an important message also to those remaining.

Establishing interdepartmental task forces to address the changes assures widespread representation throughout the organization. Frequent written and oral communication is essential to creating new organizational direction. Intradepartmental participatory planning is also an essential requirement. Ambiguity during the transition can be replaced by feelings of power and control as each employee contributes to the redesign of work and openly confronts the related issues of overload, stress, and uncertainty.

Continued evaluation of the restructuring process must occur on all levels. Understanding managers need to express the positive and negative aspects of the change in terms of short- and long-term expectations. The question "How are we doing?" is rarely addressed after significant restructuring efforts. Even bad news is easier to accept than no news, which only breeds more insecurity. Since most employees take their cues from management, it is crucial that the pattern of open communication be modeled at every level. Employees have frequently accused mid-level managers of withholding information when, in fact, these managers have been excluded from the decision-making level and are leading without knowledge. Finally, communication channels need to be reassessed from the bottom up. Focus groups, for example, can provide a means of assessing the total climate.

II. Internal and External Options

Efforts to identify internal options for employees affected by downsizing have often failed for three key reasons: first, not knowing the total organizational needs; second, not being aware of the transferable skills of the affected employees; third, lack of planning. The last area is particularly troublesome. Many examples exist of persons who were downsized, only to be asked to return to the organization a few weeks later when their contributions were critically needed. This type of situation has a terrible impact on the morale of the individual and the work group. Systematic approaches to identify and access critical skills are an important responsibility for each manager and each employee in planning the restructured organization.

Identifying external options should be an ongoing effort. More enlightened organizations are providing on-line listings of available openings in other companies. Additionally, such organizations are providing comprehensive outplacement services to help affected employees redirect their careers and build internal career security. A successful restructuring plan must offer terminated employees access to internal and external options and to high-quality comprehensive outplacement services. Taking care of those leaving is an important message to convey to remaining employees who should be included in this process.

III. Individual Employability

The new paradigm calls for independent, self-sufficient employees who can function effectively while leading or being a strong team member. This scenario requires a more comprehensive approach to the work environment. Organizations generally fall into one of two categories: maintaining the status quo or using a more enlightened approach that requires collaborative planning between managers and employees. In addition to setting and obtaining goals, both managers and employees now are required to create a vision and be sensitive to the process of achieving it. Two diverse groups of employees are likely to emerge in this demanding shift: independent and dependent ones.

Results of Change

	Individual	Organization
High	Independent	Collaborative Planning
Low	Dependent	Status Quo

Independent employees will challenge the status quo and demand answers to "what ifs." They will be sufficiently confident to recognize their skills and know what is needed to be competitive both as individuals and as an organization. The second group, the dependent employees, will resist, remain paralyzed, and avoid efforts to change the status quo. The manager's major challenge will be to encourage, support, and motivate this latter group to embrace the new paradigm. Their resistance to change is most often based on job insecurity which leads to a self-defeating cycle.

Increased training and job redesign are the foundation for achieving greater employability within and outside the organization. Knowledge of competitive markets coupled with enhanced skills provides the focus for a reenergized, restructured workforce. Independent employees, confident of their value, are most likely to remain in such a restructured organization. Dependent ones fear their value within and outside the company.

This fear must be directly and positively addressed with available training options in place (refer to Component VI, Employee Development Programs). Skills assessment requires benchmarking in three distinct areas—business, technical, and behavioral—and in three distinct dimensions: the organization, the team, and the individual. The proposed "Career Strategies Model" aligns skills and core competencies to continuous learning and measurable skills bases. Previous skill focus has often concentrated on technical competencies to the exclusion of the total business objectives and behavioral skills required, such as coaching and giving feedback. By establishing measurable standards and certification in the 3-by-3 model, individual employees and the total organization can assess strengths and deficiencies through an established plan.

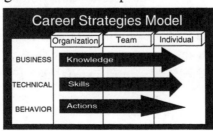

Career Strategies Model

	Organization	Team	Individual
BUSINESS	Knowledge		
TECHNICAL	Skills		
BEHAVIOR	Actions		

One of the most desired organizational outcomes, employee loyalty, is fostered by the promise of continued employability. A second by-product, flexibility, is accomplished through continuous learning. Employees equate security with their value in the workplace, which is assured by a wide range of marketable skills and the comfort that their present employment is insured as long as they add value to the organization.

IV. Morale, Motivation, and Recognition

The relationships of co-workers have often been portrayed as a close family. Losing members creates both technical and emotional voids. Failure to deal directly with the total impact diminishes the importance of each individual involved. In addition to informal discussions, workshops addressing the transitions have proven to be useful in moving from the past to creating positive future directions. Continued open communication coupled with collaborative planning creates an atmosphere of control versus one of powerlessness.

A formalized system to assist and support former co-workers in their reemployment efforts reduces remaining employees' feelings of guilt. Comprehensive outplacement services are a crucial component of such a system. Additionally, employees who contribute to the work redesign plan and develop strategies to monitor its results experience enhanced morale and a greater sense of value to the restructured organization. Motivation and recognition are intricately linked. One of the characteristics of a depressed, downsized organization is the fear of risk taking. This fear inhibits creativity at a time when it is needed most. When managers encourage individual and team contributions to profits and productivity, all benefit from short-circuiting the traditional hierarchial boundaries. The current emphasis on TQM and continuous quality improvement provides the tools but frequently overlooks concrete and immediate recognition of ideas. Creating a safe environment for risk taking is an important managerial task, especially after downsizing.

V. Work Redesign

Expecting upper management to provide the strategic plan for downsizing has been costly. Conveying the message that it is everyone's responsibility to determine continued competitiveness is crucial. Encouraging all employees to participate in shaping— not just implementing— the organizational redesign plan shifts the paradigm. This shift requires collaborative planning for functional and cross-functional areas. Anticipating and responding to customer needs must become the major component of each employee's duties regardless of level or function. Employees and managers must develop ways of openly recognizing and rewarding team and individual contributions in this area.

Managers can reenergize employees by openly and candidly acknowledging and addressing their concerns and by providing and seeking guidance and leadership around the *Who, When, Where, What, and How* approach to transition:

Who is responsible for designing and implementing the restructuring plan?

When will the downsizing begin and end?

Where will the restructuring place each employee?

What is needed from and offered to each individual during the transition?

How are these needs to be met and individuals assisted?

VI. Employee Development Programs

The major shift in designing and implementing training places the responsibility on individual employees to determine gaps in their business, technical, and behavioral skills. With well-defined and measurable skills and competencies, each employee needs to examine options in terms of continued employability. Recent trends emphasize certification as a means of documenting levels of skills and competencies. Simply taking a class is not sufficient: employees are now expected to apply the learned technical, business, and behavioral skills towards achieving organizational objectives.

The other fundamental shift is that the organization is no longer expected to meet all training needs, but to provide support and encouragement for exploring external resources as well. The major responsibility, however, rests with individuals being proactive in determining their own career needs. As stated in Component III, Individual Employability, dependent employees will resist being in charge of their careers, but this strong proactive message is essential to create a healthy organization staffed by creative, technically and behaviorally competent individuals with a strong sense of what is needed in a competitive organization.

Summary

The managerial leadership challenges of redesigning and revitalizing a downsized department involve complex issues that require multi-level collaborative planning. Managers and employees must have both direction and flexibility to create and implement the necessary restructuring plan. The resulting paradigm shift affirms the value both of departing and remaining employees and actualizes a sense of employee control and purpose.

The six components of the paradigm create a systematic plan for organizations to move forward with attention to both individual and organizational needs. Direction, support, and open communication replace the traditional lessons of silence. Remaining and departing employees emerge from the restructuring with the skills to build their own internal career security. The revitalized organization emerges stable, productive, and profitable in both human and material resources.

Bibliography

Filipczak, B. (1995, January). You're on your own: Training, employability, and the new employment contract. *Training,* pp. 29-36.

Noer, D. M. (1993). *Healing the wounds: Overcoming the trauma of layoffs and revitalizing downsized organizations.* San Francisco: Jossey-Bass.

Walter, J. H. (1991). *Career redirection workbook.* Greensboro, NC: Career Development Consultants.

Walter, J. H., & Kennedy, S. M. (1995). Career strategies model. Unpublished.

Waterman, R., Jr., Waterman, J. A., & Collard, B. A. (1994, July-August). Toward a career-resilient workforce. *Harvard Business Review,* pp. 87-95.

25

The Changing Concept of Career: Implications for Career Counseling

A. G. Watts

In the United States in particular, but in other countries too, the field of career counseling has been dominated by psychologists. Naturally so--at its heart, career counseling is concerned with individuals. But it is also a deeply socio-political activity. It operates at the interface between personal and societal needs, between individual aspirations and opportunity structures, between private and public identities. Awareness of this socio-political dimension has been more evident in Britain and Scandinavia than elsewhere (Watts *et al.*, in press).

> *If individuals are to secure progression in their learning and work, career counseling is crucial in two respects: in helping individuals to clarify and articulate their aims and aspirations, and in ensuring that their decisions are informed in relation to the needs of the labor market.*

It is also important to recognize that career counseling services are themselves social institutions. The rationale for public funding for such services stems from their value to society and the economy, as well as to individuals. At a time when pressures to reduce public expenditure are becoming ever-stronger in all countries, career counselors must be prepared to argue their case in these terms (Killeen *et al.*, 1992).

This is particularly pressing in view of the revolution which is currently taking place in the structures of work. This revolution is linked to the transition from industrial to post-industrial society. In some people's eyes, it renders career counseling, and indeed the very concept of "career," anachronistic. I believe these people are fundamentally wrong: that in the new post-industrial era, career counseling has potentially a much *more* important role to play than in the past. But to achieve this role, the profession needs to have a much clearer understanding of the changing social and policy context, and its relationship to this context.

The Work Revolution

The profession of career counseling, and the concept of career to which it relates, are creatures of the industrial age. Within this limited era, work has been regarded as synonymous with employment, and employment has been the basic source of status, of social identity, and of income. For most people, employment has been provided in large organizations: factories,commercial organizations, government bureaucracies. These organizations have provided the structures for their work lives; some employees have been promoted up the steps within the hierarchy of their organization. These people have had "careers." The rest have simply had "jobs."

Industrial models of learning have in many respects reflected and reproduced industrial models of work. Young people have been herded into schools, where they have learned the attitudes and behaviors required for their likely futures in the workplace. An important role of the school has been to sort out those destined for careers and those destined for jobs. It has done this largely on the basis of examination performance.

Within this structure, career counseling has had a limited role to play. The destiny of individuals within both education and employment has been determined largely by selection processes. Career counseling has been a limited switch-mechanism to adjust the passage of individuals from one system to the other. This is why, in most countries, career counseling systems are concentrated around the transition from full-time education to employment. In practice, the two systems have usually been so well synchronised that career counselors have not had too much to do. Their's has been a limited and marginal activity.

Now, however, the employment system is breaking down. The traditional concept of a "job for life" is dying. The pace of economic development means that organizations have to be prepared to change much more regularly and rapidly (Kanter, 1989). Employers are accordingly less prepared to make long-term commitments to individuals. Many are seeking to reduce their core workers, and to operate in more flexible ways through contracting out to suppliers and through the use of part-time workers and temporary workers. More employees are based in small and medium-sized rather than large organizations. Flatter organizational structures mean less opportunities for hierarchical progression. The numbers of teleworkers operating from home and of self-employed workers are growing. More people are now operating a "portfolio" existence in which they are engaged simultaneously in several different "jobs" (Handy, 1989). More people are experiencing unemployment.

The effect of these trends is a profound change in the nature of the "psychological contract" between the individual and work organizations. The model is no longer a long-term *relational* contract, based on security and reciprocal loyalty. Now, it tends increasingly to be a short-term *transactional* contract, based on a narrower and more purely economic exchange (Rousseau, 1995). It, therefore, needs to be constantly re-negotiated.

The new structures of work present massive opportunities, and massive risks both for individuals and for society as a whole. There is a danger that employers and individuals will become increasingly short-term in their vision, and not invest sufficiently in the acquisition of new skills which is so crucial to the competitive advantage of nations (Porter, 1990). There is also a danger of increasing division between those who are able to take advantage of the new flexible work structures, and those who are exploited or ignored by them. Such divisions threaten a decline into an ever more selfish, splintered, violent society. These are public concerns, requiring policy responses.

In managing the transition to a post-industrial society, one of the policy keys, I believe, is defining and delivering a new concept of career. Career now needs to be defined, not objectively, but subjectively, describing an individual's progression in learning and work throughout life. The retention of the notion of progression is important: career is more than mere biography. But in principle, career in its new sense could be open to all. The old definition was limited to the few who were able to secure promotion up the organizational hierarchy. But progression in learning and in work can take place through *lateral* and *horizontal,* as well as vertical movement; it can occur *within* positions; it can be effected *outside* organizational structures altogether.

The challenge, then, is to make this opportunity available to all. The market will not achieve this of itself: it is intrinsically short-term in its vision and inequitable in its effects. New social ligatures are needed to make the new concept of career accessible to everyone.

I propose four such ligatures (Watts, in press). The first provides stronger financial-support structures for individuals outside employment, to enable them both to maintain their livelihood and their sense of citizenship, and to use such time to invest in learning. The second is a more flexible and responsive learning system, which mirrors the more flexible work system. The third is a qualification and accreditation system which assesses and records individuals' learning, not only within the education system, but also elsewhere, and does so on an ongoing basis rather than simply at the entry point into employment, and makes such learning as portable as possible.

None of these will suffice, however, without a fourth ligature: lifelong access to career counseling. If individuals are to secure progression in their learning and work, career counseling is crucial in two respects: in helping individuals to clarify and articulate their aims and aspirations, and in ensuring that their decisions are informed in relation to the needs of the labor market. Career counseling is the essential lubricant to make the rest of the model work; empowers individuals in their negotiations with employers and other purchasers of their services.

Implications for Career Counseling

If career counseling is to perform the enhanced social role now emerging for it, this has major implications for its provision and methods. I propose five such implications in particular (Collin & Watts, in press).

First, career counseling must be accessible to individuals throughout their working lives. Careers in the future will increasingly be forged through a series of iterative decisions made throughout the life-span. Counseling needs to be available at all these decision points. Much of this counseling can be based within educational institutions and within work organizations. But it is also critical that individuals have access to independent counseling from a neutral base when they are considering moves between such organizations, or are currently outside them. A strategy is required to develop such access, and to co-ordinate it effectively with organization-based counseling.

Second, the role of career education in schools should be strengthened and re-cast as laying the foundations for lifelong career development. This requires paying particular attention to developing the skills of learning and of career self-management.

Third, in career counseling methodology, more attention needs to be paid to constructivist approaches and to helping individuals to develop their subjective career narrative. This focuses in particular upon three tasks: helping them to "authorize" their careers by narrating a coherent, continuous and credible story; helping them to invest their career narrative with meaning by identifying themes and tensions in the story line; and learning the skills needed to perform the next episode in the story (Savickas, 1993).

Fourth, to provide a formal frame for career narratives, career counseling services need to support individuals in the regular recording of achievement and action planning. The introduction of such practices in all sectors of education and employment has been one of the most important developments in the career counseling field in the last decade in the UK, offering regular opportunities for students and employees to review their skills and experience, their long-term goals, and the next actions required to move towards these goals.

Fifth, closer links need to be forged between career guidance and at least three other areas: financial counseling, relationship counseling, and stress counseling. Career decisions are increasingly likely to be linked to financial investment decisions. This is particularly the case in relation to investment in learning. It also, however, seems likely that pensions and other forms of social insurance will increasingly be detached from the employment nexus, and become matters in which individuals will have more powers and responsibilities. In addition, the careers of individuals within households are more and more closely intertwined. The negotiation of family roles and relationships is accordingly increasingly complex, and often requires skilled mediation. In these and other ways, social change is generating considerable uncertainty and ambiguity for individuals. Accordingly, they are prone to anxiety and stress, and require access to stress counseling when such pressures become acute. The extension of career counseling into these three related areas will require many career counselors to develop a range of enhanced competences.

Conclusion

The post-industrial era offers possibilities for more personal fulfilment for more people than has proved possible during the industrial period of our history. But it will only do so if we can develop new social ligatures that will help to bind society together. Career counseling is, I contend, one of these ligatures. This gives it a much more significant social role than ever before. If the career counseling profession can rise to the challenge, it can play an important part in creating for the post-industrial era, a just society in John Rawls's (1972) challenging definition of the term: a society we would choose to live in if we did not know what position within it we ourselves would occupy.

References

Collin, A. & Watts, A.G. (in press). The death and transfiguration of career - and of career guidance?

Handy, C. (1989). *The age of unreason.* London: Business Books.

Kanter, R. M. (1989). *When giants learn to dance.* New York: Simon

& Schuster.

Killeen, J., White, M., & Watts, A. G. (1992). *The economic value of careers guidance.* London: Policy Studies Institute.

Porter, M. (1990). *The competitive advantage of nations.* London: Macmillan.

Rawls, J. (1972). *A theory of justice.* Oxford: Oxford University Press.

Rousseau, D. M. (1995). *Psychological contracts in organizations: understanding written and unwritten agreements.* London: Sage.

Savickas, M. (1993). Career counseling in the postmodern era. *Journal of Cognitive Psychotherapy, 7(3),* 205-215.

Watts, A. G. (in press). Towards a policy for lifelong career development: a trans-Atlantic perspective. *Career Development Quarterly.*

Watts, A. G., Law, B., Killeen, J., Kidd, J. M., & Hawthorn, R. (in press). *Careers education and guidance: Theory, policy and practice.* London: Routledge.

This article draws upon ideas presented more fully in a *Career Development Quarterly* article cited above (Watts, 1996).

How Career Development is Responding to Different Client Populations

Judy Ettinger
Edwin Herr
Frederic Hudson
Diane Kjos
Fred Leong
Alice Potter
Marion Stoltz-Loike

26

Meeting the Career Development Needs of Individuals with Disabilities

Judith M. Ettinger

Overview

Individuals with disabilities lag behind those without disabilities in virtually every indicator of economic activity. In fact, the term "not working" has often been used as the truest definition of what it means to be disabled in this country. What has been done by career development specialists to improve the employment status of individuals with disabilities? How much do those who work in the area of career development understand the specific needs of individuals with disabilities?

> *...individuals with disabilities face specific barriers and challenges in their career development. Awareness and sensitivity to those issues will result in the development and delivery of strategies that can effectively meet these needs.*

It has been frequently said that ninety percent of career development issues are the same for all individuals, but many people have specific issues that need attention. Those groups might be displaced homemakers, economically disadvantaged individuals, rural youth, people of color, or individuals with disabilities. In this essay, key topics and issues pertinent to individuals with disabilities will be discussed along with several recommended courses of action.

Discussion

Career development occurs through participation in a continuum of developmental activities available through both formal and informal experiences in and outside of school. These experiences teach students how to make decisions, how to problem solve, how to be a contributing member of a team, how to set goals, and how to identify strategies for achieving those goals. Yet, due to circumstances or individual differences, some miss out on these experiences. As a result, their needs differ.

What are the career development themes and issues of individuals with disabilities that might need attention? They could include self-esteem issues, strategies for educating employers, mastery of interviewing skills that will enable applicants to effectively answer questions related to their disability, practice advocating for self, comfort with and acceptance of a disability, developing the ability to deal with insensitive questions, and deciding how and when to disclose a disability to an employer. These are not issues that can be dealt with by using a recipe in hand, but need to be approached through an understanding of the unique pattern of talents, abilities, needs, challenges, and opportunities particular to each individual.

Theoretically, what approach is the most effective? Theories are road maps and frameworks that make sense out of what we see. Traditionally, people with disabilities were looked at through a medical model. People with disabilities were seen as abnormal and were stigmatized. According to this model, the remedy for the disability was a cure. The responsibility for "fixing the person" was with the medical and rehabilitation professionals.

The medical model has been challenged by people with disabilities and an interactional model has grown out of this challenge. In this new model, disability is seen as a difference, not as a "negative" characteristic but one that is neutral in and of itself. According to this approach, the concept of disability comes from the interactions between the individual and society. The remedy is to change the interactions, i.e., to fight against discrimination and advocate for one's rights to access and equality.

Theories about individuals with disabilities are easy to put down on paper but how does our adherence to a theory or approach improve or hinder the career development of individuals with disabilities. Are we as career counselors contributing to the societal exclusion of people

with disabilities? For example, one might find that:
- parts of the counseling office are not totally accessible,
- assessment instruments are only delivered by paper and pencil,
- the career resource center does not include information about accommodations,
- staff members are unfamiliar with the Americans with Disabilities Act,
- companies who discriminate against individuals with disabilities are still allowed to use the placement office for interviews,
- the room where a one-credit career course is taught is in a room that is not accessible by wheelchair,
- the parking lot to the Career Center is half a mile away, or
- the Career Center has a policy that no one is allowed to take materials out of the Center.

Recommended Course of Action

Changing the ways in which we consciously or unconsciously discriminate against individuals with disabilities has become a matter of law. The Americans with Disabilities Act (ADA) is the most comprehensive civil rights legislation passed since the 1964 Civil Rights Bill. It is designed to end discrimination against people with disabilities in employment, public transportation, accommodations, and telecommunications. The goal is to remove all barriers that have restricted people with disabilities from achieving their fullest potential in employment and in the community. It represents the first time that changes to the environment are directly related to the notion of protecting an individual's civil rights. This bill is a direct outgrowth from the philosophy of the interaction model which advocates for access and equity. It is a system of checks and balances that attempts to balance both the needs of people with disabilities and the business interests of employers.

The portions of the ADA related to employment that must be understood to provide effective career development services are included in the following phrase: employers must provide *reasonable accommodation* to *qualified individuals* with disabilities to enable them to do the *essential functions of a job,* unless the changes impose *undue hardship* upon the employers. The phrases in italics are key phrases and need to be understood in order to comprehend the vast impact of this law on the career development of individuals with disabilities.

How could a career counselor use the language in the ADA to remedy some of the inequities that hinder the career development of individuals with disabilities? By doing thefollowing:

- We need to accept the notion that we serve all students, including those with disabilities.
- We need to establish creative partnerships with special education staff experts in meeting the specific needs of individuals with disabilities, to develop the most effective program we can, utilizing our expertise and specialists in career development.
- We need to understand the ADA and concepts such as job analysis and reasonable accommodations as they are used to protect the civil rights of individuals with disabilities.
- We need to be advocates with employers, students, coworkers, employees.
- We need to network with different groups to become effective supporters of individuals with disabilities.
- We need to know about resources in geographic areas and should maintain an informational folder for easy access by staff and students.
- We need to ensure accessibility and actively communicate about it, such as by notifying students that materials will be prepared in alternative formats on request, by posting job listings low enough to be seen by someone using a wheelchair, and by offering assistance procuring materials and serving as scribes or readers.
- We need to be sure that we include disability related materials in the career library.
- Policies need to be adapted to allow users to take materials

out of the office for extended periods of time.

• Attitudes of program staff toward students with disabilities need to be monitored and training needs to be provided to ensure that supportive attitudes are communicated when all students come to participate in career development programs.

Summary

Many career development issues are the same for all individuals. Yet, individuals with disabilities face specific barriers and challenges in their career development. Awareness and sensitivity to those issues will result in the development and delivery of strategies that can effectively meet these needs. A clear example is the impact that the beliefs and goals expressed in the ADA could have on young and inexperienced clients who need the encouragement and support of their career counselors to develop the skills they need to advocate for themselves in employment situations. The skill to affirm strengths and abilities, combines with the freedom to express these abilities through work, is crucial to the successful career development of individuals with disabilities.

References

Conyers, L. (1995). Reasonable Accommodations: What counselors need to know. In Ettinger, J., et al. *Training for delivery of effective services.* Madison, WI: University of Wisconsin School of Education, Center on Education and Work.

Ettinger, J. (1995). *Career development for individuals with disabilities.* Madison, WI: University of Wisconsin School of Education, Center on Education and Work.

Ettinger, J. (1995). Tools for improving career development services for individuals with disabilities. In Ettinger, J., et al. *Training for delivery of effective services.* Madison, WI: University of Wisconsin School of Education, Center on Education and Work.

Pimentel, R. K., Bell, C. G., & Lotito, M. J. (1993). *The Job Placement - ADA Connection.* Chatsworth, CA: Milt Wright & Associates, Inc.

Witt, M. A. (1992). *Job Strategies for People with Disabilities.* Princeton, NJ: Peterson's Guides.

27

Career Development and Work-Bound Youth

Edwin L. Herr

Overview

Career development across the lifespan incorporates perspectives on both major and minor transitions in individuals' development and includes the unique circumstances that affect some persons more frequently and with more intensity than other persons. An example of a major transition would be the individual moving from full-time employment to unemployment or to retirement. An example of a minor transition can be characterized by the person who is unemployed frequently because his skills, work habits and personal commitment are poorly developed and incongruent with the demands of available jobs. In either context, the

> *...in the formal processes beyond the family context, it is useful to conceive of the career development process [for work-bound youth] as comprised of three stages: (1) that which happens in schools; (2) the content and processes that occur during the transition from school to employment; and (3) the processes of induction, mentoring, and on-the-job training that occur in the workplace.*

transitions that occur can be expected or unanticipated, and easy or traumatic. Transitions which are unexpected and for which one is unprepared can rapidly degenerate into crises which affect one's psychological and economic coping and can presage difficulty with subsequent transitions.

In some ways, the two most dramatic transitions across the spectrum of career development are those encountered when one moves into the work force on a full-time basis and when one moves out of the work force into retirement. While both of these transitions can be complex and difficult, most observers would suggest that the transition from school to employment is the more difficult and fraught with possible complications that negatively affect self-esteem, reduce credibility with future employers, lay the bases for a jagged work history through much of one's adult worklife, and perhaps prolong exploration and trial-and-error behavior in the job search (Mangum, 1988). In contrast to these possible negative outcomes, youths who are effectively prepared for and provided support during the school-to-employment transition can gain self-confidence, assume an appropriate measure of responsibility in the adult workplace, gain maturity in their understanding and mastery of job content—as well as of the expectations of the psychological or affective work environment in which job performance is embedded—and lay the base for positive adjustment to and advancement within their work life. It is these differences in the patterns by which youth make the transition from school to employment and in the degree and type of support necessary to make the transition positive and effective that is at issue in deliberations about the career development of work-bound youth.

Discussion

The school-to-employment transition of work-bound youth, those whose primary aspiration following high school graduation is to go directly into a job rather than to college, has become an increasingly important career development issue in the United States in the past decade. The roots of this concern go back to the beginning of the Republic as reflected in the views of prominent American statespersons about the purposes of American education (e.g., Thomas Jefferson: An educated citizenry; Benjamin Franklin: Economic development through providing youth skills that are both practical and ornamental). These early views parallel contemporary issues found in the debates about how much and what kinds of academic coursework students should have to prepare them for the demands of work and citizenship in the 21st Century, fully integrating academic and vocational skills, making the schooling of all students more career relevant, and intensifying the partnership between school and employers. The concern that our international economic competitors have decided that the economic assets of a nation are not raw materials and cheap labor, but rather the literacy, numeracy, teachability, communications, personal flexibility, and commitment to life-long learning for all, not just the educated elite—the college educated. Therefore, these nations, among them Japan, Germany, Australia, and Taiwan, have had focused goals that acknowledge what students learn in school is of direct consequence to how they obtain access to, and perform in, the work force. These countries have provided mechanisms (e.g., careers education, apprenticeships, on-the-job training, employer recruitment of workers in the high school, careers officers and careers teachers in school) designed to insure that students do not flounder through the transition to employment. In contrast, the goals of education in the United States have been more diffuse and general; the school and the workplace have been more separate; and more employment-bound youth have been literally cut adrift from formal assistance in making the transition to employment than is true in many other industrialized countries.

The signs are apparent that federal and state policy-makers have begun to heed the potential economic dangers and despair associated with the historic inattention to employment-bound youth. These signs included the calls for action on behalf of this population reflected in the rationale and processes of the earlier career education movement, and the content of many reports produced during the past decade by blue-ribbon panels, (typically from the business community), calling for new paradigms of career services and career-relevant schooling. The results are reflected in recent federal policy advocating use of work-based learning for both work-bound youth and those planning to continue on to college as well as in such important federal legislation as the Carl D. Perkins Vocational Education and Applied Technology Act and the School-to-Work Opportunities Act.

Masked by or implicit in the social, economic, and political issues described above are how we, as a nation, value work-bound youth, the importance of their career development, and the content, experiences, knowledge and skills that comprise it. The term "value" is used quite directly here because it can be demonstrated that the fiscal and personnel resources, as well as the rhetorical and psychological support provided to college-bound youth, exceeds that provided to work-bound youth by a large margin compared to that which occurs in some other industrialized nations. Thus, for many work-bound youth the process of career development has proceeded without systematic support from schools, counselors, communities, or employers. In essence, many of the persons who build and maintain our homes, roads, plants, transportation and health care systems, sanitation facilities, retailing, distribution and clerical processes, come to these important roles with limited, if any, direct assistance in their choice of, and preparation for, work from the major social institutions of the nation, including school.

Recommended Actions

The career development of work-bound youth needs to be viewed as a process that is comprised of three interdependent phases: that which occurs in schools, in informal and formal transition services bridging the period from school to employment, and in workplaces (Herr, 1995). While it is possible to discuss these separately, much interaction and interdependence among the principal actors in each of the three phases is required if the career development of work-bound youth is to receive systematic, deliberate, and comprehensive support. Actions in each of these contexts through which the career development of work-bound youth proceeds needs to include the following.

Schools

The factors and influences which shape individual career development begin in the family context, probably before a person begins school. Beginning with elementary school and proceeding more or less systematically through the middle and junior high school and into the senior high school, the content, attitudes, and experiences reinforced during the schooling process can stimulate and advance individual career development or retard it. Since it is not known in a precise manner, probably not until junior high school or later, which students will be work- or employment-bound immediately following high school, all students should be exposed in schooling to knowledge bases, reality-testing experiences, work-based learning opportunities, and other career-relevant activities that help them develop self-understanding, understanding of future occupational and education opportunities from which they can choose, and career planning and decision-making skills.

There are many conceptual or research based approaches that are useful in defining the types of content and processes that are relevant to the career development of children, adolescents, and youth. In broad terms, they include perspectives which are developmental and those which are structural (Herr & Cramer, 1992). From a developmental perspective, schools that plan to systematically influence the career development of students must do so by providing experiences that are congruent with the cognitive and emotional capabilities of, and the career relevant questions asked by, students in the elementary school as contrasted with those of the junior high or senior high schools. Thus, in the broadest developmental terms, career development in the elementary schools should focus on nurturing attitudes of self-worth and competency as well as awareness of future opportunities.

It is widely acknowledged that children begin to formulate career decisions at a relatively young age. They acquire impressions of the work people do, the kinds of people employed in different occupations, and the abilities required for acceptable performance. They begin the process of formulating their own interests, perceptions of their personal capacities and how both their skills and different occupations are valued by others in the family, school, or neighborhood. Thus, career development in the elementary school is not intended to force children to make premature choices but rather to avoid premature foreclosure of choices based on inaccurate, incomplete, or biased information and stereotypes. In such instances, career development in the elementary school focuses in structural terms on awareness of choices that will be available, ways to anticipate and plan for them, and these choices' relation to personal characteristics. Students need to know that they will have opportunities to choose and the competence to do so. These students need to also begin to develop a vocabulary of self-characteristics (e.g., interests, attitudes, skills, preferences), how they are changing, and how they can use school experiences to explore and prepare for the future. Beyond these emphases, career development in the elementary schools needs to lay the base for work habits that lead to productive results in schooling and have implications for later productive work strategies in adulthood. These processes incorporate efforts to increase student feelings of self-efficacy and self-confidence as they take on and complete a variety of academic assignments, with reduced feelings of threat, and with personal assertive skills in clarifying assignments and completing them on time.

In sum, career development in the elementary school is based on evidence that styles of choice and work behavior in adolescence and adulthood are affected by the types of developmental experiences that occur in childhood. This acknowledges that feelings of personal competence to cope with the future grow with knowledge of one's strengths, with new ways to modify weaknesses, with increased skills in planning and using available exploratory resources, and with an understanding of the relationships between what is learned in school and its application in work and in other community roles.

At the junior high school level, many of the career development emphases begun in the elementary school continue and intensify in their importance. But, in addition, junior high school students tend to be more independent of their families, are capable of exploring in much broader cognitive and social contexts, and have intensified needs to acquire skills of exploration and planning as they approach their first formal choice-points of courses, curriculum, and perhaps even high school. As such, the junior high/middle school is a transition period between childhood and adolescence as well as between general and specialized education. Factors such as planfulness, knowing about and using information and exploratory resources, creating a tentative individual career development plan, clarifying values, taking responsibility for personal actions, understanding that academic and personal choices and behavior in the present have future consequences, awareness of choice or contingency factors, and using opportunities to test tentative choices become the substance of career development programs in the junior high school. Students do these things within a context where part-time employment, attention to the importance of conflict resolution, interpersonal skills and communications ability, concerns about gender differences and reducing gender bias, the classification of future occupational and educational choices, and the use of community resources become both media for career development and major emphases within it.

At the senior high level, a major developmental task within the process of career development is that of specificity of planning. The rapidly approaching requirement to choose direct employment after high school, or perhaps early marriage, full-time college attendance, or variations on these themes, intensify the importance of both self-understanding and maturity in career planning. Emerging choices and transitions from school-to-employment accent the importance of the following: integrating academic and vocational skills; choosing a curriculum and sequence of courses, which will maximize the development of skills that individual goals tend to magnify in importance; keeping one's career options open; and starting along a career ladder to employment as found in such pathways as specific vocational education curriculum, youth apprenticeships, cooperative education, or tech-prep programs. Thus, the senior high school tends to be the crucible in which work- or employment-bound youth become most distinguishable from their classmates whose career aspirations encompass college-going or roles other than direct employment.

While, again, the career development experiences of work-bound youth overlap with those of students with other goals, there are also unique career development needs of this population. They include: job search and interview skills; the need to develop respect for their occupational and technical skills and aspirations; the need to understand and develop skill in applying reading, writing, mathematics, communication, critical thinking, problem solving and teamwork skills within the work problems comprising the occupations they intend to enter; and acquisition of information about transition mechanisms (e.g., articulation agreements that the school has entered into, apprenticeships, on-the-job training opportunities, employer needs, or recruiting schemes) that will permit them to make the movement from school to work as seamless as possible.

Although space does not permit a fuller elaboration of the career development of work-bound students within the school, suffice to say that it is assumed that if the process of career development has resulted in the acquisition of the knowledge and skills pertinent to self-evaluation, self-worth and self-efficacy, educational choice, and career planning, the student will, at the end of high school, be prepared to continue his or her career development through adulthood and choose the next educational or occupational steps to be pursued. While a useful and positive assumption, the unevenness with which the career development of children and adolescents is promoted in schools at all educational levels and geographic regions, results in many young people, particularly work-bound youth, being figuratively cut adrift from either school-based or community-based support services when they graduate from school and seek full-time employment. It is this reality that has led to a growing awareness that the career development of work-based youth does not end at high school graduation or, in the case of early school-leavers, before. Rather, career development proceeds, either jaggedly or smoothly, as youth attempt to negotiate the transition from school to employment and, subsequently, the induction to and adjustment to the workplace and the performance of work. Therefore, what happens during the school-to-employment transition is a second phase of career development. What, then, happens during the induction to work is a third phase of career development which either extends or fills the void in career development that occurred during the first phase of career development.

Transition to Work

In a major sense, what happens during the transition from school to employment can significantly affect the career development of the young worker. Extended floundering and early unemployment can establish an unstable pattern of commitment to employment and a lack of credibility in employers' eyes. Such poor experiences with the school-to-employment transition can create social costs which ripple from personal unemployment, reductions in productivity, and difficulties in human resource development related to capacity building in the workforce. In contrast, a stable, smooth, and supportive transition to employment can reduce such problems and reinforce the self-confidence, purposefulness, and productivity of the young worker as he or she moves into occupational consolidation and advancement stages in their career development (Super, 1990).

Unfortunately, according to the report *From School-to-Work* (Educational Testing Service, 1990),

> The U.S. record in assisting these transitions is among the worst in the entire industrial world.... School counselors are overburdened, and helping with job placement is low on their agendas. The U.S. Employment Service has virtually eliminated its school-based programs. Our society spends practically nothing to assist job success among those who do not go directly to college. In the United States the institutions of school and those of work are separate and almost always far apart. There are limited arrangements to facilitate this transition [to work].p. 3-4)

> Most developed countries have highly structured institutional arrangements to help young people make this transition; it is not a matter left to chance, West Germany does it through the apprenticeship system, combining classroom work and on-the-job instruction. In Japan, the schools themselves select students for referrals to employers, under agreements with employers. In other countries, there is either a strong employment counseling and job placement function within the school system or this function is carried out for the student by a labor market authority of some type, working cooperatively with the schools... (p. 22)

This set of observations emphatically outlines the lack of transition services as one of the major voids in the career development of work-bound youth in the United States; it is a national issue which the federal government is now attempting to address in its work-based learning policies and in such specific legislation as the School-to-Work Opportunities Act. But, while such resources and challenges to action are important stimuli to making the career development of work-bound youth less fragmented, more comprehensive and systematic, the need to respond to the career development of work-bound youth can only be achieved if each community, school, school counselor, and related community career specialist conceives of such need as a significant one that deserves attention. One also can include the sensitivity of employers and their willingness to play an increased role in the career development of work-bound youth as a vital component in this process.

Employers

The third phase of the career development of work-bound youth has to do with how these youth are inducted into, and mentored in, the workplace; the types of on-the-job training and supervision they receive; the support systems available to them; and the advocacy of employers in their behalf. The latter includes the degree to which schools and employers engage in truly collaborative planning and communication about the knowledge, skills, and attitudes that schools can influence and how schools and employers can cooperate to shape a transition system by which the young worker can be matched to an employer and move through the application and induction process smoothly and efficiently. But the career development of work-bound youth by employers extends further. It includes how new employees are oriented to their jobs, to the culture of the workplace, and to their contributions to the mission of the enterprise. It has to do with the degree to which new or younger workers receive employer-provided training and the nature of that training. It has to do with the mentoring and information provided to new workers, the encouragement to develop loyalty and commitment to personal work values, incentives to improve one's competencies and the ability to find ways to improve how to do their jobs as part of a team of workers trying to provide the best service to customers, both internal and external to the workplace. Such concerns for young workers and for their career development is an extension of helping them gain in self-discipline, self-respect, and knowledge of how basic education fits easily into any workplace. It is also a method by which young workers refine their own reasons for working and how these can be reconciled with the expectations of the employer for the worker's contribution to the climate and the productivity of the workplace.

Summary

If the career development process is to unfold effectively and systematically across the lifespan, the influences upon it, as well as the content and processes by which to facilitate it, must be understood and acted upon.

The career development of work-bound youth overlaps in content with that of all other subpopulations of youth. But, there are unique career development needs of work-bound youth that can be identified and addressed.

This essay has suggested that the career development process of work-bound youth begins in and is significantly influenced by the family. But, in the formal processes beyond the family context, it is useful to conceive of the career development process for populations as comprised of three stages: (1) that which happens in schools; (2) the content and processes that occur during the transition from school to employment; and (3) the processes of induction, mentoring, and on-the-job training that occur in the workplace. Each of these stages has important contributions to make to the total career development process of work-bound youth; although the interaction and specific content of each of these phases has not typically been addressed beyond the school.

In sum, the career development of work-bound youth has tended to be more fragmented and less supported by school or community transition mechanisms than has been true of college-bound or other special populations. Yet, work-bound youth are major assets to the nation and facilitation of their self-esteem, skills, and career motivation and career planning deserve comprehensive and systematic attention by schools, employers, and career development specialists in each of these settings and in community agencies that can help bridge the school-to-work transition.

References

Educational Testing Service (1990). *From school-to-work.* Princeton, NJ: The Author.

Herr, E. L. (1995). *Counseling employment-bound youth.* Greensboro, NC: ERIC/Counseling and Student Services Clearinghouse.

Herr, E. L., & Cramer, S. H. (1992). *Career guidance and counseling through the lifespan: Systematic approaches.* New York: Harper Collins.

Mangum, G. T. (1988). *Youth transition from adolescence to the world of work.* Washington, DC: The William T. Grant Foundation.

Super, D. E. (1990). A life-span, life-space approach to career development. In D. Brown & L. Brooks (Eds.). *Career choice and development. applying contemporary theories to practice.* San Francisco, CA: Jossey-Bass.

28

Career Plateau Transitions in Midlife, and How to Manage Them

Frederic M. Hudson

"When we are plateaued, we are not so much actively unhappy as we are just not happy.... Most of us do not make changes in our lives until the pain in the present eclipses our fear of the future."

Judith M. Bardwick

Martha and Charlie had both plateaued in their careers. For the most part, they had achieved their goals at work, and there were few clear paths ahead with their names on them.

They were not distressed by their work roles so much as brooding over the reality issues of their lives. But since their work commitments represented their largest single time investment, they were looking for some new interface among home, work, and money issues.

There are four strategies for designing a career beyond a stagnant plateau—moving up; downshifting; moving sideways and enriching the status quo.

Now in their mid-forties, they seemed to have it made. Both of them had sustained successful careers and earned a joint income to which they had become accustomed. Their marriage of eleven years included a step-family blend of four children between the ages of seven and eighteen.

Charlie held a managerial position in a corporation he believed in; Martha was a human resources professional in a firm about an hour from their house. However, their current work routines were more habitual than challenging.

Wake-Up Calls

"Everything that happens to you is your teacher. The secret is to sit at the feet of your own life and be taught by it."

Polly B. Berends

"I'm not as willing to be overextended at work as I used to be," Martha told Charlie one evening of what they thought were small-talk exchanges. "I want to spend more time at home. The kids need me here. Do you know what I want most of all? I want more fun in my life! But I don't want to give anything up except the commute! What do you think?"

Charlie laughed, then suddenly got serious. "Everyone at work thinks I have it made," he began. "And in so many ways I know I do. But it doesn't *feel* the same any more. I get up every morning, rush to work, come home late, go to bed, and repeat it all again the rest of the week. You know I love my work, but . . . know what I mean?"

"Yes," replied Martha. "I know how easily my work consumes my best energy—usually with my full permission. But I've got to talk with you about something else. The entire human resource division at my place received notice today that we are being downsized by thirty percent. The letter made it clear that anyone who voluntarily withdraws from the company at this time will receive an excellent benefit package, including severance pay, stock options, and . . ."

"Wait a minute," interrupted Charlie. "We can't meet our monthly payments without both of our salaries. We're in pretty deep, Martha. And we're staring at college tuitions for the next fifteen years. How would we handle that?"

"I don't know," she said. "But I don't want to work as hard as I used to. Or maybe I just want to do other things more than I want to work. I don't know. If our expenses are your main concern, let's figure out how to cut back at home. I've got to put more time into the kids and my community activities. And it's about time I started living my own life. I feel a real urgency. Hear me?"

Although the conversation ended there on that evening, their midlife dialogue about work and life was just beginning.

Charlie's Plateau Alternatives

"Human beings have always employed an enormous variety of clever devices for running away from themselves...By middle life, most of us are accomplished fugitives from ourselves."

John Gardner

As Charlie was riding to work the next morning he asked himself if he had peaked in his career. His mind raced through worrisome concerns, as he carried on an endless conversation with himself, calling his career path into question:

- I feel stuck at work because no matter how hard I work, there just aren't many promotions left for people like me. Where do I go from here?
- I'm tired and weary with what I'm doing. I know my field inside and out, and it has become pretty routine and boring. What would it take for me to get excited about work again?
- I'm angry that my real talents aren't being used. I have so much more ability than this company wants, and I don't like being wasted.
- I'm even more angry that I've become personally defined by my work. My life revolves more around my work than anything else. I mean, most of the time that's all I think about. And I don't feel free to do anything about it. Maybe I've become a workaholic.
- I think I've stopped growing. I am always busy and productive, but nothing I do really distinguishes me from the other managers, and I don't have any time for significant training. I don't have the same passion for my work that I used to have. Maybe I'm over the hill.

That evening, Charlie asked Martha, "Is this what we worked so hard to get? I know we're doing well, along the path we planned, but even though we're succeeding financially, I don't feel successful. I'm working harder than ever, but not enjoying it as much. Is this all there is? Where is the passion for life that I used to have? We need more financial security so I keep my nose to the grindstone. But my work really does consume me. I don't have much of a life with you and the kids anymore. Where do I go from here?"

"I understand what you're saying," she replied. "We both scramble through the weeks, hoping the evenings and weekends will balance things out. If we're not working in our jobs, we're working at home. And in case you haven't noticed, our marriage has been on hold for years. Our sex life is pretty boring. Weekend getaways are not going to alter the treadmill we're on. We've both got to make some fundamental changes—right?" Nodding his head, Charlie silently agreed.

During the next week Charlie daydreamed much of the time—evaluating his path and searching for answers to questions he had never asked himself before—about his career direction, life priorities, family time, and the future.

Up until now he had devoted his life to just "doing his best" with whatever was on his platter—particularly his career roles. He had loved challenge and brass rings, and had always wanted more.

Now he wanted a different formula. "No matter how things turn out at the office, I want my life from now on to be different than in my twenties and thirties. As much as I love my work, I want more of my career to be focused on work items that challenge me, so I can have quality time for other things I care deeply about—outside my work world. But how can I make significant career changes without losing what I have achieved?"

He continued brooding about his deeply-held values, his triumphs and trouble spots, his unused abilities, and his latent dreams. His self-imposed life/career review took much longer than he wanted. He talked it over with close friends and mentors, and wrestled in his mind with *four alternative paths:*

- I could continue the path I've been on since I began my career—to move up into a higher leadership position in my company. I really can't imagine that I won't climb higher, but I haven't received a real promotion in ages, and I must admit that when I'm on a vacation with Martha and the kids, I seriously question moving up into more intensive roles at work, because I yearn to have a private life as well as a career.
- I could "downshift" my career to a lesser position at my company, with less pay but a schedule that will provide much more time

to design my long neglected life beyond work. I think we could downsize our financial commitments and consumptive habits— a little, at least.

- I could "sideshift" to some job in the company that would have less responsibility but about the same financial rewards. Even though I'm ambitious at work, I'm more hungry to have time to grow my life, my marriage, my family, and my leisure pursuits. Side-shifting might be smart. But everyone would write me off.

- I could take the easiest road: stay put in the job I have. At least I think I can stay. There is a lot of turbulence at work right now, but I think I'm on fairly safe ground. If I stay, perhaps I can do less so I can become more. I want more balance between home and work commitments.

Most of all, Charlie told himself, I want to march to my own drum, connected to what I love most, and committed to the directions I'm just now becoming interested in. Frankly, that's all that matters. How should I proceed?

Martha's Plateau Alternatives

"In a level business playing field, more employees than ever will be plateaued and more emphasis will be given to growing in place."

Beverly Kaye

Martha's life/career struggle was quite different from Charlie's. Her career was only one thread in the broad tapestry of her life. She was extraordinarily engaged in career, family, house, and friends. They were like multiple roles of high value. She had her hands full at work, as well as wife, mother, and householder.

"Managing a step-family of four kids is my most difficult job," she confided to a friend. "Charlie does his best to help, but he just isn't there most of the time. I've got to be, and so I work it out. But I feel exhausted, overextended, and out of synch much of the time. Sometimes it seems that all I do is help others live their lives."

"Frankly, my career is a nice relief from all of that, but now my job is on the line, and I've got to get a plan for how to proceed. Should I fight to stay in my position or take the benefits being offered and leave? I have ambitions for higher leadership roles, but maybe this isn't the time to seek them."

As Charlie brooded over his future, Martha did the same, to arrive at some new formula for balancing her life with her career. *"Will I be able to realize my promise and become the leader I always believed I could be,"* she pondered, *"or will I be more complete if I settle for less?"* Martha ended up looking at the same list of options that Charlie had devised:

- Look for a way to advance ahead to a higher position, perhaps as a director of human resources, at a company closer to home. "I know it doesn't make sense in the light of family matters," she told herself, "but I have my own life to consider too, and I've been preparing for a higher leadership position for years."

- Downshift the career at this time. "It fits my strong desire to simplify my life", thought Martha, "but it scares me to abandon my career right when I'm positioned for higher roles," admitted Martha. "Maybe I could create a job share at work." She knew that finding a "job" just for getting money didn't sound very interesting, but maybe until the children leave home it makes the most sense.

- Move sideways instead of up or down. Perhaps a parallel job in some other company. Or, take a "sabbatical" from the career and begin leadership training that might open the doors to a higher position later in life, after the children leave home. Would this jeopardize the career?

- Carve out a satisfactory work life at the current company. "I could challenge my present employer to find a place for me," thought Martha, "with more flex time and changes in my role within the department, so that in the long run I can just continue where I am. But if they find it necessary to terminate me, I'll have to shift gears fast to one of the other options."

Three Critical Plateau Transition Questions

"Life is not the way it's supposed to be. It's the way it is. The way you cope with it is what makes the difference."

Virginia Satir

To survive a midlife career plateau transition, you need to make satisfactory responses to at least three categories of questions, in order to redirect your career. Career issues at midlife are intensely intertwined with life issues, so a profound coming-to-terms with your life is most often required.

First, what do you want to do with your life *NOW*? What is your unfinished business? What are your passionate dreams, your vision, your driving interests for the years ahead? Now that you are in midlife, how can you develop your career in relation to your most vital concerns?

Second, how can you stop getting ready to live and make living your full-time business, so you are working to live instead of living to work? What do you have to do to sustain balance in your life, and pacing in your schedule? How can you make your career a vital instrument for making your life sing?

Third, how can you use your proven skills and abilities in new ways? How can you repackage your career direction within the flow of new jobs and openings taking place around you? Who can help you revise your "portfolio" of skills in synch with the job openings emerging at this time?

Charlie and Martha evaluated their plateaued lives and charted paths ahead that contained both continuities and changes. Most importantly, they felt they were at a new beginning and were now ready to live more complete lives on their own terms. They felt "in charge," again.

Four Strategies for Designing Your Career Beyond a Stagnant Plateau

A career plateau is both a gift and a burden granted to successful adults. When you arrive at a plateau, it feels at first like the positive reward you were waiting for. But after a while you feel your plateau is something you will never surpass. So you live in its shadow, feeling you have peaked and are now in decline.

Oscar Wilde once said: "The second worse thing that can happen to you is to get what you asked for." Whenever you reach your goals, there is a tendency to rest on your oars, and drift. When you do that, you begin a predictable path downhill—with defensive thinking, reduced vitality, and loss of vision for your future. You trap yourself in the very success that you thought would bring you sustained success and happiness.

So what do you do? Martha and Charlie arrived at four ways to avoid this, and to move creatively beyond their stagnant plateaus toward renewal:

1. Moving Up is the American imprint in all of our heads. Follow a linear path from beginner to expert, advancing each time on a ladder that brings increases in responsibilities, salary, and recognition. This path is still available to some, but it is not as available as it once was. Nor is the pursuit of advancement up the ladder always better for our lives.

Even if you do succeed in moving up throughout your career, you may reach a destination other than you think. As Joseph Campbell once said: "You may get to the top of your ladder only to find that it's up against the wrong wall." Charlie, for example, felt that as he moved "up the ladder of success," he became more lopsided as a person.

2. Downshifting is a major possibility for plateaued people, because today's business organizations are more flexible and malleable than they used to be. A leading career expert, Beverly Kaye, has a favorite phrase: "Up is not the only way." Downshifting is getting more from less—more life from less career absorption.

One way to do this is to contract for a job within your organization that has challenge, but less responsibility, fewer demands, and probably a smaller salary. This keeps your benefits intact, your connections with friends and career, and it frees you to begin a new life chapter.

If you can not or do not want to renegotiate work at your current place of employment, design a resume that packages your unique talents and preferences, to get you a less demanding job. Remember, there are probably many more job openings as you move down, so you may have some interesting choices.

As the post-career workplace takes shape in the late 90s, there will be abundant "temporary jobs," many of which will move like amoebas into other work opportunities. The trade-off is more freedom in place of more demands, and sometimes that's a very good deal.

Another way is to consider creating your own business. Midlife is an opportune time for the right people to take charge of their lives by becoming entrepreneurs.

Needing more money is the main reason most of us reject downshifting our lives, and many of us stay far too long on our treadmills—until we burn out, rust out, or get pushed out.Better to reevaluate the relative importance in the overall, midlife, scheme of things. "Time" is usually more important to midlifers than is "money." Can you learn to live on less and not lose your self-respect?

3. Moving Sideways is a lateral move into some position with about the same degree of responsibility and benefits that you now have. You take it because it offers new excitement and challenge. Because of the breakdown of linear careers, there are many ways that most careerists can position their portfolio of talents and accomplishments in roles that previously would not have been possible.

4. Enriching the Status Quo is a very real possibility for many of us. Don't change very much, just live differently with what you have. Alter your schedule so your work hours mesh better with your busy life. Flex time and job shares are well established in most places as an option, along with four-day work weeks and working at home.

In your own mind, shift how you measure your success from primarily your career goals to a cluster of items that might include your family life, leisure connections, and community leadership roles. Usually, you can tolerate the status quo at work much better if your life has excitement and meaning.

Remember that after you soak up the benefits and glory of reaching goals of your young adult years, you need to discover some new dream and plan so you have a vital sense of personal purpose as you lean into the wind in the years ahead. Time ahead is all you have. Design it wisely, manage it carefully, and enjoy the journey.

"If one's destiny is shaped from within, then one has become more of a creator,

has gained freedom. Here one acts as subject, author, creator."

Allen Wheelis

References

Bateson, M. C. (1990). *Composing a life.* New York: Plume.

Borchard, D., & Associates. (1992). *Your career: Choices, chances, changes* (5th ed.). Dubuque, IA: Kendall/Hunt.

Bridges, W. (1994). *JobShift—How to prosper in a workplace without jobs.* Reading, MA: Addison-Wesley.

Culp, S. (1991). *Streamlining your life—A plan for uncomplicated living.* Cincinnati: Writers Digest.

Fox, M. (1994). *The reinvention of work.* San Francisco: Harper Collins.

Hudson, F. M. (1991). *The adult years: Mastering the art of self-renewal.* San Francisco: Jossey-Bass.

Hudson, F. M., & McLean, P. (1995). *LifeLaunch—A passionate guide to the rest of your life.* Santa Barbara, CA: Hudson Institute Press.

Lifton, R. J. (1993). *The protean self—Human resilience in an age of fragmentation.* New York: Basic Books.

Murphy, J. S., & Hudson, F. M. (1995). *The joy of old—A guide to successful elderhood.* Altadena, CA: Geode Press.

O'Neil, J. R. (1993). *The paradox of success—When winning at work means losing at life.* Los Angeles: Tarcher.

Saltzman, A. (1991). *Downshifting—Reinventing success on a slower track.* New York: Harper.

29

Linking Career Counseling to Personality Disorders

Diane Kjos

Overview

This chapter discusses considerations in providing career counseling to clients who have personality disorders. A case example suggesting treatment needs of an individual with an obsessive-compulsive personality disorder is also presented.

Linking Career Counseling to Personality Disorders

An individual's personality effects career decision making, on-the-job performance, occupational success, and occupational functioning. Personality dictates the relative strengths that influence individual career development, job competencies, employment success, and job satisfaction.

> *The counselor's recognition of personality disorders and consideration for the needs of differing styles in treatment planning, including the selection and use of interventions and career assessment techniques, enhances the effectiveness of counseling and client and counselor satisfaction.*

Individual patterns of career change and career stability reflect personality style. Zunker (1994) highlighted the importance of identifying behavior patterns that can interfere with an individual's work role. He organized these patterns around selected personality disorders. The personality of the client also has an effect on the counseling relationship and plays an important role in the ultimate outcome of counseling. Little attention has been paid, however, to the relationship among abnormal personality, career development, and interventions in career counseling.

Career counselors who do not consider personality, and mental health counselors who fail to consider the career implications of personality disorders do a disservice to both the client and the counseling profession. For example, Turkat (1990) noted a case of an individual with a paranoid personality disorder who "complained of being passed up for a promotion at work" (p. 47). To set up a treatment plan based only on the work-related problem could be, according to Turkat, counterproductive. The client's guardedness and suspicion might thwart attempts to evaluate the individual's work activity. Subsequently, the client with a paranoid personality disorder may insist that the counselor provided no meaningful service and simply took advantage of the client in a time of need by not providing sufficient or appropriate help. However, ignoring the career concerns of the client to focus on the personality disorder would fail to meet the immediate felt need of the client and would also be counterproductive.

Of the ten personality disorders, the *Diagnostic and Statistical Manual of Mental Disorders (DSM-IV*; 1994), specifically links eight with occupational difficulties or impairment in occupational functioning. These include paranoid, schizoid, schizotypal, borderline, narcissistic, avoidant, dependent, and obsessive-compulsive. A case can be made for an occupational link with histrionic and antisocial personality disorders as well. A personality disorder exists only when a grouping of traits or behaviors causes either "significant impairment in social, occupational, or other important areas of functioning" (p. 633).

Many factors associated with personality disorders play a part in career development. These include the inability to make decisions, to take criticism, to get along with others, and to be assertive. Characteristics such as self-defeating behaviors, anxiety, hypersensitivity, extreme vigilance, impulsiveness, and inconsistency are also related to specific personality disorders.

It is not necessarily the traits themselves that are problematic, but the grouping of traits that create the particular maladaptive personality style. Thus, some personality traits we commonly associate with personality disorders can be seen as strengths (Ivey, 1990). Under some conditions, the vigilance of the paranoid, the high standards of the obsessive-compulsive, or the success orientation of the narcissistic may contribute to career success. When we recognize and help the client use these strengths, they can serve to enhance the client's sense of self and place in a career choice. Table 1 provides selected possible career implications and suggestions for treatment interventions based on the personality disorders of the DSM-IV.

Table 1: Career Counseling and Personal Style

Personality Style	Possible Career Implications	Suggestions for Treatment
Paranoid	Alert to deception and likely to keep information to self. May work well in areas where vigilance and confidentiality are important. Might be angry or cynical, hypersensitive to criticism, and have difficulty relating to authority figures and co-workers.	Be direct and respectful, allowing client independence and distance.
Schizoid	Works well in social isolation or jobs requiring little interaction with others. Appears distant, aloof, indifferent. May have difficulty with social contact.	Be supportive but respect distance. May need help with interview skills.
Schizotypal	Appearance of eccentricity or nonconformity masks anxiety. Could be creative with a different perspective but may have difficulty in new situations. Could work well with repetitive tasks or in a structured task with latitude for eccentricity. May daydream or have ritualistic behaviors.	Appreciate eccentricity but provide structure. Note possible need for help with social skills.
Antisocial	Generally competitive, seeking challenge and power. Can be belligerent, hostile, angry and is not apt to seek counseling as own choice. Likely to be reckless and impulsive.	Maintain limits with respect for client's need for control and distance. Teach anger management, impulse control.
Borderline	Can be intensely involved but also needs variety. Confused about career choice and may have a wide range of interests. Has difficulty with decision making and is unpredictable. Might be disorganized, undependable worker.	Provide structure and support. Help client stay on track. Teach problem-solving skills if warranted. Communicate an expectation of success.
Histrionic	Charming and sociable but also flirtatious or impulsive. Exaggerated emotional responses; easily excited, bored, angered, or frustrated. May appear phony.	Set limits; use gentle confrontation. Support and empathy are important, but watch for excessive emotionality.
Narcissistic	Portrays self-confidence. Has little or no consideration for others and hard to get along with. May be angry or hostile. Has difficulty accepting criticism or perceived rejection.	Recognize client's specialness. Confrontation can be counter-productive. Use cognitive style.

Avoidant	Is anxious to do well and generally an obedient employee. With low self-esteem, is easily hurt by criticism. Has difficulty with new tasks or assignments, changing jobs, and developing relationships.	Be supportive and empathic. Focus on learning new behaviors and building self-esteem.
Dependent	Works well with clear defined procedures. Takes and follows direction well. Fears decision making and has difficulty making them independently. Continually needs reassurance; is easily hurt by criticism and highly anxious.	Use a directive, behavioral approach with empathy and encouragement. Teach choice awareness and decision making skills.
Obsessive Compulsive	A workaholic, works well in jobs requiring dedication, loyalty and careful work habits. Sets high personal performance standards. Indecisiveness or perfectionism may effect efficiency. Tends to be highly moralistic and critical of others and have problems delegating.	Recognize anxiety, stress, and need to control. Be supportive, use client's rationality, and help client be aware of feelings as well as thoughts. Be cautiously empathic.

Effectiveness in career counseling is enhanced by the counselor's ability to a) recognize the particular traits and groups of traits that make up personality styles and personality disorders that, in turn, may inhibit or enhance career development; b) develop a treatment plan that is cognizant of career development issues and will compliment individual client style; and c) work with clients who exhibit these traits to maximize the strengths inherent in specific personality disorders.

Tailoring Interventions

As demonstrated in the following case discussion, an understanding of the relationship between personality and career choice combined with interventions tailored to the personality style of the client serves to enhance the effectiveness of career counseling.

Obsessive-Compulsive

The term workaholic might best describe the obsessive-compulsive personality style. Spokane (1991) noted that this is one of two types of clients that are most predominant in his career counseling practice. Characteristics of individuals with an obsessive-compulsive personality include the tendency to set high performance standards and exhibit precise and careful work habits, loyalty and dependability. These attributes are often compatible with jobs that require high levels of training, precision, and dedication.

Indecisiveness, procrastination, self-defeating behaviors, and perfectionism are traits used to describe obsessive-compulsive style that can effect career decision making and on-the-job performance. Haunted by the fear that any failure or inadequacy is a fatal weakness, the obsessive-compulsive individual can be unfeeling and autocratic, with little imagination or ability to tolerate or adapt to inconsistencies. This is the individual who, preoccupied with details, may have difficulty delegating tasks, complaining that no one else can do them correctly. Often seen as miserly, the obsessive-compulsive individual might hoard useless objects and old hurts.

In counseling, it can be difficult to get the obsessive-compulsive client to consider the affective component of career choice. In fact, a show of empathy on the counselor's part may be seen as ignoring the real problem (Othmer & Othmer, 1989), but by recognizing the client's anxiety and need for control, the counselor can respond to that anxiety and choose interventions that effectively maintains his or her sense of control and use the need for control therapeutically.

The obsessive-compulsive client might question each item on an interest inventory or attempt to determine just how one item contributes to the final results. The need to be perfect can lead to an inability to complete a lengthy inventory or to many erasures, thus spoiling the answer sheet. Further, some clients with this personality style will want to spend an inordinate amount of time checking out the purpose, reliability, and validity of instruments used.

Case Example: Sue.

Sue describes her current job as high-speed data entry operator for a medical billing company by saying that she has frequently received awards for her consistent accuracy, but lives in constant fear that she will make a mistake. Moreover, she believes that this very accuracy is holding her in a job that she finds extremely stressful. She complains that her co-workers are very careless and create problems that she has to clean up. She spends extra unpaid hours at work trying to be sure everything is in order and done right. For some time now, she says, she has been thinking that she needs to get out of this "pressure cooker" she is working in but she has no thought about what she wants to do. She has been trained as a medical records technician but wouldn't make as much money at that job, she reports. Furthermore, she expresses a sense of loyalty to the company for which she works.

Although, in many ways, she is an ideal employee, Sue's supervisor and fellow employees may not appreciate her critical and uncompromising style. Moreover, although Sue feels trapped in her job, much of the pressure she feels is based on her own high standards of performance and perfectionism. The counselor will want to focus on helping Sue become aware of her feelings as well as her thoughts while also acknowledging her need for control (Table 1). This may be a difficult task as it is likely that Sue will see the counselor's attempts to be empathic as inefficiency because they do not, in her view, contribute to solving the problem at hand. However, this approach will ultimately contribute to treatment success. A supportive approach that both recognizes Sue's anxiety and stress and helps Sue recognize how she contributes to her own pressure will be helpful. Directives on the part of the counselor may only add to Sue's perceived burdens. Thus, the counselor will want to allow Sue to develop her own directives and then help her evaluate her choices and actions.

As she moves toward making a career decision, Sue's pattern will include the exploration of every possible avenue, weighing and evaluating each option. In a job search, she will be organized, thorough and demanding of herself. She also will be critical of interviewers, companies she interviews with, and the counselor for inefficiencies and inattention to detail.

Summary

The enduring qualities related to personality have significant influence on the career life of the individual as well as on the counseling relationship and outcome of counseling. Aspects of personality disorders include both positive and negative characteristics that need to be considered in career choice. The individual's reaction to job loss, on-the-job pressure, management style, and the counselor's interventions may all relate to personality style. The counselor's recognition of personality disorders and consideration for the needs of differing styles in treatment planning, including the selection and use of interventions and career assessment techniques, enhances the effectiveness of counseling and client and counselor satisfaction.

Finally, because personality influences interpersonal relationships, the counselor should be aware of his or her own responses to clients, particularly when these responses may interfere with effective treatment.

References

American Psychiatric Association. (1994). *Diagnostic and statistical manual of mental disorders* (4th ed.). Washington, DC: Author.

Ivey, A. E. (1990). *Developmental strategies for helpers: Individual, family, and network interventions.* Pacific Grove, CA: Brooks/Cole.

Othmer, E. & Othmer, S. C. (1989). *The clinical interview using DSM-III-R.* Washington DC: American Psychiatric Press.

Spokane, A. (1991). *Career interventions.* Englewood Cliffs, NJ: Prentice-Hall.

Turkat, I. D. (1990). *The personality disorders: A psychological approach to clinical management.* New York: Pergamon.

Zunker, V. G. (1994). *Career counseling: Applied concepts of life planning* (4th ed.). Pacific Grove, CA: Brooks/Cole.

This chapter is a revision of the article by the same name published in the *Journal of Counseling & Development, 73,* 592-597.© ACA. Reprinted with permission. No further reproduction authorized without written permission of the American Counseling Association.

30

Career Interventions and Assessment in a Multicultural World

Frederick T. L. Leong

Overview

There are numerous challenges facing counselors who provide career assessment and interventions to an increasingly culturally diverse population in the United States. In this essay, I highlight and discuss several of these major challenges and provide some recommendations as we look towards reforming the field. The first and most fundamental challenge is how career counseling and career psychology will choose to address

> *...I would argue that such a paradigm shift [consider the cultural dimension] is necessary if the field of career counseling and career psychology is to advance in an increasingly multicultural society.*

the centrality of the cultural dimension. In an upcoming volume examining the integration of career theory and practice , Leong (in press) pointed out the central role of culture in understanding human behavior in general and career behavior in particular. A quotation from Ruth Benedict's classic book, *Patterns of Culture,* which Leong used to make his point is worth repeating here:

> No man ever looks at the world with pristine eyes. He sees it edited by a definite set of customs and institutions and ways of thinking. Even in his philosophical probings he cannot go behind these stereotypes; his very concepts of the true and the false will still have reference to his particular traditional customs...from the moment of his birth the customs into which

he is born shape his experience and behavior. By the time he can talk, he is the little creature of his culture, and by the time he is grown and able to take part in its activities, its habits are his habits, its beliefs his beliefs, its impossibilities his impossibilities. Every child that is born into his group will share them with him, and no child born into one on the opposite side of the globe can ever achieve the thousandth part. There is no social problem that is more incumbent upon us to understand than this of the role of custom. Until we are intelligent as to its laws and varieties, the main complicating facts of human life must remain unintelligible. (pp. 2-3)

Leong points out that Benedict's observation about the centrality of culture to our full understanding of human behavior, which was made over 60 years ago, has gone relatively unheeded in mainstream psychology. Currently, there seems to be a confluence of several factors, including the changing demographics in U.S. society, that make such an omission no longer tenable and the current decade is ripe for making inroads into our dominant Eurocentric paradigm. Yet, there is nothing inherently wrong with many of the components of this Eurocentric paradigm; indeed, when applied by European American counselors to European American clients, it is often the most appropriate paradigm. The problem occurs when this paradigm is applied mindlessly (Langer, 1989) and without cross-cultural validation and modification for culturally-different clients.

If the field accepts the central role that culture plays in career development and vocational behavior, then the task becomes that of identifying the various ways in which culture influences career assessment and career interventions. In a recent chapter reviewing the theoretical issues in cross-cultural career development for the *Handbook of Vocational Psychology* (Walsh & Osipow, in press), Leong and Brown (in press) observed that many scholars and counselors have already begun studying the impact of culture. These efforts seem organized around two major themes: namely, that of cultural validity and cultural specificity. According to Leong and Brown (in press), cultural validity is concerned with the validity of Eurocentric theories and models across other cultures in terms of the construct, concurrent, and predictive validity of these models for culturally different individuals (e.g., Holland's concept of congruence has been found to be predictive of job satisfaction among White Americans; Does this prediction also hold for African Americans, Asian Americans, etc. ?). On the other hand, cultural specificity is concerned with concepts, constructs, and models that are specific to certain cultural groups in terms of its role in explaining and predicting behavior within those groups (e.g., Colorism or level of melanin in skin of African Americans as a variable in vocational behavior).

Studies of the cultural validity of Eurocentric theories and models for other cultural groups allow us to identify if and when modfications to these models are needed in order for them to be valid and valuable for culturally-different clients. Studies that pursue the cultural-specificity route help identify culture-specific factors that need to be taken into account when trying to understand the vocational behavior of culturally-different clients (e.g. impact of racism on the career aspirations of African Americans). These culture-specific factors also play an important role in the career counseling and career assessment process with culturally-different clients.

Discussion

It is possible that the configuration of various social and demographic factors make it highly unlikely that we can continue to ignore the cultural dimension in what we do as counselors and counselor educators. However, the confluence of these factors notwithstanding, there is no guarantee that there will be a paradigm shift. However, I would argue that such a paradigm shift is necessary if the field of career counseling and career psychology is to advance in an increasingly multicultural society. Yet, there are powerful and longstanding barriers to such a paradigm shift, not the least of which is ethnocentricism. Despite the negative associations often attached to the notion of ethnocentricism, it should be pointed out that to be ethnocentric is the norm and not the exception. As Wrenn (1962) observed many years ago, counselors, like other human beings are inevitably culturally encapsulated.

In discussing paradigm shifts it is essential to describe first the current dominant paradigm and the points of weaknesses inherent in this paradigm (Kuhn, 1970). In a recent attempt to provide an integrative model for cross-cultural counseling and psychotherapy, Leong (in press b) pointed out that the dominant paradigm in counseling and psychotherapy is a Eurocentric one which is based largely on the assumption that psychology will identify "universal laws of behavior" which will apply to all human beings. While there is nothing inherently wrong with attempts to identify universal laws of behavior, the problems of the current paradigm in counseling are two-fold. First, there is the problem of ethnocentricism and overgeneralization. Specifically, much of the knowledge generated in psychology which is used to guide counseling and psychotherapy is based on White-European samples. To the extent that culture matters and White-Europeans comprise a unique culture among many, then the common assumption that what we have discovered is universal is by definition ethnocentric (i.e., using our cultural group as the primary frame of reference for all human beings). In addition, the ethnocentricism often leads to overgeneralization (i.e., if we are this way, other groups must be this way too). The second problem inherent in the current paradigm is that the only way that psychology can claim to offer universal laws of behavior is to accept the role of the cultural dimension and incorporate the cross-cultural methodology and perspective. To put it simply, the only way we can legitimately claim that our theories, models, and empirical relationships apply across all (or, more appropriately, "most") cultures is if we have examined these theories, models, and empirical relationships across many, many cultures.

As Leong (in press b) has pointed out, the new paradigm must integrate both the universal approach exemplified by traditional, mainstream psychology and the cross-cultural approach. According to Leong and Brown (in press), the efforts to integrate the cross-cultural dimension into mainstream vocational psychology have been organized around two major themes, namely that of cultural validity and cultural specificity. Cultural validity is concerned with the extent to which mainstream theories and models in vocational psychology are valid for culturally different groups (i.e., non-European

Americans). The conditions and circumstances where these mainstream theories have limited cultural validity may be due to the intrinsic inadequacies of these constructs and models to explain the vocational behavior of racial and ethnic minorities. At the same time, there may exist culturally-specific factors and variables which more adequately account for the vocational behavior of racial and ethnic minorities. Counselors should identify these culture-specific factors as a consequence of the limited cultural validity of mainstream theories and they must recognize the intrinsic value of culture-specific variables. Leong and Brown (in press) went on to argue that in order to increase our understanding of the career development of culturally-different individuals in this country and elsewhere, it is important that both approaches be pursued and the results integrated. It should also be noted that both approaches need to be integrated because they stand as a dialectic that interacts in a dynamic and complex fashion. For example, it may be that certain manifestations of culture-specific issues (e.g., loss of face among Chinese) that lead to problems in the cultural validity or issues (e.g., questionable responses in a diagnostic interview). Conversely, it may be that the discovery of limited cultural validity (or cross-cultural generalizability) of certain theories (e.g., a theory of career choice based solely on ability and aptitude) that lead to the search for culture-specific constructs and variables as possible explanations (e.g., use of fortune tellers to divine one's true talents).

Within the field of career counseling and career psychology, evidence for a potential paradigm shift is represented by the increasing number of both theoretical and empirical publications which incorporate the cultural dimension. For example, in 1991 Leong guest edited a special issue of the *Career Development Quarterly* devoted to the career development of racial and ethnic minorities. Two years later, a special section in the same journal was devoted to issues of multicultural career counseling (Savickas, 1993). More and more journals are devoting space to both special issues (e.g., *Journal of Vocational Psychology's* 1994 special issue on Racial Identity and Vocational Behavior and the *Journal of Career Assessment's* 1994 special issue on career assessment with racial and ethnic minorities) and specific articles in special issues (e.g., Marsella & Leong, 1995) that incorporate the cultural dimension in career counseling and vocational psychology. In June of 1995, Lawrence Erlbaum Associates published an edited volume (Leong, 1995) devoted entirely to the career development and vocational behavior of racial and ethnic minorities. Finally, in the forthcoming second edition of the *Handbook of Vocational Psychology* edited by Walsh and Osipow (in press), two separate chapters are devoted to the cultural dimension in career counseling (Fouad & Bingham, in press) and career psychology theories (Leong & Brown, in press).

Recommended Course of Action

In our profession, it has become standard practice in our publications to call for more research. Yet, with regards to career interventions and assessment with culturally different clients, the call for more research cannot really be over-exaggerated given the dearth of empirical data on the topic. If we accept the central role that culture plays in vocational behavior in general and career counseling in particular, then we need to continue to examine the cultural validity of the dominant Eurocentric theories for culturally different clients. I am referring here both to theories of career development and theories of career counseling. At the same time, we need to identify salient culture-specific factors that influence both the vocational behavior and the career counseling process with culturally different clients. In following this line of research, there is a rich source of ideas and constructs we can borrow from our colleagues in both ethnic minority psychology and cross-cultural psychology.

Certainly, career counselors cannot withhold services from culturally different clients until a strong research database has been accumulated. In the meantime, career counselors can refer to the references cited in this chapter and elsewhere in this volume as resources to guide them in their assessment and intervention with culturally different clients. The various articles, book chapters, and special issues of journals, and the new volume devoted entirely to racial and ethnic minorities (Leong, 1995) form a promising body of knowledge that should be useful to career counselors. The challenge is for practicing career counselors to master this emerging knowledge-base. However, in order for that to occur, career counselors must be convinced that such knowledge is essential to their work. Hence the battle against ethnocentrism, and the associated inertia, is a daily one. We are all creatures of habit and change is hard work. For this battle I would refer the reader to Wrenn's (1985) recommendations on overcoming cultural encapsulation (e.g., engage in long-range thinking, develop a habit of unlearning something everyday) as well as Langer's (1989) ideas and suggestions for mindfulness.

At the same time, we also need to integrate the cultural dimension into the training of future counselors with regards both to the career assessment process (e.g., see Marsella and Leong, 1995) and the career counseling process (e.g., see Fouad & Bingham, in press; Leong, 1993). If we attack the problem on both fronts by sharing existing knowledge with practicing career counselors and by providing even stronger research data and theories for future generations of career counselors, then we can be confident in meeting the continuing challenge of cultural diversity in our profession and our society.

Summary

A fundamental challenge for career counseling and career psychology over the next few decades will be how these fields choose to address the issue of the centrality of the cultural dimension. I would like to conclude by borrowing a concept from Karen Horney in framing the challenge facing career counselors who will work with culturally different clients. Like the interpersonal choices facing Horney's patients, we as career counselors have three choices with regards to cultural diversity: (a) we can move against it, (b) we can move away from it, or (c) we can move towards it. The choice is a personal one, but the consequences may affect our field's relevance and effectiveness.

References

Benedict, R. (1934). *Patterns of culture*. New York: Houghton-Mifflin.

Fouad, N. A., & Bingham, R. (in press). Career counseling with racial and ethnic minorities. In W.B. Walsh & S. H. Osipow (Eds.), *Handbook of vocational psychology* (2nd ed.). Hillsdale, NJ: Lawrence Erlbaum Associates.

Kuhn, T. (1970). *The structure of scientific revolutions*. Chicago: University of Chicago Press.

Langer. E. J. (1989). *Mindfulness*. Reading, Massachusetts: Addison-Wesley.

Leong, F. T. L. (1991). Guest Editor's Introduction. Special Issue: Career Development of Racial and Ethnic Minorities. *Career development quarterly, 39,* 196-198.

Leong, F. T. L. (1993). The career counseling process with racial/ethnic Minorities: The case of asian americans. *Career Development Quarterly, 42,* 26-40.

Leong, F. T. L. (ED.). (1995). *Career development and vocational behavior of racial and ethnic minorities*. Hillsdale, NJ: Lawrence Erlbaum Associates.

Leong, F. T. L. (in press a). Challenges to career counseling: boundaries, cultures, and complexity. In M. L. Savickas & W. B. Walsh (Eds.), *Integrating career theory and practice*. Palo Alto, California: Consulting Psychologist Press.

Leong, F. T. L. (in press b). Toward an integrative model for cross-cultural counseling and psychotherapy. *Applied and preventive psychology.*

Leong, F. T. L., & Brown, M. T. (in press). Theoretical issues in cross-cultural career development: Cultural validity and cultural specificity. In W. B. Walsh & S. H. Osipow (Eds.), *Handbook of vocational psychology* (2nd ed.). Hillsdale, NJ: Lawrence Erlbaum Associates.

Marsella, A. J., & Leong, F. T. L. (1995). Cross-cultural issues in personality and career assessment. *Journal of Career Assessment, 3,* 202-218.

Walsh, W. B., & Osipow, S. H. (Eds.). (in press). *Handbook of vocational psychology* (2nd ed.). Hillsdale, NJ: Lawrence Erlbaum Associates.

Wrenn, C. G. (1962). The culturally encapsulated counselor. *Harvard Education Review, 32,* 444-449.

Wrenn, C. G. (1985). Afterword: The culturally encapsulated counselor revisited. In P. B. Pedersen (Ed.), *Handbook of cross-cultural counseling and therapy* (pp. 323-329). Westport, CT: Greenwood Press.

31

Working: A Perspective For A New Generation

Alice E. Potter

Higher education is graduating the smallest entry-level work force in U. S. history. This trend will continue through the year 1997. Why? Because this country experienced a marked drop in birth rates between 1965 and 1975.

They are the Twentysomething Generation, the Baby Busters, Generation X, and they are redefining the role of a career in a worker's life. Complaints of this generation include that they lack maturity, exhibit a poor work ethic, hold unrealistic expectations of job duties and starting salaries, and lack professionalism. Companies particularly feel a cultural shift as they attempt to hire this generation into entry-level positions.

> *To truly understand the impact of [the Twentysomethings Generation] on our society, career counselors must understand some of their defining characteristics, among the strongest of which are a need for structure and a desire for personal attention.*

In light of the increasing number of non-traditional age career-changers available for hire today, the cultural differences appear stark. Yet, the issues at hand appear to be more than just another generation gap. The Twentysomething Generation is disillusioned. With little guidance, they navigated the trials and tribulations of a complex childhood on their own. Being small in number and relatively unrecognized as a generation during their formative years, this generation did not share the hope that together they could change the world.

However, hope is emerging. By the late 1980s, as companies began to recognize the approach of the shrinking labor pool, this generation experienced the birth of a generational identity. Schools have had to recognize a more independent generation, one that is more difficult to please. New methods of teaching are emerging which are compatible with the realities of a modified family structure. Higher education is under pressure to address the changing needs of their clientele. Companies are rethinking their human resource strategies, from hiring practices to employee motivation. School-to-work programs are being recognized for the mentoring and practical "life after college" experiences they provide.

To truly understand the impact of this generation on our society, career counselors must understand some of their defining characteristics, among the strongest of which are a need for structure and a desire for personal attention.

The Twentysomethings

This generation will be 20 - 30 years of age in 1995. At 35 million, they comprise the smallest population group ever born in our country. They follow the largest generation — the 77 million Baby Boomers. They are more culturally diverse than any previous generation born in our country. Sixty-seven percent of this generation graduated from high school, 19% will graduate from college. Of those attending college, 63% will work while in school.

Only 15% of the Twentysomething Generation was brought up in a "traditional" (two parents, one at home) household, 40% are from divorced families, and 40% were "latch-key" kids. These facts add to the confusion of this generation, for adults were seldom available to validate their identity. The Twentysomething Generation grew up with television as their primary source of both entertainment and adult role-modeling.

Today's traditional-aged college senior:
- *was born* when the news of Watergate broke;
- *was a year old* when lines were forming at the gas stations;
- *was 3* when our country celebrated the bicentennial, and when spray cans were linked to ozone layer damage;

- *turned 6* when Iran took hostages (who didn't return until they were in third grade), and when the Three-Mile Island disaster occurred;
- *was in junior high school* when the first Black Miss America was selected and deposed, when Rock Hudson died of AIDS, when crack houses started to emerge;
- *was in high school* when the stock market crashed, the Berlin Wall opened, massacres occurred at Tianamen Square, Exxon was responsible for an oil spill, and Iraq invaded Kuwait.

Current events unfolded before this generation in an "up close and personal" manner never before experienced by young people. With minimal parental interaction or consolation, these children were left to interpret events of the day on their own. As a generation, they have been raised to develop their own tastes and tendencies.

While one member of this generation may appear to be a flashback from the "hippie generation," another may seem almost "Reaganesque." Despite the appearance of being cut from different cloth, the Twentysomethings such share common threads as:

- *Self-Orientation*—measuring things in terms of "how will this affect me?"
- *Extended Adolescence*—average age of a college freshman is 26 years old, average marrying age for men/women is 26/24, 58% of Americans between the ages of 20-24 live with their parents.
- *Materialism*— access to a variety of material possessions is the norm, to do without these is considered a hardship, and with $125 billion dollars of disposable income they represent a powerful consumer group.
- *Cynicism*—while both Baby Boomer and Twentysomethings may share a negative global view of politics and daily news, the Twentysomethings' general outlook is one of helplessness and hopelessness. They lack the sense of purpose the Baby Boomers shared in their youth.
- *Expectation of fun*—reared by television as the surrogate parent, every task must be light, fast-moving, and fun.

Many of these characteristics resulted from growing up in an information age. With so much information available, our young people learned early that it can't all be digested. They constructed an internal screening mechanism to evaluate everything in relation to self. "What's in it for me?" might, in fact, be more an evaluation mechanism than an attitude — an evaluation mechanism that allows one to sift through all information and retain only what affects oneself.

This screening process persists unless an adult role model demonstrates a new pattern of relationship to the world. Unfortunately, for most Twentysomethings, this adult role modeling never occurred. The overwhelming absence of daily adult contact during their childhood has deprived them of the benefits of observing adults in daily situations. With this decrease of parental involvement, young workers transfer their unmet need to their workplace supervisors.

Twentysomethings at Work

In the 1960s and 1970s, it was common to "job hop" for a year or two after college, under the guise of finding yourself. Today, the same behavior earns this generation their "slacker" image, indicating that they lack direction. Today's Twentysomething college graduate is no longer competing only with other Twentysomething college graduates from across the U. S. for entry-level jobs. They are competing with graduates from other countries, they are competing with "re-deployed" workers who offer experience, and they are competing for fewer positions due to the global forces of down-sizing. This need to "hit the ground running" has left many Twentysomethings feeling intimidated and insecure in the workplace.

Common complaints about this generation as workers include:
- lack of understanding of power structures;
- poor work ethic;
- high expectations regarding appropriate wages;
- unprofessional communication skills;
- unrealistic expectations of "fast-tracking" to the top.

Due to technological advances, this generation grew up overwhelmed by a world of options available to them, often leaving them feeling lost. One of the necessary tasks of anyone working with this generation is to assist them in narrowing their many options down to a manageable few. One of the trends in recruiting today addresses this need. Increasingly, organizations are turning to internship programs to mentor and shape this "lost" generation. This benefits the young worker by allowing them to sample a few of their options prior to making a commitment. Internship programs further serve young workers by:

- modeling clear communication styles and interpersonal skills;
- exposing them to career-related environments;
- demonstrating how their current role in school can benefit them in the future;
- contributing to their perspective on sound work ethics;
- grounding them in the basics required for their chosen career field;
- offering them the opportunity to assume greater responsibility.

Upon completion of an internship, these students have returned to their academic institutions demonstrating a renewed sense of purpose and drive. Organizations employing interns benefit from the program's cost-effective screening process and the training it offers potential recruits. Participating educational institutions retain and graduate a higher caliber of students.

In the face of the negative publicity this generation receives in the media, it is important to note the unique perspectives or skills which they bring to the workplace. This generation is genuinely inquisitive, and at times ruthlessly honest. They can appreciate the drive to find a better, faster, more efficient way to do a task if possible. They posses advanced skills and comfort in the area of technology. The research indicating that adults will experience at least five to seven careers in a lifetime suits the Twentysomethings' desire for change and need for short-term commitment.

They also bring a more balanced perspective to the struggle many of us face in managing our personal and professional lives.

Interacting with Twentysomethings

An ever-increasing pace of change in our society has resulted in a generation that expects, and needs, a fast pace of change. They recognize change as the only constant, something with which Baby Boomers struggle. They prefer to have tasks broken up into bit-sized pieces. They learn more by seeing and doing than by listening. The good news is that this learning style is appropriate for our world today. This learning style allows the Twentysomething Generation to effectively compete and hold their own in the world today, because the world expects more and faster.

Members of the Twentysomething Generation are redefining of the needs of our clientele today. As a result, we need to redefine our methods of interacting with our clientele. As advisors, mentors, and supervisors to this generation, we must recognize that they respond positively to:

- more frequent interaction with adults who take the time to know them personally as well as professionally;
- project-style assignments which allow them taking on one task at a time;
- assignments explained in terms of what they will gain from assignment completion;
- direct recognition and praise;
- fun at work—structured play, practical jokes, cartoons, light competitions, surprises;
- small, unexpected rewards for jobs well done;
- balance between work life and home/play life.

The Twentysomething Lesson

The lesson in all this? To quote one member of the Twentysomething Generation: "The way I see the world is a result of the world I've seen." Our society underestimated the importance of adult interaction and adult role modeling upon our youth. The Twentysomething Generation clearly illustrates this for us as we watch them mature. While negative press often surrounds this generation, their independence and fight may yet win our favor.

However we choose to refer to the Twentysomething Generation, the thirteenth generation of the United States, they are our future. They comprise tomorrow's work force, tomorrow's business and civic leaders, tomorrow's parents. Through individual advising, mentoring, and supervisory relationships, we can provide them with the tools necessary to empower them in their search for belonging and contribution. By seeking new ways of interacting with young workers, keeping ourselves open to restructuring working relationships, and redefining reward structures, we open the doors of opportunity. Who knows, we may learn something about ourselves in the process!

References

Bradford, L. J., & Raines, C. (1992). *Twentysomething: Managing and motivating today's new workforce.* New York: MasterMedia Limited.

Dunn, W. (1993). *The baby bust: A generation comes of age.* Ithaca, NY: American Demographics Books.

Hudson Institute. (1987). *Workforce 2000: work and workers for the Twenty-First Century.* Indianapolis: Hudson Institute.

Howe, N. & Strauss, B. (1992). *13th Gen: Abort, retry, ignore, fail?* United States: Vintage Books.

Potter, A. (1994). *An employers guide to internships and other work-based learning experiences.* Unpublished manuscript, University of Northern Colorado, Greeley, CO.

32

Career Development Issues In Global Relocation

Marian Stoltz-Loike

As global arenas expand, greater demands are placed on companies to internationalize. While many organizations have an international presence, only a few are truly global organizations that have the flexibility to respond rapidly to the ever-changing demands of business in every location. These organizations have begun to recognize that the only way to develop employees with "global minds" is to have them address business challenges in different locations around the world. Career counselors can help employees and their employed partners be more effective on international assignments by helping them to set career goals both before and after expatriation.

Effective career development, as we approach the 21st century, means thinking outside of the box to develop new and innovative ways to meet the very different challenges posed by the global marketplace (Rhinesmith, 1993). Companies are becoming more sophisticated about preparing expatriates for international assignments by helping them understand cultural issues that impact how business is conducted in the destination country and by helping them recognize that family issues influence the success of an international assignment (Schell & Stoltz-Loike, 1994; Stoltz-Loike, 1993).

> *Career development counselors can play unique roles in helping employees and their employed partners who are transferred to other countries plan ways to develop global skills during their assignments and to reinvent themselves so as to effectively use those skills upon repatriation.*

Business leaders recognize that sending people around the world does not make them a global company. Rather, thinking globally with regard to career and business issues defines the global mind and enables businesses to address new business questions, such as: What does global hiring mean? How do you select and develop global leaders from around the world who can capably address local and international business challenges? What does it mean to develop a global product? How do you define and create a global marketing strategy?

Traditionally, companies sent employees with particular expertise abroad to fulfill technical responsibilities which involved either short-term assignments for training locals in a particular skill or long-term assignments for managing a specific project or business venture. Little thought was given to the kinds of skills that expatriates would master abroad or the impact that the international move would have on the expatriate's career. Career development counselors can play unique roles in helping employees and their employed partners who are transferred to other countries plan ways to develop global skills during their assignments and to reinvent themselves so as to effectively use those skills upon repatriation.

Career Development Challenges

Employee

During expatriate assignments, employees develop a greater breadth of understanding of their organization's global business, and a greater depth in their management skills. They develop new understanding of cultural differences and how these differences can affect business and social situations.

Companies, however, do not generally consider how relocation fits with employees' career paths. Questions regarding skills that employees may master abroad are rarely considered. Relocation is rarely introduced as a developmental assignment for employees to build a greater global business understanding. In fact, organizations usually focus on the skills that the expatriate brings to the assignment rather than considering what he or she may learn abroad. This cultural imperialism may interfere with the expatriate's ability to succeed. Expatriates may also miss career development opportunities because they are cut off from the information loop at their home office and find it hard to remain on the fast track from thousands of miles away.

Integrating career-related skills and knowledge that they have mastered during their international assignment may pose a distinct challenge for repatriates. The organization, as well as their colleagues, may express little interest in the knowledge or skills that the repatriate may have mastered. Employees themselves may find it difficult to integrate their expatriate experience into corporate life at home. They wonder how an expatriate assignment fits with their career paths and find it hard to know how to manage their own career when they return to the U.S. These frustrations are reflected in the fact that a significant proportion of returning expatriates leave their companies within one year of repatriation.

Dual-Career Couples

Most partners/spouses relocate with the employee. For these accompanying partners who were part of a dual-career couple , there are a significant number of career development challenges, because they usually relocate without a job prospect and with many employment challenges. Most companies do not offer any significant help to accompanying spouses with finding a job, although many companies will assist them in obtaining work permits or visas, whenever possible.

The greatest challenge faced by accompanying partners is the disruption to their existing career paths. Some people cannot find jobs at their levels, others have difficulty finding jobs in their industry, or their industry may not exist. For example, a position in investment banking or fashion may be non-existent or difficult to obtain in Indonesia. Alternatively, these same jobs may exist in China but they may not command the same salaries or respect that they did in the United States. In other countries, like Canada or Australia, someone from the United States would not be able to obtain a job unless they could prove that there was no one there that was qualified for that position, a challenge that can be time consuming or impossible.

Even when someone can find a job, it may be in another career field or industry, resulting in a discontinuous career path. This may have implications for their marketability when they return to the U.S. or their ability to remain current with new trends within their industry.

Definitions of "good" resumes or effective interview skills vary across the world. In the U.S., employees are expected to highlight their accomplishments and achievements. In Europe and Asia, when potential employees focus too much attention on their achievements they may be seen as self-centered and inappropriate for the job. In England, resumes are expected to be longer, more descriptive, and softer than they are in the U.S. In countries like Japan or France, educational background may be of great significance in employment, while in countries like Mexico, Venezuela, or Saudi Arabia knowing important people or being a member of the "right" family may be a valuable criterion in employment. Thus, knowing how to highlight background issues appropriately, and how to describe past experiences in a culturally appropriate fashion may impact the expatriate partner's ability to find satisfactory employment.

Career Development Solutions

To remain marketable in today's shifting marketplace requires reinventing one's self, one's career goals, and one's definitions of what it means to be a productive employee. Charles Handy (1990) claims that to address the discontinuous nature of today's workplace requires upside down thinking. Therefore, employees can no longer expect to have a neat, logical career path which is defined by their employer. Instead, employers are expecting employees to reinvent themselves to fit new workplace demands and manage their own careers so that they remain at the cutting edge of new business developments (see also, Jameson & O'Mara, 1991). For many employees, this is an extremely difficult task. Being offered an international assignment, however, forces employees to reevaluate their career directions and goals.

Employee

Career counselors can play the pivotal role of assisting employees to shift directions and plans, making their international assignment an unexpected developmental opportunity and forcing them to pay attention to their career direction. Counselors can help clients contrast their present, past, and future career paths and consider what they need to do to remain marketable. In today's changing marketplace a straight line is not the shortest path to career success.

My experience with relocation has demonstrated that the most effective way to capitalize on career development opportunities in relocation is through long-range planning, and I have identified three key areas.

Pre-departure Career Preparation. Employees who are considering an international relocation should have a routine career check-up with their career counselors, an idea that is currently being advocated by the leadership of the National Career Development Association. This involves first and foremost on-going career development support that focuses on: (1) the importance of relocation to the career path, (2) the optimal time with regard to career and family for relocation, (3) career-related skills that can be built during an international assignment, and (4) developmental activities to prepare for an international assignment. This long-range planning is appropriate whether one expects to relocate in five weeks or in five years.

Some examples include the following:

- John requests an assignment in three years, after his children enter college, to a developing country to learn about emerging markets.
- Paula requests an assignment in 5 years to allow her partner to master some portable skills and develop a more portable career.

Expatriate Career Preparation. Once an employee has been offered a relocation, the counselor can help the expatriate identify: (1) why he/she was selected, (2) the makeup of the business group in the destination country, (3) how the success of the assignment is to be evaluated, and (4) what business skills can be acquired in the destination country. Relevant business skills may include learning a new language, mastering new technical skills, or managing an international business team.

Career Repatriation Support. After repatriation, employees often find that the skills that they have mastered may not match the position that they are returning to. Counselors can help them reevaluate their career paths. Expatriates often need assistance in strategizing about new job opportunities within their companies that dovetail with the skills they have mastered abroad, and need coaching on how to obtain those new positions. They also need to identify how to reintegrate into the home office corporate culture. Regular career check-ups with expatriates can be invaluable to both the repatriates and the company by insuring that skills that they mastered abroad are integrated into both tactical and strategic organizational plans.

The following are some examples of how knowledge gained abroad may be used when employees repatriate:

- Pat learned to deal with an international team as a line manager in Indonesia and requested to be part of her company's new diversity initiative.
- Gordon coordinates a brown bag lunch series once a month. He invites repatriates and employees who are considering expatriation to gather informally and discuss what it's like to live abroad and to share specific information about living in different parts of the world.

Dual-Career Couple Concerns

For the relocating partner, relocation also provides a unique opportunity to reevaluate their career goals. For the majority of accompanying partners, long-range career planning is the only choice to empower them in the career choices they make while abroad and to maximize their workforce marketability when they return home. Counselors can focus on skill building rather than on specific job choices.

In my experience with dual-career couples, I have found that a five step approach to career opportunities for accompanying partners works very effectively. I recommend that steps one to three be undertaken before relocation and steps four and five be conducted in the destination country.

Step 1: Identifying Work-Related Skills. Counselors can assist expatriates in identifying the wide variety of skills they have mastered within their industry. These may include teaching elementary school children, developing financial products, building bridges, or doing academic research.

Step 2: Identifying Transferable Skills. Expatriates should be encouraged to identify transferable skills they have mastered in their jobs and to reframe their work-related skills into transferable skills. For example, teaching may be reframed as training; developing financial product may involve product development skills but also management, coordination and integration; building bridges may have also demanded skills in managing a multicultural team and long range planning and development activities. Academic research may be reframed as research and development, or writing and planning.

Step 3: Identifying Long-Range Career Opportunities. Counselors should encourage expatriates to identify career paths during the expatriate assignment, as well as long-range goals for three years and for five to ten years after repatriation. Together with the counselor, the expatriate can explore the feasibility of each career path and identify skills necessary to perform successfully in each career path. Expatriates can then gap the difference between the identified goal and the transferable skills that they have already mastered. Next, they can explore job, volunteer, educational, or entrepreneurial opportunities to develop those skills.

Step 4: Learning about the Job Market. Counselors can provide expatriates with essential information about the local job market, including local employers, trade magazines, professional associations and publications. Additionally, they can help the employees arrange informational interviews when appropriate. Counselors, themselves can obtain some of this information by forming and using international networks of counselors, and through listings and information in the World Wide Web.

Step 5: Resumes and Interviews. A counselor in-country can provide invaluable information on the appropriate form for resumes and help the expatriate master market-appropriate interview skills. The counselor can also coach the expatriate regarding how to highlight some of the skills that they have mastered prior to relocation, and assist them in customizing their resumes to the local job market.

Summary

For career counselors, as well as for their clients, there are many new opportunities in the global marketplace. Some of them include the following:

- Develop international networks of career development professionals;
- Incorporate information on working in a global marketplace;
- Learn about key skills necessary to manage globally;
- Look at succession planning from a cross-cultural perspective.

Globalization and international assignments provide specific challenges to expatriates, but also offer unique opportunities to reevaluate career goals and identify new developmental career strategies. Career counselors can play pivotal roles in helping their clients be successful both at home and abroad.

References

Handy, C. (1990). *The age of unreason.* USA: Harvard Business School Press.

Jameson, D., & O'Mara, J. (1991). *Managing workforce 2000: Gaining the diversity advantage.* San Francisco: Jossey Bass.

Rhinesmith, S. (1993). *A manager's guide to globalization: Six Keys to Success in a Changing World.* NY: Irwin Publishing.

Schell, M., & Stoltz-Loike, M. (1994). Importance of cultural preparation to international business Success. *Journal of International Compensation and Benefits, 2,* 47-52.

Stoltz-Loike, M. (1993).Work and family considerations in international relocation. *Journal of International Compensation and Benefits, 2,* 31-35.

Innovative Tools and Techniques That Maximize the Effectiveness of Career Development Interventions

David Campbell

Mary Heppner

Ed Jacobs

Janet Lenz

Albert Pautler

Gary Peterson

Robert Reardon

James Sampson

Denise Saunders

33

Psychological Development Surveys

David Campbell

Psychological surveys differ widely in their formats, both at the item (input) level and at the scale (output) level. Some of the more popular item formats include True-False, Like-Indifferent-Dislike, and the Likert format, with five to seven choices which are often labelled "Strong Agree" to "Strongly Disagree." The scale formats include, among others, standard scores, stanines, percentiles, type scores, quadrant scores, and raw scores.

When working with multiple surveys in the assessment process, each professional is expected to be intimately familiar with the technical characteristics of each survey used, especially if the resulting data have some unpleasant implications for the client. In the development of the Campbell Development Surveys, a deliberate attempt was made to simplify the situation and keep the important survey characterisitics constant.

While these varying formats usually serve their intended purposes well, this variety makes life difficult for both professional users and their clients. The professional user—counselor, psychologist, or human resources professional—has to be familiar with the unique features of each survey, and then has to transmit that knowledge to the client in everyday language. For example, the professional has to know that a score of 60 on the *California Psychological Inventory* (CPI) is a full standard deviation above the mean in the *psychologically healthy* direction, while a score of 60 on the *Minnesota Multiphasic Personality Inventory* (MMPI) is a full standard deviation above the mean in the *pathological* direction. Furthermore, the same score of 60 on the *Myers-Briggs Type Indicator* (MBTI) is near the top of most MBTI scales while a score of 60 on the *Wechsler Adult Intelligence Scale* (WAIS) is so low that the person may require institutional care. In an even more complex situation, on the *Strong Interest Inventory* (SII) a score of 60 on the Basic Interest Scales indicates that the respondent has scored one standard deviation above the general population average whereas a score of 60 of the Occupational Scales indicates that the respondent has scored one standard deviation above the average of the members of that occupation. Thus, the same numerical score of 60 has vastly different meanings from survey to survey, or even within the same survey.

When working with multiple surveys in the assessment process, each professional is expected to be intimately familiar with the technical characteristics of each survey used, especially if the resulting data have some unpleasant implications for the client. In such cases, the client will often strenuously question the process: Why were these specific statements used? How were the measuring scales constructed? How were they normed? How stable are the scores? Who scores high and who scores low? Why should I trust these scores? In a typical battery of current surveys, the answers to these questions can differ from survey to survey.

In the development of the **Campbell Development Surveys**, a deliberate attempt was made to simplify the situation and keep the important survey characteristics constant. Thus, when a user becomes familiar with any one of the CDS surveys, he or she is immediately familiar with all of them. Further, a deliberate "user-friendly" strategy was followed, especially in the presentation of results, so that naive users could quickly grasp the meaning of the scores. Arcane jargon was avoided, and graphic presentations were used wherever possible. As a result, most everyone can quickly understand the results from each CDS survey. This frees the counselor or other professional user from spending so much time on "test interpretation" and allows more time for discussion of the underlying dynamics of the individual's personal situation. Each survey is listed next, followed by a discussion of their common characteristics.

The Battery of Campbell Development Surveys (CDS™)
The CDS battery includes the following five surveys. With a few minor variations, they all have the same item format, the same standard score format, the same scale construction method, the same norming strategy, the same profile layout, and the same kind of supporting documentation. They differ only in item content and in areas of application.

Campbell Interest and Skill Survey™(CISS®), a career planning instrument that covers both vocational interests—"What I like to do" — and vocational skills— "What am I confident I can do."

The CISS has 29 Basic Scales covering specific areas such as Science, Fashion, and Financial Services, and 60 Occupational Scales such as Attorney, Librarian, and Athletic Coach, all organized into seven conceptual Orientations— Influencing, Organizing, Helping, Creating, Analyzing, Producing, and Adventuring. Each scale has two scores, one for reported interests, the other for reported skills. The results are used to help guide individuals to those areas of the occupational world where they are likely to be most interested, and where they are most confident of their performance. When used with groups, the CISS is also helpful in team building situations. (Campbell, Hyne, & Nilsen, 1992)

Campbell Leadership Index™(CLI®), a leadership characteristics questionnaire completed by the Self and three to five observers chosen by the Self.

The CLI has 22 scales covering specific leadership areas such as Ambitious, Considerate, and Flexible, organized into five conceptual Orientations -- Leadership, Energy, Affability, Dependability, and Resilience. Each scale has two scores, one based on the Self's responses, the other based on the Observers' responses. The results help respondents understand how they are perceived by others on these important leadership characteristics. Discrepancies between Self and Observers in either direction are particularly useful in charting further self-development activities. (Campbell, 1991)

Campbell-Hallam Team Development Survey™ (TDS™), a team effectiveness survey designed to be completed by each member of a working team and by selected outside observers.

The TDS has 18 scales covering areas such as Coordination, Motivation, and Planning, clustered into four major categories -- Resources, Efficiency, Improvement, and Success. Each team respondent receives a profile showing how they evaluated their team's characteristics, versus how the other members of their team evaluated the team. An optional procedure also allows comparisons with outside observers, using the same 18 dimensions. (Hallam, G. H. & Campbell, D. P., 1995)

Campbell Organizational Survey™ (COS™), a comprehensive, versatile, and normed employee attitude survey covering important features of organizational life.

The COS has 17 scales covering areas such as Supervision, Coworkers, and Quality, and it has an Overall Index, which is used in two major ways: first, as a job satisfaction survey where respondents can see how they evaluated their working situation compared to a normative standard base of "typical employees in typical organizations"; second, as an employee attitude survey where clusters of employees can be compared across departments, divisions, different geographical locations, or any other desired groupings. In this survey process, employees receive back a personal profile, showing how their results compared to any designated group. (Campbell, 1990; Campbell & Hyne, 1995)

Campbell Community Survey (CCS), a normed community survey covering important aspects of community life.

The CCS has 18 scales covering areas such as Education, Health Services, and Community Pride, and it has an Overall Index, which allows residents to see how they evaluated their community compared to a normative standard base of "typical residents in typical communities." Each respondent can also be compared with designated subgroups within their own community. This survey, which is in its 7th pre-publication version, will likely be published in late 1995 or early 1996.

Common Features of the Campbell Surveys

Item format. The choice of item format is important because it influences the quality of data available for the assessment process. If the format is primitive or confusing, the resulting data will be primitive and misleading. Further, if respondents find the item format poorly planned or foolish, they may not take seriously the task of completing the survey. In general, respondents do not like item formats that force them into a restricted range of choices, such as the two choice True-False format, or formats that force them to choose between two or more equally attractive alternatives, e.g. "Which adjective is most descriptive of you: kind, creative, or responsible?"

Based on earlier experiences, a six-point response scale has been chosen for each of the Campbell Surveys, with choices ranging from "Strongly Like" to "Strongly Dislike," or from "Always" to "Never," or from "Strongly Agree" to "Strongly Disagree," depending on the specific survey.

These six-point scales have proven to be quite satisfactory. Virtually all respondents accept the format without comment, and the resulting scores produce stable, meaningful, and valid distributions.

Item content. Once the decision has been made to construct a new survey in a particular area, such as career planning or team performance, items relevant to that area are prepared; this selection of specific items is undoubtedly the most "artistic" step in the development of a new survey. The items usually come from the author's personal and professional experience, from ideas gleaned from the work of other researchers, from the writings of theorists, from focus groups of representative respondents, and from colleagues and staff members. For each CDS survey, this initial item pool always contained at least twice as many items as were eventually used.

Multiple waves of tryouts identified troublesome items which were either re-worked or rejected; the surviving items then constituted the final survey form.

Survey construction. With the exception of the CISS Occupational Scales, the CDS scoring scales were constructed by clustering together items using two criteria: first, statistical intercorrelations, and second, common sense. By clustering together several items related to the same theme, scales were created that are more reliable than single items taken alone.

The CISS Occupational Scales were constructed by comparing successful, satisfied members of occupational samples with a general reference sample of workers from a wide range of occupations.

Norming. The CDS scales were normed in the following manner: a wide range of relevant samples, each containing from several dozen to several hundred respondents, were surveyed. Using both statistical measures and visual inspections of the sample distributions, a central point was selected to represent the population mean for each scale. The same technique was used to estimate the population standard deviation. These two raw score statistics were then used to calculate T-scores for each respondent. The net result of this procedure is to equate "the population norm" to a mean of 50 and standard deviation of 10 on each scale of each survey. Because a wide range of samples was used, containing thousands of respondents, these population statistics are quite stable.

Profile layout. The visual presentation of the survey scores can have a substantial impact on how the scores are interpreted. While the numerical scores are more important in a scientific sense, the visual presentation usually has a more vivid impact on how the scores are actually used.

The Campbell Surveys all have the same profile layout, showing the individual's scores against a population norm. When the survey has two sets of scores, such as the CISS where each scale has both an Interest and a Skill scale, or the CLI where each scale has both a Self and an Observer score, the two sets of scores are presented in a manner that permits the simultaneous comparison of both scores against the relevant population norms.

Procedural checks. Each CDS answer sheet is scanned by computer and scorers look for indications of gross distortions in the response patterns. Although the number of problems is quite small, and the average user may never see a single "Doubtful" profile, when a significant problem does appear, the user is alerted.

Applications of the Surveys

The Major Functions of Psychological Surveys. Psychological surveys have become ubiquitous. From their beginnings in educational, military, and mental health institutions, they have spread widely. Surveys are now used not only in these traditional settings, but also in corporate retreats, prison rehabilitation programs, church-sponsored marital enhancement weekends, "charm school" programs for high-ranking military officers, motivational sessions for athletic teams, military intelligence studies trying to predict the personalities of foreign leaders, ghetto programs working to keep teenagers in school, and prestigious Park Avenue receptions focused on volunteer, team-building sessions for charitable fund raisers. They have even been used in the halls of Congress to help our elected leaders work together more effectively. Whatever the setting, psychological surveys usually serve the following three major functions.

*First, to focus attention. . .*Most psychological surveys have several scales covering a variety of topics, and each survey inevitably calls attention to whatever topics are represented by its particular scales. If a survey has an Extraversion scale, then attention will be focused on extraversion; if a survey has a Mechanical Interests scale, then attention will be focused on mechanical interests; if a survey has a Depression scale, then attention will be focused on depression. Thus, the initial choice of item and scale content will usually drive the decision about whether or not that survey is seen as relevant for particular applications.

*Second, to structure conversations. . .*Most psychological surveys provide normed scores for each of their scales, and the level of the individual score usually determines the nature of the conversation about that scale. For example, a conversation with a client about a high score on an Extraversion scale will be different from a conversation about a low score on that scale. Thus, the definition of "high" and "low" scores—the norming process—will structure the nature of the conversations about the scores.

Third, to suggest future implications. . . .Survey scores are almost always used to suggest future implications of current characteristics. For example, "With your high score on Extraversion, you will probably enjoy working in situations with a wide range of social interactions. You may have trouble with tasks that can be intensely lonely or individualistic, such as writing or data analysis."

The Specific Applications of the Campbell Surveys

Within this framework of "The Major Functions," each of the Campbell Surveys have their own specific individual applications, which are often obvious, and which are described in greater detail in each of the Survey Manuals. The Surveys are also complementary, and can often be used together in beneficial ways. For example, the CISS, the career survey, is often used as an "ice-breaker" in team building sessions before the results of the TDS are discussed with the team; the latter results tend to lead to intense discussions, and some warm-up activities are often useful. Because the surveys have been designed with common characteristics, these complementary uses are easier to achieve than with a typical battery of mixed surveys.

References

Campbell, D. P. (1991). *Manual for the Campbell Leadership Index.* Minneapolis: National Computer Systems.

Campbell, D. P., & Hallam, G. H. (1995). *Manual for the Campbell-Hallam Team Development Survey.* Minneapolis: National Computer Systems.

Campbell, D. P., & Hyne, S. A. (1995). *Manual for the Campbell Organizational Survey* (2nd ed.). Minneapolis: National Computer Systems.

Campbell, D. P., Hyne, S. A., & Nilsen, D. (1992). *Manual for the Campbell Interest and Skill Survey.* Minneapolis: National Computer Systems.

34

Adult Career Transitions: Assessing Psychological Barriers and Resources

Mary J. Heppner

Karen was 39 when she came to the Career Center for counseling. She had grown up in a working class neighborhood in a northern industrial city. She and her husband had moved to the midwest to find work after the factory her husband worked for had massive job lay offs. Karen had secured a job as a secretary in the Dean's office of a small college. She had done secretarial work ever since she graduated from high school. She presumed that is what she would continue doing. The Dean she worked for had other ideas for her. He wanted her to go to college and earn a degree. He would pay for all her expenses through the college's staff tuition remission program. Although a generous offer, it terrified Karen. She had no idea what she could be. The Dean had suggested she go for career counseling on the same campus at which she was employed. The counselor used a battery of interest and skill assessment measures and provided extensive information about majors and careers that would be good matches for Karen's personality. The counselor encouraged Karen to explore these career

> *No matter how effective the counselor is in assessing skills, interests, and work-related values; no matter how psychometrically sound the instruments used to make this assessment are; no matter how well equipped the resource library; the fact remains that if adults have psychological barriers or faulty belief systems about themselves, the work world, or the transition process, and these barriers are left uncovered, the progress of these adults will be slow to nonexistent.*

options more fully and make a decision among them—that was six months ago. The Dean noted Karen's lack of progress and again referred her to career counseling, this time at another college in the area. This time the counselor didn't focus on Karen's interest or skills, and didn't seem as concerned about finding the appropriate match. This time the counselor focused on Karen's core beliefs about herself and the world of work. The counselor assessed Karen's psychological resources and barriers in this career transition. Karen's counselor determined that Karen had virtually no belief in her ability to be successful either in college, or in a profession following college. She had no role models from her own background who had accomplished this and she had never been encouraged to pursue any higher goals. Karen also worried about the impact this transition would have on her marriage and the self-esteem of her husband who had not completed high school.

Karen is one of the 40-million Americans currently in some form of career transition. A large number of factors are causing adults like Karen and her husband to reevaluate their lives and career plans. Large scale changes in our society, such as the change from a manufacturing, goods producing, industrial base to an information and service oriented society, has affected the lives of millions of Americans. Some of these changes are involuntary while others are voluntary, involving adults going back to school for their own personal growth, for career advancement or change. Whatever the reason for the career transition, the fact remains that with the change comes a critical need for greater understanding of the adult-career-transitions process. Up until recently, career planning was viewed as happening in adolescence: choices were made, a life structure was set in motion and that was that. Many of our existing theories of career choice or career maturity are based on that premise. Subsequently, relatively little is known about the factors particularly relevant to adults in career transition.

Of central importance is the issue of what factors affect career transitions in adults. It is evident to practitioners that there are individual differences in an adult's ability to move through the career reevaluation and change process. Some individuals do so with little difficulty while others may continually try, but they never move from where they are to where they want to be. There are a number of external or environmental factors that impact an adult's progress— such as sexism, racism, and ageism—which all affect the structure of opportunity available to adults. These external variables have been written about extensively in both the popular and professional literature. Much less attention has been given to assessing internal, psychological barriers and resources adults bring to the career-transition process.

Reasons for this lack of attention to psychological resources and barriers in the career-transition process have been well documented. The idea that the career-planning process is a streamlined three part process—identifying interests, matching with appropriate occupational information, and making an decision—goes back to Parsons and his 1909 *Choosing a Vocation.* This method still has many strengths today. In cases like Karen's, however, the importance of also examining psychological issues that may be obstacles to this three-part progression is critical. Although we frequently read of the importance of not dichotomizing personal counseling and career counseling (Hackett, 1993), Karen's story personifies the danger in doing so.

No matter how effective the counselor is in assessing skills, interests, and work-related values; no matter how psychometrically sound the instruments used to make this assessment are; no matter how well equipped the resource library; the fact remains that if adults have psychological barriers or faulty belief systems about themselves, the work world, or the transition process, and these barriers are left uncovered, the progress of these adults will be slow to nonexistent. It is the role of the career counselor to help clients recognize their beliefs, barriers, and resources; to build on their strengths and find ways of countering their barriers. Only then will dreams start becoming realities.

Although the field of career development has developed numerous psychometrically sound measures to assess career interests, values, and skills, there have been, until recently, no measures designed to help clients assess and understand internal, dynamic psychological processes that may get in the way of the career-transition process. Two recent instruments appear to hold promise in this area. Krumboltz's Career Beliefs Inventory (1988) and Heppner's Career Transitions Inventory (1994). These instruments will be briefly described and recommendations will be provided for their use with adults.

The Career Transition Inventory (CTI; Heppner, 1991) is a 40-item, Likert-type instrument designed to assess an individual's internal process variables that may serve as strengths or barriers when making a career transition. The responses of the items range between 1 (strongly agree) and 6 (strongly disagree). Factor analytic studies revealed five factors: (a) Career Motivation (Readiness), (b) Self-Efficacy (Confidence), (c) Social Support, (d) Internal/External (Control) and (e) Self vs. Relational Focus (Independence-Interdependence). High scores are positive and indicate that the person is perceiving him/herself to be doing well in that area, low scores indicate barriers.

Career Beliefs Inventory (CBI; Krumboltz, 1988). This tool reports to measure "beliefs that block people from achieving their career goals" (Krumboltz, 1988, p. 1). The inventory contains 96 items, answered on a 5-point rating scale from "strongly agree" to "strongly disagree." It yields 25 scales plus an Administrative Index to estimate response accuracy. These 25 scales are organized under 5 headings: *My Current Career Situation, What Seems Necessary for My Happiness, Factors that Influence My Decisions, Changes I Am Willing to Make, and Effort I Am Willing to Initiate.*

What both of these instruments have in common is that they provide a vehicle for understanding the assumptions and perceptions that individuals hold about themselves and the work world. Whether these constructs are referred to as psychological resources (Heppner, 1991), or beliefs (Krumboltz, 1991) these instruments seek to provide information to the counselor and client about how clients are perceiving their world. This awareness is the first step in trying to target specific interventions. These instruments serve both the purpose of deepening the career counseling process and of giving the client and the counselor a common language.

In Karen's situation, she was administered the CTI. Through this assessment, she indicated that she had extremely low self-efficacy beliefs, and extremely low social support. Her independence score was also low. Her readiness and control were moderate. Thus, through this assessment the counseling sessions could be much more targeted to understanding Karen's barriers and building on her strengths. For example, from the theoretically rich and practically useful work of Hackett and Betz (1981), and the numerous researchers who have built on their seminal work, we now have strong evidence that self-efficacy beliefs are critical to individuals' persistence and successful accomplishment of career-related tasks. Since Karen's self-efficacy beliefs were low, her counselor worked with her on setting small goals and having success experiences in accomplishing them. This kind of "performance attainment" along with appropriate modeling and verbal reinforcement are specific, targeted interventions which may be vitally important to promoting Karen's progress in her career transition. Her counselor also was able to challenge her belief system that she could not "rise above her station" as Karen put it, without bringing about negative consequences in her marriage. In counseling, Karen also developed ways of gaining more social support in her new locale.

In essence, in using Karen's story as an example of one adult in career transition, it is illustrative of the need to help clients as whole people, complete with the full range of psychological strengths and barriers, faulty beliefs and intertwined personal and professional lives. We must move beyond the sole use of matching to a more complex understanding of the unique dynamics that both promote and limit adults' self-actualization.

References

Hackett, G. (1993). Career counseling and psychotherapy: False dichotomies and recommended remedies. *Journal of Career Assessment, 1,* 105-117.

Hackett, G., & Betz, N. E. (1981). A self-efficacy approach to the career development of women. *Journal of Vocational Behavior, 18,* 326-339.

Heppner, M. J., Multon, K. D., & Johnston, J. A. (1994). Assessing psychological resources during career change: The development of the career transitions inventory. *Journal of Vocational Behavior, 44,* 55-74.

Krumboltz, J. (1988). *The Career Beliefs Inventory.* Palo Alto, CA: Consulting Psychologist Press.

Parsons, F. (1909). *Choosing a vocation.* Boston: Houghton Mifflin.

35

Impact Therapy and Career Development Groups

Ed Jacobs

Group counseling is seen as a valuable means of working with clients in treatment centers, abuse shelters, schools, etc., but many counselors have not considered the value of groups for career development issues. Groups can be a helpful tool in career development because members can gain valuable information by sharing, exploring, and hearing others talk about career choice and adjustment to the world of work (Davis & Horne, 1986; Herr & Cramer, 1992; Perovich & Mierzwa, 1980). In this brief article, I focus on an Impact Therapy approach to leading effective career development groups.

Impact Therapy is a multi-sensory approach to counseling which advocates active participation on the part of the counselor. Impact Therapy encourages the leader to generate and build interest and hold, shift, and deepen the focus of the group. It is the leader's responsibility to cut off and draw out members and to try to make the sessions interesting, helpful, and thought provoking. Impact Therapy states that counseling should be clear, concrete,

> *Three of the main tenets of Impact Therapy are "People don't mind being led when they are led well," "Group counseling should never be boring," and "The group leader is primarily responsible for what goes on in the group."*

and engaging. Three of the main tenets of Impact Therapy are "People don't mind being led when they are led well," "Group counseling should never be boring," and "The group leader is primarily responsible for what goes on in the group" (Jacobs, 1994b, pp. 8-9).

The PPFF Map

To be an effective leader, one must be able to organize what he or she is doing. I use the PPFF map (**Purpose, Plan, Focus, Funnel**) to give me this organization.

Purpose. The leader must be clear as to the purpose of the group— career exploration, career awareness, or job hunting— each has a different purpose (Herr & Cramer, 1992). Probably the biggest mistake when leading groups is the lack of clarity of purpose. The leader needs to be clear when setting up the group and screening potential members since members with very different needs can cause the group dynamics to be such that the group cannot be successful. Once the purpose is clear, the leader then plans a group that is interesting, using information from the many theories, inventories, and tests that have been set forth by career development experts.

Plan. Another major mistake with career groups is the leader does not take time to plan each session in detail. Career groups absolutely should be planned. This insures that the leader has a good idea as to what he or she is trying to cover in any given session. The warm-up phase should be planned to last from 3-10 minutes. Time should be allocated for the closing phase, which should also last from 3-10 minutes, depending on the purpose of the group and the length of the session. The middle, or working phase, should be planned to last the majority of the time. I suggest that leaders write out their plans and have estimated times for the various activities so that they have a good sense of how time will be spent in a given session. By writing out plans, the leaders can clarify what they are trying to accomplish during the session and how they are going to focus and funnel the session.

Focus and Funnel. In order to be effective in a career development group, the leader needs to concentrate on important issues such as peer influence, job skills, or work stress. The leader should always try to focus the session on meaningful material. Many leaders make the mistake of letting the group members try to focus the group and thus it never happens. Funneling in a group refers to really zeroing in on an issue or a person so that there is impact. Impact occurs when a member, or many of the members, feel they have learned something or gained some new insight. In different groups I have led, members have talked about how much their parents play a part in their decisions about work; how much they worry about approval at work; how little satisfaction they get from their careers; and how they want to change careers but are afraid. Funneling these topics tends to have impact. Too often, groups never focus and funnel because the leader allows the group to drift along, hoping that it will go deeper, or, when it is going to a more meaningful level, the leader allows a member or members to shift the focus, thus preventing funneling to an impactful level.

Skills for More Impactful Groups

Below, I briefly discuss a number of exercises and leadership skills that can be utilized to maximize the benefits of your career development groups. In another publication, *Group Counseling: Strategies and Skills* (Jacobs, Harvill, & Masson, 1994a), I discuss in great detail these and many other creative exercises that can be valuable in career development groups.

Use of written exercises. Written exercises help members focus on a task; everyone has answers or conclusions they can comment on as a result of completing some written scale, test, or inventory (Herr & Cramer, 1992). One important skill is finding material that fits the purpose of the group and is interesting for the members. There are many different scales, tests, and inventories that can be easily integrated into a group format. Other written exercises that are valuable include sentence completion exercises or making lists of such things as personal characteristics, possible jobs, or fears.

Use of Rounds. The round is the most useful tool that I use in leading groups because it gets everyone to talk and yet does not allow for anyone to take over the group. The round is an exercise where everyone is asked to respond with a word, a phrase, or a brief comment. The response can range from some aspect of a written exercise or question the leader might want discussion on such as, "In a word or a phrase, how has your progress been regarding your career search?" or "What are two things you have learned from the interest inventory?" By using the round, members are involved because they are sharing and they get to hear other members' comments. By hearing members' comment, the leader then can assess the members' energy, trouble spots, commonalities, etc. Rounds can be used effectively in assessing who wants to work on some issue by simply saying: "Let's do a round or 'yes' or 'no' if there is something you want to work on regarding your factors in seeking a career." This helps the leader learn if anyone has some issue he or she wants to discuss in group. A 1-10 round regarding job satisfaction can be very helpful. The round can be one of the easiest, quickest, and best ways for locating and building energy in a session.

Movement exercises. If the leader is not careful, some career groups can become rather slow moving or boring. Therefore, movement exercises can be extremely valuable in that they are energizing. I refer to movement exercises as any activity that has members out of their seats. (I am not referring to forms of dance therapy or yoga, which are valid movement exercises but usually not relevant for career development groups.) There are a number of movement exercises that can be helpful.

Progress toward goals: Members line up side by side and are asked to then move forward as much as they feel they are making progress in reference to the goals (career choice, getting a job) they set for themselves at the beginning of the group. This tends to get members focused on the idea of progress and how far they have come and how far they have to go.

Difficulties in reaching your goals: This is a good exercise for members to experience the obstacles in the way of their career path and the difficulty in reaching their career goals. Members line up on two sides facing each other about 4 feet apart. One person steps out of the line and goes to the front and looks down the space created by the members. The member is asked to envision their goals as being at the other end and tell the other members how she sees her road to her goals—such as "it is going to be very hard at first, then easy, then hard again"— so the other members can step in the way and simulate the experience. Since this is an active, somewhat rigorous exercise you will need to caution the members about this. If members know each other well, they can add verbal comments that are appropriate, such as playing the part of some family members or friends or the voice of fears and doubts in her head. The leader may want to let everyone do the exercise and then discuss the many things that come up or the leader may want to allow one person to move through the land and then focus and funnel on that person, then proceed to the next person.

Value lines: A very simple but useful movement exercise is to have members line up in the center of the room behind one another and then designate the wall on their right as one thing and the wall on their left as another. I then ask the members to move to the spot that best represents how they feel, seeing the space between the walls as a continuum. Some examples that I use are:

Winner .... Loser
Big City .... Small town
Work with few people .... Work with lots of people
Leader.. Follower
Lots of variety .... Routine tasks

Having members move along the continuum usually energizes the members and much discussion is generated.

Processing exercises. The most important skill in using exercises is the processing of them. Exercises are used to generate discussion or to get members more focused on some particular issue or aspect of their personality. Any exercise that is conducted should have a purpose and the leader should try to process the exercise so that their is some lasting impact for the members. Too often leaders let the discussion after an exercise drift along and do not focus and funnel the discussion to a meaningful level. It is absolutely essential that the leader have in mind how to use the exercise in a meaningful way and what issues may be brought up, focused on, and funneled.

Cutting off. To be effective, a leader must be able to cut off members and direct the discussion to more meaningful topics or to different members (Jacobs, Harvill, & Masson, 1994a). If I were asked what is the hardest thing for most group leaders to learn, I would say it is the ability to cut off members in a timely and appropriate manner. Far too often, due to fear of hurting members' feelings, leaders do not cut off dominating members or discussion that is irrelevant or boring. In my career groups I tell my members during the first session that one of my responsibilities as a leader is to monitor the flow of discussion and, therefore, there will be times that I may have to cut off some stories or discussion.

Summary

Career development groups can be quite valuable if they are led well. The leader needs to be active and know the purpose of the group. A good map to use is the PPFF map which gives organization to any group that is led. PPFF emphasizes the importance of purpose, planning, focusing, and funneling each session so that there is impact. The leader should feel that it is his or her responsibility to energize the group and make it as interesting as possible. A number of ways to do this is by using written activities, rounds, and movement exercises. Two essential leadership skills are cutting-off members when it is appropriate and processing exercises so they are meaningful.

References

Davis, R. C., & Horne, A. M. (1986). The effects of small group counseling and a career course on career decidedness and maturity. *Vocational Guidance Quarterly, 34,* 255-262.

Herr, E. L., & Cramer, S. H. (1992). *Career guidance and counseling through the lifespan* (4th ed.). New York: Harper Collins.

Jacobs, E. E., Harvill, R. L., & Masson, R. L. (1994a). *Group counseling: strategies and skills* (2nd ed.). Pacific Grove, CA: Brooks/Cole.

Jacobs, E. E. (1994b). *Impact therapy.* Odessa, FL: Psychological Assessment Resources.

Perovich, G. M., & Mierzwa, J. A. (1980). Group facilitation of vocational maturity and self-esteem in college students. *Journal of College Student Personnel, 21,* 206-211.

36

Negative Thinking and Career Choice

James P. Sampson, Jr., Gary W. Peterson
Janet G. Lenz, Robert C. Reardon
Denise E. Saunders

For many years counselors have noticed that some individuals experience great difficulty in making career choices. In counseling, some clients do not make good use of assessment and career information resources. As a result, these clients fail to benefit fully from career counseling services offered to them. By identifying clients who are likely to experience difficulty in career choice, counselors can assess client needs effectively and design specific strategies to remove barriers to effective career problem-solving and decision-making.

This led us to explore the literature on how negative thinking influences career choices. We identified numerous misconceptions, self-defeating assumptions, myths, private rules, self-defeating statements, irrational expectations, dysfunctional cognitions, and dysfunctional career beliefs that were identified from research and counseling practice

This article explores how theory and research were used in a career center to develop career counseling resources to help clients identify, challenge, and alter negative career thoughts. Based on our experience, recommendations for practice with various types of clients are provided.

Identifying, Challenging, and Altering Negative Career Thoughts

Here at the Florida State University Career Center, we noticed that as many as one-third of the clients seeking assistance appeared to have difficulty in benefiting from our career counseling and information services. For example, some clients struggled in responding to assessment items. Other clients did not make good use of career information resources, even when modeling and follow-up support were available. Some clients found it difficult to assume responsibility for decision making, expressed considerable dependency on others, or expected "magical" or "quick" answers to complex and long-standing problems. Finally, some clients consistently failed to follow through on mutually agreed upon career-exploration activities.

Instead of assuming that the clients were simply "not motivated to change" or "not ready,"we chose to take a more proactive approach. We decided to apply a theory-based approach to deal with this problem. Using Holland's theory, we experimented with the Identity scale of My Vocational Situation (MVS; Holland, Daiger, & Power, 1980) to identify clients with low vocational identity who would likely need additional assistance to make effective use of our career services. Vocational identity involves clarity and stability of self perceptions and decision-making confidence (Holland, et al., 1980). We began to allocate our more time-intensive and costly interventions, such as individual counseling or a career-planning course, to clients with low vocational identity.

Although encouraged, we still believed that there was something missing from our services. In an attempt to improve further the effectiveness of our career services, we broadened the theoretical basis of the Center to include a cognitive information processing (CIP) approach to career problem solving and decision making (Peterson, Sampson, & Reardon, 1991). This approach involves using two key concepts—the pyramid of information processing domains and the CASVE cycle—to help clients and counselors better understand career problem-solving and decision-making and, as a result, make more effective use of counseling services offered through the Center.

The pyramid of information processing domains answers the question, "What do clients lack in the essential components of career problem-solving?" This includes: 1) self-knowledge, 2) occupational knowledge, 3) decision-making skills, and 4) metacognitions (self-talk, self-awareness, and control and monitoring). The CASVE cycle provides a guide to the decision-making process and includes the following: 1) realizing that a problem exists that needs to be solved *(communication)*, 2) understanding the nature of the problem and potential solutions *(analysis)*, 3) expanding and narrowing alternatives *(synthesis)*, 4) choosing an alternative that optimizes costs and benefits *(valuing)*, and 5) following through with the actions needed to implement a choice *(execution)*. In addition to helping clients make a current career choice, the CIP approach attempts to enhance clients' problem-solving and decision-making skills to help clients better cope with the inevitable career changes that will occur in the future (Peterson, et al., 1991).

The CIP approach led us to pay more attention to all facets of career problem-solving and decision-making, namely, self-knowledge, occupational knowledge, decision-making skills, and metacognitions. According to the theory, career decision-making effectiveness is directly related to client awareness and to control of self-talk about self-knowledge, occupational knowledge, and decision-making ability. As we listened more carefully to clients who were experiencing difficulty making career decisions, we noticed that these clients verbalized considerably more negative self-talk.

This led us to explore the literature on how negative thinking influences career choices. We identified numerous misconceptions, self-defeating assumptions, myths, private rules, self-defeating statements, irrational expectations, dysfunctional cognitions, and dysfunctional career beliefs that were identified from research and counseling practice (Sampson, Peterson, Lenz, Reardon, & Saunders, 1994). This literature suggested that negative thinking among some clients was a major barrier to effective career decision-making.

We then developed a 30-item card sort of dysfunctional career thoughts. Each card had a dysfunctional thought on one side and a reframed (more appropriate) statement on the reverse side. Clients sorted the cards in terms of how much they agreed with each statement. When clients indicated they agreed with a statement, they were asked to read the reframing statement to challenge their thinking and then discuss their thinking with their counselor. In this way, the client and the counselor collaboratively worked to remove cognitive barriers to career problem-solving and decision-making.

Our experience with the card sort indicated that clients were able to identify and challenge their negative thinking. We had two concerns, however, about using the card sort. First, the process was time consuming for the counselor, which restricted the number of clients who could use this approach and limited the utility of this resource for client screening. Second, we were concerned that the card sort did not adequately cover all of the key aspects of career problem solving and decision making.

We decided to improve the cost-effectiveness of our assessment of dysfunctional career thoughts by creating a brief paper-and-pencil instrument that could be quickly administered, hand scored, and immediately interpreted. Potential items were generated from two sources. First, we generated a total of 248 items across all domains of the Cognitive Information Processing model (Peterson, Sampson, & Reardon, 1991). This procedure maximized the likelihood that key aspects of career problem-solving and decision-making were included. Second, using the literature on dysfunctional career thinking to sensitize us to important issues, we noted negative statements made by our clients and then categorized the potential items according to the theory. The final 48 items were selected on the basis of psychometric quality, lack of bias concerning gender, ethnicity, and social desirability, and the capacity to differentiate clients from non-clients (Sampson, Peterson, Lenz, Reardon, & Saunders, 1994).

The resulting Career Thoughts Inventory (CTI; Sampson, Peterson, Lenz, Reardon, & Saunders, in press) is a measure of dysfunctional career thinking. While dysfunctional thinking in career problem-solving and decision-making cannot be measured directly, it can be inferred from an individual's responses to test items that reflect dysfunctional career thoughts.

> Career thoughts are defined as outcomes of one's thinking about behaviors, beliefs, feelings, plans, and/or strategies related to career problem solving and decision making. Regardless of whether CTI items refer to behaviors, beliefs, feelings, plans, and/or strategies, all items reflect dysfunctional

thinking that inhibits effective career problem solving and decision making (Sampson, et al., 1994, p. 2).

The CTI is designed to be used for *screening* and *needs assessment,* as well as a *learning* resource for the client. By using the CTI as a regular part of the counseling intake process for *screening,* the total score can be compared to national and local norms for high school students, college students, and adults so as to identify which clients are likely to experience more problems in career problem-solving and decision-making. These clients can then be provided with the additional help they need in making career choices. Individual items can be discussed with the client for *needs assessment* (or diagnosis) to determine the specific nature of dysfunctional thinking. Then, specific interventions can be recommended to reduce problems in career choice.

One of the recommendations we make to our clients is to complete "Improving Your Career Thoughts: A Workbook for the Career Thoughts Inventory." This workbook is used as a *learning* resource to help clients identify, challenge, and alter negative thoughts that impair career problem-solving and decision-making; clients then take concrete action to follow through with career choice. The workbook is based on the assumption that career cognitions can be modified through learning (Keller, Biggs, & Gysbers, 1982). The workbook adopts a typical approach to cognitive restructuring used in counseling. Corbishley and Yost (1989) observed that interventions for dysfunctional cognitions involve evaluations both of the "old" cognition and of less dysfunctional "new" beliefs. CTI items help to provide a source for "old" dysfunctional career thoughts. After reading reframing stimulus statements contained in the workbook, clients write out new, more appropriate, career thoughts. The workbook also includes the development of an individual action plan. Counselors can help clients disconfirm prior dysfunctional career thoughts by creating and using an individual action plan for career exploration and decision making within the supportive context of a counseling relationship. In order to avoid stereotypical labeling, the term "negative career thoughts" is used in place of "dysfunctional career thoughts" in all client materials.

Our initial experience with the CTI is that clients with higher scores do experience more difficulty in career choice. This observation is supported by preliminary validity data on the instrument. For example, as dysfunctional career thoughts increased, vocational identity and career decidedness decreased (Sampson, et al., 1994). Exploring the specific nature of dysfunctional thinking with clients helps to quickly identify key issues that need to be examined in counseling. Concepts from the CTI, along with ideas drawn from the CIP approach, provided a common language that facilitated communication between clients and counselors. Initial experience with the CTI workbook has also been encouraging. Clients report that they have become more aware of how their negative thinking makes it more difficult to engage in effective problem solving and decision making.

What We Have Learned From Our Experience
The process described above occurred over a period of fifteen years. We can summarize what we have learned to date as follows:
1) Some clients needed more help than others to benefit from our career services. We found that dysfunctional thinking was a key barrier to effective career choice. Improved services were achieved by identifying clients with barriers early in the counseling process and then helping them to recognize, challenge, and alter the negative thoughts that impaired their career problem-solving and decision-making, and take concrete action to follow through with career choice.
2) The professional literature provided a wealth of information, wisdom, and divergent opinions that helped to stimulate our critical thinking about the effectiveness of our services and about potential options for innovation and improvement.
3) Theory improved our practice by providing a concise model for understanding how to redesign and evaluate our services, as well as for guiding the development of assessment and learning resources for clients and training materials for staff. Also, since no single theory is totally sufficient for guiding service delivery, an integration of several theories was most practical and effective.

4) The changes that we initiated have taken time and resources to achieve positive results. Some changes were successful and were incorporated into our services, while other changes were not cost-effective and were dropped. Also, the ultimate success of our innovations was directly proportional to the quality of our staff training.

Recommendations

Given what we have learned from our experience, we recommend the following:

1) Screen clients for barriers to career problem-solving and decision-making prior to recommending career assessment or career information resources. If dysfunctional career thoughts are a barrier, help clients to: a) understand the nature and impact of their negative thinking; b) identify, challenge, and alter their most problematic negative thoughts; and c) take action to follow through with career choice, which can further disconfirm their prior dysfunctional career thoughts.

2) Use the professional literature as a foundation for critically evaluating and improving the delivery of career services.

3) Integrate several theories that are compatible with staff beliefs and experience to assist with program design and evaluation and the development of local resources for clients and staff.

4) Balance the willingness to innovate with an understanding that effective change is built step by step with regular staff input and training.

References

Corbishley, M. A., & Yost, E. B. (1989). Assessment and treatment of dysfunctional cognitions in career counseling. *Career Planning and Adult Development Journal, 5(*3), 20-26.

Holland, J. L., Daiger, D. C., & Power, G. (1980). *My vocational situation.* Palo Alto, CA: Consulting Psychologists Press.

Keller, K. E., Biggs, D. A., Gysbers, N. C. (1982). Career counseling from a cognitive perspective. *The Personnel and Guidance Journal, 60,* 367-371.

Peterson, G. W., Sampson, J. P., Jr., & Reardon, R. C. (1991). *Career development and services: A cognitive approach.* Pacific Grove, CA: Brooks/Cole.

Sampson, J. P., Jr., Peterson, G. W., Lenz, J. G., Reardon, R. C., & Saunders, D. E. (in press). *Career Thoughts Inventory.* Odessa, FL: Psychological Assessment Resources, Inc.

Sampson, J. P., Jr., Peterson, G. W., Lenz, J. G., Reardon, R. C., & Saunders, D. E. (1994). *Career Thoughts Inventory: Professional manual [research edition].* Odessa, FL: Psychological Assessment Resources, Inc.

37

The High School Transition Process

Albert J. Pautler

In this essay I describe some of my recent research and work dealing with high school graduates' transition to the next phase of their lives. Some of my ideas have resulted from the influence of writers whose work appeared in *High School to Employment Transition: Contemporary Issues* (Pautler, 1994).

The report of the William T. Grant Foundation (1988) *The Forgotten Half: Non-College Youth in America* had a major impact on my present program of research and interest. This report clearly spelled out the difficulties experienced by the so called "forgotten half" (really the forgotten 70%) who will go through life with less than a college degree. This report is must reading for those interested in the plight of the non-college graduate in the United States.

> *I argue that all high school graduates need equal attention in their transition to the next phases of their lives. School districts need to consider a management plan that will report to the community the transition plans of all high school graduates.*

A simple framework for analysis of the transition process from high school follows. Upon graduation most graduates will exit in one of the following ways: some graduates will go on to further education; some will enter military service; some will enter employment. and the remaining graduates will flow into the pool of the unemployed or underemployed. These are rather traditional exit points for most high school graduates. This process is described in some of my earlier work (Pautler, 1994a).

This essay describes four major areas of immediate concern to school-to-work (STW) transition, work-based learning, and career education and development. These four themes are as follows:

1. How do they exit your school?
2. School transition follow-up studies;
3. Countdown to graduation;
4. The handover process

Discussion

In this section I describe the four major themes to be developed in this essay. I would encourage you to give serious consideration to these themes and perhaps engage in further development and research in these areas.

How Do They Exit Your School

My framework for analysis of how graduates exit from high school is simple. High school graduates exit school in one of three basic ways: (1) Some graduates will go on to further education including community college, college, trade and technical schools, universities, etc.; (2) Some graduates will seek and enter employment upon graduation from high school (this includes the military); (3) Others may flow into the pool of the unemployed for either a short or long term stay.

Most high schools like to report data in June, July, and August about the college entrance rates of their recent graduates. In the area in which I live it is not uncommon to see percentages of 70 to 95% going on to further education. Seldom are mentioned the remaining 5 to 30% not included in the college-bound group. I find this to be improper—mention should be made of the transition plans of all graduates.

I argue that all high school graduates need equal attention in their transition to the next phases of their lives. School districts need to consider a management plan that will report to the community the transition plans of all high school graduates.

Most will agree that the K-12 school curriculum is mainly directed and focused on the preparation of graduates for further education, mainly college programs. Two exceptions may exist: One is for those students who select a vocational education program, which may include tech-prep programs. The other is for special education students who are required by law to have a school transition plan.

I encourage school personnel to give serious attention to the normal exit program for high school graduates. Several things should be considered in this discussion and three ideas follow.

School Transition Follow-up Studies

In recent years I have been involved in the development and refinement of high school graduate follow-up studies. I argue that *all school districts* should develop an empirical data base of the school transition experiences of high school graduates. What I have in mind is much more than the senior year plans of those about to graduate in June.

When I speak or write about this most people ask, "What about the dropouts?" I respond, " I am interested in what happens to high school dropouts. Dropouts need help and attention. My interest is focused on the high school graduates. Someone else needs to demonstrate concern for the dropouts." Just let me attempt to deal with that group which may be considered the forgotten 70% of the high school graduates.

National statistical data indicates that 25 % of persons over age 25 have competed an associate degree, bachelor degree, or higher professional degree. Within this 25%, about 6% have associate degrees. Therefore, I feel on rather safe ground to state that in the United States about 25 percent of the population over age 25 has an associate degree or higher. (U.S. Department of Commerce, 1993)

The New York State Education Department (1994) reports that about 85% of the 1992 high school graduates entered some form of institution of higher education. These institutions include four-year and two-year degree granting and other postsecondary programs.

The point is a wide gap exists in those who report going on to some form of further education and those completing degree-based programs. It appears that about 75% of the U.S. population will go through life without a two- or four-year degree.

Based upon the previous facts, I argue that all school districts should attempt to develop a follow-up system that follows recent graduates for at least two years after graduation and preferably for four years. The two-year system will at least give some indication of those who complete a two-year associate degree or the first two years of college. This should provide the district with some empirical data on student transition experiences, including those attending college, entering employment, entering the military, or *flowing into the pool of the unemployed.*

I have been involved in two major projects dealing with school transition studies. The Cheektowaga Transition Study involved four school districts over a three-year period of time. This was followed by a multi-district study, involving ten school districts, which followed a random sample of graduates one and two years after school completion.

I have come to the conclusion that the best way to do such studies is by taking a random sample of 25% of the graduates from the entire class two years after graduation. I have learned not to waste time or resources by mailed surveys. Use telephone survey techniques. The best time for data collection is during the college winter break or during the summer. You may want to try a stratified random sample such as we did in New York. We used a sample of Regents' diploma, high school diploma, and vocational completers for our sample population. It seemed to work well for us.

The data can be helpful in feeding information back to the school-improvement team, TQM committee, and curriculum committee. The basic idea is to improve the curriculum for future students.

Countdown to Graduation

Recently I was asked to serve on a school-to-work (STW) funded Workforce Preparation program for the Buffalo (NY) Public Schools. The grant was for about $300,000 and involved four out of some 70 schools in the school district. It was a pilot project for one year and involved a K-5 school, a 6-8 school, and two high schools.

It is difficult, if not impossible, to make many changes in a school system of some 48,000 students during a one-year program. Of course the idea is to seek additional funding for more years and more schools. This project involved several partners including the local community college, Erie County Community College.

For such a short-term project I argued for the development of some system of school transition. Each and every high school graduate should be turned over to some next agency upon graduation. In order to put such a plan in operation it was first necessary to make plans for the transition of the graduates. I wrote a plan that I called *Countdown to Graduation* that could be implemented between January and June of 1995 for the graduates of June 1995.

This was a six-month plan, due to the circumstances of the grant and time frame. It is a start only. The Countdown involved students, faculty, staff, and parents. During each month an activity took place to assist *all* those planning to graduate in making their transition to the next phase of their lives. This involved further education, employment, and the U.S. military.

Ideally, the countdown to graduation from high school should begin with the entry point into high school. It may be that this is already the goal and function of the guidance staff within the school. It does appear that those students planning to go on to further education upon high school graduation are given much greater attention than those not planning on further education. I believe that *all* students deserve equal attention in preparation for high school graduation.

The Handover Process

The fourth and final theme of this essay is concerned with the handover process and the handover card. I argue that every high school graduate should be handed over to some next agency upon graduation from high school. For lack of better words, I suggest that each high school graduate be issued some form of handover card in addition to the high school diploma.

In years past, the high school diploma, served as this handover card. The high school diploma was the "formal" document guiding the graduate into the workforce or some form of further education. I am no longer sure that this is any longer the case. I suggest that school districts attempt to put in place a formal process of handing over the graduate to some next agency. This would involve serious discussion about the handover process and the development of some type of handover card.

Most high schools are viewed as places to prepare for further education—college. That group of graduates going on to college and accepted prior to high school graduation are handed over to the various colleges that they plan to attend. This includes all types of formal education: community colleges; private trade and technical schools; and apprenticeships.

Those graduates planning to enter employment and accepted for full time employment are handed over to the employer. In this category I include those graduates entering the United States military upon high school graduation.

It is the last group that presents the most problems. Those graduates not going on to further education, entering the military, or obtaining full-time employment are most likely to flow into the pool of the unemployed. It is this group that is most in need of further services upon exiting from high school. The problem is what services are available and who can provide those services.

I suggest three possible courses of action for this group of graduates. First, that prior to graduation these students be taken to the local office of the State Employment Agency and encouraged to register for employment. Second, that arrangements be made with local community colleges to assume the future advisement role for these high school graduates. Third, that the school district inform the graduates that the high school guidance staff is available for help. In some districts this role is provided by the adult education evening school program.

Students, now graduates, should not just be turned out into the world and allowed to sink or swim. Each graduate should be turned over to some next agency for additional help, support, and encouragement. Some form of handover process or handover card may be of help in this effort.

Summary

I have attempted to deal with the topic of high school transition based upon four major themes. These themes were concerned with exit theory, follow-up studies of graduates, countdown to graduation, and the handover process. Each of the four themes was described in some limited detail based upon the length of this essay.

I would encourage interested readers to expand on these four themes to meet the individual needs of their own organizations. The process of school transition is based upon years of research on career and vocational development and is not designed to be a short-term solution to issues of school transition.

In closing, I believe that each school district must have an empirical database on the transition experiences of their graduates. I believe that each school district should have a system of guidance services for *all graduates* not just those going on to further education. I believe that *each high school graduate should* be handed over to some next agency upon high school graduation. What do you believe?

References

Grant Foundation. (1988). *The forgotten half: Non-college youth in america.* Washington: The William T. Grant Foundation.

New York State Education Department. (1994). *New York state statistical yearbook.* Albany, NY: New York State Education Department.

Pautler, A. (1994). *High school to employment transition: Contemporary issues.* Ann Arbor, MI: Prakken.

Pautler, A. (1994a). How do they exit your school? *Tech Directions, 53*(4), 34-35.

U.S. Department of Commerce. (1993). *Decennial census, minority economic profiles.* Washington, DC.

A Look to the Future of Career Development Programs and Practices

Sharon Anderson
Lynne Bezanson
JoAnn Bowlsbey
Larry Burlew
Beth Durodoyne
Dennis Engels
H.B. Gelatt
Bryan Heibert
Carolyn Kern
Juliet Miller
Howard Splete
Garry Walz

38

Career Counseling: An Emotionally Intimate Relationship Requiring Ethical Consideration

Sharon K. Anderson

Introduction

In career counseling there continues to be a growing concern and interest with professional ethics. The career counseling literature has included discussions of various topics as they relate to ethics (Engels, Minor, Sampson, Splete, 1995; Hafer, 1992; Schmeiser, 1995; Spokane, 1991). These topics include: pressure to carry a large case load; testing, instrument choice, and administration; release of information; fees; competence; referrals; confidentiality and limits of confidentiality; advertising; and cultural differences. However, there is little if any discussion concerning ethics and the relationship between the career counselor and client.

> *The client invites the career counselor to participate in overt or covert exploration of these intimate issues of life. Career counselors are responsible to maintain an ethical relationship with their clients in the midst of this exploratory process.*

This omission is interesting in light of the National Career Development Association (NCDA)Ethical Standards. The standard encourages career counselors to be "...aware of the intimacy in the counseling relationship..." (NCDA Ethical Standards, 1994). One possible reason for this omission could be that career counseling is merely perceived as a nonpersonal, cognitive process that involves intellectual exploration of career options. The session(s) include a discussion of outcomes from assessments, identifying skills and interests, and exploring training and career options. This description of the interaction sounds rather sterile and null and void of any intimacy between the client and career counselor.

A more likely reason for this gap in the literature could be that certain aspects of the career counseling relationship (i.e., the personal and intimate aspects) have not received their due attention. Indeed, career counselors may experience the counselor-client relationship as personal; yet, the relationship, in contrast to other counseling relationships, may seem impersonal and less than intimate. For example, it may be easier to perceive of intimacy occurring if the client has a cathartic moment during a personal counseling session. Although there may not be a cathartic moment, the interaction between the career counselor and client does include a level of intimacy similar to other counseling relationships. When clients investigate career options they are really exploring core issues such as belief systems and values; personal development and identity; and investment of self in society. In addition they are deciding upon a future lifestyle that in turn can impact relationships.

Engels et al. (1995) suggest career counseling explores "such concerns as self-understanding; broadening one's horizons; work selection, challenge, satisfaction, and other intrapersonal matters;...communication, and other interpersonal phenomena; and lifestyle issues..." (p. 134). The client invites the career counselor to participate in overt or covert exploration of these intimate issues of life. Career counselors are responsible to maintain an ethical relationship with their clients in the midst of this exploratory process. The potential intimacy in the relationship and ethical behavior on the part of the career counselor are an important part of the career counseling process and need to be addressed. Therefore, the purpose of this paper is three fold: 1) to highlight and address (through two case scenarios) the intimate nature of the career counseling relationship and the importance of ethical relationships with clients, 2) to provide a brief discussion of ethical principles as they relate to the career counseling relationship and form a foundation for ethical relationships with career clients, and 3) to discuss training issues to better prepare career counselors to establish and maintain ethical relationships with clients.

Case Scenarios

As previously stated, intimacy between the client and career counselor can occur on an overt or covert level. The following two case scenarios illustrate the intimacy that can occur in the client-career counselor relationship. Identifying client information has been changed to maintain client confidentiality.

In the first case scenario a Hispanic couple was referred to the author for career counseling. The husband was thinking of a career change. He was in his mid 40s and had been making a lucrative income until the last few years. The wife, also in her mid 40s, had taken care of the household for a majority of this marriage, but had taken a job outside the home when her husband's income began to dwindle. The job was distantly related to her college degree. During the history intake she explained that she obtained her college degree some 20 years ago after her first marriage failed. At that time she had herself and a young child to support. The wife's degree was not very marketable and now she was trying to decide if more school was necessary. Both clients completed a battery of assessments. The results of the assessments were discussed. In the process I became aware of each client's deeper core issues. The wife valued a relationship where the husband was the main economic provider. Part of her decision to marry this man was his ability to provide financially for her and her child. She believed this was his responsibility. Both of them recognized that his new career would not be as profitable as his current one. The husband did not value his current career. He felt stifled, almost suffocated, in his present job. He no longer valued the career choice he made in his twenties. He wanted to invest his time and energy in another area that would allow his creativity to bloom. Emotions erupted; the assessment outcomes were no longer the focus. Each client was sharing a deeper part of himself or herself and, as their career counselor, I was invited to be part of this intimate exploration. Sometimes the intimate, deeper issues are tucked away behind the details of skills, interests, and career options.

In a second scenario a young, Caucasian male client was recently relieved of his duties within a world-wide organization. The organization provided one last service: career counseling. In the course of reviewing assessment outcomes, he shared brief yet revealing information about his relationship with his wife and the impact that his career decisions would have on their relationship and her career desires. He no longer valued his experience with this organization and wanted no connection with this system. The organization employed the wife and she wanted to maintain her connection with them. Due to this and other issues, the status of the relationship was uncertain. He displayed no emotion as he shared this. It was clear, however, that he was sharing intimate information about his relationship with his wife. He invited me to help him explore what his career decision meant for different parts of his life.

In these two examples a level of intimacy developed between the clients and myself. They shared intimate aspects of their lives. I heard heartfelt conflicts that centered on career decisions. As previously stated, the NCDA Ethical Standards encourage the career counselor to recognize intimacy in the relationship. Furthermore the Ethical Standards encourage the career counselor to "avoid engaging in activities that seek to meet their personal needs at the expense of the client" (NCDA, 1994). This is important guidance as well. The career counselor is in a position of trust. When a career counselor engages in certain activities to meet personal needs this violates the client's trust and betrays the counseling relationship. For example, in the first case both the husband and wife were sure that finances would be a problem if the husband made this career change. Both agreed however that his new career choice could eventually be very profitable. It was a risk he was willing to take. Hearing their distress, I could have offered them money as a financial investment in the new business. As their career counselor I was aware that the husband needed financial backing to start this new business. The wife was distressed and did not want additional responsibility for the family income. Without much forethought I could have considered my offer an act of kindness. If they had accepted this offer I would have created a dual role relationship between these two clients and myself.

A dual role relationship is a blending of roles that have different obligations and expectations (Kitchener, 1988). For this case I would have had two roles; I would have been in the counselor role and would have been in an investor role and personally/financially interested in the outcome. Whether the outcome was positive or negative these clients would have figuratively "owed me." In this case I would have been financially involved with my clients. In addition I would have placed my personal need to increase my finances over my clients' need to have an objective person help them sort through this difficult decision. My ability to be objective and effective in the career counseling process and relationship would have been hampered if not totally eliminated.

In the second example, I might have been attracted to the client. To act on this attraction and initiate or accept an offer to pursue contact apart from the career counseling relationship would have established a dual role. I could have rationalized this decision by thinking, "We only met once and the main topic was career choice." By this action I would have put my personal needs ahead of my client's professional needs. Again, I would have misused the intimacy in the professional relationship, violated the client's trust, promoted my personal need, and eliminated my ability to stay professionally objective.

Ethical Principles and the Career Counseling Relationship

Counseling relationships involve three key principles: beneficence, nonmaleficence, and fidelity. Beneficence and nonmaleficence are closely related. Beneficence means "doing good for others" and nonmaleficence is defined as "above all do no harm" (Kitchener, 1984, p. 47 & 49). Fidelity translates into "'faithfulness,' promise-keeping, and loyalty" (Kitchener, 1984, p. 50) in a relationship such as a counselor-client relationship. (See Beauchamp& Childress, 1994; Kitchener, 1984 for further elaboration on ethical principles.) Typically, the career client comes voluntarily to counseling expecting that his or her concerns and issues will be the primary focus in the counseling relationship and interaction. Because of this expectation they trust the career counselor with information and details of their lives that then foster intimacy in a professional relationship. The client expects the career counselor to be faithful in the counseling relationship by doing good and not doing harm.

In both case scenarios the clients shared intimate parts of their lives. They came to career counseling expecting that their welfare would be my primary concern. They expected me to act faithfully in my role as career counselor and to do good. In other words, they expected me to uphold ethical principles of beneficence, nonmaleficence and fidelity. I would be able to better fulfill their expectations and my ethical obligations as I stay aware of the trust and intimacy in the relationship and make certain the client needs are foremost in our interaction.

Recommended Course of Action for Training

In training career counselors, faculty and supervisors alike can help students understand the counseling relationship and the ethical issues by discussing three key areas. First, a client and career counselor do have a relationship and many times intimacy will be a characteristic of the relationship. The interaction and the relationship are built on trust and the client expects that the career counselor will do good and be faithful in their professional obligation. Second, dual role relationships can occur in career counseling as well as other types of counseling or therapy. Novice career counselors might assume that one session does not constitute a counseling relationship. In reality, a relationship, whatever type it might be, begins with introductions and intimacy which are part of the counseling interaction. When a dual role relation occurs professional objectivity can be lost, client expectations of the counselor go unmet, and the client's needs are in competition with the counselors needs. Faculty and career counselors in the field must model the importance of keeping professional boundaries. Last, but not least, future career counselors need to understand their code(s) of ethics and use them as guides for ethical behavior (Hafer, 1992).

Conclusion

In summary, career counselors play a special role in the lives of people who receive career counseling. The counseling relationship between the career counselor and client is similar to any other counseling relationship. Clients share intimate details of their lives in the process of exploring career options and making decisions. Career counselors will do well to stay aware of the intimacy in the relationship, maintain their professional role and appropriate boundaries, and keep the client's needs as the primary focus.

References

Beauchamp, T. L., & Childress, J. F. (1989). *Principles of biomedical ethics* (3rd ed.). New York: Oxford University Press.

Engels, D.W., Minor, C. W., Sampson, J. P., & Splete, H. H. (1995). Career Counseling Specialty: History, development, and prospect. *Journal of Counseling and Development, 74,* 134-138.

Hafer, A. (1992). Introduction, potential private practice problems and ethics. In A. Hafer (Ed.), *The nuts And bolts Of career counseling: How to set up and succeed in private practice.* Garrett Park, MD: Garrett Park Press.

Kitchener, K. S. (1984). Intuition, critical evaluation andethical principles: the foundation For ethical decisions in counseling psychology. *The Counseling Psychologist,* 43-55.

Kitchener, K. S. (1988). Dual role relationships: What makes them so problematic? *Journal of Counseling and Development, 67,* 217-221.

National Career Development Association, (1994). Ethical standards. In D. W. Engels (Ed.), *The professional practice Of career counseling and consultation: A resource document* (2nd ed., pp. 26-33). Alexandria, VA: Author. (Reprinted from Ethical Standards, by the National Career Development Association, 1991, Alexandria, VA: Author

Schmeiser, C. B. (1995). Ethics in assessment. *Eric Digest,* EDO-CG-95-23. Greensboro, NC: ERIC/CASS.

Spokane, A. R. (1991). *Career intervention.* Englewood Cliffs, NJ: Prentice-Hall, Inc.

39

Career Development In Canada: An Emerging National Strategy

Lynne Bezanson & Bryan Hiebert

Over the past 10 years there has been growing concern in many segments of Canadian society that young people need better preparation for the transition into adult life. Given the complexity of social issues, the changing nature of work, and a shifting societal structure, many felt that young people need a wider repertoire of skills to navigate the social system and plan their careers. Realizing this, a series of meetings was begun in 1987 that led to a major national initiative for the Creation and Mobilization of Counselling Resources for Youth (CAMCRY). CAMCRY was funded with 7.2 million dollars from the federal government and approximately 9 million dollars of partner contributions, making it the largest counselling research and program development initiative ever undertaken in Canadian history. Through CAMCRY, 41 projects were undertaken at 16 colleges and universities to make a dramatic improvement in the way career counselling was approached with youth.

In the 1990's we are evolving a proactive capacity for collaboration and pulling together. Increasingly, we are inclined to share resources and pool our energies so that consumers have access to quality career and employment counselling and exemplary career development programs.

During the past three years, the Canadian Labour Force Development Board (CLFDB) has commissioned a series of task forces to investigate various issues needed to promote informed decision making. The Report of the Task Force on Transition into

Employment (1994) contained many recommendations pertaining to career counselling. To develop a database to inform policy formation, the CLFDB commissioned a survey of career and employment counselling in Canada (Conger, Hiebert, & Hong-Farrell, 1994). A common finding in both the transition task force report and the survey was that there needed to be a united leadership focus behind career development in all regions of the country. It appeared that many young Canadians were "falling through the cracks" in the social safety net, and comprehensive and coordinated action was needed. In response to these needs, a series of leadership forums on career development was planned and the resulting vision for national leadership emerged.

Career Development: An Emerging
National Strategy

The Need. Massive changes in the labour market—the structure of opportunity, globalization, and the very nature of employment—are leaving our working lives in a state of "permanent flux." Staying with a single employer is now the exception; several careers in different fields are rapidly becoming the new norm. Moving back and forth between education and work is expected, and periods of unemployment are commonplace. These shifts represent enormous changes in the relationships between individuals and organizations, and in the nature of paid work. These changes significantly alter the role career development services need to play.

High school students increasingly need (and parents expect) services which motivate them to complete school and make sound decisions regarding post-secondary training and education. Openness to lifelong learning, increased personal responsibility, flexibility and adaptability, although important at every stage of a career, are now essential attributes for graduates and entry-level workers. Career education, once considered optional, now belongs squarely in the mainstream of core curriculum. At the same time, increasing numbers of workers need periodic assistance in order to make informed decisions about their place in the labour market, and to acquire the employability skills needed to become/remain successful. As a result, there is unprecedented demand by Canadians for career development services to assist in managing change effectively and economically.

Leadership Forums

In recognition of the need to be more proactive in the career development area, four "Leadership in Career Development" forums were held between January and March 1995, in Newfoundland, Nova Scotia, New Brunswick, and Saskatchewan. The sessions were developed and facilitated by the Canadian Guidance and Counselling Foundation.

The forums focused attention on the current state of career development services: How well are the services responding to demand and need? What are the gaps? What needs to be changed? Over two hundred participants tackled the issues and debated action strategies.

Forum discussions were organized around five key issues: Leadership, Delivery System, Demonstrating Value, Standards and Training, and Professional/Technical Support. This paper focuses on themes consistently raised in all four provinces and on consensus about what needs attention most urgently.

What Do We Mean by Career Development?

Career development is, as the words suggest, a "developmental" learning process that evolves throughout our lives. The subject matter of career development learning includes three major areas: self-awareness/preparation, opportunity awareness, and decision and transition learning.

Career development services, as they have evolved in Canada, encompass several specialties. Career education is delivered in schools and post-secondary institutions. It helps students understand what motivates them, what they value, and how they want to contribute to society. It provides them with knowledge about the labour market; skills to make sound choices about education, training, and working options; and career planning tools needed to begin to pursue a career direction. Career counselling is available from community agencies and private practitioners. It helps individuals clarify their aims and aspirations, make informed decisions, manage career transitions, cope with unplanned career changes (including sudden unemployment) and be self-directed in managing their employability. Employment counselling is available from Canada Employment Centres, provincial employment agencies and outplacement organizations. It helps individuals clarify their employment goals, understand and access job opportunities, make sound decisions about upskilling and retraining, and learn skills they need to look for and maintain jobs.

Views From Four Provinces

Leadership

The issue. The forums confirmed that leadership in career development is generally fragmented and has limited influence. Fragmentation was illustrated by the fact that the forum was the first opportunity for many of the participants to exchange ideas and experiences with others working in different areas of career development.

While participants acknowledged that career development belongs more squarely on the social policy agenda, lack of leadership and a small voice makes it easily ignored. Limited understanding of the career development area frequently constrains people in positions of influence from advocating effectively on behalf of practitioners or consumers. Policy makers who attended said they did not turn to the profession for leadership and vision in establishing directions because practitioners do not act as a unified group and there is not a single professional association or other point of contact.

The consensus. From the discussions in the forums, several items of consensus emerged pertaining to leadership. There is strong motivation to move to a new model of collaboration and there is recognition that career development needs to involve new partners: economic recovery commissions, provincial labour force development boards, employers, labour organizations, and consumers; and a "Leadership Council" in career development is needed, drawing from the expanded list of partners. Rather than focusing on career development practice and practitioners (the role of a professional association), it would focus outward on building bridges to public policy. It would undertake specific roles, notably: public education, think tanks, influencing decision makers and policy makers to collaborate, and problem-solving.

Delivery System

The issue. Career development services are provided in many different organizations: classrooms, guidance offices, human resource departments, community agencies, private practices, and employment agencies. Although finding your way to the right service should be easy, it isn't. A transparent delivery system was recognized as fundamental—and as one of the greatest challenges.

Of the many hurdles to be overcome in bringing coherence to the existing system, three stood out: efficiency, disconnectedness, and gaps in the service system.

The consensus. Four themes emerged in the very difficult area of coherence in the delivery system, and there was agreement in all provinces on initial action steps: share information, educate the consumer, focus on consumers, and highlight new roles for key players. The following groups were identified as critical players in building a better delivery system.

Education. Career education needs to be experienced by every student. Some ministries of education have reversed decisions made over the past 20 years to drop requirements for career education as part of basic education. This reversal is in line with recommendations echoed in many sources, including the Report of the Canadian Labour Force Development Board's Task Force on Transition into Employment, "Putting the Pieces Together" and the Canadian Guidance and Counselling Foundation's "Ready for Change: Career Counselling and Development in the 90s."

In addition, a broader range of careers need to be promoted. The traditional tendency to over-value the professions cheats the 60% of students who do not pursue post-secondary training out of a full opportunity to explore and create their futures.

*Community.*Community agencies can play a collaborative role in building for, and with, consumers a delivery system which is clear, publicized, and rationalized. Such a system would have an agreed-upon starting point for consumers before branching out to a range of services. In building a system which is more coherent and has less duplication, it may be necessary for some deliverers to give up certain services and assume others.

Workplaces. The roles and responsibilities of employers and unions in career development and human resource development must be more clearly defined—not only in building their own internal work force, but also in incorporating these services as part of outplacement or downsizing. Tools and education may be required to assist them in implementing these as essential core benefits. Sharingresources is essential. Many employers and unions already have exceptional programs within their own operation which have enormous potential for reaching the growing displaced worker population.

Facilitating Agency. A body which assumes a facilitative and catalytic leadership role is needed to focus the many sectors and many players on the issue of coherence in the system. While no particular organization was identified to undertake this task, labour force development boards were generally seen as being well positioned in provinces where they exist. Participants also identified an initial objective: agree on the first points of contact for consumers. This would reduce duplication significantly. It would also mean that some agencies would have to give up delivering these initial services, or provide them in a collaborative structure. Although this was a potentially troublesome aspect of this proposal it was, nonetheless, recognized as a basis for building a sensible continuum of service.

Governments. Recognizing that governments, especially at the federal level, are moving out of direct delivery of career development services and entrusting them to others, forum participants want governments to ensure that policies and practices are in place to guide this process. In particular, they expressed the view that government leadership is essential to strengthen agencies' capacity to deliver services. This capacity-building must address access to labour market information, training, and professional and technical support.

In the Unemployment Insurance program, as well as in emerging social program trends such as "workfare," recipients are now expected to access employment counselling services as a requirement for their entitlement. Secondly, governments need to fund agencies on the basis of collaborative models. Currently, many agencies must compete for a common pot of resources, even on an annual basis. This system is the antithesis of what is needed to build collaboration and coherence in the delivery system. And, overall, government is the key mechanism for national coordination and leadership in building career development services.

Training and Standards
The issue. Training career development practitioners and specialists has not been taken seriously by Canadian educational institutions. While some francophone universities offer career development programming, no anglophone university program specializing in career development exists. Career development has not quite made it as a recognized specialization in the university stream; it has fallen between the cracks of psychology and education. It has been seen as a "poor cousin" by faculties of psychology, because of its emphasis on what can crudely be called "normal development and decision processes" and its reliance on economics and sociology as companion disciplines. Similarly, it is seen in faculties of education as peripheral to specific subjects included in core curriculum. A few community colleges have begun to offer programs, yet more quality programs are needed.

As a result, organizations providing career development services have purchased privately or developed in-house training to meet their needs for knowledge and skills. As well, a great deal of learning on-the-job has occurred. There are many examples of clinical psychologists, identifying themselves as career specialists, who have acquired their specialized learning completely outside the framework of their formal studies. The result is a mixed bag: practitioners who have learned practical skills through informal routes; practitioners who need upskilling to be effective at delivering career services; and a lack of standards of basic practice to guide practitioners, employers, and—ultimately—consumers.

Much course development work has been underway in the past few years. Nonetheless, while quality training now exists, it remains uncoordinated and unanchored. The need is not for more curriculum for practitioner training, but for organizing what is now available around a standard of basic practice that applies the principles of lifelong learning. In this era of high unemployment, career development services are a high-demand area. Yet no compulsory requirements/standards for service exist. It is widely recognized within the field that the area is ripe for abuse, attracting those who are not qualified to practice or to teach career development.

The consensus. The following points of consensus pertaining to training and standards emerged.

The training of practitioners in career development, a specialty in its own right, must be taken seriously. The quality of practice has enormous personal, social, and economic consequences to consumers. Roles must be revised for critical partners, including universities (especially faculties of education and counselling), community colleges, professional institutes, and institutes for open and distance learning. These partners have much to work with by building on the excellent courses that already exist.

There is an urgent need for core competencies which establish the minimum knowledge and skill levels needed to call oneself a career practitioner. A national collaborative effort is called for to capitalize on the best of what diverse organizations have already developed. The resulting competencies would provide grounds for provincial endorsement and a foundation on which to build multiple specializations for practice. The core competencies would help to diminish the current fragmentation by providing a common language across the field. They would also provide much needed consumer protection by guaranteeing a basic standard.

The training system must be practitioner-driven and inclusive, recognizing a wide range of educational backgrounds and on-the-job experience. Building blocks include prior learning assessment, flexible entry and a minimum of three delivery methods. One delivery method should be non-institutional ("without walls") and available through a range of professional development offerings which are recognized upon completion by a professional organization that has national credibility in career development. The remaining two might be institutionalized within community college and university settings and lead to diploma and degree credentials. All three should reflect basic underlying competencies.

Over time, an additional important component can develop if institutions endorse the principles of inclusion and seek to broaden their scope beyond a purely academic system. There is potential for an inclusive credentialing system which contains at least three recognized levels of credentials. The core competencies would apply to three specializations: a Professional Career Development Institute Certificate; a Diploma in Career Development granted at a community college; and a university degree in Career Development (Bachelor's and eventually Master's degrees). This would regulate the profession, recognize the qualified practitioner, and assure the consumer of quality.

Demonstrating Value and Professional/Technical Support

In the four forums, participants selected the issues they saw as most critical for their attention during the day. Only one forum addressed the issue of evaluation and demonstrating value. No forum chose to address "professional/technical support" as a discrete topic; participants' consensus was that it was an aspect of the leadership issue.

New Brunswick forum participants agreed it is very important to have evidence of the value of career development services in order for them to be reasonably resourced, especially when there is such competition for scarce funds. Frustration was expressed about the lack of sharing of frameworks to support service delivery. The working group identified the need for consensus on what outcomes can be expected of career services. They noted fragmentation in the systems, citing the example of federal departments and provincial governments developing and using different evaluation methodologies to measure the same outcomes. Participants provided strong evidence that a good deal of evaluation is being conducted. They raised concerns that the instruments and/or methods may be inadequate and inaccessible, because they remain internal to agencies and programs, and they suggested there may well be a great deal more knowledge and expertise that has not been reported.

Initiating a National Strategy

Unanimously, the forums were seen as the impetus for an important action agenda to make quality career development services more accessible. Participants demonstrated an interest in sharing best practices, experiments in delivery which had been tested, information, and problem-solving. This confirms the potential for a national career development strategy which could make a very significant contribution to the life/work of all Canadians. Three first steps for initiating a national strategy for careerdevelopment are outlined below.

Establish a Leadership Council

Groups involved in career development should work in partnership to establish a "Leadership Council," These partners would be drawn from federal and provincial governments, ministries of education, professional associations, community-based agencies, economic recovery commissions, business, labour, and consumers. The Leadership Council would exist for a period not longer than 3 years, to accomplish the following specific tasks.

Public education . Educate Canadians about resources and services to help them manage their career futures; and normalize the use of these services.

Standards. As the national body that recognizes and endorses standards for practice in career development. (Standards would be developed in a collaborative initiative separate from the leadership council). Because this Leadership Council would represent all major jurisdictions, it would also be ideally positioned to endorse core competencies which would govern practice across all sectors.

Think-tank. Conduct at least one forum to engage policy makers and experts in an examination of critical aspects of career development. The objectives would be to increase the profile of career development on the public policy agenda, promote public education about it, and contribute to understanding and practice.

Catalyst. Build a service continuum by charting and implementing coherent services and overcoming barriers to collaboration.

Take Collective Action

Vital players can take immediate steps to advance career development. These vital players include: governments, education, community-based agencies, workplaces, and career development experts. It is important to secure agreement among these critical players to initiate the actions, with defined milestones, that are essential to a successful national strategy.

Governments. As departments move away from direct delivery, it is nesessary to ensure that other deliverers are able to assume service responsibility; assist in building the capacity of organizations to meet new demands; facilitate technical and professional support needed to develop and sustain quality career services; and promote policies and standards to ensure access to career services for all Canadians who need them.

Education. Some of the initiatives for education to address include: career education for all students throughout the elementary and secondary school system; in-service training for active teachers so they are able to deliver career education effectively; career education as an integral part of teacher and guidance counsellor training and specialization in universities; and focus on learning respect for work of all kinds to ensure that the career planning needs of youth moving from school to employment, as well as school to post-secondary, are addressed.

Community-based agencies. Community-based agencies need to work together to make consumer access to services more transparent and easier, and collaborate to organize a continuum of service based on a common point of entry and no unnecessary duplication.

Workplaces. Workplace initiates where leadership can be demonstrated include leadership in championing new roles and responsibilities for employers and unions, and partnering by medium and large employers to provide effective labour adjustment, career planning and transition programs for employees of small businesses.

Career development experts. In the nest five years, career development experts can begin the collaborative process needed to establish standards for career development practice that are inclusive and accepted across jurisdictions. They can negotiate a professional training strategy and work in partnerships to achieve this goal. Such a strategy will include at least the following: continuing and distance education and/or summer institutes in at least four regions throughout Canada; diploma programs using the good program models already offered at Sir Sanford Fleming and George Brown Colleges (in Ontario) and Concordia College (in Alberta); and specialized degree programs in career development at universities in at least six provinces, distributed geographically across Canada.

Create a Mechanism for National Coordination

Access to advice, support, innovative tools, and evaluation methodologies is critical. However, in order to be maximally effective, there needs to be an operational mechanism for national coordination, professional and technical support, and sharing best resources and practices. For example, if the training delivery system is to profit from having access to courses which have been tested, there needs to be a coordinating centre to make the availability of courses known. Much information exists which is not currently being used to capacity. What is needed now is not new money and development, but time, expertise, coordination, professional support, and a mechanism to make the best use of what exists. Partners across all sectors will then be able to access professional and technical support, remain current, and sustain a strong career development network.

Conclusion

We Have a Beginning

These early steps toward a national strategy will help to make quality career development services accessible for Canadians. The strategy will put into practice the commitment to sharing excellence and promoting lifelong learning in practical ways that support personal, economic and social goals. It will accomplish this by: responding to the need for leadership that involves new, critical partners; providing professional and technical support to all sectors in which career development services are delivered; inciting governments, education, communities, and workplaces to take on new responsibilities related to the career futures of Canadians; establishing standards to unite the field, give a common language and meet consumers' needs; moving universities and community colleges to recognize the specialization of career development and provide appropriate training; establishing a Professional Career Development Training Institute to offer ongoing training for practitioners; placing career development services in the mainstream; and supporting education about career development services and how to access them.

A Call to Action

In today's labour market, career planning and preparation are necessary for all Canadians. Career and employment counselling must be an integral part of identifying training needs and structuring training opportunities. Career and employment counselling needs to be more broadly available, particularly in smaller communities where existing services are limited. Career guidance and counselling in elementary, secondary, and post secondary schools also is needed to prepare young Canadians—not only to establish initial career directions—but also to acquire the employability skills needed to make successful transitions in a rapidly changing labour market. Young people must learn how to assess workplace realities, and to seek opportunities for developing both the generic and specific skills they need to get and keep employment.

This paper is a call to action. It can be a starting point for building further consensus and adding other dimensions to the strategy. Many partners and organizations are well positioned and committed to moving a national strategy forward: the Canadian and provincial labour force development boards; the provincial representatives who participated in the four forums that generated ideas for this paper; the Canadian Guidance and Counselling Foundation (CGCF); the regional groups who are coordinating career development initiatives across Canada; Human Resources Development Canada (HRDC) at National Headquarters and in Regional offices; the National Life/Work Centre in New Brunswick; and the Career Information Partnerships—to name a few.

This emerging national strategy reflects many of the unique attributes of career development in Canada. In the 1990s we are evolving a proactive capacity for collaboration and pulling together. Increasingly, we are inclined to share resources and pool our energies so that consumers have access to quality career and employment counselling and exemplary career development programs. New partnerships between business, education, and service delivery organizations are emerging. In several provinces, career development "action groups" are forming, which bring all career development players to the table to do strategic planning for improvement in the field. A national momentum in career development is growing. If this collective approach continues, we will embark on process of national collaboration and implementation of a well-considered national strategy designed to make very real differences in the career lives of Canadians.

References

Center of Education and Work. (1994). *Improved career decision making (ICDM)—A multi-media program.* Madison, WI: University of Wisconsin at Madison.

Conger, D. S., Hiebert, B., & Hong-Farrell, E. (1994). *Career and employment counselling in Canada.* Ottawa, ON: Canadian Labour Force Development Board.

Task Force on Transition into Employment. (1994). *Report of the Task Force on Transition into Employment.* Ottawa, ON: Canadian Labour Force Development Board.

Watts, A. G. (1994). *Lifelong Career Development.* Cambridge, England: CRAC/Hobsons.

This paper was originally published in January 1996 by the Canadian Labour Force Development Board (CLFDB) under the title *Career Development: An Emerging National Strategy.* It is reprinted here with the permission of the CLFDB.

40

Serving All of Our People in the 21st Century

JoAnn Harris-Bowlsbey

Overview

Those of us who have spent our lives in career development would readily affirm that every individual needs to possess knowledge and skills that would outfit him or her to make satisfying career choices across the life span. We acknowledge the centrality of the worker role in career since it has such a large influence on overall life satisfaction, income, lifestyle, available colleagues, and socioeconomic class.

> *Almost nintey years after Parsons...we continue to fail to meet the standard that we know we must uphold: helping people of all ages, colors, and characteristics to not only make satisfying, well-informed choices but, even more importantly, learn and internalize a process for doing that again and again across the life span.*

Yet, now almost ninety years after Parsons laid the groundwork for our profession, we continue to fail to meet the standard that we know we must uphold: helping people of all ages, colors, and characteristics to not only make satisfying, well-informed choices but, even more importantly, learn and internalize a process for doing that again and again across the life span.

This short paper offers a personal analysis of this challenge and makes some concrete suggestions for coming closer to meeting it as the profession enters the 21st century.

Discussion

The need to possess career planning skills is as old as the human race itself. Adam and Eve doubtless sought alternate occupations after the Fall, and Biblical Joseph made one of the greatest career transitions of all when he made a move from shepherd on his father's sheep farm to Executive Director of Pharaoh's estate. Yet, the pace and nature of change is vastly different as we approach the 21st century from what it has been at any single point of history.

Let me illustrate the nature of that change by taking two benchmarks in my own life and in concomitant career development theory. I graduated from college in the early fifties, about the same time that Super was publishing his life-span theory for the first time (1953). As in his theory, I assumed that I would enter an occupation immediately after college and that I would pursue it or some near iteration of it over my entire lifespan, moving upward as I gained more education and experience—and so it has been for me. I moved easily from exploration to establishment to maintenance, and it's too early to know about decline. As time passed, I was able to contribute more, have a higher income and lifestyle, and accumulate security for the retirement years because of the paternalistic support of an organization that provided a high-quality fringe benefits package. My life has been a good illustration of the early Super life-span theory.

But, what about today's youth entering the job market? They find a job less easily than I did right out of school; they enter a world which is characterized by an obsession with productivity and cost- and quality-competitiveness, one whose employers are driven by whatever it takes to get the competitive edge, not by their concern for the welfare of employees. It is interesting that Super's last statement of his theory (1990), the Arch of Determinants, looks quite different from his first statement. Notice in Figure 1 that an individual's career is sustained by two columns of equal importance: the internal characteristics of the individual (interests, abilities, values, talent, needs, etc.) and the nature of the external environment (employment practices, employment outlook, corporate policies, etc.).

Super has adequately captured the nature of the change between the fifties and the nineties. There must be a dramatic change in our

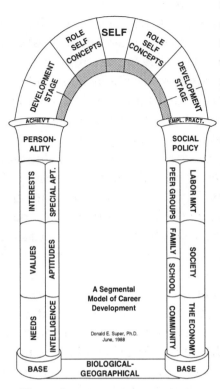

Figure 1

theory, assumptions, and practice of career guidance. If ever it was an adequate assumption that we only need to work with young people to make a one-time, good vocational choice, that assumption is vastly inaccurate today. The fact is that we need to work with all individuals of all ages to help them understand the nature of the changed world of work and to help them develop a set of planning and transition skills that will take them from where they are into a constantly changing future.

Besides our reticence as a profession to understand clearly the changed nature of assumptions as they relate to career development, we have not believed our own theory sufficiently to understand the nature of counselor selection and type reinforcement. Borrowing from Holland's theory (1985), we know that the typical counselor code is SAE. The predominant position of the S means that guidance practitioners, by innate nature, want to work with individuals to help them by the skilled use of verbal and interpersonal skills. Dealing with individual problems and crises often requires creativity (the A) and some influencing of others (the E). Inherent in the code seems to be the propensity for dealing with crisis-oriented personal adjustment problems much more than with passage through the normal developmental tasks.

Skills for the development of programmatic efforts (I) in an organized way (C), making wise use of technology (R), are missing from the typical counselor code. Yet, developing plans which can be implemented for all persons, making appropriate use of technology, absolutely requires the possession of R, I, and C skills by counselors. Further, our counselor education programs, on the whole, reinforce and commend the strong skills and activities and seldom teach or reinforce the kinds of activities and skills related to strong program development and systematic delivery of services. Because my personal Holland code is ISE, I realized very early in my career that I would have limited contribution to the field if I could only provide individual counseling to five students per day. That realization motivated me to use my skills to conceptualize, with others on my high school guidance staff, how a computer could be programmed to simulate the kinds of "interviews" or activities that a good counselor would provide to a student. The discipline of computer logic helped me to define a systematic process of career planning which could be delivered by a computer in a standard way, though personalized, for all users. Later, I not only developed more advanced versions of this computer-delivered systematic process, but also presented a similar model through career planning curriculum. The development and use of my strong I personality component eventually allowed my work to influence thousands of students every day rather than five. My point here is that we need to attract a proportion of young people into our field who have interests and skills quite different from the usual type. We need to train and reinforce the ICR or IRC types for development and delivery of services to all.

A third contributor to the problem has been the nature of the environmental press in which counselors constantly live. That press causes them to be chameleon-like in the sense that they are required to spend their time in ways either dictated by individual work environments (such as having to discipline or make schedule changes) or by the then-current political agendas (tech-prep, drug abuse, or teen pregnancy, for example). The environmental press always includes budget concerns: either that the guidance budget is inadequate or that it must be spent in specific ways. Like extracurricular activities, guidance functions are often one of the first programs to be cut back when there is insufficient money for everything.

Possible Approaches to Amelioration

Being beset by an impossible assignment with insufficient resources can be a catalyst for creative thinking and planning. This may be the dilemma of our profession. We may have to make the best of the assignment and resources we have, since getting more resources may not be a possibility. So, what can we do with our challenge?

First, leaders in our profession need to continue to help practicing counselors understand changed assumptions about the work world and its jobs and about the workers who fill those jobs. The new assumptions about jobs include the following:

- A smaller percentage of them will require a baccalaureate degree, but they will require higher and higher levels of technical and communication skills.
- Organizations in which these jobs are located will continue to be hard-pressed for survival in the global society and will seek a combination of high productivity, high quality, and low cost. This need will perpetuate the practices of downsizing, reorganization, hiring of temporary workers, and allocation of significant parts of production to offshore sites.
- Many jobs and their settings as we know them today will either disappear or be radically changed. Because of ever-emerging technology, a much larger proportion of workers will work at home and many job descriptions will change with frequency.

New assumptions about the workers who will fill these jobs include the following:

- They must be high-skilled and oriented to productivity as a goal.
- They must be capable of frequent transition from job to job and location to location and must readily acquire new skills.
- They must be independent in terms of their ability to manage their own careers and financial well-being.

A second approach to meeting our challenge is to "professionalize" the guidance profession. Increased professionalization is always related to three things: improving the content knowledge and operational skills of those in the profession; training and making effective use of people at paraprofessional levels; and making effective and appropriate use of technology.

Translated to our profession this means:

- Continuing to upgrade the knowledge and skills of professional counselors through more content related to career development theory and practice in their graduate programs (including supervised practice specifically in career development/planning) and through a nationwide network of training opportunities.
- Training and certification of paraprofessionals, often called career technicians, who can help with the task.
- Continuing to improve the content and functionality of computer-delivered career planning systems, the computer literacy of counselors, and the training that assists professional and paraprofessional counselors to use computers wisely to supplement their services.

A third approach is the acceptance and support by the profession of additional avenues for delivery of career planning services to the nation's people. We see the beginning of that trend with the Employment Service One-Stop Centers and the ACT Transition Centers, both designed to provide career planning services to the community-at-large. These centers should be staffed by certified professional and paraprofessional career counselors. With the growth of computer network services, including Internet, career planning services should be available in this mode, linked to human support services via one-to-one interviews, group interaction, or telephone. Trained professional career counselors should develop and design these services and their attendant support.

Conclusion

For the well-being of our people and our society, we must fulfill our mission of providing high-quality career planning services to everyone. The needed paradigm shift, counselor type selection, and environmental press are significant challenges which can be overcome by the development of new awarenesses, new counselor selection and training standards, and the better utilization of technology-based career planning systems in a broadened arena.

References

Holland, L. (1985). *Making vocational choices: A theory of vocational personalities and work environments.* Englewood Cliffs, NJ: Prentice-Hall.

Super, D. E. (1953). A theory of vocational development. *American Psychologist, 8,* 185-190.

Super, D. E. (1990). A life-span, life-space approach to career development. In D. Brown, L. Brooks, and Associates (Eds.), *career choice and development: Applying contemporary theories to practice* (2nd ed.). San Francisco: Jossey-Bass.

41

Career Counseling is Not Mental Health Counseling: More Myth Than Fact

Larry D. Burlew

Myths are created to entertain, enlighten, and/or explain the unexplainable. However, myths can inhibit change and development if they are believed to be fact and held as gospel truth. This situation is occurring within our profession as a "battle" rages to label career counseling as something other than counseling. The battle involves the myth that career counseling is limited to information giving, decision making, and placement. In turn, career counselors are relegated to a "restricted" position with respect to enhancing the mental health of human beings. If we continue to ignore the voices of the myth promoters, then many others will have no option but to accept the myth as truth. On the other hand, career counselors can stand shoulder-to-shoulder and say, "You've got to be kidding!"

> *Potential clients, as well as other counselors, need help in understanding that there is not career stuff, but just stuff. There is only stuff because the client is only one person, not two separate individuals who can clearly discuss one type of issue while excluding the other.*

I repeat, "You've got to be kidding!" A counselor who defines career counseling as something other than mental health counseling is prematurely diagnosing a client's emotional stability. This premature diagnosis occurs because such a counselor's mind is already made up. A client with a career concern is only looking for information about the world of work, is only interested in learning more about her/his interests, abilities, and work values, or is seeking help in making a career decision. Such a client is certainly not experiencing enough anxiety or disequilibrium to warrant more serious, "personal" counseling (i.e., mental health counseling), or is she/he?

I hope that potential clients reading this article are now saying, "You've got to be kidding." Clients present problems to career counselors that are multifaceted, just like problems presented to a feminist counselor, a family counselor, or a gerontological counselor are multifaceted. The following career concerns illustrate this point.

- I've worked for a long time but nothing's ever really satisfied me. I feel empty inside but want work that helps fill that emptiness.
- My boss is awful and treats me like dirt. I'm afraid of men like him. I don't think I'll last long in this job.
- What will happen now that the company knows I'm gay. My career is ruined.
- Every company I've worked for thinks that Latinos are lazy. I can't seem to get ahead. I wonder if I stand a chance here in the United States.

A client could walk into a counselor's office with any of these career concerns. Limiting the work with any of these clients to information giving or career decision making is a disservice to the client, bordering on being unethical. Counseling with these clients remains within the career development framework (i.e., how all the client's issues led to the current career anxieties), yet the client is experiencing as much anxiety and disequilibrium as she/he would about a dysfunctional relationship.

This article shares a philosophy about the nature of mental health counseling as it relates to career counseling. The article is educational in nature, challenging the myth about career counseling and beginning with the fact that, "Career counseling is mental health counseling."

Career Client Issues

Gold and Scanlon (1993) found that career counseling may be shorter in duration than other types of counseling and that "the shorter duration in counseling may reflect counselor uncertainty as to how to best serve this population, relegating career counseling to test-and-tell and termination" (p. 189). The shorter duration easily occurs when counselors believe that career counseling is something other than mental health counseling. I believe that counselors who buy into the myth that career counseling is not mental health counseling are "therapy-phobic" and, therefore, limit the services they provide to their clients. This automatic limiting of services partially accounts for career counseling being shorter in duration.

For example, suppose Lorenzo came into a counselor's office with the statement, "My boss is awful and treats me like dirt. And, I'm afraid of men like him. I don't think I'll last long in this job. Can you help me find another job?" A career counselor who is therapy-phobic might respond with, "It sounds like you're in a terrible situation. Let's take a look at the type of job you're doing and see what your options are." After exploring what Lorenzo does in advertising, such a counselor might say, "Now let's determine what other types of companies are available in this area doing your type of work." This counselor might even explore Lorenzo's current work environment, determining what is absent, seeing if he can find it at his present job but, if not, teaching him to evaluate work environments during the interview.

While these issues are important, the therapy-phobic career counselor above superficially split the client in two, career issues and personal issues. This "splitting" of clients with career concerns may account for the shorter duration in counseling; after all, only half of the problem has been addressed. Peterson and Nisenholz (1991) believe that "one commonly desired outcome of counseling is to help clients beome more self actualizing, or more fully functioning, or more closely approximating their highest levels of potential" (p.6). If we continue to split clients, they can never reach their "highest levels of potential" because we're only dealing with half the truth, half the problem.

Let's not split Lorenzo from the scenario above and treat him as a whole person. A career counselor who is not therapy-phobic might respond with, "You're really tense about work, the way you're being treated, and see finding another job as the way out." Lorenzo might agree with this and share that he's from a very traditional Mexican family. Men are supposed to be strong and able to defend their honor. Since graduating from college with a degree in advertising, he's left one job after another. He has trouble with extremely critical supervisors, particularly male supervisors. He feels that the criticism attacks his honor as a worker. However, he feels he can do nothing about his honor being challenged; rather than be fired for challenging a supervisor, he quits. The counselor might respond with, "It must be hard to get a strong message from your culture and find that it's hard to carry it out in your place of work." Lorenzo tells you that it is hard. He also tells you that he takes his "failures" in defending his honor out on his wife and family. He runs around and drinks and, on occasion, has hit his wife. He doesn't feel good about hitting his wife, and resents work even more for "making him do this."

With this information, what potential are we talking about? Lorenzo wants to be a successful advertising executive, yet he wants to uphold his honor as a man. If we don't work with the whole Lorenzo and address only the "career part," then the outcome of counseling is that Lorenzo will find another job. In doing so, the issues motivating the job-hopping pattern are never addressed, and Lorenzo's anxiety and disequilibrium are simply put on hold until the next time. In some ways, Lorenzo's beliefs that the workplace doesn't support a man's honor and that the workplace is causing him to drink and hit his wife are reinforced, because they were not fully processed during counseling. He leaves counseling with the same beliefs with which he started. Additionally, when Lorenzo experiences the same pattern at the next job, he now has a new belief, "See, that counseling stuff doesn't work."

Therapeutic Conversation Taps Into the Mind

In a manuscript that I'm currently working on, I address the issue of "dissolving the separation of individual theory." I find it amusing that we try to separate clients into personal "stuff" and career "stuff," because any stuff is coming from the same place . . . the mind. In my manuscript, I write the following:

Potential clients, as well as other counselors, need help in understanding that there is not career stuff, but just stuff. There is only stuff because the client is only one person, not two separate individuals who can *clearly* discuss one type of issue while excluding the other. I try to clear this confusion up early in my work with clients by explaining that there is no way to separate issues with which clients come into counseling because they're housed in one body, one mind, and one soul (i.e., The Total Individual). You can't pull a person apart and dissect mind and spirit issues as clearly as you can separate, for example, the heart from the rest of the body (Burlew, in progress, p. 14). Therefore, clients come into counseling sessions ready to deal with all "stuff," and the stuff is housed in the mind and soul, both of which are housed in one body.

Therapeutic conversations, then, tap into the mind and soul of clients. Most people agree that the mind is our mental arena and thus agree that career concerns stem from the mental arena. They also agree that career concerns are dissected, examined, and reformed during therapeutic conversations.

However, while some readers clearly see Lorenzo's concern as a mental health counseling concern, they consider a college student being forced to choose a major in her junior year is not . . . not what? Not stemming from the mind? Not part of a therapeutic conversation? Not serious enough to be a threat to the student "approximating her highest levels of potential" (Peterson & Nisenholz, 1991, p. 6). Not serious enough to be affecting her mental health? Answering "yes" to these questions is what I addressed earlier as prematurely diagnosing a client's emotional stability. With regard to this myth about excluding career concerns from the mental arena, I write:

We know that when the body has problems we call a medical doctor. We also know that when we're "sick" with anxiety or worry, we may call our medical doctor, but eventually we would see a mental doctor, thus a mental health practitioner. Similarly, we might enlist the help of a Shaman for a true spiritual ache for meaning. So, if a client has anxiety over a career problem, the logical place to place that is in the mind, since the problem is housed there as compared to the body or spirit. Therefore, a mental health practitioner would be consulted. If you are not willing to place career problems in the mental health realm, even with symptoms like anxiety, stress, depression and dysfunctional behavior, then in which other realms would you place it? (Burlew, in progress, p. 14).

When you take the college student's concern out of the mental arena (i.e., the mind), you approach her with a preconceived notion, a predetermined diagnosis about the direction and seriousness of her problem. This premature diagnosis opens the door so that a counselor can limit services. Limiting services leaves the counselor open to unintentionally harming a client by not addressing a client's complete problem. When a counselor believes the myth that career counseling is not mental health counseling, the myth guides the diagnosis; the client becomes less important as a human being with unique problems. Is this what you want to do?

What is Mental Health Counseling?

Accepting the fact that career counseling is mental health counseling probably depends on how one defines mental health counseling. Therefore, logical questions to ask are: 1) What is mental health counseling?; and 2) Exactly why doesn't career counseling fit under this umbrella? Counselors may perceive that mental health counselors deal only with pathology, mental illness, diagnosis and/or institutionalization. My immediate response to that is, "Absolutely not." Whether we call ourselves Licensed Professional Counselors, Licensed Professional Mental Health Counselors or Clinical Mental Health Counselors, I propose that most of us were trained within traditional Counselor Education programs. Many of these programs were housed in Colleges of Education.

These programs stemmed from developmental and community agency models that taught that mental health was on a continuum. On one end of this continuum is mental illness, but on the other end, is mental health. Along the continuum are common issues, such as self-esteem, relationship, sexual abuse, depression, and life satisfaction. Included within this continuum are the career issues, and most of the practitioners specializing in career counseling were trained in traditional Counselor Education programs.

With regard to my own training, I consider myself a Licensed Professional Counselor with a specialization in career counseling. I was trained to deal with the whole person, the complete mental health/ mental illness continuum. I never believed that mental health counseling meant mental illness counseling (even though I completed an internship at a psychiatric hospital). I believe that clients present their problem in an open, accepting environment that does not prejudge what issues contributed to that problem, nor do I restrict the sessions to a particular "specialty" (e.g., career development). However, I always practiced only within the ACA (1988) ethical guideline of "recognizing [our] boundaries of competence and providing only those services and using only those techniques for which [we] are qualified by training or experience" (p. 1).

Therefore, I assert that career issues are like any other type of client issue, in that they stem from the mind of the client and affect the client's mental well-being. Additionally, I assert that most career counselors are trained to deal with the whole person and with most issues that affect the career issues (e.g., self-esteem). Career counselors must decide for themselves what type of training they received, and whether they can provide total mental health services to their clients. However, I must warn career counselors against being therapy-phobic, because we have too often heard that we are not mental health counselors. Don't let the myth guide you; be an informed practitioner and provide those services for which you have been trained.

Some mental health counselors, however, do rigidly perceive mental health counselors as specializing in mental illness or want to follow the DSM-IV and the medical model as their Bible. I say, "Fine, but then don't force all practitioners to follow the same model or define themselves similarly." Additionally, don't assume that the training of career counselors focuses only on career development and certainly don't tell us how to provide treatment to our clients. I can work with a gay client coming out, having low self-esteem, feeling depressed, and experiencing an unstable career pattern. I can do so because of my previous training in Counselor Education, my work experience with gay clients, ongoing professional development, and my specialization in career counseling. So, does career counseling fit under the umbrella of mental health counseling? What do you think?

Conclusion

This article confronts a myth that is pulling our profession apart. Instead of uniting under one professional identity— professional counselors or mental health counselors— we split into many. We fight amongst ourselves about what services can be provided and who is an acceptable service provider, even though most of us evolved from Counselor Education programs. In some way, I envy social workers; they don't seem to have this problem. Once a practitioner has been trained, the social work profession *supports* all members in personally deciding the types of problems and clients with which they can work. And, they are smart enough not to exclude any of their own members. Their message seems to be, "We are trained social workers. We are all equal. We work with clients." Our message seems to be, "We are trained counselors. We are all *not* equal. And some of you should not work with clients."

So why do we make it so difficult for us to become a profession as strong as social work or psychology or medicine? What's pulling us apart? Why can't we trust our members to practice within the scope of their training and competence and still be professional counselors, regardless of specialties? Why is it that we can't accept that career counselors were trained in traditional Counselor Education programs and are able to treat the whole client? When we unite and quit splitting our profession, then the American Counseling Association (ACA) will grow from its current 58,000 members to the 200-300,000 members who are professional counselor practitioners. Like the social workers, the profession of counseling will then say, "We are trained counselors. We are all equal. We work with clients." The rest we will trust to practitioners to practice within the ACA ethical guidelines. When this happens, then the question, "Is career counseling mental health counseling?" becomes a thing of the past.

References

American Counseling Association. (1988). *Ethical Standards.* Alexandria, VA: ACA.

Burlew, L. D. (In progress). *Career counseling: A mental health perspective.*

Gold, J. M., & Scanlon, C. R. (1993). Psychological distress and counseling duration of career and noncareer clients. *The Career Development Quarterly,* 42, 186-191.

Peterson, J. V., & Nisenholz, B. (1991). *Orientation to counseling* (2nd ed.). Boston, MA: Allyn and Bacon.

42

Career Counseling and Credentialing

Dennis W. Engels, Carolyn Kern
& Beth Durodoye

Major changes in the substance and conduct of work have modified forever the relative simplicity, continuity, and stability of employment for many people in our Information/ Communication Age. Previously secure forms of employment are tenuous today in the face of major and rapid downsizing and shifts in the production and delivery of goods and services. In a fluid global economy, jobs which previously lasted for generations do not last even a life time.

In a world of abrupt and massive social, political, and economic change, uncertainty and fear abound. People who never before required assistance with their career development need help today in learning to manage their careers. To compete effectively in the high-skills, high-wages, and rapidly changing global economy, the United States must have workers with high-level skills

> *Ultimately, no counselor education program will ever provide sufficient preparation for a lifetime of professional service. Yet, rather than advocate existing entry level standards followed by a lifetime of continuing education, ACA and NBCC advocate entry level standards that greatly exceed a traditional master's degree.*

and knowledge and the resilience to market those competencies. Counselors, especially career counselors, have the potential and competence to serve a major role in helping individuals, employers, and, ultimately, nations, identify, define and address these issues assertively. However, determining counselor competencies tied to appropriate standards faces frequent debate. This article offers input to the dialogue.

Competencies and Ethical Standards

Major landmarks in the development of career counseling and career counselor credentialing emanate from the work of pioneers in career theory and practice as well as the work of several organizations, most notably, the National Career Development Association, (NCDA), founded in 1913 as the National Vocational Guidance Association. Perhaps most significant among NCDA's numerous contributions to career counselor credentialing are the identification of competencies, the development of preparation standards and ethical standards for career counseling, and the initial development and implementation of career counselor certification. (Engels, 1994; Engels & Dameron, 1990; Loesch & Vaac, 1993). NCDA has also made great strides in addressing the vital roles of paraprofessionals in facilitating career development.

There is general agreement that career counselors need competence in such general mental health counseling areas as individual and group counseling, individual and group assessment, program management, consultation, counseling theory, specific populations, supervision, ethics, and research. Beyond these general counseling emphases, NCDA's career counseling competencies constitute most of the required knowledge and skill base for career counselor preparation and credentialing. These are extended by adding emphases on career development and by furnishing competencies in Information Resources and Career Development Theory (including extensive emphasis on career counseling and related practice).

NCDA's Ethical Standards parallel the Ethical Standards of the National Board for Certified Counselors (NBCC) and provide the consensus value set which sanctions, governs, and guides professional behavior in career development work in general and career counseling in particular. These ethical standards are updated as circumstances merit. It should be noted that a career counselor might be accountable simultaneously to more than one set of ethical standards, for example, a NCCC is accountable to the ethical standards of the NBCC, but if that person is also licensed in a state, he or she would be accountable to that state's licensing requirements and ethical standards and related laws, as well as the ethical standards of any and all professional counseling or other mental health organizations to which the person belongs.

Credentials

Credentialing formally defines, sanctions, and regulates professional behavior through licensing, registry and /or certification. Credentialing protects the public from unscrupulous practices and governs professional behavior (Bradley, 1991). In career counseling, the most longstanding and universally recognized credential is that of National Certified Career Counselor (NCCC), certifying a master's degree in counseling, additional expertise, and supervisedexperience in career counseling and career development, along with successful completion of a national career counseling certification examination.

Counselors, psychologists, and other licensed mental health providers may have expertise in career counseling, however, as authors, we found no specialty licenses in career counseling, even in states, such as Texas, which have laws related to some aspects of career counseling, most notably laws aimed at protecting the public in for-profit ventures in career placement. Generally, licensed practitioners are required by their licensing bodies and ethical standards to be truthful in advertising or in describing their expertise. Someone seeking career counseling is well advised to inquire as to the practitioner's competence in this area. Both NCDA and NBCC publish consumer guidelines designed to help the public make good choices in selecting a counselor or a career counselor.

As noted above, the major career counselor credential appears to be that of the NCCC. Although NCCC credential, examination, and certification process was initially established by NCDA's National Council for Credentialing Career Counselors, NCDA decided to turn the credentialing process over to NBCC. Since that transition, both NCDA and NBCC have worked to refine and promote career counseling, while continuously working to improve all aspects of the career counselor credentialing process.

Career counseling is a specialized form of counseling aimed at helping people make wise career plans and decisions, while balancing their multiple life roles. Career counselors possess general and specific competencies and abide by multiple, generally complementary, ethical standards. Credentialing serves to protect the public and the profession.

Our changing world and societies portend a great need for career counseling provided by competent professionals. As stated earlier, demands for career assistance are likely to increase--much has been done to move beyond the primary work of Frank Parsons. It is more than interesting that the U.S. Labor *Secretary's Commission on Achieving Necessary Skills* (SCANS),a commission of representatives of business, industry, labor, education, and government identified as future necessities for work, many competencies which counselors acquire, refine, and demonstrate, and, in turn, share and promote with clients. In the light of these necessary skills and changing world economy, longstanding counselor competencies and practices may provide much to facilitate America's continued global competitiveness and American's individual and collective competence for positive growth and empowerment.

Entry and Continuing Education

In the preparation and regulation of career counselors, one concern merits special attention at this writing. According to the "psychology of more" (Looft, 1991), humans have a tendency to assume that if something or some process is good, more of that entity or process will be better; the psychology of more is manifest in addressing new situations by continuously increasing requirements, restrictions, and aspects of almost any human process. Unfortunately, this quantitative fixation may sacrifice quality and promote unintended exclusion. While refinements in practice, preparation, and credentialing have been forthcoming, it is necessary to base improvements on systematic research and evaluation, rather than to allow artificial or temporary stimuli to lead to permanent changes in preparation, credentialing, and practice standards.

One operational example of the "psychology of more" is the American Counselor Association's (ACA) 1994 counselor licensure model, which exceeds requirements in over 95% of counselor education programs in the country and also surpasses the 1994 Accreditation Standards of ACA's own accrediting body, the Council for Accreditation of Counseling and Related Educational Programs (CACREP, 1994). Similarly, the NBCC's 1995 decision to require a 50% increase in its required hours of post master's supervision, parallels ACA's increase, although little or no data support such changes and little or no informed consent of practitioners or aspiring professionals was obtained. Such increases in preparation requirements fly in the face of credible data gathered by the SCANS Commission which echo numerous studies and speculations suggesting the need for life-long learning. Former models of a complete or completed education—a turn-key or set-it-and-forget-it education—are outmoded today. The senior author's friend who graduated from college and worked his way up to the presidency of a major international corporation over the course of 30 years is a contemporary anomaly. Based on the changing nature of knowledge and the concurrent need for life-long learning, professions and bodies such as ACA and NBCC are likely to require continuing education throughout the professional life of practitioners. Yet, ironically, by expanding the entry requirements for initial credentialing, these same organizations require that a new professional possess knowledge and skill far beyond what CACREP, the ACA accrediting body, acknowledges as an appropriate preparation *before* being credentialed. Several implications seem clear.

Ultimately, no counselor education program will ever provide sufficient preparation for a lifetime of professional service. Yet, rather than advocate existing entry level standards followed by a lifetime of continuing education, ACA and NBCC advocate entry level standards that greatly exceed a traditional master's degree. By discounting the vast majority of existing statutes that require less than 60 credit hours and less than 3000 hours of supervision, ACA has done the public and aspiring counselors a grievous disservice. Although the ACA legislation model advocates protecting the public, its exclusive standards keep vast numbers of the public from the services of licensed professional counselors. Perhaps most distressing in the rarified atmosphere of the ACA stance is the effect on already under-represented populations in the counselor and ACA ranks. Increasing the opportunity costs obviously excludes prospective counseling students of modest or poor income levels. Increasing the quality of existing preparation standards, programs, and continuing education seems much more sensible than merely expanding entry requirements.

Aside from this major concern regarding entry requirements, there is a rich history of progress both in professional development and in professional service in career counseling andcredentialing. Future opportunities suggest strong challenges and promises for career counselors and those who regulate the profession.

References

Bradley, F. O. (Ed.).(1991). *Credentialing In counseling.* Alexandria, VA: Association For Counselor Education And Supervision.

Council for the accreditation of counseling and related educational programs. (1994). *CACREP accreditation standards and procedures manual.* Alexandria, VA: Author.

Engels, D. W., & Dameron, J. D. (1990). *The professional counselor: competencies, performance guidelines and assessment.* Alexandria, VA: American Association For Counseling And Development.

Engels, D., (Ed.).(1994). *The professional practice of career counseling and consultation: A resource document.* Alexandria, VA: National Career Development Association.

Loesch, L. C., & Vaac, N. A. (1993). *A work behavior analysis of professional counselors.* Greensboro, NC: The National Board For Certified Counselors, Inc.

Looft, W. R. (1971). The psychology of more. *American Psychologist.* *26,* 561-565.

43

Developing A Future Sense

H. B. Gelatt

Overview

I started out as a child. Perhaps you did too. While growing up I became more and more adult-like and less and less child-like. This seemed like a good process of development for me — and I thought it was good for everyone. But now I'm not so sure. Perhaps you also have some doubts. Everything seems to be changing so I'm sure growing up (life/career development) isn't what it used to be. But what should it be? Most people would agree that growing up is desirable, but maybe that's because it's the only "direction" we know how to grow. Growing up, in only one direction, may not be the best developmental strategy in turbulent times. Maybe we should optimize our life transitions by learning never to stop growing and to grow in many directions. If the times are turbulent, (constantly changing, disorderly, chaotic) maybe our career development will be the same.

My own career development has been constantly changing. I have had my doubts and changes of mind all along the way. I started out as a champion of rational, logical, sequential decision making and made a "career" out of it. But then I became uncertain and changed my mind. Being uncertain wasn't in vogue in those days and changing one's mind wasn't "good" professional behavior for an "expert" on decision making. But now I am advocating being uncertain and promoting changing one's mind as appropriate strategy for future career development.

> *...we will need to learn to keep changing our minds. Our minds will need to become as changeable as our environment. That makes future sense.*

Is it possible to develop by constantly changing and being uncertain?

Is it desirable? I believe it is both possible and desirable. My proposal for reforming career development will involve growing and developing every which way. Many of us will have to learn to recover some of our "child-like" ways: being playful, creative, receptive, curious, and eager to learn. Others may need to learn to grow out of some adult disabilities picked up during these turbulent times: futurephobia, info-mania, mind's eye myopia, reverse paranoia. But most of all, we will need to learn to keep changing our minds. Our minds will need to become as changeable as our environment. That makes *future sense.*

The idea being presented in *Developing Future Sense* is that growing up (and career development and life transitions) is a process not an outcome, a journey not a destination. The goal is to remain green, child-like, unfinished — to grow and grow and grow. To keep growing means to keep learning and changing. Optimizing life transitions in the future might best be accomplished by optimizing our capacity to change. Keeping an open mind about what we *believe, see, and think* will lead to more effective changes in what we *do.* Obsolete beliefs, narrow views, and limited thinking might be restricting what we do in our life transitions. An openness to change will mean first changing the way we *sense the future.*

Future sense is what I call a new way of *seeing* the future — which leads to a new way of *thinking* and *doing.* Future sense does not spell out how to foretell the future or which road to take on the journey into the future. Our trip to the future takes us on to uncharted waters, into uncertain terrain, where the topology is constantly changing. On this journey we don't have a simple choice between the road *more* traveled and the road *less* traveled. We must choose a road *never* traveled. We have to learn to be willing (adventurous) and able (resourceful) to go where no one has gone.

There is no well-beaten path, no riskless route, no guided tour to the future. Future sense does not provide a road map or a pilot's manual. It is more a philosophy of traveling.

We only have five senses because that's all we believe we have. What we believe, and what we don't believe, determines how we *see, think,* and *do.* Future sense may be that elusive sixth sense which is based on what we believe.

"The minute you make up your mind that what you believe makes a difference, it will make a difference in what you believe — and what you see, think, and do."

Discussion

Have you ever been to the future or met anyone who has? The answer, of course, is no, you haven't. By definition the future doesn't exist, and never will because when it happens, it becomes the present and then quickly becomes the past. If the future never exists, how can you know what *your* future will be? The answer, of course, is you can't. Another way to perceive the future is that it resides only in the mind's eye. In this sense, the future lies right behind your eyes. "All things are created twice. There's a mental or first creation and a physical or second creation" (Covey, 1989, p. 99). Future sense focuses on this first creation, where the future is invented. "We do not... create reality, but we are essential to its coming forth. We evoke a potential that is already present" (Wheatley, 1992, p. 36).

Career development, like the future, is unknown and unpredictable. If the future needs to be invented, career development needs to be reinvented. Other reformers are currently reinventing government, corporations, and schools in order to make them self-organizing, self-renewing, learning organizations, that is—organizations that keep *growing*. However, organizational self-renewal will occur only if *individuals* are capable of reinventing themselves. Future sense means inventing the future while reinventing oneself.

One's career journey today is said to be taking place in "permanent white water." Conventional career planning (the logical, scientific approach) probably won't be sufficient in such a turbulent environment. Something more creative and fluid will often be required. Conventional planning is like following a blueprint—a linear, left-brain, by-the-book approach. Creative career planning, on the other hand, is like using an artist's palette—a non-linear, right-brain, by-the-vision approach.

But we don't have to choose between either conventional or creative planning. Our old way of seeing, thinking, and doing separated everything into *either - or:* career or personal, left brain or right brain, work or play, job or family, child or adult, employed or unemployed, tangible or intangible, this or that. Future sense's new way of seeing, thinking, and doing will interconnect everything into *both—and more:* both career and personal, both job and family, both child and adult — and more, etc. Reforming career development will involve moving from either-or, to both-and more. Both and more is systems thinking. Systems thinking is called the fifth discipline (Senge, 1990). "Systems thinking is a conceptual framework ... to make the full patterns clearer, and to help us see how to change them effectively" (p. 7). By adopting this conceptual framework, career development would *see the whole patterns* of change rather than focusing on "snapshots" of isolated parts of a system. Our profession would then focus on improving whole systems instead of solving individual developmental problems. *Breaking things into parts may prevent us from seeing the whole.*

This "simple" change in mind-set will have a profound affect on career development. For example, there are different ways to plan your career: One way is to predict what the future will be and prepare for what is predicted. This way is logical, conventional career planning, and it is the way education decides what students should learn on their way from school to work. However, *predicting what is probable may inhibit discovering what is possible.*

Another way, intuitive creative planning, is to imagine what you would like the future to be and create what you imagine. This creative approach to career development isn't the conventional wisdom today because most of us *believe* in the logical and *don't believe* in the intuitive. If you don't believe in something you don't employ it. Furthermore, we don't educate people in the skill of imagining and we don't reinforce those who already use it. Dreaming in school and in the workplace is actually frowned upon. And others haven't learned how to visualize precise, positive futures. Most of us dread in a precise way and dream vaguely. Why not balance both rational and intuitive strategies into our "mainstream" career development? What would happen if we expanded our techniques from predominantly collecting, analyzing, and processing information to eliciting, developing, and processing imagination proportionately?

Another example of applying this new mind set is in the skills required of the worker in the evolving workplace: self-reliance and teamwork. This is not an oxymoron, if you are thinking *systems*. Self-interests and system-interests are reciprocal — if you see the whole. Career development wouldn't separate self and system, management and staff, independence and dependence, etc. Employers and employees would begin to declare their interdependence.

Finally, future sense's new mind set would require career development to change its major focal point. "What do you want to be when you grow up?" is the number one question in career planning, and goal setting is the number one strategy. Future sense would change our view to focus on the journey — on the *process* of growth and change. Adults keep asking children what they want to be when they grow up because they are looking for new ideas. New ideas about growing and developing are created right behind our eyes, in our minds eye, using our new way of seeing, thinking, and doing.

Recommended Course of Action

In order to develop a future sense, versatile techniques and tools will be required. The following are strategies suggested by the author. It is hoped there are many more already in use and others to be invented.

One source of new techniques is "Positive Uncertainty," (Gelatt, 1991; Gelatt, 1992), a personal, decision-making philosophy (maybe it is a personal paradigm) that helps you imagine and create possibilities and see the whole (both and more). Its paradoxical principles are

- be focused and flexible about what you want;
- be aware and wary about what you know;
- be objective and optimistic about what you believe;
- br practical and magical about what you do.

It recommends techniques and tools such as treating goals as hypotheses, imagining best-, worst-, most-likely outcomes; shifting personal paradigms; using "What else?" questions; treating memory as an enemy; testing the "vision" of the eye of the beholder; rehearsing future scenarios; treating beliefs as prophecy; engaging in an internal debate dialogue; hunting for hardened habits; treating intuition as real; visualizing probable-possible-preferable futures; replacing the anchor of the past with the pull of the future; dreaming impossible dreams; trying on other "spectacles" for a different "view"; using metaphor as method to monitor your mental maps — and more.

Another source of career development techniques comes from future sense's recommendations for overcoming four new neuroses created by the career anxiety related to life's transitions in turbulent times. The following is a summary of these neuroses, their causes and proposed cures (Gelatt, 1993).

Future Phobia
> *Definition:* Fear of the future
> *Disability:* Leads to avoidance
> *Cause:* Dread of the unknown
> *Cure:* Positive Uncertainty

Info-mania
> *Definition:* The idolizing of information
> *Disability:* Limits creativity
> *Cause:* Compulsion to know
> *Cure:* Using both your I's: Information & Imagination

Mind's eye Myopia
> *Definition:* Inability to shift view
> *Disability*: Restricts flexibility
> *Cause:* Concrete convictions
> *Cure:* A malleable mental map

Reverse Paranoia
> *Definition:* Belief you're following someone
> *Disability:* Stifles self-reliance
> *Cause:* The "visionary leader" fallacy
> *Cure:* A declaration of interdependence

Developing future sense involves becoming a dreamer and a doer, combining pie-in-the-sky and feet-on-the-ground strategies, balancing achieving goals with discovering them, balancing using facts and fantasy, balancing reality testing and wishful-thinking, balancing responding to change and causing change. This involves a reinvention of career development.

Summary

Before children become "grownups" they are full of questions, because they love *learning*. Adults have answers, because they love *knowing*. In this case, knowing becomes the antithesis of learning. Future sense, as a philosophy of traveling a turbulent road where no one has been, encourages us not to "arrive," not to grow up, to remain childlike, to keep learning — to keep an open mind.

There is no device, no matter how sophisticated, that can equal the power, flexibility, and user-friendliness of the human mind. All we have to do is believe in it, and learn how to keep it open. Career development can reinvent itself by developing a future sense.

References

Covey, S. (1989). *The 7 habits of highly effective people.* New York: Simon and Schuster.

Gelatt, H. (1991). *Creative decision making using positive uncertainty.* Los Altos, CA: Crisp Publications.

Gelatt, H. (1992). A new vision for counseling: How to create the future. *Counseling and Human Development, 25,* 2-10.

Gelatt, H. (1993). Future sense: Creating the future. *The Futurist, 27,* 9-13.

Senge, P. (1990). The fifth discipline. New York: Doubleday Currency.

Wheatley, M. (1992). *Leadership and the new science.* San Francisco: Berrett-Koehler Publishers.

44

A Career Counseling Collage For The Next Century: Professional Issues Shaping Career Development

Juliet V. Miller

An Invitation

Earlier this year, I attended an art retreat. One of the media that we worked with was collage. We sat around a giant table, thumbed through magazines, and clipped pictures that attracted us. While I worked, I selected images that I like — a carved polar bear, a brilliant yellow woods with the white birch bark gleaming through the trees, a Tiffany stained-glass window highlighted with deep blues and purples. I began to feel the deep sense of community as all sixteen women sipped coffee and clipped favorite images. When I got tired, I circled around the table and found scraps that others had discarded.

> As I sorted and arranged the clippings that I have put in my collage, I found four themes that provide a unifying center point. These four themes apply to clients, to career helpers, and to the profession. These themes are resilience, balance, cyclical, and community.

Finally, we took large sheets of paper and began to arrange the pieces. Rather than forcing the pieces into some predetermined mode, I just moved them around. Turning, cutting, and rearranging. Finally, the collage told me that I was done. It was just right and I was to let it be.

As I write this article, I am going to practice what I learned that day. I will describe for you the pieces that I have collected recently in my work as career counselor and as executivedirector of the National

Career Development Association (NCDA). Then I will develop a collage that presents some of these pieces in a way that has meaning for me. As you read, I invite you to add pieces that you have found, to borrow any of mine, and to build your own collage that can inform and inspire your work as a career helper.

Images for the Collage

Images from My Clients

My clients have been one of the greatest influences on my view of the professional issues in career development. Listen to these views that I hear from them:

> The answers to career planning lie outside of myself.
> I have little ability to identify my own career path.
> Career planning and change are logical and should be accomplished easily and quickly.
> Success in career depends on selling myself.

The dominant message from my client is that career planning is a rational process that should be completed easily with brief assistance from career helpers. Call this view "the science of career planning." It seems that a balancing image might be called the "art of discerning career ." This is an image that I have described in greater detail in my remarks prepared for the NCDA 75th Anniversary President's Symposium (1993). In this image, career planning is seen as a creative, internal process that ebbs and flows throughout life. Here, clients centered in self, are involved in various creative activities such as dream work, art, journal writing, and metaphor that support the active authorship of their own life stories.

Images from the CDQ Issue: How Personal is Career Counseling?

I remember an article in the Special Section of the *Career Development Quarterly* (1993) entitled, "How Personal is Career Counseling?" In one article "Career Counseling Practicum: Transformations in Conceptualizing Career Issues," career counseling practicum students process their changing perceptions of career development and career interventions. Here are some images from that article:

I initially thought that I should avoid discussing anything personal with her. I was sure this would not be difficult because I was providing career counseling. I am embarrassed to admit how naive I was. My client's indecision was connected to family issues and her identify as a woman. Not only was it impossible to avoid personal matters, but their resolution was the path to the client's achieving individuation and making a college-major decision. (Patricia J. Dauser, p. 182)

Prior to practicum, I thought that career counseling was a very different and easier endeavor than personal counseling, and that there would be little "therapy" involved inhelping people with career concerns. I soon discovered that career concerns were as personal and complex as other presenting problem; career issues need to be viewed from the same developmental perspective as personal issues. (Stella Dial, p. 184)

Images from the APA Division 17 Vocational SIG Conference

Last Spring I attended a conference at the Ohio State University organized by the Vocational SIG of APA's Division 17 for Counseling Psychology. Several important images emerged from that conference. The first focused on career counseling practice theory. While we have a rather rich body of research and theory on career development, we have only sketchy theories of career counseling. This void creates a screen on which helpers may project many images. For example, career counseling is really therapy with vocational issues being the presenting problem. Or career counseling is an educational process where clients learn specific career exploration and job-search skills. I found these extreme images confusing and longed for a clearer, more integrative picture. This need was supported by many at the conference.

Another suggestion at the conference was that there is a need for practice to inform research. The exciting image of practioner-researcher teams working collaboratively throughout their careers was an image that I knew I wanted for my collage.

Images from the California Career Conference

In November, I attended the California Career Conference. During these two brief days, I collected several images for my collage. William Bridges (1994) overviewed his new book, *Job Shift*, starting with this image:

> Our organizational world is no longer a pattern of jobs, the way that a honey comb is a pattern of those little hexagonal pockets of honey. In place of jobs, there are "part-time and temporary work situations". . . Today's organization is rapidly being transformed from a structure built out of jobs to a field of "work needing to be done." (p. 1)

What does this mean for our clients who are living through this transition? Career resilience—the capacity to sense environmental situations —center on personal goals and employ a variety of career strategies to navigate the shifting organizational climate, was one suggestion. Viewing oneself as self-employed, even within the organization, is another picture. This marks a shift from the idea of filling a job to the notion of identifying, contracting and delivering vital services in the flux of changing personal and organizational needs.

At lunch, someone recommended that I read the book, *When the Canary Stops Singing* by Pat Barrentine (1993). This is a book about feminine viewpoints on management.

> Perhaps women were to business what the canary once was to the coal miners . . . When the canary stopped singing, it was a warning that the environment was too toxic for living creatures. Perhaps women in business are harbingers of a needed transformation. (p. 9)

This book provides important organizing concepts that I connected with deeply as one who is a career helper. Interdependence, balance, community, openness to change, and courage to act.

A second book, *The Adult Years: Mastering the Art of Self-Renewal* (1991) by Frederic M. Hudson has provided a frame that I find powerful in guiding my work. I like this image that Hudson presents:

Living in the 1990's feels like being on a raft floating down a commanding river ... Sometimes when it is calm our journey is fairly effortless; we can moor the raft in an eddy near a meadow and camp for a while. At other times, the white waters of the river test every skill we have as we slide over rocks and rapids and swirl about in unforeseen direction. (p. 51)

Hudson captures several concepts that others have also discussed. We need to help our clients view their lives as cyclical (cycles in a gradual upward growth) versus linear, in a straight line.

Images from My Field Contacts as NCDA Executive Director

In May 1994, I became the Executive Director of the National Career Development Association. Several images emerge as I scan back over the past several months. I see the vast diversity of members that we have in the Association. NCDA has around 20 special interest groups that focus on special interests by setting (community college, business and industry, military, or private practice), life-career stages (youth, adult, or retirement), clients groups (HIV Seropositive, cultural diversity, women's issues or men issues). This reinforces the vast diversity within our field.

I am struck by the need to find a sense of community for many types of helpers in the career development field. NCDA is supporting the work of the NOICC Career Development Training Institute at Oakland University to clarify the competencies needed for less than master's level career facilitators. Our new product, *The Professional Practice of Career Counseling and Consultation: A Resource Document* (Engels, 1994) reflects our visions of career development, career counseling competencies, consumer guidelines, various career specialities, and ethical standards.

Career counseling is getting national recognition. Here are two examples that highlight this. I have received calls from two outplacement firms wanting to identify career counselors in specific geographic areas. They are aware that outplacement services cannot meet the deeper career development needs of all clients and they want to refer to career counselors. A SOICC director, who is developing a plan for one-stop career centers, wants involved NCDA members as qualified providers of career counseling services.

Many of our calls at NCDA headquarters are from consumers, the press, and the public. These inquiries reflect both the intense need for career services and the continuing confusion about how to be wise consumers of those services. Here is a sample of those questions and concerns:

> What type of career helpers are there? What are the qualifications of each?
>
> What questions should I use to interview a career counselor before hiring one?
>
> Why do other people decide to seek career counseling?
>
> How long does career counseling usually last?
>
> What can I expect to happen when I go to see a career counselor?

I am moved by the intense need for our services and somewhat pressing weight of these demands. Recently, I heard someone suggest that since people are experiencing so much pain around issues related to work and career, career helpers are in a central position as healers in our society. This idea rings true for me.

Creating the Collage

Well, enough clippings. I hope that as I described my clippings, you conjured up some of your own. Now it is time to build the collage.

The new workplace provides the environment in which career clients and career helpers must function. Dominating this environment is the new adult-to-adult contract between employers and employees. This leads to a new vendor attitude on the part of employees. They are sensing organization needs and suggesting services to meet these needs. They are assuming responsibility for negotiating their tasks and rewards. Feminine concepts are defining successful organizations through an increased awareness of the need for community and cooperation.

Career helpers are being challenged to reassess the basis for their work. There is a recognition of the danger of creating a dichotomy between career and personal counseling. Several writers are reminding us that career is personal. Another issue is the need for a theory of career counseling. While we have had career development theories, we lack career counseling theories that might inform the work. Another suggestion has focused on the need for practice to inform research. There has been the suggestion that we need practioner-researcher (not faculty-student) teams that come together in community to inform each others work. Finally, are we practicing an art or a science? Too often our clients view us as the ones who have facts and techniques to "cure" their career pains. Many counselors are looking at the art of career counseling that addresses personal stories and creative inventions to help clients clarify and take ownership of their careers.

Several professional issues grow out of the trends. It is time to look at all career providers as a community of helpers. There are a variety of career helpers including career counselors, career facilitators, career technicians, career management specialists. We have developed counseling specialities (school, clinical, career, gerontological). Is it time to clarify the variety of career specialities? Our clients deserve full assistance for their career needs. The profession needs to define and respect the unique strengths of various career providers. We are already beginning to see a pattern of referral and cooperation among practitioners. Perhaps it is time to formalize this within the professional.

Consumer protection continues to be a primary need. If career providers are "healers for a troubled time," it is vital to help the public become wise consumers of career services. We need to continue to strengthen our consumer rights and responsibilities statements. We need to increase our public information services. We need to collaborate with other groups such as the National Board for Certified Counselors and the California Career Registry to help the public identify qualified career providers.

Job creation for career helpers is important. There is an embarrassing demand for career counselors on the part of the public. Often my private practice clients want to know how to become a career counselor based on the fact that they have waited six weeks to two months to see me. They are sure that it is a high-demand occupation. But the real issue is the need to provide quality, life-long career services at a reasonable cost to all people. Jane Goodman, NCDA President, has focused on the need for a periodic career check-up. Congress is looking at the myriad of federally-funded career services and noting overlap, gaps and lack of evidence of effectiveness of services. As professionals, we need to clarify the strengths of our community of career helpers, address these strengths through appropriate referral, and inform organizations of the need for career helpers, whether in educational, community, private practice, or corporate settings.

As I sorted and arranged the clippings that I have put in my collage, I found four themes that provide a unifying center point. These four themes apply to clients, to career helpers, and to the profession. These themes are resilience, balance, cyclical, and community. Resilience is the capacity to adapt to a changing situation while maintaining and nurturing one's core self. Balance is the capacity to hold opposites . For example, the capacity to balance work and other life roles or to view career counseling as both an art and a science. Cyclical is the notion of change as a never- ending process. The goal is not to fix the situation permanently, but to note where we are in the cycle and to honor our current needs. Cyclical has to do with timing. Is it time to act or is it time to rest? Finally, community is an important theme for our time. We need to avoid pseudo-community where we assume we are all the same, and reach for real community in which we embrace our differences while maintaining our interdependence.

References

Barrentine, P. (Ed.) (1993). *When the canary stops singing: Women's perspectives on transforming business.* San Francisco: Berrett-Koehler Publishers.

Bridges , W. (1994). *Jobshift: How to prosper in a Wworkplace without jobs.* Reading, Massachusetts, Addison-Wesley Publishing Company.

Engels, D. K. (Ed.). (1994). *The professional practice of career Ccounseling.* Alexandria, VA: National Career Development Association.

Hudson, F. M. (1991). The adult years: Mastering the art of self-renewal. San Francisco: Jossey-Bass Publishers.

Miller, J. V. (1993). *The art of discerning career.* Paper presented at the National Career Development Association's 75th Anniversary President's Symposium at the American Counseling Association Convention in Atlanta, GA.

Warnke, M. A., Kim, J., Koeltzow-Milster, D. Terrell, S, Dauser, P.J., Dial, S., Howie, J., & Thiel, M. J. (1993). Career counseling practicum: Transformations in conceptualizing career cssues. *The Career Development Quarterly, 42(2),* 180-185.

45

Adult Career Counseling Centers Train Career Counselors

Howard Splete

Need for Training

The workplace, both in the United States and internationally, has changed dramatically. The Secretary's Commission on Achieving Necessary Skills (SCANS, 1992) found that a majority of students leaving school lacked the knowledge or foundation to locate and hold good jobs in the current economy. Many companies are down-sizing and many of those adult employees in job transition also lack skills or knowledge in career development. The need to provide our citizens with the best support in their career exploration, preparation, and placement is evident. Career development counselors can provide this support in educational, business, community agency, and private practice settings. The question is—are our career development counselors appropriately trained?

> *As the need for professional career counseling increases, counselor education preparation programs should develop and implement adult career counseling centers as part of their programs, not only to train students and conduct appropriate research, but to provide needed career services to community adults.*

Based on an analysis of national surveys, Gazda (1991) saw the need to reassert the role of the counselor in aiding others in their career development. He proposed that counselors obtain additional expertise and upgrade their skills in career work. Recent surveys have indicated an immediate need for better training of career development counselors. Larrabee and Touma (1995) found that counselors in both pre-service and in-service career development courses were not exposed to the full array of career counselor competencies and lacked training in practical skills. Results of a similar survey by Hoppin and Splete (1994) support the need for career development facilitators to update their skills through experiential hands-on activities with supportive curriculum and supervision.

The overwhelming majority of master's level programs designed to prepare professional counselors include at least one course in career development. The programs that are Council for Accreditation of Counseling and Related Educational Programs (CACREP) accredited require course work to include *Lifestyle and Career Development*— studies that provide an understandingof career development theories; occupational and educational information sources and systems; career and leisure counseling, guidance, and education; lifestyle and career decision making; and career development program planning, resources, and evaluation (CACREP, 1988). An increased emphasis on career counseling in counselor preparation can be seen in the continual upgrading of career development standards, which includes knowledge and skills in multicultural issues, life roles, computer applications, supervision, ethical and legal issues, research and evaluation, and in the CACREP recognition of specialty preparation standards for career counseling (Engels, Minor, Sampson, & Splete, 1995).

The National Career Development Association (NCDA), in its publication, "The Professional Practice of Career Counseling and Consultation: A Resource Document" (Engels, 1994), lists ten needed competency areas for professional career counselors. They include individual counseling skills related to career development counseling.

Three experiential sub-headings are:
1. Ability to plan, implement, and evaluate counseling techniques designed to assist clients to achieve the following:
    a. Identify and understand clients' personal characteristics related to career.
    b. Identify and understand social contextual conditions affecting clients' careers.
    c. Identify and understand familial, subcultural and cultural

structures and functions as they are related to clients' careers.

d. Identify and understand clients' career decision-making processes.

e. Identify and understand clients' attitudes toward work and workers.

f. Identify and understand clients' biases toward work and workers based on gender, race, and cultural stereotypes.

2. Ability to challenge and encourage clients to take action to prepare for and initiate role transitions by:

a. Locating sources of relevant information and experience.

b. Obtaining and interpreting information and experiences.

c. Acquiring skills needed to make role transitions.

3. Ability to support and challenge clients to examine the balance of work, leisure, family, and community roles in their careers.

These counseling skills can be learned and practiced in adult career counseling centers, such as the University of Rochester Adult Counseling Center (URACC). This center provided adult career counseling based on a developmental life-span model (Gladstein, 1994). URACC was directly tied to a faculty academic unit, the Center for Counseling, Family and Worklife Studies (CFW) at the University of Rochester. The counseling at the center was designed to help clients resolve discrepancies between identity and experience, increase discrepancy awareness, and assist clients with modifying a restricting environment. This center also emphasized community service, training, research, and evaluation.

Oakland University has developed and operated an adult career counseling center for the past 12 years. Potential career counselors gain experience in the center, as they participate as interns, practicum students, graduate assistants, volunteers, or career class students. It should be emphasized that all participants work under the supervision of a faculty member or licensed professional counselor.

Center Services

The Adult Career Counseling Center (ACCC) at Oakland University has been staffed primarily by graduate assistants and interns who are called career advisors. The goals of the ACCC are to:

1. Provide career exploration and planning opportunities to community adults at no charge.
2. Train faculty, staff, and students in the use of career guidance practices for adults.
3. Support research efforts in promoting effective career guidance practices for adults.

ACCC objectives and activities are:

Goal 1: To provide career exploration and planning opportunities to community adults at no charge.

Objectives	Activities
To aid clients in self-analysis relating to their interests, values, abilities and experiences.	Review of past work history Use of career assessments Use of DISCOVER and SIGI PLUS
To provide job information pertaining to careers of interest, such as salary ranges and job growth rates nationally and/or in Michigan.	Use of Discover, SIGI PLUS, MOIS and OOH.
To aid clients in the process of taking the next step—including school or training program selection, resume preparation, honing interviewing skills, and informational interviewing.	Use of Harris SELECTORY and Expert Resume Writer. Provision of individual counseling sessions.

Goal 2: To train faculty, staff, and students in the use of career guidance practices for adults.

Objectives	Activities
To train faculty and staff.	Through periodic in-service sessions.
To train students.	Through experiential assignments in CNS 640, 664, and 675 Graduate Counseling classes.
To train area counselors.	Through in-service sessions.

Goal 3: To support research efforts for a better understanding of the career developmental sphere, ultimately promoting better career guidance.

Objectives	Activities
To support Master's level research.	ACCC advisors conduct research. CNS 560 and 660 projects are facilitated by the center.
To support Doctoral research activities.	Provide facilities and support to research efforts.

The Adult Career Counseling Center (ACCC) provides services for adults who are seeking guidance in reviewing their career possibilities. The ACCC provides career information, counseling, advice in resume preparation and interviewing skills, and referral information at no charge. Four graduate assistants, students in the Oakland University Master of Arts in Counseling Program, facilitate the ACCC services.

Two career guidance programs—DISCOVER for Colleges and Adults and SIGI PLUS—are available on micro-computers at the ACCC. These systems aid adults in learning how their interests, abilities, life experiences and work-related values are related to possible occupations and/or educational and training opportunities. The Michigan Occupational Information System (MOIS) is also available on micro-computer for clients seeking specific Michigan career information. Recently, the ACCC has made two new resources available to its clients: the Harris SELECTORY and Expert Resume Writer. The Harris SELECTORY provides information on companies where center users might conduct informational interviews or investigate employment opportunities. The computer program Expert Resume Writer allows clients to view and customize sample resumes provided in the program.

Additionally, clients have access to printed resources at the ACCC, including course catalogs from educational institutions in Michigan, career information books (e.g., Dictionary of Occupational Titles) and a wide range of practical books concerning the processes involved in the career search, such as *What Color is Your Parachute?*, *The Damn Good Resume Guide*, *Re-careering at Mid-life*, and *Job Choices 1994.*

Additional appointments can be made with counselors through the Practicum Counseling Center by clients desiring more in-depth career or personal counseling. Referral information about other career counseling and training programs is also available.

The counseling process used at the ACCC is as follows:

1. ACCC clients schedule two, two-hour appointments.
2. First the career advisor gathers background data and conducts an intake interview to establish the client's purpose for using the center.
3. After clients are provided with an overview of the computer programs, they may use DISCOVER for Colleges and Adults, SIGI PLUS and/or MOIS, depending on their specific needs.
4. Assistance and explanation of computer results are provided by the advisors.
5. At the completion of the client's second visit, the counselor conducts a short exit interview to help clients formulate their next step. Additional appointments may be scheduled

for computer use, assessments, or resume preparation. Referrals may be made to the Practicum Counseling Center or other university and community resources depending on the specific needs of the client (Splete & Davis, 1994).

Counseling Student and Department Involvement in the Center

Perhaps the key component in providing career counseling experience to master's level students is that this experience be part of class requirements. Many opportunities to acquire career counseling skills are provided in a variety of courses. The introductory career counseling course in the Oakland University Master's program, CNS 640: Career Development Theory and Practice, is based on students obtaining knowledge, understanding and experience related to the recommended NCDA career counseling competencies. These competencies are presented in Splete's (1992) "Using the National Career Development Guidelines in Training Career Counselors." Each student in this course is expected to become very familiar with the ACCC and its computer-assisted programs, assessments and other resources. They are required to use the ACCC in working with their class career clients. Instructor supervision and feedback is provided during this class assignment. Also at Oakland University, many practicum level students (CNS 664), advanced career counseling students (CNS 675), as well as interns (CNS 666) use the ACCC in working with their clients. These students gain valuable hands-on experience with clients by learning to administer and interpret a variety of career assessment instruments, including the Strong Interest Inventory, and by working with clients on the computer guidance systems. Practicum and intern level students have the ability to follow through with clients in individual counseling sessions. The experience Oakland University students gain from using the ACCC is invaluable.

The counseling department is extremely supportive in including the ACCC as part of its counselor preparation program. Mention of the facility is made in promotional materials of the counseling program. Released time is provided for an instructor to coordinate the center and supervise the four graduate assistant career advisors.

Financial support for the non-fee services has come from the university budget, as administrative officials strongly believe in providing this community service as part of the university's overall mission.

Development of a Center

In developing a university career counseling center for community adults, it would be appropriate to:

1. Review the needs of community adults for this service by contacting community agencies, businesses, and governmental agencies. The review could promote this service as supportive or collaborative to the other groups— not as an attempt to take their clients. An advisory task-force could be helpful.

2. Review the university, school, and department understanding and support for the concept of providing this service and the related functions of training and research.

3. Draft a pilot project for staff and student involvement which would include the necessary financial support for graduate assistantships, faculty released time, facilities, equipment, and resources.

4. Obtain administrative support for the pilot project with an evaluation process included.

5. Complete the pilot project and note revisions. Ask for continued involvement and support by administrators, faculty, and the community.

6. Establish an advisory committee, including university, business, governmental, and community agency personnel to provide input and suggestions.

7. Continue to evaluate, revise, and publicize the center's services annually. This can be done through a report of clients serviced, training provided, and research done. This information should be shared with university officials, local newspapers, community agencies, and professional associations.

8. Continue communications with other agencies and institutions to look at possible improvement of services and

involvement in collaborative efforts such as "One Stop Career Centers."

In planning an adult career counseling center, provision of the following resources should be researched:

1. Adequate space and facilities to include a reception area, private computer and counseling rooms, and a large room for staff meetings and group presentations
2. Full-time receptionist
3. Computer-assisted career-guidance programs
4. Computer hardware
5. Computerized DOT
6. Multi-media career development programs
7. Information on apprenticeships and volunteer field experiences
8. Career materials and job possibilities relating careers to high school, community college, and university career majors
9. Comprehensive faculty supervision of career advisors.

Summary

Career counseling experiences during pre-service master's level programs better prepare professional career counselors for their jobs. Adult career counseling centers seem most appropriate in providing these experiences under proper supervision. As the need for professional career counseling increases, counselor education preparation programs should develop and implement adult career counseling centers as part of their programs, not only to train students and conduct appropriate research, but to provide needed career services to community adults.

References

Council for Accreditation of Counseling and Related Educational Programs. (1988). *Accreditation procedures manual and application.* Alexandria, VA: Author.

Engels, D. W. (Ed.). (1994). *The professional practice of career counseling and consultation: A resource document.* Alexandria, VA: National Career Development Association.

Engels, D. W., Minor, C. W., Sampson, J. P., Jr., & Splete, H. H. (1995). Career counseling specialty: History, development, and prospect. *Journal of Counseling & Development, 74,* 134-138.

Gazda, G. M. (1991). What recent survey research indicates for the future of counseling and counselor education. In G. R. Walz, G. M. Gazda, and B. Shertzer (Eds.), *Counseling futures* (pp. 11-26). Ann Arbor: ERIC Counseling and Personnel Service Clearinghouse, University of Michigan.

Gladstein, G. A. (1994). *Changing careers: A ten year demonstration of a developmental life-span approach.* Rochester, NY: University of Rochester Press.

Hoppin, J., & Splete, H. (1994). *Training needs of career development facilitators.* Stillwater, OK: National Occupational Information Coordinating Committee Training Support Center, Oklahoma Department of Vocational and Technical Education.

Larrabee, M., & Touma, S. (1995). *Training needs of career development practitioners and trainers.* Stillwater, OK: National Occupational Information Coordinating Committee Training Support Center, Oklahoma Department of Vocational and Technical Education.

The Secretary's Commission on Achieving Necessary Skills. (1992). *Learning a living: A blueprint for high performance: A SCANS report for America 2000.* Washington, DC: U.S. Government Printing Office.

Splete, H. H. (1992). Using the national career development guidelines in training career counselors. In J. Lester (Ed.), *From pilot to practice: Strengthening career development programs* (pp. 55-73). Stillwater, OK: National Occupational Information Coordinating Committee Training Support Center.

Splete, H. H. & Davis, J. (1994). *Adult career counseling center eleventh annual report.* Rochester, MI: Oakland University.

46

Using The I-Way for Career Development

Garry R. Walz

An increasingly popular and influential way for people to conduct their lives, e.g., send messages, order things, network with others, see/hear the latest news, locate important bodies of information and further their education is to use the Internet (The Net) or, in more generic terms, the Information Highway (I-Way). So ubiquitous has it become that the popular press regularly features articles such as addiction to the Net, giving up real-life (RL) for "life before the screen," children's access to pornography and gross materials, the use of the Net to foment hate campaigns, and discussions by pop psychologists on virtual affairs and infidelities by married people on the Net.

> *The I-Way for counselors can be about human values, sharing personal views and thoughts with others without fear of disapprovaal, and eliminating responses to what a person thinks and feels based on her/his color, race, religion, social/economic status, etc.*

Clearly, as persons across the globe rush headlong to "get a life," the I-Way will occupy an important niche in their lives exercising a potent influence on how people spend their work and leisure times, with whom and how they communicate, and from what means they learn about new events. One would believe that anything as ubiquitous with such seemingly boundless potential to significantly influence the behavior of both children and adults would result in a zesty dialogue among career counselors and other mental health specialists as to the implications of this revolution in information and communication for the practice of counseling and career interventions.

Such, however, does not appear to be the case. There does appear to be considerable interaction by those who are regular surfers of the I-Way. However, the more traditional forms of professional communication, e.g., journal articles, professional presentations or ERIC documents, are sparse in their treatment in contrast to coverage of other contemporary hot topics such as multiculturism, ethics, new legislative initiatives, etc. If this seeming ignoral of the potential of the I-Way to influence career counseling is as widespread as it would appear, then it is both puzzling and troubling—puzzling because career counselors have been in the forefront in the use of computers in counseling, e.g., computer assisted career guidance (Walz, 1970), and troubling because a literal revolution is underway in the larger world and we are not discussing and responding to how this revolution in communication is affecting the makeup of the people we seek to help and counsel, and how this new force could be used to optimize the very ways we provide career counseling and career development (Walz, Gazda & Shertzer, 1991).

It is with the belief that what is needed is more thoughtful imaging of potential outcomes and less overloading of technical information that leads me to focus my attention on what I believe are powerful new resources that the I-Way offers which can assist us in responding to the many vexing and challenging tasks which confront all who would seek to facilitate the career development of others. Said in the most direct terms, "What can the I-Way do to help us be better career counselors?"

Proactive Strategies for Counselors
Using the I-Way

The following four suggestions are intended to assist counselors to optimize their use of the I-Way.

1. Change our mental set regarding the new information tools from viewing them as pieces of advanced technology to viewing them as a process for furthering human connection and interaction.

My experiences in discussing the I-Way with countless groups and organizations is that the common image of the Net and the I-Way is one that involves a high level use of computers involving skills that rcquire considerable time, expense and special training to acquire. There are two negative consequences of this overblown negative stereotype. First, the technological framing of the I-Way with all the accompanying anxiety persons possess over learning how to use new technologies intensifies the "internetaphobia" that adults in general experience (career counselors too?). This perception has also probably reinforced the views of many that the Net is for computer nerds only. The unfortunate result as regards career development is that many active career counselors and specialists see using the I-Way as so demanding and complex that "getting on" is deferred to sometime in the future.

A second, even more detrimental consequence, is a generalized perception and response that the I-Way is only tangentially related to the intimate and interactive nature of career counseling. The I-Way is perceived as probably having utility for accessing information and data, but certainly not an important component of career counseling and the career development process. The point, therefore, needs to be made and passionately pursued that the real potential of the I-Way for career specialists is to enhance and extend connections between the career specialist and client/student to the benefit of both. It brings an enabling function to the career development process allowing counselors to deal more intensively and extensively with clients and students. It also allows counselors to overcome problems of distance and time to offer opportunities for networking and interacting not otherwise available. The I-Way for counselors *can* be about human values, sharing personal views and thoughts with others without fear of disapproval, and eliminating responses to what a person thinks and feels based on her/his color, race, religion, social/economic status, etc. Admittedly, it will take some imaginative planning on the part of the counselor to realize the full potentials of the I-Way for facilitating career development. However, unless counselors envisage the potential positive outcomes in *human* terms, and have a positive mental set towards using the I-Way, they will never undertake the requisite steps to capacitate themselves and apply it to their career counseling contacts.

2. Create virtual libraries of career development resources for use
   by career counselors, students, clients, parents, and teachers.

A Website on the Net offers a highly attractive opportunity for career counselors to access career resources for use by themselves and/or by students, parents, and clients. The advantage of the virtual library over a traditional library is that it does not require a large expenditure of funds to purchase physical copies of career resources. Instead, virtual libraries use career materials presently on theNet or materials which are specially added from ERIC or other public sources. Because the library is on a Website, other Net users with the appropriate software can search the virtual library "card catalog", to locate what they want, and then call up the items for their use on their own Net connection without leaving their computer. A special feature is the ability to download and print long documents so as to minimize online time spent scrolling and scanning the screen. The virtual library also has other important features such as easy updating and no lost or checked out books.

Jeanne Bleuer and I are currently heading a project funded by NOICC which is focused on creating a model of a virtual career library for parents and students to assist them in making career plans and decisions. The virtual library plus training packs on how to establish and train persons in the use of the library will be available in Summer '96.

The great advantage of the virtual libraries is that they are dynamic and can be customized to meet the needs of special user groups, e.g., students studying career development in a counseling theories class, parents wanting to be good career mentors for their children, and career specialists who want a listing of relevant Web sites to "hot link" to and download additional career resources in full text form.

3. Prepare *all* students in how to use a computer and the Net for
   self- development and career planning.

Recent statistics compiled by the U.S. Department of Education reveal a dramatic difference in the use of computers by students at all grade levels by racial makeup (Lappin, 1995). Whites are far more likely to have access to computers in their schooling than either

Hispanic or Black population sub-groups. When one considers that computer competency may be the single most important skill a high school graduate needs to obtain employment, this statistic assumes great importance. Without this competency, even a high school diploma may be of minimal assistance. Even traditional industries which previously sought high school dropouts for their mills and factories now require computer competency for many of their jobs. Of special importance is the *level* of computer skills needed by students. Rote learning and basic word processing skills are relatively less important, while the ability to do database searching, problem solving, and locating special resources is in large demand. Students who have a constructivist approach to computer usage, who see it as useful in responding to their own special needs and interests will develop computer competencies for use on the I-Way which not only meet their personal needs and interests, but also have important occupational applications as well. For students who have limited access to computers and whose immediate environment is not computer rich, access to the interactive Internet options such as Listservs, chat boxes and MUD's through their schools may provide the incentive to get "wired" and in the process develop useful computer skills with occupational applications. The ability to communicate, problem solve, and network electronically is an essential life competency which counselors can assist all students to acquire.

4. Promote the use of Internet "tools" which offer great promise for moving career development and career counseling to a higher and more interactive level.

Counselors differ considerably in their intervention styles and how they choose to relate to and interact with counselees. As frequently discussed in the articles in this monograph, some counselors have a diagnostic and assessment bent. In a similar vein, some career counselors have a predilection for augmenting their one-on-one career counseling with activities that enhance a client's perceptions of what is entailed in different choices and actions. Though hard to classify or describe, they have a common emphasis on front loading the decision matrix by providing the participants with insights they ordinarily would acquire through actual training and work experience. Examples include *shadowing* (following an actual worker while he/she performs her/his job); *behavioral tryout* (performing job samples to see if one gets the knack of a job); and *computer assisted career guidance programs* which can combine a number of the activities in a unified way.

With the advent of the Internet, a new and challenging array of interactive activities are available. Though not developed with counselors in mind, they lend themselves to creative and imaginative uses by career counselors. Data regarding the efficacy of these innovations is sparse. However, the feedback of participants gathered either formally or informally is invariably highly favorable to the process and the outcomes. Following are brief descriptions of two of these interactive Net options.

a) Moderated and Participant Limited Interprofessional Listserv.

Listservs are a common feature of the Net today with literally hundreds of participants. Easy to join, they cover whatever topics the participants are interested in raising questions about or offering suggestions on. Their strength is the ease of entry and withdrawal while the drawback is the sheer volume of messages any given person will receive.

The innovative format to be used with the ERIC/CASS CATS (Counselor and Therapist Support System) Listserv is distinguished by the selection of a host (an expert on the topic under discussion) who reviews and edits all comments before they are posted. The host regularly adds comments and asks questions of the participants to help keep the discussion focused.

b) Multiple-User Domains.

A descendant of the Dungeons and Dragons fantasy role playing game of the late 1970s and early 1980s construct new selves through social interaction with other players in a virtual community. According to Turkle (1995), there are now over 500 MUDs in which hundreds of thousands of people participate. Most players are in their twenties and thirties, but some are as young as eight or nine. "MUDs provide worlds for anonymous social interaction in which one can play a role as close to or as far away from one's "real self" as one chooses" (Turkle, 1995, p. 12). They offer an unparalleled opportunity to ".. express multiple and often unexplored aspects of the self, to play with their identity and to try out new ones" (Turkle, 1995, p. 12).

Persons who are active participants describe the activity as among the most compelling they have experienced. Some go as far as to suggest that because of the opportunity to explore different personalities and "to be whom you want to be," life in a MUD should have equal status and importance as real life (RL). One student, in obvious awe of his experiences, reported to me that "if you are going to get involved in MUDs, you had better be prepared to see your GPA drop a full point."

Foremost among those doing serious research on MUDs is Sherry Turkle (1995) who is researching the impact of the computer on our psychological lives and how it (the computer) can lead persons to a deepened and multiple sense of identity. There appears to be little or no direct research and/or experimentation with MUDs with career development in mind. The potentialities, however, are exciting. If the choice of a career is an expression of a person's self concept, it behooves us to maximize opportunities for counselees to more fully explore their self concepts. The nature of a person's interactions with other persons of both similar and dissimilar occupational identity is an important determinant in a person's job satisfaction. Participants in an occupational MUD would have the opportunity to try out different career identities and note both their satisfaction with a given occupational identity and perhaps more importantly, how they feel about other people's response to them as a skilled technician, engineer or personal services representative.

The above descriptions are illustrative rather than definitive. There are many imaginative uses where a MUD would be beneficial to a person exploring a first career choice or contemplating a career change. Though seemingly complex, in actuality, MUDs do not require sophisticated hardware or software. It is probable that with further research they will be an additional powerful career development tool which a career counselor could judiciously use with clients/students.

c) Internet Relay Chat.

Another interactive computer mediated activity is the Internet Relay Chat (IRC), sometimes called "chat boxes." They have similarities to the MUDs in that the participant can open a channel (usually with a name or topic) and interact with others. Participants speak to one another as if they were in the same room. It can be highly interactive, even hectic. The IRCs offer "real time" interaction (communication is spontaneous and on-going) with other people, personal anonymity if desired, and the opportunity to assume alternate identities. Usually less scripted than a MUD, they provide people with a comparatively easy way to connect with others on topics of mutual interest. One particularly powerful option they provide is to assist a person to experience another identity as a means to better understand how the other person feels, e.g., a male assuming a female identity to be sensitized to sexual harassment. Topic-oriented interaction is also common where participants (with or without passion) can share their views on topics important to them.

Anyone who has participated in an IRC can attest to the power of the experience—so powerful, in fact, that a syndicated columnist recently reprinted the compelling (and often negative) experiences that participants had described to her. Suffice to say, powerful experiences can cut both ways —positive and negative. With the proper structure and timely interventions by a "leader" if needed, the IRC offers a relatively easy way for persons to interact on cognitive topics or a more personally focused self exploration.

5. Use ERIC database searching for personal decision making and professional renewal.

Not too long ago people who wanted to search the ERIC database via computer had to go to a university or other public library. There they could either: a) request a professional information specialist to conduct an online search using a commercial online service provider such as BRS or DIALOG; or b) conduct the search themselves at one of the library's SilverPlatter CD-ROM work stations. Unfortunately, unless the library was highly subsidized, the online search could be quite expensive and it often took up to a week to obtain the printout of the search results. While searching ERIC via the library's CD-ROM station is free and the results are immediate, these very advantages make CD-ROM work stations very popular. In fact, in many University libraries, both students and faculty have to sign up a month in advance for a one-hour time slot.

Two recent developments have changed all this; and people can now obtain free and/or inexpensive access to the ERIC database from their own home computers. The first development is the availability of ERIC on the Internet. Several universities as well as the U.S. Department of Education offer access to ERIC through their Web and gopher sites. For example, AskERIC offers search capability at the URL http://ericir.syr.edu/ERIC/erichtml. Users can also telnet to ericir.syr.edu, login as "gopher," hit Return/Enter for the password, then follow the instructions.

The second development is the release of a low-cost ERIC on CD-ROM product by the National Information Services Co. (NISC). Available through the ERIC Processing and Reference Facility, the current NISC disc contains the complete ERIC database including full-text ERIC Digests for 1980 to the present at a cost of only $25. An archive disc (1966-1979) is also available for $25. A one-year subscription with quarterly updates of the current disc costs $100 and the complete set with archive disc costs $125. Hardware requirements are: 1) any DOS-capable, IBM-compatible computer (but 386-level or greater is recommended); 2) any CD-ROM drive; 3) color or monochrome monitor; and 4) 150K RAM available (512K without extended memory).

By using these tools, career counselors and career development specialists can easily stay on top of what's new in the literature. For further information on either Internet or CD-ROM access to ERIC, contact the ERIC/CASS Clearinghouse toll-free at 1-800-414-9769, by e-mail at ericcass@iris.uncg.edu or by FAX at 910-334-4116.

Career counselors can reap major benefits from ERIC database searches in two major ways. First, is to search a particular question or problem where they need the best and most up-to-date research and literature. Using the NISC CD-ROM, a person can select the level of his search (novice to expert) and within minutes on his/her home computer print out the results of the search. Who hasn't had a vexing problem where quick reliable information was needed for making an important decision? A second use is to create a personal renewal system where, quarterly, a person searches the new CD-ROM on topics of ongoing importance to him/her, e.g., assessment and minorities, girls' career development, etc. Both search strategies are needed by a career counselor who wishes to be professionally and ethically sound by making her/his decisions on the best available information.

The Lucky Seven—Taking A Leap Forward on the I-Way

The following seven recommended actions are neither difficult to accomplish nor hard on the budget. They will, however, be a major leap forward on the I-Way.

1. *Get Online!* You can't reap the benefits of the I-Way unless you can cruise the I-Way and utilize what cyberspace has to offer. What is required? Not much. A computer with a modem and a CD-ROM; an Internet Service provider (through your school, university, community, or a commercial provider, e.g., AOL, Prodigy); and the appropriate browser, e.g., Netscape, Java, etc.

2. *Identify a friendly, local mentor and reserve time to browse, surf and experiment!* Find an associate with high nurturing needs who will be available to answer questions and demonstrate. Allow time at home to play with all the options and goodies. Remember, it's hard to go wrong or make serious mistakes.

3. *Access several relevant Web sites.* The ERIC/CASS and newly introduced NCDA Web sites are good for starters. Through them you can link to other "rich lodes" of career development information and resources. The NCDA page will particularly be helpful to you in keeping attuned to important happenings in career development.

4. *Join a number of Listservs with different foci and sophistication.* Keep your cutting edge sharp by participating in "free forum" open Listservs and focused moderated Listservs. You benefit by joining Listservs with different expectations in mind for each. Check the Web sites of different counseling organizations, gophers and indexes on the Net to identify attractive options. And don't hesitate to get off if it isn't serving your needs!

5. *Purchase ERIC on CD-ROM and develop skill in the use of the different search strategies.* The capacity to do on-demand searches when you need them far outweighs the modest expenditure that a CD-ROM NISC DISC will cost you. Having the best information available when you want it will become addictive. You will make better decisions and take more appropriate actions.

6. *Undertake your own personal experimentation with innovtive options on the I-Way.* IRCs, Moderated Listservs, MUDs, and Newsgroups are just some of the more visible options. By experimenting with them, you can sharpen your use of technology to more effectively deliver different aspects of career development. Some, if not most, will not work for you or only in very limited fashion; but you won't know until you experiment.

7. *Share your successes and difficulties on the I-Way by writing about them for ERIC/CASS.* There is a real dearth of materials available on facilitating "career development in turbulent times," especially as regards innovative and technologically driven interventions. ERIC's general policy of accepting material based on content and quality rather than style, length, etc., makes ERIC an attractive source for authors who have a meaningful message to deliver, but not the time to prepare a finely word-crafted article. It also bears repeating that by

having an article in ERIC you speak to a worldwide audience and increase the engaging opportunities of networking with others on the I-Way.

Conclusion

A recently stated goal of President Clinton is that every school in the U.S. be wired for the Internet by the year 2000. Mega communication corporations have loudly proclaimed their goal of having the Information Superhighway enter every home by the turn of the century. However unduly optimistic these goals are, and in many ways they are both unrealistic and inappropriate, they foretell a new age in communication and learning throughout the world. The opportunities to access important bodies of information, the ability, from your home, to communicate and network with persons around the globe quickly and inexpensively with print, sound, graphics, and animation, and most of all to do so interactively will change forever how we learn. Given this true paradigm shift in the tools and the process of learning, the ultimate question for career counseling is from whence will career development be offered and delivered? Will it be through the use of traditional educational methods, or will it be a resculpturing that optimizes the fit between the needs of individuals for personalized lifelong learning and the expanded capabilities of technology to customize learning to fit individual needs. How individually and collectively that question is answered will greatly influence the future and vitality of career development programs.

If the "medium is the message" what message is contemporary career development delivering?

References

Coulter, P., Howley, C. B., Kerka, S., Smith, S., & Walz, G. (Eds.). (1995). K-12 computer networking. *The ERIC Review, 4* (1).

Lappin, T. (Ed.). (1995, December). Students with home computers. *Wired,* p. 70.

Office of Educational Research and Improvement. (1995). *Getting online: A friendly guide for teachers, students, and parents.* (ERIC 95-5029). Washington, DC: Author.

Turkle, S. (1995). *Life on the screen: Identity in the age of the Internet.* New York: Simon & Schuster.

Walz, G. R. (1970). Technology in guidance: A conceptual overview. *Personnel Guidance Journal, 49* (3),   175-184.

Walz, G.R., Gazda, G. M., & Shertzer, B. (1991). *Counseling futures.* Ann Arbor, MI: ERIC Counseling and Personnel Services Clearinghouse.

A Summing Up and a Leap to the Future

Garry Walz
Rich Feller

47

The Summing up and a Leap to the Future

Garry Walz & Rich Feller

As you piece together a book that has many parts, you find yourself albeit unwittingly forming conclusions as regards what is important. Some thoughts or themes stand out. You say to yourself, "That's something important! I want to remember that!" Such has been our situation in assembling this book. Our "Summing Up" is the result of a few ideas that had a strong impact on us. Sometimes they were worth remembering because of the singular power they possessed—one reading and we were "hooked!" Other times a message seemed important because it was repeated by so many of the writers. There seemed to be a common consensus that it was important, and we thought so too.

Therefore, we have put down, in no particular order, a few ideas that influenced our thinking. Our intent was to informally model a process we think is important, i.e., summing up central concepts and sharing them with others. If you read what we have to say and disagree, but go on to identify what attracts *you,* we have been successful. Each of us needs to sort out from all the information before us that which is important enough to remember.

1. There is an emerging consensus that what every worker needs is a core set of survival skills—resilience, the capacity for continuous learning and improvement, the ability to network and team, skill in using technology effectively, willingness to take calculated risks and learn from setbacks, etc. Important skills all! Can career counselors contribute to the learning of these and other equally important survival skills? Probably, but few writers believe they are doing so now. What will it take to facilitate learning these skills and to give them a high priority in

career development?

2. The need for revisiting counselor training emerges again and again. However, the *need* for change generates a greater consensus than does the prescription. Some of the recommended changes may be more a matter of counselor selection than counselor training. In a nutshell, a number of writers are calling for career counselors to be better prepared to deal with the whole person (the career *client*) not just her/his career situation. It is a "career counseling plus" with attention to personality dynamics, mental health, disabilities, and negative thinking that needs, among many things, to be dealt with *before* there is a concerted focus on career considerations. The argument for this added "whole person dimension" is rooted in making the career counseling take hold or penetrate. A series of dysfunctional personal characteristics are seen as overshadowing or precluding effective career counseling work. The logic behind the argument is powerful, but questions abound. How much broader or deeper counseling is necessary or desirable? Should we be thinking of the model as clinical counselors who have additional preparation in career development? From an economic standpoint, how much specialized training can we reasonably expect to be the norm for career counselors? Once raised, the question of the adequacy of a career counselor's "clinical training" doesn't go away easily.

3. Running through the conceptions of many of the authors is a clear conviction that knowledge and skill in the use of the new technologies, e.g. computers, multimedia, Internet and video, are essential components of the of the armamentarium of the complete contemporary counselor. Equipped with technological "know-how," counselors can more easily relate to Twentysomething and younger students/clients who cut their learning teeth on video games, TV, and computers. Technological expertise also empowers the counselor with additional counseling and facilitation tools, extends the number of clients and the distance at which clients can be served, and offers increased opportunities for the counselor to serve as a mentor and co-counselor. While

many writers speak of the need for counselors to use technology, the resistance to its use and the obstacles to its greater utilization are infrequently dealt with.

4. One of the most pervasive areas of agreement by the writers has to do with the increasing recognition of the importance of the environment in individual career development. While individual psychological characteristics are still seen as important, the influence of the workplace, the family and the immediate environment are seen as setting limits and determining how influential individual characteristics are in affecting career development and occupational behavior. Large numbers of our writers are calling for a more realistic appraisal of the work place, what opportunities actually exist for self-realization, and how persons can be equipped to cope with a bumpy, pot-holed road— a *more frequently traveled* road that is both more challenging and unpredictable than previous career development conceptions would suggest. This "new found" realism about the workplace seems to have become a rallying point for a career counseling initiative that is both more inclusive of persons of differing backgrounds and experiences, and more willing to confront environmental challenges that have previously been ignored or glossed over.

5. "Is career counseling for everyone?" This could be the question of many writers who career planning and decision making to be available to all youth and adults, rather than the few who fit a neat, prescribed mold. Cultural diversity, pluralism and multiculturalism is the norm and the strength of the United States. Will we confront our cultural differences and customize the delivery of career development to the needs of each sub group? Or will we ignore the differences and put the onus of adjustment and change on those persons not now adequately and appropriately served? The answer to the question, "Is career counseling for everyone?" would, for many of our writers, be a resounding yes. But even though most deserving, the task is a daunting one that will require a firm resolve. Is there a sufficient collective resolve for such an initiative to be successful? There had better be if

career development is to become a viable component of "getting a life" for all people.

6. From whence does a professional movement or trend draw its knowledge? Clearly psychology is seen as the watershed from which our theorists, scholars and researchers draw their inspiration and ideas. Few of our writers would distance us from psychology, but many would multiply the wells from which we draw our sustenance. Organizational and industrial sociology, manpower, industrial economics, and anthropology are some of the disciplines which some writers believe are essential if we are to become a part of a national strategy for human resources development. If we are to offer a potent punch strategy to the public policy makers who will decide what will make the most compelling national initiative we will clearly need to add to our psychological base the wisdom of other highly respected disciplines.

More illustrative than definitive, we hope these brief summaries will nonetheless facilitate your own "leap to the future!" Hopefully, they will encourage you to identify for yourself what from among the abundant ideas presented are those that are sufficiently compelling for you to act on now!

Contributors

Sharon Anderson, PhD.
    Licensed Psychologist, state of Colorado
    School of Education
    227 Education Building
    Colorado State University
    Fort Collins, Colorado, 80523
    (970)491-6861 FAX: (970)491-1317
    e-mail: Sanders@lamar.colostate.edu

M. Lynne Bezanson, M.Ed.
    Canadian Guidance and Counseling Foundation
    202-411 Roosevelt Avenue
    Ottawa, Ontario, K2A 3X9
    (613)729-6164 FAX: (613)729-3515
    e-mail: cgcffcoc@magi.com

Henry Borow, Ph.D.
    Licensed Psychologist, state of Minnesota
    565 Otis Avenue
    St Paul, Minnesota, 55104
    (612)645-1723

JoAnn Bowlsbey, Ph.D.
    ACT, Educational Technology Center-East
    Executive Plaza 1-Suite 200
    11250 McCormick Road
    Hunt Valley, Maryland, 21031
    (410) 584-8000 FAX: (410) 785-1714

Larry D. Burlew, Ed.D.
    Associate Professor, Barry University
    ADSOE/Counseling Program
    11300 NE 2nd Avenue
    Miami Shores, Florida 33161
    (305) 899-3000

David Campbell , Ph.D.
    Center for Creative Leadership
    850 Leader Way
    Colorado Springs, Colorado, 80901
    (719)633-3891 FAX: (719)633-2236

William Charland
   Senior Fellow
   Center for the New West
   1625 Broadway-Suite 600
   Denver, Colorado, 80202
   (303)572-5452 FAX: (303)572-5499

Cal Crow, Ph.D.
   Center for Career and Work-Related Education
   Highline Community College 25-5A
   P.O. Box 98000
   Des Moines, Washington, 98198-9800
   (206) 870-3784 FAX:(206)870-3787
   e-mail: nwcooped@halcyon.com

Beth Durodoye, Ph.D.
   LPC, NCC, Assistant Professor
   Dept of Counseling, Development and Higher Education
   Box 13859
   University of North Texas
   Denton, Texas, 76203
   (817)565-2910 FAX: (817)565-2905

Dennis Engels, Ph.D.
   LPC, NCC, NCCC, Regent's Professor
   Dept. of Counseling, Development and Higher Education
   Box 13859
   University of North Texas
   Denton, Texas, 76203
   (817)565-2910 FAX:(817)565-2905
   e-mail: Engels@wp.unt.edu

Judith M. Ettinger, Ph.D.
   964 Educational Sciences Building
   1025 W. Johnson Street
   Madison, Wisconsin, 53706-1796
   (608)263-4367 FAX: (608)262-9197
   e-mail: jettinger@soemadison.wisc.edu

Rich Feller, Ph.D.
   Rich Feller is Professor of Counseling and Career Development at
   Colorado State University.
   School of Occupational & Educational Studies
   Room 222, Education Building
   Colorado State University
   Fort Collins, Colorado 80523
   (970) 491-6879 FAX: (970) 491-1317
   e-mail: feller@cahs.colostate.edu

H.B. Gelatt, Ed.D.
> Licensed Psychologist, state of California
> 1936 Kay Drive
> Los Altos, California, 94024
> (415)967-8345 FAX: (415)960-7076
> e-mail: 76761.2373@compuserve.com

Norman C. Gysbers, Ph.D.
> Professor
> Department of Educational and Counseling Psychology
> University of Missouri-Columbia
> Columbia, Missouri 65221
> (314) 882-7731 FAX: (314) 882-5440

L. Sunny Hansen, Ph.D.
> NCC, NCCC, APA Fellow, School Counselor, state of Minnesota
> 139 Burton, 178 Pillsbury Drive
> University of Minnesota
> Minneapolis, Minnesota 55455
> (612) 624-4885 FAX: (612) 625-4063
> e-mail: hanse001@maroon.tc.umn.edu

Tom Harrington, Ph.D.
> 201 Lake Hall, Dept. of Counseling Psychology
> Northeastern University, 360 Huntington Ave.
> Boston, Massachusetts 02115
> (617) 373-5938 FAX: (617) 373-8892

Bryan Hiebert, Ph.D.
> CCC
> Department of Educational Psychology
> University of Calgary
> Calgary, Alberta T2N 1N4
> (403) 220-0770 FAX: (403) 288-0028
> e-mail: hiebert@acs.ucalgary.ca

Mary Heppner, Ph.D.
> Psychology Department
> 210 McAlester Hall
> University of Missouri
> Columbia, Missouri 65211
> (573) 882-6485 FAX: (573) 882-7710
> e-mail: psymary@&mizzou1.missouri.edu

Edwin L. Herr, Ed.D.
NCC, NCCC
Office of Associate Dean for Graduate Programs
Research and Technology
College of Education
241 Chambers Building
The Pennsylvania State University
University Park, Pennsylvania 16802-3206
(814) 863-1489 FAX: (814) 865-0555
e-mail: elh2@psu.edu

Kenneth B. Hoyt, Ph.D.
Kansas State University
Department of Counseling and Ed. Psychology
369 Bluemont Hall
1100 Mid-Campus Drive
Manhattan, Kansas 66506-5312
(913) 532-6500 FAX: (913) 532-7304

Frederic M. Hudson, Ph.D.
The Hudson Institute of Santa Barbara
3463 State Street, Suite 520
Santa Barbara, California 93105
(805) 682-3883 FAX: (805) 569-0025

Ed Jacobs, Ph.D.
Counseling, Rehabilitation, and Counseling Psychology Department
502 Allen Hall, West Virginia University
Morgantown, West Virginia 26506-6122
(304) 293-3807 FAX: (304) 599-6683
e-mail: 74352.1403@compuserve.com

Frank Jarlett
3634 Tierra De Dios
Escondido, California 92025
(619) 745-1090 FAX: (619) 741-2863

Carolyn Kern, Ph.D.
LPC, NCC
Assistant Professor
Department of Counseling, Development and Higher Educ.
Box 13859, University of North Texas
Denton, Texas 76203
(817) 565-2910 FAX: (817) 565-2905

Diane Kjos, Ph.D.
Division of Psychology and Counseling
Governors State University
University Park, Illinois 60466
(708) 534-4904
e-mail: gdkjos@uxa.gsu.bgu.edu

Richard L. Knowdell
NCCC, Charter Fellow of The Outplacement Institute
Knowdell is currently the President of Career Research and Testing, Inc.
President, Career Research & Testing, Inc.
2005 Hamilton Avenue, Suite 250
San Jose, California 95125
(408) 559-4945 FAX: (408)559-8211

John D. Krumboltz, Ph.D.
Licensed Psychologist, state of California
School of Education, Stanford University
Stanford, California 94305-3096
(415) 723-2108 FAX: (415) 725-7412
e-mail: jdk@leleand.stanford.edu

Janet G. Lenz, Ph.D.
NCC, NCCC
Career Center, University Center - Fourth Floor
Florida State University
Tallahassee, Florida 32306-1035
(904) 644-9547
e-mail: jlenz@admin.fsu.edu

Frederick Leong, Ph.D.
Ohio State University, Department of Psychology
142 Townshend Hall, 1885 Neil Avenue
Columbus, Ohio 43210-1222
(614) 292-8219 FAX: (614) 292-4537
e-mail: leong.10@osu.edu

Juliette N. Lester
2100 M Street, NW
Suite 156
Washington, DC 20037
(202) 653-5665 FAX: (202) 653-2123
e-mail: noicc@digex.com

Rodney L. Lowman, Ph.D.
Licensed Psychologist, state of Texas
Development Laboratories
6 Chelsea Blvd., Suite E
Houston, Texas 77006-6203
(713) 527-9235 FAX: (713) 527-8130
e-mail: devlabs@ix.netcom.com

Esther E. Matthews, Ed.D.
Professor Emerita, University of Oregon
832 Lariat Drive
Eugene, Oregon 97401
(541) 343-2448

Carl McDaniels, Ed.D.
NCC, NCCC
Professor, Counselor Education
Virginia Tech
Blacksburg, Virginia 24061-0302
(540) 231-6890 FAX: (540) 231-7845
e-mail: cmcd@vtvml.cc.vt.edu

John McFadden, Ph.D
NCC, LPCS
Department of Educational Psychology
University of South Carolina
Columbia, South Carolina 29208
(803) 777-7797 FAX: (803) 777-3068
e-mail: jmcfadden@ed.sc.edu

Juliet V. Miller, Ph.D.
NCC, NCCC, Licensed Professional Counselor, state of Ohio
Executive Director, National Career Development Association
317 Kertess Avenue
Worthington, Ohio 43085
(614) 436-8004 FAX: (614) 436-6116
e-mail: millerncda@aol.com

W. Larry Osborne, Ed.D.
NCC, Licensed Professional Counselor, state of North Carolina
Department of Counseling and Educational Development
The University of North Carolina at Greensboro
Greensboro, North Carolina 27412-5001
(910) 334-3433 FAX: (910) 334-3433
e-mail: osbornel@dewey.uncg.edu

Samuel H. Osipow, Ph.D.
Diplomate, American Board of Vocational Experts
Licensed Psychologist, state of Ohio
Department of Psychology, Ohio State University
1885 Neil Avenue Mall
Columbus, Ohio 43210
(614) 292-1748 FAX: (614) 292-4537
e-mail: sosipow@magnus.acs.ohio-state.edu

Albert J. Pautler, Ed.D.
Teacher and School Administrator
Professor of Education, Graduate School of Education
University at Buffalo, 478 Baldy Hall
Buffalo, New York 14260
(716) 645-3164 FAX: (716) 645-2481
e-mail: apautler@ubvms.cc.buffalo.edu

Gary W. Peterson, Ph.D.
215 Stone Building
Florida State University
Tallahassee, Florida 32306-3001
(904) 644-1781
e-mail: gpeterso@garnet.acns.fsu.edu

Alice E. Potter, M.A.
University of Northern Colorado
Career Services, Kepner Hall 0025
Greeley, Colorado 80639
(970) 351-2681 FAX: (970) 351-1182
e-mail: alice@cs.univnorthco.edu

Anna M. Ranieri, M.A.
Licensed Marriage Family Child Counselor, state of California
663 San Juan Street
Stanford, California 94305
(415) 328-6942 FAX: (415) 328-6942
e-mail: ranieri@leland.stanford.edu

Robert C. Reardon, Ph.D.
NCC, NCCC
Career Center, University Center - Fourth Floor
Florida State University
Tallahassee, Florida 32306-1035
(904) 644-9777
e-mail: rreardon@admin.fsu.edu

Lee Joyce Richmond, Ph.D.
NCC, NCCC, Licensed Psychologist, state of Maryland
Loyolla College
Education Department, 4501 North Charles Street
Baltimore, Maryland 21210
(410) 617-2667 FAX: (410) 617-5095
e-mail: ljr@loyola.edu

George Ritzer, Ph.D.
Department of Sociology, University of Maryland
College Park, Maryland 20742
(301) 405-6418 FAX: (301) 314-6892
e-mail: ritzer@bssl.umd.edu

James P. Sampson, Jr., Ph.D.
NCC, NCCC
215 Stone Building
Florida State University
Tallahassee, Florida 32306-3001
(904) 644-1286
e-mail: jpsampso@garnet.acns.fsu.edu

Denise E. Saunders, M.S.
NCC
Career Center, University Center - Fourth Floor
Florida State University
Tallahassee, Florida 32306-1035
(904) 644-9778
e-mail: dsaunder@garnet.acns.fsu.edu

Nancy K. Schlossberg, Ed.D.
Center of Human Services Development
Department of Counseling
3229 J.M. Patterson Building
University of Maryland
College Park, Maryland 20742
(301) 405-4571 FAX: (301) 405-4576

Howard Splete, Ph.D.
NCC, NCCC, Licensed Professional Counselor, state of Michigan
1539 Biggers Drive
Rochester Hills, Michigan 48309
(810) 370-4173 FAX: (810) 370-4202
e-mail: splete@oakland.edu

Marian Stoltz-Loike
    Director
    Global Intercultural Programs
    Windham International
    55 Fifth Avenue
    New York, New York 10003
    (212) 545-8918 FAX: (718) 380-1758
    e-mail: compuserv: 10215,204

Anna Miller-Tiedeman, Ph.D.
    NCC, Who's Who Among American Women, Who's Who in the West
    LIFECAREER Center
    1078 La Tortuga Drive
    Vista, California 92083-6441
    (619) 726-6700 FAX: (619) 724-0083
    e-mail: anna@mailhost2.csusm.edu

David V. Tiedeman, Ed.D.
    Professor of Higher and Postsecondary Education, University of Southern
    California, Emeritus
    Who's Who in America, Who's Who in the World
    1078 La Tortuga Drive
    Vista, California 92083-6441
    (619) 726-6700 FAX: (619) 724-0083
    e-mail: dtiedema@waldenu.edu

Jane H. Walter, Ed.D.
    NCC, NCCC, NCLPC
    1030 West Market Street
    Suite 215
    Greensboro, North Carolina 27401
    (910) 274-0820 FAX: (910) 274-0032
    e-mail: janewalter@aol.com

Garry R. Walz, Ph.D.
    NCC, Senior Research Scientist
    Director & Professor Emeritus, University of Michigan
    ERIC/CASS, School of Education
    101 Park Building, UNCG
    Greensboro, North Carolina 27412-5001
    800-414-9769 FAX: (910) 334-4116
    e-mail: walzgx@iris.uncg.edu

A.G. Watts
    National Institute for Careers Education and Counseling
    Sheraton House, Castle Park
    Cambridge CB3 0AX
    00-44-1223-46027 FAX: 00-44-1223-311708

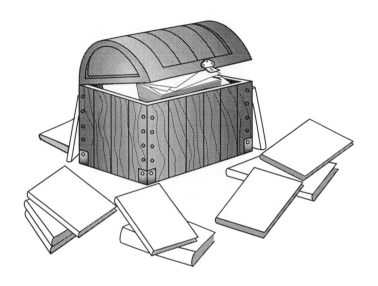

SPECIAL
RESOURCES

ERIC/CASS
Web Site

**University of
North Carolina at
Greensboro
School of Education
101 Park Building
UNCG
Greensboro, NC 27412**

One of the best sources of career related information is the Web sites of relevant organizations. A useful first step is to access the home page of ERIC/CASS and through it pull up relevant career resources and/or "hot links" with other Web Sites.

Through ERIC/CASS, the U.S. Department of Education's extensive educational resources can be accessed as well as special services of the ERIC system (AskERIC, Access ERIC and other ERIC Clearinghouses). In the Spring of 1996, NCDA will have an operational Web site which can be accessed directly or through ERIC/CASS. Contact NCDA (614-436-8004, FAX 614-436-6116, or e-mail at millerncda@aol.com) or ERIC/CASS (1-800-414-9769, FAX 910-334-4116, or e-mail at ericcass@iris.uncg.edu) for details!

Among the specific resources available on the ERIC/CASS Web site are:
- Full text ERIC/CASS Digests
- Information on forthcoming conferences and workshops
- Shopping mall of publications and resources
- Search capability of the ERIC database through the U.S. Department of Education
- Information on forthcoming ERIC/CASS Listservs
- Access to other members of the Counselor and Therapist Support System - CATS :
    National Association of School Psychologists
    National Board of Certified Counselors
    National Career Development Association
    American Psychological Association - School Directorate
    Canadian Guidance & Counseling Foundation

Item No. EC 199 $19.95

**COUNSELING
EMPLOYMENT
BOUND
YOUTH**

Edwin L. Herr

Counseling Employment Bound Youth

Edwin L. Herr Ed.D.

At long last, we have the monograph which so many persons have needed and sought out for such a long period of time—*Counseling Employment-Bound Youth*. Employment bound youth, a large and vital segment of our population (20 million plus) and future labor force, have been largely ignored in the literature on careers and on counseling and guidance. This neglect has clearly been to the great detriment not only of the young people themselves but to our country's vitality and competitiveness in the rapidly expanding global economy.

In seven vital and compelling chapters, Dr. Herr covers the topics which make this monograph both a thought piece and a practical handbook. The basic topics covered are:

- *Employment-bound youth: Diversity in characteristics, opportunities and support*
- *The emerging economic investment for employment-bound youth*
- *Career development for employment-bound youth in schools*
- *The school-to-work transition for employment-bound youth*
- *Career counseling for employment-bound youth*
- *The counselor and related career interventions*
- *Epilogue—Challenges to and the future of career counseling and guidance*

In masterful writing that offers a broad and comprehensive overview of the challenges faced as well as specific recommendations for how school, business, and communities can and should respond, Dr. Herr has produced a thoughtful yet eminently practical book. This compelling monograph is directed towards counselors, career specialists, teachers, administrators, policy makers and community members who are desirous of providing practical assistance to employment bound youth.

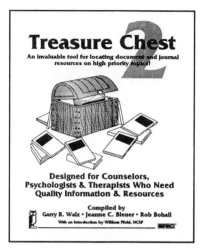

Treasure Chest 2

Garry Walz, Jeanne Bleuer and Rob Bohall

An invaluable tool for locating document and journal resources on high priority topics.
Designed for counselors, psychologists and therapists who need quality information and resources.

- Indexes over 82 high priority topics in counseling, education and psychology
- Provides abstracts on relevant ERIC document and journal entrees for each topic
- Offers practical suggestions on how to use and contribute to ERIC
- Provides ERIC digests on many of the topics which offer expert analysis of the topic and suggest practical and effective interventions
- Provides information on relevant World Wide Web sites with specific information on how to access them
- Updated biannually

What Every School Counselor, Psychologist & Therapist
Needs to Offer...

Family Counseling in the Schools

by J. Scott Hinkle & Michael Wells

This ground-breaking monograph combines a sound theoretical orientation with eminently practical approaches for offering family counseling in school settings. Written by two knowledgeable and experienced counselors, this monograph will be equally useful to persons new to family counseling or experienced family therapists. All readers will benefit from the large number of innovative and highly useful interventions and family counseling techniques which it presents.

- *"This book is unique in the amount of help it offers counselors who want to do family counseling"*
- *"A gold mine of useful approaches and techniques"*
- *"The authors are clearly experts in family counseling with a great deal to offer all of us."*

Among the exciting and useful areas covered in this book are:
- A Systems Perspective in the Schools
- Systems Theory and School Counseling
- Training in Family Counseling for School Counselors
- Additional Family Counseling Approaches in the Schools
- Family Counseling Technique in the Schools
- Family Assessment and the School Environment
- Special Clinical Issues in the Schools: Abuse, Anorexia, Substance Abuse, Attention Deficit/ Hyperactivity Disorder, and Antisocial Behavior
- Issues of Divorce and Marital Conflict
- A Family Approach to School and Community Crisis Management
- Case Contributions from School Counseling Professionals
- Appendix : Suggested Reading List in Family Counseling for School Counselors

Saving the Native Son: Empowerment Strategies for Young Black Males

by Courtland C. Lee

In this greatly expanded and revised edition of the highly acclaimed earlier publication on *Empowering Young Black Males,* Dr. Lee has provided a monograph which is both comprehensive in its coverage (from grades 3 through adolescence) and brimming with practical ideas and interventions. It is a highly thoughtful and probing account of the needs and challenges facing Black youth. It also provides action packed training modules which are unique in the breadth and depth of the activities which they offer. An idea of the richness of the contents can be readily seen by a review of the chapter headings:

- *The Black Male in Contemporary Society: Social and Educational Challenges*
- *The Psychosocial Development of Black Males: Issues and Impediments*
- *African/American-American Culture: Its Role in the Development of Black Male Youth*
- *"The Young Lions": An Educational Empowerment Program for Black Males in Grades 3-6*
- *"Black Manhood Training": An Empowerment Program for Adolescent Black Males*
- *Tapping the Power of Respected Elders: Ensuring Male Roles Modeling for Black Male Youth*
- *Educational Advocacy for Black Male Students*
- *"S.O.N.S.": Empowerment Strategies for African American Parents*
- *White Men Can't Jump," But Can They be Helpful?*
- *"The Malcolm X Principle": Self-Help for Young Black Males*
- *A Call to Action: A Comprehensive Approach to Empowering Young Black Males*

Counselors, psychologists, social workers, therapists and teachers will find this an immensely rewarding monograph to read and a highly useful resource for responding to the plight of young Black males. This monograph can be the start of a constructive and effective program for young Black males

ASSESSMENT IN COUNSELING & THERAPY

William D. Schafer, Ed.D. Guest Editor

ERIC/CASS
School of Education University of North Carolina at Greensboro
Greensboro, NC
in collaboration with
the Association for Assessment in Counseling

This ERIC/CASS Counseling Digest Collection is an indispensable resource for acquiring knowledge of the latest research, practice and professional developments relating to assessment in Counseling & Therapy.
William D. Schafer, Guest Editor

This collection:
- Explores the topic in depth in 34 authoritative digests for each topic
- is written by acknowledged experts
- Includes ERIC searches on the major themes of the digests
- Compresses a large amount of information into a highly readable and interesting format
- Provides individual digests that can be distributed in classes and in-service training sessions
- Offers a selected body of additional resources
- Are written to facilitate decision-making and action-taking
- Provides useful information in a special "resource pack" on how to use and contribute to the ERIC national database

Exemplary
Career
Development
Programs &
Practices

The Best from
Canada

Produced by ERIC/CASS in
collaboration with the Canadian
Guidance and Counselling
Foundation

EDITED BY
Dr. Bryan Hiebert

EXEMPLARY CAREER DEVELOPMENT PROGRAMS & PRACTICES: THE BEST FROM CANADA

This "First of its Kind" publication highlights the tremendous activity in research and development focused on career development which is occurring across Canada. Spurred on by the leadership of the Canadian Guidance and Counselling Foundation and the CAMCRY project to create viable career development resources, a remarkable quantity of high quality materials have been developed. So impressive have been the resulting products of this national initiative in career development, that ERIC/CASS has devoted an entire digest collection to the Canadian initiative in career development.

Forty-eight substantive digests are dispersed between nine major topics with a tenth devoted to an introduction by ERIC/CASS Director, Garry R. Walz.

The nine topics are as follows:

- National Canadian Initiatives in Career Counseling

- Career Counseling With Specific Populations

- Career Education in Schools

- Approaches to Career Counseling

- Career Counseling Methods and Techniques

- Delivery of Career Counseling Services

- Evaluation of Career Counseling

- Issues Needing to be addressed in Career Counseling

- Summary Comments

Two additional sections contribute greatly to the utility of the publication. The first section is devoted to ERIC data base searches on each of the nine special topics and include both relevant journal and document entries.

The second special section, *Using and Contributing to ERIC*, is designed to help all users of the publication in being more effective users of the total ERIC system plus learn how they can write and contribute to ERIC as well— both very useful learnings in their own right.

The uses for this digest collection are limitless. It is as useful for the practitioner as for the scholar or educator; and will prove invaluable as a general reference guide or source for information on specific questions.